T0369520

The Sixty-seventh Book of the Holy Bible by Elijah the Prophet as God Promised from the Book of Malachi.

iUniverse, Inc.
New York Bloomington

The Sixty Seventh Book of the Holy Bible By Elijah, the Prophet from Malachi 4:5.

iUniverse books may be ordered through booksellers or by contacting:

iUniverse
1663 Liberty Drive
Bloomington, IN 47403
www.iuniverse.com
1-800-Authors (1-800-288-4677)

ISBN: 978-1-4502-4341-4 (sc)
ISBN: 978-1-4502-4343-8 (ebook)
ISBN: 978-1-4502-4342-1 (dj)

Printed in the United States of America

iUniverse rev. date: 8/9/2010

Table of Contents

Dedication

The works of Elijah, the prophet are written for all the children of the world that would love all the gifts a child richly deserves. In addition, to the adults that believe all people living in the true kingdom shall not want of money or any other gift an adult believes, they richly deserve. In God's Kingdom, any problem of pain in a family must be overcome or the sorrows. What is required to start is quoted below!

We must use the Holy Bible to see the return of King Jesus Christ and His organization to start the beginning of heaven on earth. Since He has told us all things, we should be able to create the love required to reach for the true glory of God. The book is dedicated to all that believe in what is written after the kingdom is formed and the clergymen learn how to talk.

Chapter 1.   The Mystery of God.

To understand, the mystery of God, you must start with the book of Revelation or God stating the future. What is obvious in scripture or the sacred text? The Holy Bible is not complete as the book from Revelation 10:1 to 10:10 was left out for a reason. Seven thunders are fear and the New and Old Testament requires fear as the beginning of all wisdom (knowledge). The Old Testament is an eye for an eye, and a tooth for a tooth, and extract a pound of flesh. The New Testament is an eye for an eye, and shove the bodies under the Altar. King Jesus Christ has written, there is no reason to change one word of the Old Testament. The New Testament is an update on fear for the church to include John 3:16 and they are gatherers, not hunters. Fear is to be understood and joy for the congregation. The book you are about to read is required by all clergymen and the congregation are secondary to the people that have the right heart and must learn.

This book cannot be read like a novel, but a test of education. The clergymen must study each word, even centuries in the future. This book must last like the Holy Bible or longer than heaven and earth.

Man has written so many versions of the Holy Bible and we are to live by every word, so I will just use the King James Version. Now we can start with one set of words.

From the book of Revelation.

Rev 10:1 And I saw another mighty angel come down from heaven, clothed with a cloud: and a rainbow was upon his head, and his face was as it were the sun, and his feet as pillars of fire:

Rev 10:2 And he had in his hand a little book open: and he set his right foot upon the sea, and his left foot on the earth,

Rev 10:3 And cried with a loud voice, as when a lion roareth: and when he had cried, seven thunders uttered their voices.

Seven thunders, that is fear. Fear is the beginning of all wisdom (knowledge) and must be taught on the great and dreadful Day of the Lord or Good Friday. Many passages define the judgment on the government and they must be trained to live by every word. If you know of a church that does not train the politicians on the tree stories, you should grant them a copy of this book. By the grace of God, you are saved since there is nothing you have to do. God has planned it all for you and that is His Grace (work), or the entire Holy Bible. You are to teach the congregation to live by every word, which is the grace (work) of the clergymen. The Holy Bible is the clergymen's cross to bear. Do not let them stand in front of you and just read it. For example, the new engaged couple must be trained on marriage before they say "I DO", not by the divorce court. That would be potentially child abuse.

Back to the book of Revelation.

Rev 10:4 And when the seven thunders had uttered their voices, I was about to write: and I heard a voice from heaven saying unto me, Seal up those things, which the seven thunders, uttered, and write them not.

Rev 10:5 And the angel which I saw stand upon the sea and upon the earth lifted up his hand to heaven,

Rev 10:6 And sware by him that liveth for ever and ever, who created heaven, and the things that therein are, and the earth, and the things that therein are, and the sea, and the things which are therein, that there should be time no longer:

The end is only one election away (2012) and there is not much time left. The time left is a short time or the year of Our Lord 2014 AD. The eighth beast is well known by me and should be by every church employee of the King of Peace. The eighth beast is a beast, yet not a beast, yet he is a beast. The beast is already a beast, but he has the wrong title to be called the eighth in the year of the Lord 2008 AD. All church locations by now should know the names of the first seven beasts and the eighth was campaigning he will continue to be a dragon as President John F. Kennedy. Also, congress does not have the information from the book of Mark in mind. When I see their faces, I know they are easily deceived by their present foolish story of salvation. Where is the church that formed the kingdom and the clergyman learned how to talk?

Back to the book of Revelation.

Rev 10:7 But in the days of the voice of the seventh angel, when he shall begin to sound, the mystery of God should be finished, as he hath declared to his servants the prophets.

Rev 10:8 And the voice which I heard from heaven spake unto me again, and said, Go and take the little book which is open in the hand of the angel which standeth upon the sea and upon the earth.

Rev 10:9 And I went unto the angel, and said unto him, Give me the little book. And he said unto me, Take it, and eat it up;

and it shall make thy belly bitter, but it shall be in thy mouth sweet as honey.

Rev 10:10 And I took the little book out of the angel's hand, and ate it up; and it was in my mouth sweet as honey: and as soon as I had eaten it, my belly was bitter.

If you do not understand the above or know of any person that does not understand the above, you had better find Elijah, the prophet. You are blessed if you receive a copy of this book even if you do not understand how fear is applied, today. Fear is the beginning of all wisdom (knowledge) and must be taught on the great and dreadful Day of the Lord, Good Friday. Only a penanced man can get off this world alive, not a man of unpardonable sins. The church must end all Cardinal sins of the clergymen. The congregation will not and cannot forgive their sins until they do. The clergymen must repent of their deadly sins.

Here is the mystery of God, where He will train an angel to write about the seven thunders in modern times or fear. Fear is the beginning of all wisdom (knowledge), yet we have to reach for, there is nothing to fear but fear itself. How can a book result in my mouth sweet as honey when I speak and my belly was bitter as I tried to swallow my pride and the wisdom made me sicken? He told us to eat of the book as He has told us to eat of His body. A location that does not teach fear is not a valid church location, since fear is the beginning of all wisdom (knowledge). The common sense logic is that all of us could have saved billions of lives if we were not in penance and all worked together for common causes. On the great and dreadful Day of the Lord or Good Friday, the church must teach fear. The future as a challenge has resulted in the implementation of the Lord's Prayer as the only permanent solution. Many church locations have taught about the new beginning or the end in the year of Our Lord 2000 AD. The new beginning is the clergymen giving King Jesus Christ His virgin bride or His kingdom. The greatest joy of the clergymen would be to be part of that trial of the new beginning. The clergymen must read the book and their belly will be bitter, but for the love of the world, they must use their mouth to overcome their total displeasure. I, the author, am God's angel and have known the true future for a long time and I desire to get the little book in your mouth, so my grandchildren are safe.

Now from the book of Malachi.

Mal 3:1 Behold, I will send my messenger, and he shall prepare the way before me: and the LORD, whom ye seek, shall suddenly come to his temple, even the messenger of the covenant, whom ye delight in: behold, he shall come, saith the LORD of hosts.

Mal 3:2 But who may abide the day of his coming? and who shall stand when he appeareth? for he is like a refiner's fire, and like fullers' soap.

NO ONE COULD STAND; THE HOLY BIBLE ALREADY CONTAINS THE TRUTH.

Notice temple not church. You are to delight in Elijah, the prophet. Do not go to the temple, but you must complete the story of the church, first. King Jesus Christ will meet us in Israel, once we complete all the tests of scripture in the church world. All He promised for Israel will be disregarded if the tests of the church world are not desired by the people and the penance will continue for seven times longer. Adam stated in principle to God in the Garden of Eden, I need to do it myself. The Holy Bible states in principle, I have told you all things. The church has a book that always ends up with a life a thousand times better than the end. Many still talk about the end, which means the church is not teaching how to live by every word.

Now to continue from the book of Malachi.

Mal 3:3 And he shall sit as a refiner and purifier of silver: and he shall purify the sons of Levi, and purge them as gold and silver, that they may offer unto the LORD an offering in righteousness.

Mal 3:4 Then shall the offering of Judah and Jerusalem be pleasant unto the LORD, as in the days of old, and as in former years.

Mal 3:5 And I will come near to you to judgment; and I will be a swift witness against the sorcerers, and against the adulterers, and against false swearers, and against those that oppress the hireling in his wages, the widow, and the fatherless, and that turn aside the stranger from his right, and fear not me, saith the LORD of hosts.

Gold is money and from Israel, silver is peace. After peace the silver becomes money in the year of Our Lord 2800 AD. Can you say the offering of Jerusalem should be pleasant to the Lord today with all the killing the Middle East has produced? All should judge Israel as a life nine hundred times better than the end as the time of King Jesus Christ, not the Israel of today. All judgment is contained in the Holy Bible. Anyone who judges as a voter or does not vote shall be judged or a judge in court. No person could call himself a human being and live without judging; therefore, all people must be judged on Judgment Day or the day you die. Do not listen to a man that states not to judge by voting or any other judgment a human being must make. That human being must be judged by the saints or the men that must obey the Ten Commandments without sin, the church employees of King Jesus Christ. The Holy Bible states, we must identify the man of sin. So Elijah the true representative of Our Gods will be like Paul in scripture to reform the church. Like Paul, he will not be paid by any denomination or be a clergymen. All in the book of Malachi

6

3:5 will be judged, but notice the stranger as he comes into your perfect church and does not know the tree stories or the path to a small door, he should not be driven away. A passage like, I do not want you to do a job you do not want to do requires a tree where God is the trunk, the passage is the branch, the leaves are the ideas, and the fruits of our labor are the children growing up trained to do a job, they desire to do. Since statistically all over the world, the children as adults are not getting the jobs they were trained for or many cannot get a job at all, you realize the churches must create the tree stories to be called a church. All judgment is contained in the Holy Bible and copied in fear for Adam to start to learn how to live without fear.

Now to continue from the book of Malachi.

Mal 3:6 For I am the LORD, I change not; therefore, ye sons of Jacob are not consumed.

Mal 3:7 Even from the days of your fathers ye are gone away from mine ordinances, and have not kept them. Return unto me, and I will return unto you, saith the LORD of hosts. But ye said, Wherein shall we return?

Mal 3:8 Will a man rob God? Yet ye have robbed me. But ye say, Wherein have we robbed thee? In tithes and offerings.

Can you believe our present clergymen are stealing from God? They have a blasphemous mouth, worship Satan, and refuse to implement the Lord's Prayer, which is the new beginning, thereby robbing God. King Jesus Christ stated you denied me the tithes, which is what joins the people to the government like income tax and use of currency, not money to people trying to make the congregation feel guilty to raise money. God is saying the churches are wrong. King Jesus Christ can train the politicians through the church to double the best Adam can do in money. The clergymen should have trained people listening to the failure of Adam as an economist. All I can do is copy the words from the Holy Bible and let the church locations learn. The above, like all the rest of the Holy Bible is true. The wisdom in the Holy Bible, I can easily understand. God will not return if you have any questions to ask. He has told us all things, so the clergymen already have the answers. We must live by every word, not just read it. He will join us in Israel, not the church. When they form the church with the seven names from the book of Daniel and book of Revelation or I saw seven churches, they will have to write questions and then answer. A question should be, "What is God's Covenants?" The answer is for all locations to determine what the minimum requirement is to run a church, like the education requirement on how to live by the Ten Commandments to eliminate the clergymen's sins. Another question should be, "What is the book of Galatians for?" The answer is for the church to lord over the courts and teach the judges to have the right heart for John 3:16. King Jesus Christ is the Lord and the saints that run the church are to be the lords. The court comes to the church for the story of salvation, the church does not go to the court for John 3:16.

Now to continue from the book of Malachi.

Mal 3:9 Ye are cursed with a curse: for ye have robbed me, even this whole nation.

Mal 3:10 Bring ye all the tithes into the storehouse, that there may be meat in mine house, and prove me now herewith, saith the LORD of hosts, if I will not open you the windows of heaven, and pour you out a blessing, that there shall not be room enough to receive it.

The entire nation of the church of America has robbed God. All church locations take His Name in vain to prove you should provide money. Bring ye all tithes into the storehouse. The meat from the Altar requires the church the train the politicians on the economic model of King Jesus Christ, which I will cover later. In the kingdom, no one worries about money, so if you notice billions of people worried about money, you know the kingdom has not formed or I saw seven churches. Certainly the clergymen should worry about money today as money is the only goal of the church. In the United States, the Holy Bible and clergymen should agree, the problem is with the rich. The Holy Bible has stated the problem, but not the people of the church in away that can be resolved. How can the rich (wicked) learn to have the shackles released if they do not know they are in shackles and what it takes to have the right heart for John 3:16? Have you heard a president (foolish Bush) state the children should not have health care because there are too many? He loves trillions for military, but the children cannot have health care because there are too many. He does not have the right heart to say he worships the God of Heart. Do you know about the hanging judges in courts or judging without mercy? Have you noticed the violence of the curse of thy children, as the church has driven them away? The complete curse of God is covered later.

Now to continue the book of Malachi.

Mal 3:11 And I will rebuke the devourer for your sakes, and he shall not destroy the fruits of your ground; neither shall your vine cast her fruit before the time in the field, saith the LORD of hosts.

Mal 3:12 And all nations shall call you blessed: for ye shall be a delightsome land, saith the LORD of hosts.

Mal 3:13 Your words have been stout against me, saith the LORD. Yet ye say, What have we spoken so much against thee?

Mal 3:14 Ye have said, It is vain to serve God: and what profit is it that we have kept his ordinance, and that we have walked mournfully before the LORD of hosts?

Mal 3:15 And now we call the proud happy; yea, they that work wickedness are set up; yea, they that tempt God are even delivered.

The future heartland of the world, where King Jesus Christ is going to make a stand is going to be blessed above all others. How will He bless you or the people of the United States of America? He will bless you by every word of scripture as America becomes the research and development arm of God (heartland) and He wrote the Holy Bible for the church to use the words to create Standing Historical. Elijah, the prophet will give you the branch story or a path to the small door.

The politicians are in shackles and the church is in denial, yet God is the ruler of time and space. Have you heard of shackle less churches? They cannot tell God what to do. If you tell God what to do that you should do like ending the divorces, you are taking God's name in vain. Where is the humility for King Jesus Christ when many blame Him for everything Adam is doing wrong? All prayers must define their call to action in His Name. Do not write or speak a prayer telling God what to do. God will help those that helps themselves, not people that do not work together like for daily bread from the politicians that state they represent the God of Heart, not trillions to create hell on earth. War is hell. There is no hell like a woman scorned as her children cannot get daily bread, health care, education, and/or a bright future for her children. All children must receive the gift of a bright future for your children to live in peace. Have you heard about the American children in orphanages without parents and they have to beg for a toy at the holidays? Are the people of the United States representing the God of Heart? Have you heard about the clergymen sending the Italian Mafia to heaven and they are killing your children with guns and drugs?

Now to continue the book of Malachi.

Mal 3:16 Then they that feared the LORD spake often one to another: and the LORD hearkened, and heard it, and a book of remembrance was written before him for them that feared the LORD, and that thought upon his name.

The book of remembrance is critical to the leaders of the Holy Cities for their story of salvation and developing and maintaining the right heart to represent the God of Heart. As I have defined, it is a book of good deeds of the congregation of each denomination and Standing Historical. When the leader of that denomination dies, he must have the composite of all critical good deeds led by the Mother of Inspiration (clergymen) in his mind and soul. Standing Historical must replace most of the Holy Bible to be taught. The church has no written Standing Historical, written to biblical standards. The clergymen start a war against the 666 beast. War is one of the four words to learn for the millennium. You must have the right heart for John 3:16 as the church must obey God, not God must obey the church. Do not listen to a location that states, I must wait for God to return. They must find Elias and Elijah, an angel and prophet from the books of Mark and Malachi. King Jesus Christ will return when He receives His virgin bride back. That is the church of today that the animals the ass and oxen makes the clergymen look bad. At least the animals know their own cribs. That knowledge makes the clergymen worst than fools.

Now to continue the book of Malachi.

Mal 3:17 And they shall be mine, saith the LORD of hosts, in that day when I make up my jewels; and I will spare them, as a man spareth his own son that serveth him.

The jewels are the church employees of King Jesus Christ that are the saints that judge the world because they love the

11

children and their families. King Jesus Christ judged you because He loved you. The church employees of King Jesus Christ must become the meek who inherit the earth and the saints. They get John 3:16 back, when they start to form the kingdom. The only ones are God's chosen ones that He will be involved with, not the Antichrists running a church. Elijah only concern is if he cannot use his hand to write good laws.

Now to continue from the book of Malachi.

Mal 3:18 Then shall ye return, and discern between the righteous and the wicked, between him that serveth God and him that serveth him not.

Mal 4:1 For, behold, the day cometh, that shall burn as an oven; and all the proud, yea, and all that do wickedly, shall be stubble: and the day that cometh shall burn them up, saith the LORD of hosts, that it shall leave them neither root nor branch.

Mal 4:2 But unto you that fear my name shall the Sun of righteousness arise with healing in his wings; and ye shall go forth, and grow up as calves of the stall.

Fear is the beginning of all wisdom (knowledge) and the seven thunders in the book of Revelation. You must teach people to fear His name. The good people of your congregations will love fear. The bad people must change. In Israel at the time of writing the New Testament, life was nine hundred times better than the end. In Israel, it was an eye for an eye and tooth for a tooth, and extract a pound of flesh or Death Penalties. The fear in the church world is an eye for an eye and shove the bodies under the Altar. The results will be the end of divorces over time. The Holy Bible states in the year of Our Lord 2008 AD, I pity the women of suck or women with children. That sorrow will always occur without fear. With fear the trial by fire shall burn like an oven, where the politicians will always grant the children all the gifts children richly deserve like health care, good education, money where families do not worry about money, and a bright future, children richly deserve. Today in America, our politicians have stolen a bright future from many millions of our children and their families. Around the world, the number is great with a countless number of unnecessary deaths. One death of a child is one too many. Let me repeat, with fear, one unnecessary death of a child in the world will result in the world shaking and all the world of the nations of church to work hard to avoid the unnecessary death of a second child. Today millions die and many just teach, I will forgive all the unpardonable sins (deadly sins). Unpardonable means they cannot be forgiven. The congregation should desire to hear what the employees of King Jesus Christ will teach about unpardonable sins on the great and dreadful Day of the Lord. The church must find the man of sin.

To earn your wings, you must w (work) in (in) g (Gods) s (servant) or the meaning of wings. May all of the congregation of all the world get their wings from the church, when they are reborn again at the age of the King being baptized.

Now to continue from the book of Malachi.

Mal 4:3 And ye shall tread down the wicked; for they shall be ashes under the soles of your feet in the day that I shall do this, saith the LORD of hosts.

Mal 4:4 Remember ye the law of Moses my servant, which I commanded unto him in Horeb for all Israel, with the statutes and judgments.

Mal 4:5 Behold, I will send you Elijah, the prophet before the coming of the great and dreadful Day of the Lord:

Mal 4:6 And he shall turn the heart of the fathers to the children, and the heart of the children to their fathers, lest I come and smite the earth with a curse.

The curse is in Chapter 27 The New Beginning of Refiner's Fire, and Like Fullers' Soap in a memo titled THE END. The curse is eternal death for the entire world.

Elijah, the true prophet has achieved all that is above and understands all that is written, but must stop before Israel and the work in the church world must come first. Elijah grants you the information required for the great and dreadful Day of the Lord or Good Friday. Part of the curse of God is the children will be violent and not be like the children parents richly deserve, because man of the cloth does not care to seek God's knowledge. Adam cannot abandon his children and live with good Domestic Tranquility caused by Adam himself. The passage will come true anywhere where religion and families abandon Thy Children and I will abandon you and the penance will continue for seven times longer. The world is in penance and the way out is to implement the Lord's Prayer using the Universal Church format granted in the year of Our Lord 1200 AD. The format was used to form the American government and wrongfully abandoned by the church. The curse will be automatic by society training the children without God and the penance will continue for seven times longer or fourteen thousand more years. Many have taught the end shall come, but in the year of Our Lord 2008 AD, many do not believe it all happens in one generation or the year of Our Lord 1992 to 2016 AD. The eighth beast is already a beast and his name is available to me and any church location by now should know the names of all eight. He is a beast but not a beast, means he does not have the right title to be called the eighth beast in the year of Our Lord 2008 AD. He will go through a five-month period, ending in November. The process will be completed in January in the year of Our Lord 2009 AD, when President Barack Obama takes office.

All churches shall develop and teach the Tree of Life and the Tree of Knowledge from the Garden of Eden to create the perfect church. The way to the small door is huge today, but the church must be gatherers of all knowledge. The way to a perfect way of life can be found and must be taught. That is what Adam stated he needed God to let him do it himself in the Garden of Eden. Now is the time for Adam to grow up and achieve being like Gods (saints) in thy kingdom come. As the clergymen are saying now, "You know, I have to wait for King Jesus Christ to return." Why? As the Holy Bible states, I have told you all things. We already have the skill. What is required is the will and the desire to work together for the common good.

What is the requirement? When a stranger enters your perfect church or one of the seven and he does not know the door stories or Tree of Life and Tree of Knowledge, do not drive him away. That information must be consumed by the trial by fires and maintained by the gatherers of all information, the church.

What are some of the other greatest mysteries in the Holy Bible?

Jacob stated, "I guess my name is Israel." The reason was, he did not have a clue as to what that meant. This is the beginning of the first power of eight, Israel.

The prophecy of the crucifixion in one thousand years. The purpose was to inspire Israel in longing for a savior, to show us the meaning of the gift of John 3:16, to write a new beginning for the church world and update the temple, a transition of power to the meaning of the heart in judgment, His only begotten Son to rule, and to forgive the Israeli man for his sins as King Jesus Christ used the word jealousy against us to make the prophecy come true. This is the second power of eight.

How could King Jesus Christ send Elias back and why would he be able to restoreth all things when men are claiming how brilliant they are and none of the people that state they represent Him could do it? Mark 9:12.

How could King Jesus Christ send a man back in a war to end all wars of European descent to write the small book on fear to be taught on the great and dreadful Day of the Lord or Good Friday and add to the Holy Bible? Malachi 4:5 or the third power of eight writing the book from Revelation 10:1 to 10:10.

Our Father as written, rested on the seventh day. In the Holy Bible, King Jesus Christ has told us all things. The millennium story was in the year of Our Lord 2000 AD. How could the present time complete with the reality of the seventh day He rests. Many will tell you the Holy Bible was started about six thousand years ago. Now, we are in the seventh day and we are to finish the Six Day Creation Story. How could man ever believe He has told us all things, we are to finish the Six Day creation story, and the seventh day He rests? The only answer is He has given us the knowledge to create in His name, the faith of the unseen the work through hope, for the next thousand years. Could any man believe through the church, we could write prophecies that produce mystery and intrigue for all humanity to be taught at the Altar? I say man through the wisdom of the Lord can do it as He has told us all things. He will meet us in the temple and be against all nations of the church, so the seventh day he rests in the church environment. May joy through church and happiness through government be the many glad tidings, you hear on all world news media.

The Holy Bible in its entirety is a mystery. Our Gods put the world in penance, when King Jesus Christ divorced us back in Israel for the church disobeying three times and refused to help us. The passages are clear that no one understands what the Holy Bible means and what the chapters are for. The Holy Bible states to form the kingdom and learn how to talk. Today, God has compared the wisdom of the clergymen to the animals the ass and oxen and the animals know their own crib. The clergymen cannot compete with the animals on their knowledge of religion. Adam has created his own religion and it is failing the world. Once the religious leaders accept that reality, the

Holy Bible has a new meaning of a planning book and very easy to understand. Only true Gods could write a book where one hundred percent of everything the clergymen are doing is wrong and once they accept the true fate all the answers to all mankind's sorrows can be resolved if you can find a place where people can congregate. The church is the ideal format for people to congregate and the language for them to use is the language of business or English as scripture explained to them, two thousand years ago.

So the great miracle of scripture is the clergymen are doing one hundred percent of everything wrong. They do not even know what the chapters are for like the book of Galatians is used for them to lord over the courts. The definitions of words like evil, nation, needs, want, and the list goes on as they have the wrong definitions. Once they form the kingdom, they learn the Holy Bible is a planning book and all their questions about scripture at this time can be answered. So the church uses the same book and the penance is beginning to end, as they get John 3:16 back for forming the kingdom.

What would be left is what we expect in outer space. God is the ruler of time and space, so Adam would desire to create or meet the men in God's image, beyond our little world. Our Father's Kingdom is vast. Our pleasure is He has granted us His only begotten son and we should expect the same in other worlds.

The greatest mystery of all is how God can turn Adam into being like Gods. From the Garden of Eden it is written that once you are responsible for good and evil you will surely die. That must occur when the clergymen form the kingdom. Once you know how to manage good and evil you will be like Gods. The flaming swords of the Garden of Eden protected the knowledge of the Tree of Life and Tree of Knowledge. God's angel has the way for the clergymen to be in a quest for knowledge from the Garden of Eden to turn into people like Gods called saints to judge the world. God judged you for the year of Our Lord 2000

AD in the book of Revelation. The clergymen must judge the world because they love the members of all congregations. The knowledge has been hidden since the beginning of time and now Adam through the training of a man by God can have the technique. The way is a path to a small door or the best way of doing everything.

Let us look at Luke 17 to gain an insight.

Luke 20 And when He was demanded of the Pharisees, when the kingdom of God should come, He answered them and said, The kingdom of God cometh not with observation:

Luke 21 neither shall they say, Lo here! or, Lo there! for, behold, the kingdom of God is within you.

What is written is if all church employees of King Jesus Christ work together, we can form the kingdom, because we have the skills and the Holy Bible tells us how. I have written the Chapter "Stairway to Heaven" to summarize in detail what the Holy Bible states. Have you heard a man state, "You know, I have to wait for King Jesus Christ to return?" He is trying to form the kingdom by observation. He does not desire to work, but just have our Gods do everything, which violates the words Adam used in the Garden of Eden. Adam told God, he needed to do it himself. The Holy Bible is written that way. God was right in the Garden of Eden as Adam will live in much pain until he implements God's wisdom. We must develop the third power of eight. If the Holy Bible would allow God to do the work of Adam, do you believe He could have been the son of the leader of the Roman Empire. Now He would define the answers and we could evolve to create the Holy Roman Empire. Wait He has told us all the answers, so we can evolve, if we work, not take pride in ourselves that we can tell Our Gods what to do. They tell us what to do and the clergymen must obey like a slave. They must form the kingdom and learn how to talk. In two thousand years in penance, Adam has not learned how to talk. Speak, yes but talk no. The path to the small door is huge, not the best way of doing anything like the Holy Bible teaches us to live by every word.

Lo here, lo there are the clergymen blaming others for not being as good as themselves, yet none try to form the kingdom, so they can learn how to talk. Once you learn how to talk, your questions become something you can ask and then learn the answers from scripture. Until you ask the questions, you will not discover the answers. No church location can say you know I can read the Holy Bible better than the church down the street. That is blame and must end in a kingdom. If that was true, the location must reform the church to save the souls of the people violating the Commandments or not in a good quest for knowledge.

From the book of Luke 17

Luke 22 And he said unto the disciples, The days will come, when ye shall desire to see one of the days of the Son of man, and ye shall not see it.

In the Holy Bible, there are many occurrences of the use of the word forsaken. When they say I have to wait for King Jesus Christ to return, they sound forsaken, as they know not what they do. They seek the story of observation rather than work together for common causes. The one that is very important and only done once is the Lord's Prayer and the book of Daniel. The entire world is in jeopardy of the end and the only answer is the Lord's Prayer, which the average clergymen desires to avoid. I have not found one that is interested as they continue their desire to forsaken their required deeds, which is correctly called the end shall come from the eighth beast or the famine. The ultimate famine is caused by the pen.

From the book of Luke 17.

Luke 23 And they shall say to you, See here; or, see there: go not after them, nor follow them.

All you will here in a church is the little achievements such as I must provide the daily bread. The Lord's Prayer states for the church to tell the governments to give us this day our daily bread. Many have written that only my literature is good. They qualify for, "Some of the stories are so great (not many), that if you could get to the very elect (clergymen) all you would do is deceive." The reason is the Holy Bible can only be understood if you use it to form the kingdom, not try to convince people, you understand it. Do not follow the clergymen that thinks small, instead they must think about working in an organization more powerful than all the governments. The government comes to the church for salvation, not the church goes to them for reality. The Holy Bible states all people talk like little children. King Jesus Christ will not return until you have no questions to ask. How could an Antichrist state, "I have to wait for King Jesus Christ to return?" Does he have a million or so questions to ask? If the first question is, "What do I do first?" You should know the Holy Bible gave him the answer.

From the book of Luke 17.

Luke 24 For as the lightning, that lighteneth out of the one part under heaven, shineth unto the other part under heaven; so shall also the Son of man be in his day.

Through the seven Holy Cities of nation against nation and kingdom against kingdom, all the clergymen are trying to produce the best life for the congregations. The church personnel (saints) will judge the deeds to declare what stories of sorrows they have put to rest like abortion, divorces, and lack of money. The church is around the world and will be heard in a kingdom. The news will be trying to learn more than you should discuss. Instead of being in the news for bad deeds like the priests abusing the children, the church will drive the news to glad tidings. Today the news is mostly blame. The church must train television not to blame. If you build it, they will come. The congregation will love fear, the congregation creates. Have you heard the politicians working to eliminate prisons as the Holy Bible states? I told a politician that and she thought I was crazy. How could she win an election with something that is not possible? In a kingdom, the congregation would call that a miracle. The Son of man is the christ of the church. King Jesus Christ will return with His christ. His christ will help you write the sermons to eliminate prisons thereby policemen. The miracle of all possible through a kingdom is impossible for the congregation to believe today. All is possible in a kingdom, if it is good. The best way to start the hope through God is to copy His thousand year plan out of the Holy Bible, go to the city of angels, make a movie, and show it in all locations as lightening under the skies.

From the book of Luke 17.

Luke 25 But first, must he suffer many things, and be rejected of this generation.

This is well used, but the church is rejected by the children (God's Children of 777 design) today or especially teenagers to twenty-one. How can it be that the employee's of King Jesus Christ shall be hated above all others for My name's sake? This book will answer that question completely.

From the book of Luke 17.

Luke 26 And as it was in the days of Noah, so shall it be also in the days of the Son of man.

Luke 27 They did eat, they drank, they married wives, they were given in marriage, until the day that Noah entered into the ark, and the flood came, and destroyed the rest.

You are waiting for the Son of man to return. Domestic violence is great in the country, USA. We foolishly go to a foreign country to end the bomb squads in American police departments. The guns are killing our children and the American courts are a land of chaos and confusion, the man with the gavel. We have not evened learned how to sell houses, but our prisons are full. Our schools cannot educate the fallen angels (God's Children of 777 design) to think about money and education go hand in hand. Many fallen angels know, they can earn money on the streets. I like the America of old or New York City in the year of Our Lord 1900 AD. We are one American election away from the end of American civilization as God has told us all things. Adam has proven the Story of Noah's Ark is kind.

From the book of Luke 17.

Luke 28 Likewise also as it was in the days of Lot; they did eat, they drank, they bought, they sold, they planted, they bought, builded;

Luke 29 but the same day that Lot went out of Sodom it rained fire and brimstone from heaven, and destroyed them all.

Luke 30 Even thus shall it be in the day when the Son of man is revealed.

Have you gone to New York City in the year of Our Lord 1900 AD in literature? The police officers did not carry guns. It was a city (NEW) where love and marriage was the way and our government was zero dollars in debt. They paid off the loans to quickly but they were out of debt at federal. Now, you go to New York City and ask the police department to get rid of their guns and the businessperson, they would refuse. We have many fallen angels in our prisons raised by the women and the men get the better paying jobs on average. Our credit card bills are high and if you believe a two (yes two) percent mortgage is good, you would be mistaken. The only cost of interest for a purchase must be zero. The United States Federal Government is the greatest debtor nation in the world and contains many citizens that are in want of money. Hundreds of billions go to the wealthy as our government has established gambling in our stock and commodities trading for the rich of this world. Many rich do not use the money to create goods and services for a billion plus people in jeopardy. Should America take pride in the religion of New York City and our commitment of our government to its children in health, wealth, and wisdom? Do we have a city we would like to get Lot to leave, but there would be no place to go. Fire and brimstone of God will be replaced by guns, drugs, bomb squads, smart bombs over Iraq or the fire and brimstone you delivered unjustly, and lack of hope without John 3:16. The Battle of Armageddon will be started by Adam in the United States of America, be run by only American citizens against American citizens, and we cannot recover. The penance from the days of Israel will continue until Adam proves he desires to live in God's Kingdom as defined by the Lord's Prayer. Adam will repeat the mistakes he made in Israel. When the Son of man is revealed, we will understand we avoided the Battle of Armageddon in the United States, because we agreed to obey the will of God. Man finally saw the way, truth, and light. The will of God and the will of Adam must agree to achieve a life one thousand times better than the end. The women must receive their ways on wars and children.

Do you know what country contains the city of sin or Sodom? Iraq is a place where we Americans had sent fire and brimstone equivalent from the heavens or Smart Bombs. You can read about the two hundred million (Salvation Army if you form the kingdom) allowing Smart Bombs to drop from heaven and taking John 3:16 away from the entire world. The one third dead are the foolish Americans (Republicans) that voted for the beast Bush in the year of Our Lord 2000 AD. The inaction of the clergymen killed the entire world and the end is where the clergymen allow America to be destroyed because the banks fail and the poor with guns will inherit the United States. You allowed the people to live by the sword and America will die by the new sword called the gun. Have we convinced the puppet government to love a land of freedom like America where children's lives are less important then the ability to put military weapons in our children's hands? Domestic violence is on the rise in America, but Americans continue to waste resources on what Elias calls "Hell Machines". Where is the future of our United States children? Is that what you desire for the land that contains Sodom? The United States is teaching them to live by the sword and die by the sword.

From the book of Luke 17.

Luke 31 In that day, he which shall be upon the housetop, and his stuff in the house, let him not come down to take it away: and he that is in the field, let him likewise not return back.

We have what we call "Whistle Blowers". I like their new names of "Salvation Restorers". They are people that love their land and cannot stand injustice to remain. Today, when they report a problem, the government or businessmen can use threats to produce silence. On April 3, the year of Our Lord 2008 AD, the Whistle Blowers where in Congress on national television. We must teach not to let the wicked go to perdition because they believe they have the right to threaten, rather than learn. The people we can call the "Whistle Blowers" require a new title of honor and they must be allowed to shout from the highest rooftops. If you have FBI agents in the field, do not stop him from defending against the crime syndicates. You leave the men in the field and do not work against them. The American courts protect the crime syndicates from the FBI. There is to be no rest for the wicked. That Congress news item and American FBI shall be written in Standing Historical (666 beast books) and added to the training courses of the church lording over the courts in the book of Galatians and the politicians in the book of Timothy.

Let Elijah, the prophet teach bottom up planning as Ross Perot of the election in the year of Our Lord 1992 AD promised. Since he did not understand how to do it within a company, state, or the entire country, let Elijah, the prophet teach you. He did not know how to do it in business because the words of the Holy Bible were not in place as it defines how.

From the book of Luke 17.

Luke 32 Remember Lot's wife.

What do you believe Lot's wife should do but obey God. If she turns as Eve or Lot's wife lost, penance will be in her life. The church must teach the women (King Jesus Christ's educators) to become great women and obey King Jesus Christ in the wedding vows and beyond. The word obey in the wedding vows is to obey King Jesus Christ, not her husband when his ideas are foolish. A single woman that goes out with a married man in a romantic setting will go into penance. All women are sisters and must be trained not to abuse children in divorces. Israel used fear to end divorces in great numbers and the churches must learn to do the same. The women will love the fear of God, not what Adam believes.

From the book of Luke 17.

Luke 33 Whosoever shall seek to save his life shall lose it; and whosoever shall lose his life shall preserve it.

King Jesus Christ is looking for the clergymen who are willing to die for the Lord's Prayer and the ones that refuse and seek to save their lives shall die. The clergymen must go through the story of resurrection. The Chapter Stairway to Heaven covers this completely.

From the book of Luke 17.

Luke 34 I tell you, in that night there shall be two men in one bed; the one shall be taken, and the other shall be left.

Gays cannot be married in the church. See the Chapter, "The Word Lust" and many clergymen must change to one voice. The two men through education and the women believing in love and marriage will be true as the answer is as God has written. Do not blame or try to make the men feel guilty. A sermon must not attack a person in gospel armor.

From the book of Luke 17.

Luke 35 Two women shall be grinding together; the one shall be taken, and the other left.
Luke 36 Two men shall be in the field; the one shall be taken, and the other left.

When the church creates the kingdom and good food becomes a problem, get the governments to invest in producing food not guns. Look for modern farming ideas as in America and the farming equipment, not just labor to be used, without modern equipment. All countries must have surplus good food. The church must create the concept of the food of the Gods.

From the book of Luke 17.

Luke 37 And they answered and said unto him, Where, Lord? And he said unto them, Where so ever the body is, thither will the eagles be gathered together.

Read the Chapter on the one world government for your nation in the Chapter "The Seventh Trumpet Story" and the body is the women or body of the church.

Let us look at the Lord's Prayer for other mysteries or focus on the word debt.

Luke 11:2 And he said unto them, When ye pray, say, Our Father which art in heaven, Hallowed be thy name. Thy kingdom come. Thy will be done, as in heaven, so in earth.

Luke 11:3 Give us day by day our daily bread.

Luke 11:4 And forgive us our sins; for we also forgive every one that is indebted to us. And lead us not into temptation; but deliver us from evil.

Luke 11:5 And he said unto them, Which of you shall have a friend, and shall go unto him at midnight, and say unto him, Friend, lend me three loaves;

Luke 11:6 For a friend of mine in his journey is come to me, and I have nothing to set before him?

Indebted that is money. Learn how the wicked love to pay and why!

The greatest mystery in modern times is how the world can be down to one prayer or the Lord's Prayer. Adam without God is just a fool and the Holy Bible is clear. The clergymen and His employees must form the kingdom to learn how to talk. Adam is about to create the end due to the pen and refuses to change. Let us review the Lord's Prayer for what is known.

What is the easiest to achieve by all humanity that represents King Jesus Christ? Give us day by day our daily bread. All church locations will teach future politicians the importance of daily bread to their salvation. The politicians must have the right heart from the book of Luke. The congregation will be taught that if they do not love children, they do not love Our Gods. They should listen to the politicians for daily bread and/ or understand what to do if the greatness of good food of Our Gods are not in your world.

Thy kingdom come is the first requirement for His return. The clergymen in Standing Historical will have to write, why they were so reluctant to grant God His kingdom.

As in heaven is like in heaven on earth, do not send your policemen out to kill them because they will not go to school. You are to get rid of prisons, which is easy to do, but takes longer than it should, because Adam is reluctant to change. That is well covered in the Holy Bible. The church will create God's Children of 777 design as one voice, in heaven on earth. The children are born and God appoints their souls. Spare the rod and spoil the child comes into all churches as requirements. The church cannot help raise a child today and must describe why in Standing Historical. The requirement is 777 design as one voice. All church locations must be the same even though there are, I see seven churches or seven names on the door with seven Holy Cities.

The church does not know what the word evil means, but became responsible for good and evil on January 1st in the year of Our Lord 2000 AD at one hour past midnight. Since they

28

were responsible for something they could not even define, they were dead spiritually.

The clergymen were instructed to absorb all debts and they being the most evil organization the world will ever experience, they kept distorting the words; And forgive us our sins; for we also forgive every one that is indebted to us. Start with forgive every one that is indebted to us comes from the Old Testament on usury laws. Indebted is money and American children and taxpayers are the greatest debtors in the world. The Nation of Israel is a nation of priests required to obey the Ten Commandments, so the sinners are the church priests.

A great mystery is the entire world is down to implementing the Lord's Prayer and His employees that must live by every word, but he does not have a clue of what the Lord's Prayer does and means. The reality of the their lack of knowledge must be covered without using evil spirits to hide their beliefs. They will realize what they did before they die. King Jesus Christ summarized in:

Luke 17:33 Whosoever shall seek to save his life shall lose it; and whosoever shall lose his life shall preserve it.

King Jesus Christ is looking for the clergymen who are willing to die for the Lord's Prayer and the ones that refuse and seek to save their lives shall die. The church must go through the story of resurrection.

God is the ruler of time and space. One hour past midnight in the year of Our Lord 2000 AD, the Gateway to Perdition was opened. Fear is what this book is about but I desire to write is what man may do in outer space. In the majority of science fiction literature, they blow up planet earth as serpentines. Many examples must be maintained, which is causing children to be violent. I wrote in my first book that we should stay on planet Earth, because what is at stake is the human race. Let us believe Adam does not desire to live through more penance and decides to obey God. We must live by every word of the Holy Bible. The Holy Bible is the cross the church employees of King Jesus Christ must bear as slaves or the word obey.

When we achieve the technology to reach the stars in our journey, what would be the purpose? First, the challenge is there. Second, we have to establish goals. The first goal may be to explore the worlds close to ours and seek knowledge. We may send rockets without man to see what is there. When we determine we desire to go, we would send a ship called "The Star of Bethlehem". The internal design of the crew will be the temple of Israel or the Eternal Temple. Population and change shall be designed. What an exciting time when man returns.

What if he finds worlds of life back in the dark ages, he must avoid. What if he finds life advanced to the point past the beginning of implementing the Lord's Prayer. Our space ship will look for equivalent to this world or seven Holy Cities. He will desire to obtain a copy of the seven Holy Bibles and the 666 beast books of Standing Historical, the 777 design for God's Children (one voice), and music. That must be the design for this world and beyond. The seven Holy Bibles can be away for us to translate their language into ours. Do not accept the knowledge of the Tree of Life or the Tree of Knowledge. Adam must create that knowledge without outside help. Yes, do not even accept the cure for cancer or grant it. If he colonizes, he will leave a copy of the Old Testament maybe and prepare for away to bring the new. We would love to see a new beginning of Israel and the Heartland. Maybe Our Father would manage until He can send a new only begotten son. You have a realistic chance to train future children and societies on God is the ruler of time and space. Do not go too far in what you believe or try to achieve, remember God is the ruler of space. We know what the people will look like as we can see an image in the mirror. The worlds and planet earth will be the same after we implement the Lords Prayer or seven names on the door and I see seven churches using the Universal Church format including the seven Holy Cities.

If you do not understand what I wrote above, you will find the knowledge contained within this book exciting and rewarding to learn. Your belly will be bitter, but your mouth will be sweet as honey. Book of Revelation 10:10 And I took the little book out of the angel's hand, and ate it up; and it was in my mouth sweet as honey: and as soon as I had eaten it, my belly was bitter. The words of the book of Revelation 10:10 must be met. Are you aware of the figure of speech or drink of my blood and eat of my body.

The church may write and produce some realistic movies of what they believe the future of exploration of outer space is by keeping in mind the challenges of scripture. I am a prophet, yet even I as a representative of God, would joy in seeing a well-played movie of real conversations not meaningless "fire at will". As science goes closer to exploration, may you keep the prophecies up to date through literature and films leading the way through being the Mother of Inspiration. God will never give you more to do than you can achieve; however, without God the best Adam can do is fail himself. The Holy Bible is true as Adam is doing one hundred percent of everything wrong. He has a book that always ends up with a life one thousand times better than the end and you can ask why Adam even discussed the end in the year of Our Lord 2000 AD. King Jesus Christ judged Adam in the past because He loved you. Can the clergymen become the saints to judge us because they love us or will their pride continue and the end will come?

Always believe in yourself. You as an individual can achieve equivalent to Divine Intervention if granted a chance. Your work will be the third power of eight and important to the world. No location shall consider they are small if they have a means of contacting people like on a telephone or a computer.

The next good tribulation the world will ever experience could be through you, if you are willing to be a leader.

Thy kingdom come as a challenge cannot be beaten by any work of man and yet God has created a value for all of you to be like a God like John, a saint. As a saint you control the Tree of Life and the Tree of Knowledge as gathers.

Chapter 2.   Stairway to Heaven

What a strange story to write in a book on fear (the seven thunders), which is required for the great and dreadful Day of the Lord or Good Friday. The reason is the clergymen of today are in one hundred percent fear and fear is the beginning of all wisdom (knowledge). If they do not change, the civilization as we know it will disappear. The only chance this world has is for the clergymen to implement the Lord's Prayer. Any other way will always result in Adam destroying everything Adam worked to inherit. The World Wide Web will teach you the clergymen will argue with you on why you should not try to obey God and live by every word like the Lord's Prayer. They will imply there are more important things to do rather than give Our God His Kingdom. I have heard their words or the kingdom is already formed because I am here. They do nothing more than lie as false witness by disobeying the Ten Commandments. You as a clergymen are in penance and they must learn what they did before they die. The clergymen must experience death. All the prophecies must come true and be understood.

What has Elijah done to help them? I wrote a presentation and created the words, so they can do it themselves. I grant you some of the letters I have sent. I have also gone to their locations. The name below is not the only locations. Paul is an auditor to be created by the church. King Jesus Christ is the only one that can save souls. Why can Paul claim he can save souls? It is because he is reforming the church. By reforming the church is the only way a clergyman can save souls. Read Corinthians 4:3 as the hardest thing to do is to judge yourself. I have covered the techniques in other writings in this book.

This is not the first letter I sent to a man worse than a fool or the Antichrist.

January 6, the Year of Our Lord 2008 AD
First Baptist Church
Appleton Road & W. Jackson St
PO Box 276
Belvidere, IL 61008-5800
Antichrist Rev. Rex A. Rogers

RE: Kill the Messenger

Now, you know whom the Antichrist is that is creating all that you see and hear as bad or as the Holy Bible states, Adam. What is good is nothing or the Noah's Ark story from God is kind. That I can prove. The new beginning can be only a few years away with your help. As Elias, I can form the kingdom and the book is complete or, "The Antichrist God's Version". You should realize why the book has that title. As Elijah, I can end ninety percent of the divorces in a kingdom in twenty years and the prophecy will be found to be easy. You must get the hearts of the children back with fathers or the fallen angels will be with the women and you will have babies having babies and your prisons will be filled with little ones that were small and great that did not go to the right school in the church environment. Have you heard of Pro-life or the opposite of the hearts of the fathers back with the children. You cannot believe you will not reach for the greatest tribulation (reward) a clergyman can see or the return of King Jesus Christ, once you have no questions to ask. I have copied King Jesus Christ thousand-year plan for the government from the Holy Bible and you can prove it from scripture. Can you allow all the people you see to die in the Battle of Armageddon, which starts in the United States because you do not need to hold a meeting?

You are responsible to find Elijah if you believe you cannot form God's Kingdom by yourself. The Universal Church format, which was granted in the year of Our Lord 1200 AD, has seven names on the door and seven Holy Cities. If you understand reality because of your blasphemous mouth, you worship Satan. If you stay with the gospel about Christ as defined in the year of Our Lord 31 AD, as Matthew 24:14 states, the end shall come. The Holy Bible is not the word of God. It is His plan. I have contacted you in the past and all you desired to do is kill the messenger.

The teenagers of America do not like organized religion so you believe that is not your problem. Let me kill the messenger. The teenagers do not like their parents getting divorces and you say I do not give a damn. I will kill the messenger. I am perfect. Why would I desire to change? All I have to do is con the congregation out of their money and I can tell them how great I am. Have you told the congregation about your version of Faith Healing? The Holy Bible states, you are taking pride in yourself and not humility for King Jesus Christ. The Holy Bible states you are asleep at the Altar. Why would you desire to change when you judge yourself as perfect? You must judge the world as a saint. The Holy Bible states you have the wrong heart for John 3:16 as you worship Satan. I can prove that statement. Can you prove King Jesus Christ's messenger is wrong?

I am Elijah to teach you how to end divorces so you can get the hearts of the fathers back with the children or teenagers back to the church. I am a prophet that can end millions of children dieing each year due to a famine (money). Do you desire to kill the messenger? A great amount of money is required and King Jesus Christ states I will double the best Adam can do. I have King Jesus Christ's thousand-year plan for the one world government of Israel for the United States. Do you need to kill His messenger and tell the congregation, "You know, I have to wait for King Jesus Christ to return?" The Holy Bible states He has told you all things, so you should know all the answers. Are you lying to the congregation and yourself? May you die without any possibility for John 3:16 as you desire to kill the teenagers that have a message or Elijah? You have the wrong heart for John 3:16.

Are you killing the messengers of the Italian Mafia and lying to the men that are failing themselves? They are in shackles and as failures cannot be saved. Are you killing the messenger of the families whose children die of drugs? The Italian Mafia has the wrong heart and the church does not care or are the Son of Perdition. Do you judge the politicians violating the book of Mark and becoming the Mark of the Beast? No, you are the Son of Perdition.

King Jesus Christ has judged you because He loved you. Do you judge the world of yours because you love the people that are dependent on you to hear the living word? The Holy Bible is clear. Do you have seven churches with the Universal Church format? Where is your Holy City? You are just the sinner that must repent and the Son of Perdition.

I have asked you and your peers to check what you must teach on the great and dreadful Day of the Lord or Good Friday. If you desire to check, you can correct and send to me. If you agree you should ask Elijah, "What should I do next?" If you take no action, just resign from the church or do the Millstone Story. You will find it impossible to be saved. You have a heart that is different from your God of Heart as you have the heart of Satan or heart of failure of yourself.

What is required of you? I have created a presentation and a voice file. You must read, listen, learn, reproduce some papers and set up a meeting. The rest I have done for you. You will learn more about religion in less than one hour than you have learned in your entire lifetime. It is time for Adam to grow up and learn how to talk. King Jesus Christ will not return until you have no questions to ask. The seals are for communication within a kingdom. The 666 beasts are books of Standing Historical or the history of your denomination in each nation where you have a presence. The beasts are the politicians you start a war to avoid their failures as human beings. The 666 beast books are to last longer than heaven and earth or from Here to Eternity, a measure of time. May a thousand zeros of time be short in terms of the effective use of the Holy Bible to resolve any problem in this world through one hundred percent theology!

Elijah

Richard Cartwright
430 Pembroke Rd SW
Poplar Grove, IL 61065
Tel # 815-765-0161
Elijah lives at Candlewick Lake, has a daughter and grand children living in Elk Grove Village, and can prove all that he has written.

The four words of the millennium are fear, war, jeopardy, and joy. I have not heard your understanding of how the words apply for the next thousand years.

The purpose of the church is to allow Our Gods to appoint a soul to a new life that has a future that they desire to inherit. As defined in Israel that life must be one thousand times better than the end, so one hundred percent of all people desire to worship God. How well do you believe the church has done when millions of children die each year? God has told you to stop sending Him little ones small and great. The Holy Bible states for you to form the kingdom and learn how to talk.

Memo started on January 31, the year of Our Lord 2008 AD

We must find the Antichrist before the world can progress and King Jesus Christ will return. Well, we should start out with what is known. You give me a sign.

In Israel, the antichrist forced God to divorce the church and put the clergymen in penance, since they refused to obey God. He is waiting for His virgin bride the church and kingdom.

First, the Antichrist came in an era of peace and prosperity. He speaks many tongues. He takes pride in himself, not humility for King Jesus Christ.

The year of Our Lord 2000 AD became the "Age of Accountability" as King Jesus Christ named the age.

The four words of the millennium story for the next one thousand years are war, fear, joy, and jeopardy. We must learn the meaning and use of the words.

We had a millennium story of many that talked about the end in the year of Our Lord 2000 AD.

All knees where to bow down to the King in the year of Our Lord 2000 AD or just before the beginning of the millennium.

The Antichrist will make useless eighty-two percent of the standing armies led by a man of European descent.

King Jesus Christ is the King of Peace and His clergymen are the Prince of Peace. We have to find the Prince of the princes or the leaders of the seven Holy Cities.

I heard Pastor Murray of FOX television make a good statement when he said, "The Antichrist is a clergymen teaching false doctrine." Any location violating the smallest of deviations from scripture will not be perfect and will qualify. I will add that to my information on who the Antichrist is. If you notice anyone deviating from scripture in the smallest detail, you have a moral responsibility to reform the church and save his soul.

I saw the two-hour documentary from Benny Hinn of TBN. I would not add anything to the two hour documentary he had on who the antichrist is. I would just discard it as fantasyland. The program was foolish wisdom or what the Holy Bible would call evil spirits. The church does not know what the word evil means.

In Israel, the antichrist is where the clergymen disobeyed God three times. Are you sending Him little ones small and great despite He tells you to stop doing that? In a kingdom, the easiest thing to do is feed the children. The Holy Bible states, I do not care what they eat. Can you believe in a fool that believes he is better than God or a clergyman?

Can you add to the definition so we can find the Antichrist?

Many saw the false prophet in Jerusalem when Pope John Paul II was going to use the power of creation to destroy a city in Israel.

Satan was in the only Holy City.

King Jesus Christ gave us a summation of the book of Daniel in the Lord's Prayer. The book of Revelation states I saw seven churches. God has judged the seven churches and many have claimed the Church of Philadelphia or a church of liars is a good church to attend. See Gerald Flurry on Sunday on WGN. The first five are not considered acceptable. Where are the nonaligned churches in the seven names?

The Catholic Church is the seventh as they are to poor.

The Catholic Church is bad and any location other than a Catholic location is worse than bad or terrible.

39

King Jesus Christ judged us long ago and before because He loved us. The saints are to judge the world for the same reason.

King Jesus Christ has told the clergymen all things, so they have the answers, like the seals are used for communication in a kingdom. The 666 beast books are written Standing Historical or the history of the denominations of each nation.

The United States started out as a nation in the year of Our Lord 1776 AD and President Abraham Lincoln invited the Jewish man in and made us a country of two nations. Today the church has allowed twenty-one hundred religions or nations in the United States.

Israel was a nation of priests; therefore, the clergymen are to obey the Ten Commandments and become the saints in the church world. Since they are the priests, they become the man of sin and unpardonable sins are a great concern of a clergyman in a kingdom. They cannot take pride in themselves, but must live by every word of the Holy Bible, thereby take humility for King Jesus Christ. Their cross to bear is the Holy Bible.

The Universal Church format was granted to the church in the year of Our Lord 1200 AD and contains a Holy City. Now, you must have seven denominations with seven Holy Cities. The book of Revelation states I saw seven churches.

King Jesus Christ has stated if you abandon Thy Children, I will abandon you and the penance will continue for seven times longer. The end is where the church abandons His children (angels) of 777 design or to twenty-one years old. Many adults are leaving the major denominations for the nonaligned or leaving the church entirely. I have gone to many almost empty church locations. The teenagers of America do not like organized religion and most have left the church. All churches do not work together to form the kingdom and get them back. The clergymen are in penance and all they have is good intentions. The road to hell is paved with good intentions.

Where are the good deeds? Is it on the 5 o'clock news? I see blame, not glad tidings.

The Holy Bible states the church has gone backwards from the year of Our Lord 1900 AD until today and the wax is cold. In New York City in the year of Our Lord 1900 AD was a nation of love and marriage and the US government was zero dollars in debt. Today, New York City is a place of abortions and divorces and our government is the greatest debtor nation in the world. Scripture proclaims the wax is cold.

King Jesus Christ stated how it would be with Lot. In the year of Our Lord 1900 AD you would move Lot to New York City. Today you would desire Lot to leave New York City, but there would be nowhere for him to go. The wax is cold. What has the Antichrist achieved in the last one hundred plus years? They have gone backwards and the wax is cold. The clergymen have made everything worse.

Fear is the beginning of all wisdom (knowledge). Are the churches teaching the crime syndicates, they are in shackles or are the clergymen the Son of perdition?

Should the clergymen send President Herbert C. Hoover to the true Heaven in the year of Our Lord 1932 AD for his good works for America or was he taking the world on the road to hell? The Antichrists have shackle less churches and believe they are better than God is and can violate the Holy Bible. Is that considered humility for King Jesus Christ? King Jesus Christ put the wicked in shackles, not the people in prisons.

Can you add to the definition, so we can find the Antichrist?

The Antichrist speaks many tongues as the Holy Bible states the language of the church should be English, so the clergymen can communicate in the church environment.

777 design for children on how to help raise a child must be one voice across America and the world. That is the age born

41

to twenty-one. King Jesus Christ states, we cannot go to Israel to learn how to raise a child. All locations add to the enlighten power as one voice, but do not drive them away. The clergymen refuse to work together to help raise a child using one voice or the same in all locations.

The fallen angels are with the women. Many single women raise the boys without fathers as marriage has become much less important than in the year of Our Lord 1900 AD in America. Many fallen angels are raised in part by the police officer not the church. The angels are the children of 777 design. Pro-life and divorces are the opposite of getting children back with biological fathers and biological fathers back with children.

Children do not like divorces, so the Antichrists drive them away. They send the parents to divorce court or the land of chaos and confusion to receive marriage counseling. The Holy Bible contains the rules on divorces, not the judge in a land of total failure. All a judges should be able to do is divide up the money to the advantage of the children, not the adults.

All laws are bad that are important and the church refuses to train the politicians on how to write New Testament laws or equivalent in government to faith and wait and all that is left is love.

The politicians like foolish George Bush has violated the book of Mark in a big way and some clergymen state all the laws are good. They refuse to train from scripture, but state you know you are saved. King Jesus Christ saves, not the clergymen. Divorced people are not saved. Only a penance man can get off this world alive. Satan cannot be saved. Satan is part of the penance you receive for violating the Holy Bible. You are doing one hundred percent of everything wrong and the wax is cold.

The clergymen claim they can save souls which violates the Holy Bible. The only way they can save is by reforming the church. I have never heard of any success in reforming the church. Where are the seven Holy Cities and the Universal Church format that is the only acceptable way?

I know the Antichrists are the clergymen that refuse to implement the Lord's Prayer and live in the kingdom as defined by the Universal Church format of the year of Our Lord 1200 AD.

The church must develop the reality of the Tree of Life and the Tree of Knowledge from the Garden of Eden. That can only be developed in a kingdom. Elijah, the prophet or King Jesus Christ's true representative can teach you how to form the kingdom as the greatest tribulation the world will ever see.   The kingdom story or the Lord's Prayer by the church is the best story man can create and the only chance to avoid the end.

The Holy Bible states for the church to find Elijah, the prophet. What has the Antichrist done to find Elijah and what tests did he use to verify?

The Holy Bible states when you are running your perfect church with the door (tree) stories well understood by the congregation, what should you do when a stranger enters your church? Do not drive him away when they do not know the tree stories. Where are the Antichrists creating a perfect church and the tree stories are well known?

The 666 beast books are recorded Standing Historical written to biblical standards as the clergymen start a war against the politicians if they are beasts. One name is Life of US (U.S.) Catholic. Life of Mexico Catholic is another.

The seals are for communication within a kingdom.

The Four Horsemen are defining what war the churches are in against the beasts or what is bad (sorrows).

We are past the seventh beast and the eighth beast is already a beast but has the wrong title in the year of the Lord 2008 AD to the end as scripture defines. I have to update at this time in that the year of Our Lord 2012 AD is the last election in the

United States unless the church does divine intervention or the third power of eight.

The eleven hundred and fifty days in the book of Daniel is for the aligned churches. The twenty- three hundred days are for the nonaligned churches.

Unless you shorten the days (form the kingdom) no flesh is saved (no John 3:16).

Once the clergymen start to form the kingdom and learn how to talk, they get John 3:16 back as they have the beginning of the right heart. Men that worship Satan as today have the wrong heart.

The clergymen must go through the story of resurrection to get John 3:16 back and reverse the end.

All that refuse to implement the Lord's Prayer cannot be saved. They have the wrong heart as the ones with the blasphemous mouth that worship Satan now.

I can prove Satan was with us and will be around for only a short time longer or the year of Our Lord 2009 AD as he will retire. He was in the Holy City on television in case you missed it.

Send your updates to comfortingod@mchsi.com. I will add to the summation.

What other names has God called His clergymen? The names my be more but I will list the ones I heard.
1. Antichrist.
2. Prince of Darkness not Prince of Peace.
3. The lawless ones not the meek that inherit the earth as they eliminate prisons.
4. The sinner not the congregation as they are in jeopardy, not sinners. The church is to identify the man of sin. The priest calling the congregation a

sinner is blame and a sin. The church is not a nation of priests, like the temple of Israel.

5. The Son of Perdition. They do not teach people the true meaning of John 3:16 and from the book of Luke to have the right heart.

6. Any other names that He has used to inspire the priests must be found in the Holy Bible and defined in Standing Historical or 666 beast books.

When the clergymen write the Standing Historical of the United States or any other location, it will be apparent why they will be hated (loved less) than anyone else for my Name sake as prophecy defined.

February 6, the year of Our Lord 2008 AD

First Baptist Church
Appleton Road & W. Jackson St
PO Box 276
Belvidere, IL 61008-5800
Rev. Rex A. Rogers

Re: Elijah

I believe your greatest problem is King Jesus Christ cannot send a man back from the true Heaven to help you. King Jesus Christ did not forsaken you; He sent Elijah and trained him to help. All you desire to do is work against all others of your denomination and you are afraid to ask a question.

The true representative of Our Gods would be like Paul, Daniel or all others you find in the Holy Bible. If you truly believed in King Jesus Christ, you would believe His representative would have a small horn (not like a Pope in voice recognition). All he would try to do is what prophecy foretells or be a true prophet of God and at least be able to get the hearts of the fathers back with the children. That would mean ending divorces and children born out of marriage. To get the children back with fathers, you have to get the women married not work on Pro-life. Pro-life violates the Holy Bible.

Look in the mirror and ask yourself a question, "If a man tells you he can implement the Lord's Prayer and start the beginning of heaven on earth, should I take a small amount of time to listen?" I will give you a series of questions you can start with.

The Holy Bible states to stop sending me little ones small and great. How would I get the money to do that all over the world? The answer is simple for God's prophet.

One of the biggest problems in American churches is marriage is not that important and the teenagers do not like organized religion. How can I solve that problem? In heaven on earth or the Lord's Prayer that challenge should be easy, but whether they go to a church or not does not matter today. The divorce rate is over fifty percent. Elijah can solve that problem in a kingdom of seven names on the door, as the book of Daniel requires. Today you have thirty-six names on the door (denominations) and half nonaligned with gays and demons running to marry.

To end the above problems, you would tell me you are too small. King Jesus Christ cannot send you a person to add a book to the Holy Bible. Not all the people in the Holy Bible can exist or a man in the year of Our Lord 2008 AD. I have been asking you to consider, what is the best you can do without me? Would you say marriage would disappear and I will send Our Gods additional billions of little ones small and great? Are you sure, you have the heart of Our King? I can prove whom you worship.

To end the problems, I have created a presentation that would allow the smallest church to be able to start the beginning of heaven on earth if they have a telephone. What advantage do you have over me? Pride is a deadly sin, but I agree with the Holy Bible which states I am to handicapped to do it myself. I do not run a church and the Holy Bible is clear as to what title I should seek now. Are you to handicapped to do it yourself? The answer is yes. What you seek is the prophecy of five denominations and one thousand signatures.

In addition to you being able to create the greatest tribulation (reward) the world will ever see His Kingdom, prove you desire to obey Him, and you can end what is poor within your world like health care, education, daily bread, marriage, abortions or anything that is the beginning of the sorrows. Now, King Jesus Christ will return. I can grant you the plan for any sorrow described here and any other that are major. King Jesus Christ will return when you have no questions to ask. You would expect King Jesus Christ to be able to fulfill the prophecy of Elijah to complete the Holy Bible.

Do you know of any organization that desires to implement the Lord's Prayer? I will go anywhere I have a chance to stop the Battle of Armageddon, which starts in the United States in less than one decade or the end. On the web, all I found were losers that need to work against implementing the Lord's Prayer so King Jesus Christ cannot return. The clergymen must first prove they desire to obey Him as if you should believe a slave would or the clergymen must teach the congregation to live by every word of the Holy Bible. If you know of any organization that desires to implement the Lord's Prayer, please send me their contact information and I will try.

What would it cost you but maybe a hour of your time to ask, "How can I start heaven on earth and how far can I go? What should I do next?" Of all the items you work on, can one hour to end millions of unnecessary deaths of children be too much for your Gods to ask of you? I am the true Elijah and I am not taking God's name in vain.

Elijah

Richard Cartwright
430 Pembroke Rd SW
Poplar Grove, IL 61065
Tel # 815-765-0161

Elijah lives at Candlewick Lake, has a daughter and grand children living in Elk Grove Village, and can prove all that he has written.

I will start your work to bring you and all others to the new beginning. Do not expect me to copy all the Holy Bible requires you to do, but you must in a Vow of Silence (silent war) challenge yourself and your peers to answer all questions you may have. One may be God's Covenants. The answer would be for you and your peers to determine what the minimum requirement is to run a church. Standing Historical is the history of your church in each country as you work against the politicians that violate the book of Mark and develop the Mark of the Beast should be recorded. Do not forget the politicians that fail to blow the trumpet and one person dies. For example, the Mark of the Beast should be called Hoover Ville in the year of Our Lord 1932 AD, yet President Herbert C. Hoover desired to be president again. The format is in the Holy Bible. The Mark of the Beast in your forehead is the politicians we see representing King Jesus Christ that have the knowledge from the book of Mark. When we see them, we know they are trained by the church.

How would an individual clergymen get heaven on earth started? Where does an individual start? I have developed the first meeting presentation and the words of the presentation. The first part is the presentation and the words of the presentation follow.

The Beginning of Heaven on Earth

The Supper (Last Supper) Meeting

Kingdom First

1. Change anything that is bad into good.
2. Reach God is amongst us.
3. Develop the leaders of the church and family as royalty.
4. Reach for heaven on earth.

VG 1

God's Plan

I do not want you to do a job, you do not want to do.

A want is a demand that the government must satisfy.

I	I	I	I
0	7	14	21

49

VG 2

The New Beginning or the End

1. Continue Gospel about Christ (31 A.D.) Book of Matthew.

2. Start Gospel of Christ (Holy Spirit 6th Sense).

3. Book of Daniel go to Perdition for clergymen and congregation on earth.

4. The end or a new beginning.

5. Start heaven on earth.

6. Eliminate what is poor like poverty.

7. The Beasts

VG 3

MIRACLES WITHIN OUR HANDS.

What is the greatest miracle in which you have a copy?

The Holy Bible

Once you form the kingdom, you realize you require seals for communications. Other questions can be answered, as the Holy Bible is a planning book. King Jesus Christ plan is for you to teach the world to plan or it is one hundred percent theology. In a kingdom the Holy Bible will be understood by all clergymen. The Holy Bible contains the tests the clergymen must go through before King Jesus Christ will return. Only when His Father is satisfied all tests are completed will King Jesus Christ meet us in the temple of Israel, not church.

VG 4

Notes

Once you form the kingdom all your questions are answered as King Jesus Christ has told us all things. Therefore, you have had the answer to granting the church world a life that is one thousand times better than the end or humanity destroying the world as recorded through the failure of Adams. The difference is you have a book that you can plan anything. When one hundred percent of the congregation can plan their inheritance (future), you are at one thousand times better than today. You should realize that a million men will work together as seven Holy Cities and yet all will define what to do to raise God's Children of 777 design. You develop a book of needs is where is documented and at the age of King Jesus Christ baptism, you ask a member of the congregation. "Are you saved and ready to be reborn again or do you require more education?"

Do not go into King Jesus Christ computerized planning technique yet, but His system is covered in books or a path to a small door.

Therefore, King Jesus Christ divorced you when the church of Israel disobeyed three times and He did not help you, so Adam has done one hundred percent of everything wrong. Without God, Adam is just a fool.

God's Government Plan

1. King of kings and nation against nation.

2. Understand one world government for US.

3. Do not cover but provide handouts.

4. Change of today 2009 A.D.

5. Develop goals (Prophecy) for 2050 A.D.

6. Receive schools 2800 A.D.

7. Plan for the year 3000 A.D. as covered in scripture.

8. Review for the next meeting.

VG 5

How to get started.

1. Explain Moses Laws.

2. Cover King Jesus Christ Words on Moses Laws.

3. Develop meaning of Church Laws.

4. God's Name in Vain.

5. Vow of Poverty.

6. Vow of Silence.

7. Change committees to King Jesus Christ technique not Adams.

VG 6

Reference reading notes and not part of the presentation.

Holy Bible

Entire book The Antichrist God's Version written by Elias. In Mark 9:12, Jesus stated, "Elias will come first and restoreth all things." A copy can be obtained from www.iuniverse.com. That is the first book from the book of Daniel.

Chapter on most miracles is Chapter 18 &19. You will understand the power of heaven on earth.

From Chapter 24 page 274 & up on Church Law.

Read the sixty-seventh book of the Holy Bible or this book.

Chapter 3 and 4 of sixty-seventh book of the Holy Bible contains over twenty-five thousand words of prophecies or miracles people would state is not possible today or create the wall of hope. What is shown is the faith of the unseen. The call to action or hope will put the stories to rest as the church is run by mysteries and intrigue.

One world government comes as documented below. It is a commitment of the one party that represents King Jesus Christ in the King of kings. One government led by the two hundred million members plus of the Salvation Army with gospel armor in the Heartland of the world or USA. The political party will be named Health, Wealth, and Wisdom. The Heartland is the land where King Jesus Christ will make a stand or He stands for every word of the Holy Bible. I can explain the passage, "I do not want you to do a job you do not want to do.", to explain why it is 100% theology. One World government will be published in the book, sixty-seventh book of the Holy Bible. I will use the handout to explain.

The Supper Story is a requirement of the church, which makes the smallest location a very powerful voice. A clergymen invites twelve peers or some number and they do the "Last Supper" story except do not make your first your last. The smallest location can have a voice for the entire world if he has a good idea.

When you read, you will become like Moses or a man without a country. You will become royalty. Your children will wear the color purple and if you have a wife and the women see her purple cloth at the market, you will reach God is amongst us.

Holy Spirit Possessions is in sub chapter 9 of Chapter 24.

Holy Spirit and Holy Ghost are in Chapter 17 where I am Paul.

You may ask about Communion and what you will have to develop or 777 design. We can spend too much time together to explain it all. As you develop, all will be understood.

Once you have your Church Laws ask each to start all over with twelve of their peers. Now you have the confidence of many not just a small group. You are ready to go to upper leadership and others like the pope in Rome.

Reference is from the book, "The Antichrist God's Version" available on the web at www.iuniverse.com and other locations. The Author is Elias of Mark 9:12.

Next is the presentation from the word file.

When you hear this presentation, you will understand the meaning of Revelation 10:10. And I took the little book out of the angel's hand and eat it up and it was in my mouth sweet as honey and as soon as I had eaten it my belly was bitter. From Revelation 10:4. When the seven thunders had utter their voices. Seven Thunders, that is fear!!!!!!!!!!!!!!!!!!!!! What are the four words of the millennium? The four words are jeopardy to joy, war, and fear.

You are looking for the sixty-seventh book of the Holy Bible. The one God told St John not to release at that time, but save it for modern times, right now. The sixty-seventh book of the Holy Bible was the book by Elijah as trained by King Jesus Christ, the mysterious messiah.

Now GO TO THE FIRST VU GRAPH.

Well, I would like to welcome you to the beginning of heaven on earth. God has given us the challenge for us to lead the way. As the Holy Bible said the first thing we have to do is form the kingdom and learn how to talk. The book of Daniel, we seem to know is a book, we do once. In there it says you have eleven hundred and fifty days and twenty-three hundred days. King Jesus Christ has given us a summation of the book of Daniel, where the aligned churches like the Catholics and us, we go through the eleven hundred and fifty days to implement the Lord's Prayer. That will take forty-two months. We get everything done in eleven hundred and fifty days and review all until the forty-two months of time has expired.

We are trying to do is get our upper management, the leaders of our particular denomination to recognize in terms of King Jesus Christ's plan, most work starts right at the local church level. Once they develop the concept, then it is presented to upper views. The first thing we have to do is figure out what King Jesus Christ expects us to do, when we have a kingdom. Well naturally, we should write down everything we consider being a sorrow and turn it into good or jeopardy to joy. That challenge seems rather simple to do. So we just write down anything we think is bad and turn it into good. Well, let us start with we have a number of people that are dieing of unnecessary deaths in our country, the United States. We have children eating out of garbage cans. We do not have Universal Health Care unless you believe in what the government is doing in the year of Our Lord 2009 AD. What was signed came at a price of bribery and the model for the entire world as developed by Elijah will prevail. What I hear is you must purchase health care or else. The rich are bidding up the price of health care stocks as fortunes can be made. Maybe other techniques should apply as developed by Elijah and approved by the church. There does not seem to be enough money to go around to overcome the sorrows of the country, yet in a kingdom no one worries about money. We must resolve what the Holy Bible calls the sorrows and eliminate the problems as fast as we can.

The government seems to be all in the world of blame. Foolish President Bush used extensive blame in the year of Our Lord 2004 AD election as defined in the Holy Bible. Senator John F. Kerry spent a lot of money reacting to that blame. All we hear from campaigning is they blame, worst blame, more blame and the congregation does not learn about what they are trying to achieve. So one of the things we desire to do is to form the one world government. The just finished campaign between Senator John McCain and Senator Barack Obama was the same. What won was not the views of Senator Barack Obama, but through a vast amount of money convincing the voter Senator John McCain and foolish George Bush would be the same results in the economy. Where is President Elect Barack Obama's great economic miracle that won the election because of his good ideas for change and recovery? Our president was not qualified to run, but was ten times better than his opponent Senator John McCain. Our president is not an idea man as he never introduced a new piece of legislation for his term in office as a senator. What is missing is the blood of a just man to end the black plague or the word blame. King Jesus Christ gave all of His blood (there was nothing left) and the clergymen do not give their blood to end the word blame, but say Lo here and Lo there when they talk about others.

What are we trying to achieve? We are trying to reach God is amongst us. What does the Holy Bible say? We become prince. For example in the Prince of Peace, we always teach King Jesus

Christ is the Prince. In reality, the prince is the clergymen and we are in charge of Domestic Tranquility. Domestic Tranquility most of us have not heard that word for a long time. That was the beginning of the United States of America with the laws of liberty.

When we are wearing the color purple as royalty and we go into the grocery store, people see God is amongst us. When we are driving our cars with the special color purple, people see God is amongst us with all denominations the same. When we go to any celebration, or rally, or any place that we meet including from the Altar, they see God is amongst us. We have formed a kingdom.

What we have to do is develop the leaders of the church and their families as royalty (the Holy Bible defines you as a saint). Israel was a nation of priests. When you obey the Ten Commandments as a clergyman, you become saints as in comparison with the rest of the people and you are to judge the world. King Jesus Christ judged you long ago because He loved you. You are to walk a mile in His footsteps, so you judge the world because you love the congregation. We should understand our children would be wearing the color purple. What are we trying to reach? Every place in the Holy Bible that said God would do, we as a work force through a kingdom can achieve. What is required is a place where people can congregate and a plan. King Jesus Christ has told you all things. We are to reach for the Lord's Prayer and creating heaven on earth. We are the chosen ones to lead the way. God will not give us more than what we can do. You think of a prayer as your call to action in His name.

Next VG

God's Plan.

We are going to learn what God's Plan is. Anything in the Holy Bible that God said He or we are to do that is His employees must achieve. For example, King Jesus Christ states to get rid of prisons. The kingdom and politicians can achieve if we work together in any nation. King Jesus Christ admits, we can do it better because the congregation goes to the church. What is required is a place where people can congregate, so we must stay at the Altar. The mothers of a billion children will demand 777 design and thy children of 777 design will prosper. Another example, we are going to reach for one of the passages in the Holy Bible, so we can learn and train our upper management on what the Holy Bible actually does and what God's Plan is. We are creating the beginning of the tree story for your perfect church. The Holy Bible states God's Plan is one hundred percent theology or planning from the Holy Bible. By the Grace of God, you are saved. There is nothing you have to do. The grace of God is His work or the entire Holy Bible. What is missing is the grace of the clergymen as the wax is cold. The passages are there. The church is to teach the congregation on how to live by every word. King Jesus Christ planned it all, so there is nothing you have to do because the plan is already there. We will start out with a passage, I do not want you to do a job, you do not want to do. A want is a demand the government must satisfy. We shall not want. Now in order to understand this passage, many of us would say God tells us not to take a job we do not want to do.

In the United States, what is happening is that ninety percent of the students are taking the wrong careers in college. It was on national television. The Federal Reserve in the year of Our Lord 1999 AD stated that ninety percent of the college graduates are taking the wrong courses. In other words, we train them for a job they do not want to do. Unfortunately, what that means to us is that is something that is bad or a sorrow. According to the Holy Bible if you allow that to continue that becomes a sin for the clergymen. He must develop the Holy Spirit words to inspire the resolution of the problem. If we fail to create the Holy Spirit words, we should realize what will happen to us. Also many millions of people cannot find a job even one they do not want to do. That is fear as it is bad government and bad laws. Therefore, you are trying to change everything that is bad, that becomes our sins and turn it into something that is good. We cannot do it ourselves because it is a demand the government must satisfy.

So in order to start this off, we should take out a piece of paper, take your pencil, and draw a straight line and mark off 0 years, 7, 14, and 21.

That is 777 design as one voice or all church locations the same. You can relate this to the temple at thirteen or 77 design, where all temple locations are the same. The Rabbi should add seven more years. We start when the children have hair on their head and the temple should add seven more years to twenty. In the church we become adults at twenty-one. Any church location that does not have this is failing the children of your world. You are abandoning the children. Where is the right heart for John 3:16? King Jesus Christ said it is one hundred percent theology. In addition, He stated we cannot go to Israel to learn how to raise a child.

We are looking to see what affects our children the most in education, when they are at the age of a teenager. A problem in education today is one hundred and sixty thousand children cannot go to school. In addition, we have thirty million children on happy pills turning many A & B students into D & E. In the year of the Lord 1939 AD, the major problem in schools was gum, not happy pills. Where is the Exorcist story or the clergymen getting the Demons out of the children minds? You should know the clergymen helping to raise a child is one of the main functions of a church. One of the instructions King Jesus Christ said is a woman is His educator. They have to come through the church to learn the procedures. We have some responsibilities too. We are going to do a communion for a child at seven years old. The children are God's angels. They are to talk at the Altar and our senators must be trained to listen to them for John 3:16. We are in charge of Domestic Tranquility and seven is very young to learn this. One of the lessons, we need to teach is how a child should turn the other cheek. We sit down in front of them, but the women have done some preliminary work in teaching on how to turn the other cheek. We tell them we are in charge of their safety because Domestic Tranquility, they may not understand. They are to be safe in the schools and in the neighborhoods. That is our responsibility. In order to achieve, we require their help. We are trying to explain what they should do if they get in a bad situations of being a bully that interferes with Domestic Tranquility. We are looking to them to seek their guidance in terms of what we have to achieve. As you are going along, you are trying to get the children, especially the teenagers, to do presentations. When they run across situations where they have a chance to turn the other cheek, we should learn. We have simple plays maybe ten minutes or maybe a half hour on the twelve days of Christmas or anytime during the year, where you are showing the younger children on how to turn the other cheek. A child shall lead the way. Who is giving you the answers? We learn from the teenagers that have gone through the experiences. You are asking the teenagers to help you teach the younger children on how to turn the other cheek and they are very involved. A child that is the solution usually does not become the problem.

You are working on a problem of we do not want you to do a job, you do not want to do. In the thousand-year plan when you read it, you will have a possibility of two years in kindergarten. The children can start first grade better prepared. For the seventh and eighth graders, we will have the educators try to determine which children shall go to high tech schools, where they have a higher potential to be doctors, physicists, programmers as opposed to the regular schools. You are trying to separate them out because we desire high tech in this country because of the technology of the future, which is incredible. We are trying to look at our plan of 777 design and we are coming up with fourteen years. That is when they are going into high school. What are you trying to do but teach the Holy Spirit words? Write this down, sixth sense or six words of common sense, "Play it Cool, Stay in School". You mark that as fourteen years old that you are teaching. You are going into communions and so you are asking the children at that age. "Are you prepared to go into high school and learn what career you should be taking when you graduate from high school and or college? The first item you have to consider is:

1. Is money.
2. Is money.
3. Is money.
4. Is challenge.

It is up to us to fill in the blanks as to what sermons we are going to teach the teenagers at that age. The question they should answer is, "The IQ I possess, how can I serve myself best? Yes, I said serve myself best." The teenagers may desire to know for families that are without want what allowance they should have, but let us not go into that right now. Let us stay with the fact we need to teach them, "Play it Cool, Stay in School" or the Holy Spirit words. We are trying to overcome the fact that ninety percent of the students are taking the wrong courses in college. We are not even talking about graduating from high school.

What are you doing to fill in the blanks between fourteen and twenty-one, especially just before seventeen and one half? The twelve days of Christmas must be developed where in a sense the children run the church (a new beginning). In the twelve days of Christmas period is just before the time they are going to graduate from high school. For some children that grew up in your congregation, they have gone through high school and that is as far as they have gone. As electricians, they are learning equivalent to some college education in the labor unions. The truck drivers at UPS are learning how to get the packages delivered or what other manager's courses are designed, but exclude the children that go to college. They are to tell you how they picked the career, they ended up with. The first time you try, it is not very good, but as the years go on, you get more children graduating from college and from high school. You are finding out that someone needed to be a lab technician. They did not go to a high tech school, but they went to a junior college or technical school, or being Mr. Good Wrench that requires many technical skills in order to fix the cars in modern times. They must interface with the computers to be able to access the web and read all the instructions on what potentially could be wrong with a product. As you do that, you are developing plays. We call them Career Day plays. You start in the beginning with strictly with college first. Somebody is going to be an engineer, a rocket scientist, a clergymen, whatever the stories are on how to get started. You get those people to write down some plays. How did they pick the career? What were the problems they had to over come in schools, what their counselors told them, and all other types of information? As life goes on, you are developing the plays for hundreds of years. You realize these plays get to be very good as Career Days. Think about it, you have access to these children after school. You have the upper hand in complimenting the demand, the want. A want is a demand the government must satisfy. I do not want you to do a job you do not want to do. The passage becomes part of the tree story. That is a demand. We shall not want. You can compliment the government in a way because the people are still with you.

You must have the twelve days of Christmas and you have Career Day. Well, that becomes quite a challenge when children are learning how to turn the other cheek, do songs of praise to God about turning the other cheek, and songs of praise to God about the careers, they can do. A song, Onward Christian

Soldier as to war in terms of becoming a labor union person or a programmer as a career. We keep going and every day, every year, and every century goes by, you are looking at the numbers and you wonder why. The numbers seem to improve greatly at first, it is true, but then you are getting down closer to none. The number never seems to change and you are suffering for your faith waiting for those days of your great grace.

NEXT VG

If you need to know God's Plan, you have to understand the new beginning or the end. Back in the year of Our Lord 31 AD, what did you do? You decided to go into the gospel about Christ and the book of Matthew 24:14, "And this gospel of all the kingdom shall be preached in all the world for a witness unto all nations and the end shall come." The mystery is in the word this. The Holy Bible is not the word of God, it is His plan. The Holy Bible states by now you should be teachers, not preachers. The word of God is how you are getting the children into the right careers. A mind is a terrible thing to waste. Is it possible for one hundred percent of all the people in the world to have a good job and a job they want to do? The only answer possible is yes in God's Kingdom.

The Holy Bible is God's Plan, not His words. Many people talk about they are hearing the Holy Spirit words, but they are reading God's Plan. The Holy Spirit words are, "Play it Cool, Stay in School." I do not want you to do a job you do not want to do. That becomes the word of God. Therefore, what you have to do to achieve the new beginning is start the Gospel of Christ, Holy Spirit, sixth sense (six words of common sense) as you have written in front of you. You can go into sermons about divorces, where the sixth sense words are, "For the love of God's Children". All across the world, you are teaching and developing the sermons. The words seem to imply what you are trying to do. The sixth sense sermons becomes the Holy Spirit words for the group of sermons.

As a clergymen, you cannot possibly develop all of the techniques that are possible. You use a computerized program. It is the path to the small door. Let us assume on divorces you have seven sermons that are used quite a bit and there are ten in file. You have access to it as a leader of the church. You are putting a number in there when you are using a file. You have a count as to what is current or not. Three of the sermons are really out of favor, but someone in your congregation comes to you with an idea, or you have an idea listening to somebody and you create a sermon. What denomination are you? Yes, you are one of the seven, from the book of Revelation or I saw seven churches. You put the sermon in there and it becomes available for all the other clergymen like yourself to access. Do they care at all? No, they do not care at all, what denomination you are. You find out no one decides to use it, what should you do? Delete. What if you find out a hundred thousand clergymen, like yourself desire to use it? You have done something great. Here you are a little church in Montana and you have had an influence on South America and Russia. Sixth sense goes that way. You are not by yourself any more. You have a computerized system, which includes an outline of the sermon, and the voice file. You have to decide on the right ones. The Holy Bible states, you have to do time management. There is only so much time.

Getting back to the ones that desire to disobey King Jesus Christ and not implement the Lord's Prayer, you have to go through that also. King Jesus Christ put you in penance way back when you disobeyed in Israel and He divorced you and refused to help you. In Israel and after is the antichrist that came before. You have been on your own for all these years, all these centuries and the answer has always been to implement the Lord's Prayer. Therefore, what you get as far as the power is derived is, "If God is for you, who can stand against you." The only answer is you always work for no one. You are trying to teach "For the Love of God's Children" in divorces. You are trying to find those families that are against you. You teach the children are better off if you stay married.

What happens to those clergymen that unfortunately do not need to implement the Lord's Prayer at a particular location? They die a second death and cannot be saved. They go by the way of Satan. There is a sense of urgency on this change. What happens if you fail to implement the Lord's Prayer? You are failing yourself because you are not becoming royalty. You are not having all the pleasures of developing the techniques of the Holy Spirit. As defined in the book of Luke, you have to believe in John 3:16, but in order to qualify you must have the right heart. If you have a blasphemous mouth, taking pride in yourself, you will worship Satan. That is not going to give you John 3:16.

Unfortunately, what happens is the true end shall come or God will give you the curse of more penance because of your inaction. The famine at the end times is not for daily bread as most clergymen desire to work at. If it was, they are really failing at it. Every time you turn around there are more people going into poverty requiring daily bread. That is really a want or a demand the government must satisfy. The famine at the end time is for the word of God. If you look in the Old Testament, it is the usury laws and interest baring investments that are affecting us. That shall be the end of civilization, as we know it unless the government goes through and does what King Jesus Christ told you to do. The United States of America became the greatest debtor nation in the world, our currency is green, and it becomes buyers and sellers remorse. That means the dollar collapses completely and we have to get a political party that will get us out of debt, but you can read more about that later.

What we need to talk about is we need to start heaven on earth. Once you form the kingdom and you learn the Holy Bible technique, you desire this one world government. Many people say, the poor are in poverty and that cannot change. There is nothing we can change; however, the clergymen have a Vow of Poverty and they shall not be poor. So poverty is a little more of a definition that will evolve once you understand that poor is something like bankruptcy court, poor is like earthquakes, more like hurricanes where people suffer like Louisiana and the government does not have the money to solve the problems or does not try. If you form the kingdom, it is rather easy for us through a one-world government to end the defined sorrows because Elijah already has a thousand year plan that states how easy it is to do. As a matter of fact if you form the kingdom, you wonder why anyone ever worked long on poverty, because it is so easy to eliminate. The suffering of the clergymen is waiting for this poverty to disappear all around the world. Part of the tribulation becomes past the Seventh Trumpet Story because you formed the kingdom and you formed this one world government. The only country, we have a plan for is for the one world government of Israel is for the United States. That is all it stands for.

Part of the prophecy is unfortunately an extreme, great failure on our part. Unless you shorten the days, no flesh is saved. The Garden of Eden story states that once you are responsible for good and evil, you will surely die. The clergymen do not know what the word evil means. What no flesh is saved means is John 3:16 has disappeared and the way to get it back is to implement the Lord's Prayer. From the book of Daniel, it is eleven hundred and fifty days even though it is forty-two months. We get everything done in eleven hundred and fifty days and then we must review everything and make sure we have everything in place. Twenty-three hundred days are for the half that are the nonaligned church locations. That is seven years. At that time seven years, if you fail to join the kingdom, agree to work on the Lord's Prayer, and become one of the seven denominations, your soul is sacrificed because you failed yourself and you go the way of Satan. That is fear for the clergyman.

A quick review of past the Seventh Trumpet Story. You will be given a copy of the thousand-year plan for the government of the United States. The Seventh Trumpet Story is from the Old Testament where King David's son was granted through Our Father a reprieve from all killing wars. We will still use the Seventh Trumpet Story name to intrigue. Now, Israel could work on good wealth creation. Well, ending wars if you form the kingdom is rather easy to do. King Jesus Christ desires to become the wall. It is not difficult for you to understand, but what you must understand is the eighth beast is the end past the year of the Lord 2012 AD.

The Holy Bible has the number seventy-two from the number, 2000 is 1928. What happened with the usury laws and money in the year of Our Lord 1928 AD? The famine was the money just disappeared. You should remember President Franklin D. Roosevelt had to put five billion dollars in the banks. Today, that would be five trillion dollars. All the money just disappeared. Therefore, the first beast is President Herbert C. Hoover and he was so great that he could run again in the year of Our Lord 1932 AD. The Mark of the Beast was called Hoover Ville where he violated the book of Mark. That must be part of Standing Historical. Unfortunately, many of the clergymen would vote for foolish Hoover, now. So who is the second beast? The second beast is President Richard Nixon. Some people remember him from being impeached, but not the bad impact, he had on the economy. Who is the third beast, Ronald Reagan? Who is the fourth, George H. W. Bush. Now, we have to go back before the millennium story started and count the other beasts. How about Dwight D. Eisenhower starting the cold war in the fifties? The last one you are looking for before the millennium story is President John F. Kennedy. President John F. Kennedy got us involved in Vietnam and Cuba. Now, you have six beasts. What is a beast? In the Holy Bible a beast is a king that in our time thinks more about winning the election than serving the taxpayers. Since they were not responsible for their actions, King Jesus Christ had us in what I call "play pens." He was treating us like little babies and the answer has always been to form the kingdom and learn how to talk. They did not go to Perdition. We have to go into the Age of Accountability, where foolish Bush is the seventh beast, the Red Dragon. There is one left. Before that story started, it was millstone two names, Ronald Reagan, George Bush and one name left George Bush. King Jesus Christ was telling us who was going to be president of the United States in the year of Our Lord 2001 AD. We should record is that the eighth beast is the next one coming along or Senator John McCain or Senator Barack Obama. Senator John McCain has promised he will violate the book of Mark, becoming the Mark of the Beast and he promises he will be a dragon. The Pale Horse of Death is supposed to cut off his ugly head or the end shall come. He will refuse to pay his bills and the usury laws will destroy the American economy just as President Herbert C. Hoover did. Senator Barack Obama has become a dragon for political reasons and cannot be saved. He now qualifies to be the eighth beast. If you had Standing Historical, you would know why the Battle of Armageddon starts in the United States. America will again be in bankruptcy court, but instead of us having time under President Franklin D. Roosevelt with twenty-five million Americans with some religion involved walking the streets unemployed, we will have twice that with fifty million, as the population is greater and they will have guns. We cannot recover! I repeat. We cannot recover! The Battle of Armageddon starts in America. Therefore, we live by the sword, we will die by the sword, and it is the end. The end shall come. That is exactly what the Holy Bible says. Whom are we trying to fool, when King Jesus Christ tells us exactly when and how? The church never paid attention to, "Some governments are taking us on the road to hell." Chapters twenty-one through twenty-five of Elijah's literature will explain the economy of the end.

Next VG

Miracles within our hands. What is the greatest miracle in which you have a copy? It is called the Holy Bible. Once you form the kingdom, all your questions are answered, as King Jesus Christ has told you all things. The Holy Bible states you do not understand it, which is true. The antichrists of the past forced Our Gods to put you in penance. As the Holy Bible and reality of life is true, you are doing one hundred percent of everything wrong. Once you form the kingdom you use the same book and are doing one hundred percent of everything right. That book can only be written by Gods to achieve their desired results. You must learn to obey not create your own way. I have never met a clergymen that understands what the book of Galatians teaches. It is when the clergymen lord over the courts and provided special training in the seminaries. Once you form the kingdom and answer your questions by Standing Historical, the Holy Bible is understood as one hundred percent theology. One item is what are God's Covenants? You think what the minimum requirement in running your church is. We had the answers to grant in the church world a life that is one thousand times better than the end or Adam destroying the world as recorded as Our Gods have warned us. The difference is you have a book you can plan anything. When one hundred percent of the congregation can plan their inheritance, their future, you are at a life one thousand times better than the end. You should realize that a million men will work together through the seven Holy Cities, yet all will define what to do to raise a child of 777 design or one voice. You develop the book of needs where as documented at the age of King Jesus Christ, you let a member of the congregation tell you why he is saved and ready to be reborn again and qualified to be granted his wings.

The church must read the words and develop Standing Historical or the history of their denomination in a country. You must combined all written Holy Bibles into just one version all

70

locations must use. To live by every word, requires you to know what the words are and not have fifty different versions.

NEXT VG

I am not going to go into King Jesus Christ's computerized planning technique yet, but the system is covered in certain literature and in the Holy Bible as a path to a small door. As you study the Holy Bible, you can understand the advantages of seals as communications, which come out of the seven Holy Cities as King Jesus Christ's christ gives us the sixth sense or Holy Spirit words. King Jesus Christ will return with His Christ, which are located in the seven Holy Cities and rides the White Horse in concept. It should be rather easy for us to develop the sermons and put the information in the file. You do require a computerize system for communication and the use of the seals. In case a famine occurs, you are explaining to the Holy Cities, where it is and what extent you see it to be. They will come and rescue. Their job as upper management is to coordinate with all those involved, whether it is just a city, a state, a country, or the entire world. That is their role. The role of the clergymen of the church locations are to be the first line of defense against the tyranny of man or beasts that desire to invade our lands.

Some people do not seem to understand this one world government. King of kings and a nation against nation. What that means is we know who King Jesus Christ is and the kings are the crown leaders. Therefore, when we develop the end of famines, poverty within a country, demands of money, as we know it becomes nation against nation. Every nation stands on its own merit and the Holy Bible says whoever is not written in the book of life (that is the book that forms the kingdom and we document this change into), will be cast in the lake of fire (trial by fire). When we end poverty for those members that go to our church, naturally we will drag along the temples and disestablishment organizations and end poverty in their lives. The book that establishes this is Life of US (U.S.) as Standing Historical versus Life of Mexico that is their Standing Historical. When you understand this one world government from the USA, one party we have in the United States will be trained by the church from the book of Timothy as we train the future politicians to be like a bishop and coordinate the efforts of a governor, or the mayor, or the president. We will authorize who is qualified to represent King Jesus Christ. Also, in the book of Galatians is where we train attorneys to run courts and to be Scripture Attorneys. The training courses becomes like a seminary or special training course. We use the same techniques, we used before like the Holy Bible said do not let the government steal our houses. We are training them in the beginning, but as the people involved get the real ideas, the actual stories like in the Holy Bible where King Jesus Christ used the parables, we change. We get the parables together and build that into our training courses. We will teach that all over the world. The clergymen should train people that represent God through government is planning or one hundred percent theology.

We will be given a thousand year plan, which I am not going to cover. The chapter title is "The Seventh Trumpet". When you review it, look at the change of today, the prophecies for the year of Our Lord 2050 AD, the schools of the year of Our Lord 2800 AD, and the plan for the year of Our Lord 3000 AD. You may write down some of those items that we will review for the next meeting. It is too much to go into right now. What you shall have to review is the Wall of Hope where thousands of men will fill in the words and should be used by the government in their house of legislation and/or outside the governor or president's office. The Wall of Hope is a fifteen by thirty wall in our church summarizing the sorrows (jeopardy into joy in our world of city state or country. Many items are copied from the Seventh Trumpet Story. What should we go into?

NEXT VG - VG 6

We should be ready for our next session. First, you have explained Moses Laws which all of you are very familiar. King Jesus Christ said how great Moses Laws were and we are to sing the songs of Moses or Moses Laws equivalent. King Jesus Christ has already covered the words on Moses Laws.

What do we have in the church? We have to develop what is called Church Laws. We need some for the single and married church type people like ourselves. What happened with Moses Laws? The congregation tried to live by them. Therefore, instead of the Ten Commandments which does not apply in the church world to the congregation, but it does apply to us as the clergymen, we need to use Church Laws. A Church Law is a law the clergymen and other employees of King Jesus Christ are required to obey.

One of the Church Laws from the Holy Bible is taking God's Name in Vain. We know we are not supposed to do that. We are to be "sure" of what we teach from the Altar.

We can talk about the Vow of Poverty. We the clergymen are suppose to raise our children like the son of a carpenter. We should know what type of income we should have.

When we go through this book of Daniel we do once, we have a silent war. Therefore, we have to explain the Vow of Silence. The Vow of Silence is we do not put this forming the kingdom on national television. What happens ever time we have a little problem? The news desires to cover how bad we are. We go through what we call a Vow of Silence or the silent war as described in the book of Daniel. If we start out with Moses Laws, Church Laws is rather simple because if that gets out without being covered in the Vow of Silence it is not to bad, but some of the other items required, maybe.

What we are going to do is use the technique of King Jesus Christ of not forming committees. We are going to write down what we feel should be three Church Laws or more. We are going to bring them back to the next meeting and put them on the black board and summarize and see if we end up with ten or what number it is. The church must learn the wisdom of someone seconding a motion. They now are responsible to carry forward that idea to resolve its usefulness. Do not let a committee vote three to two to end a great idea.

What do we do with this? When we come back, we should try to get more people like ourselves to do the same meeting. What we should do then is we have a list of signatures just like the preamble days when we started America. We are signing what we need to start to create heaven on earth. We will use that to go to our upper management and then to go to the Vatican. The requirement to go to the Vatican is five denominations and one thousand signatures. We will present what we have as the chosen ones. Then we will start it over there because you have such an understanding of what God's Kingdom is. The thousand-year plan is just incredible when you go through and read it. We require a new one-world government for the other countries, but at least we have one for the United States, which is very well defined. We have a good understanding of Church Laws and its meaning, Moses Laws. We cannot go any further than that because it is up to the Icons, the upper management to authorize the rest of the work because that cannot be done at local levels. We do have to create the seven Holy Cities representing the seven names on the door. We have to get to the leadership of our denomination. They bring us to the leaderships of the other denominations.

Once we get this established, we should take this one world government plan and turn it into a Hollywood movie. We go to the City of Angels or Los Angeles, California and seek out a studio that will do it at cost plus. They have the marketing available. We become the actors in it. We write the script. When it goes in the theaters, Hollywood gets their cost plus and we end up with all the rest of the money, plus the right to the DVDs, and any future sales. This could be worth a billion dollars and up to us. How are we going to use the money? The church requires the money to create the seven Holy Cities, to get the computers required, and anything else that is necessary. If you are a Lutheran Church and you started in Germany, you would desire to buy a thousand acres and put up a church, put up an office building, develop your private network for communications, and establish your Holy City, like the Vatican. You must keep the money for the seven Holy Cities. Do not lose control of the movie.

What do the politicians get out of this? If you listen to them campaigning right now, they talk like little children. They do not seem to have anything of real value. They are trying to make others look bad, blame and no real long-term objectives or goals. All the politicians are reacting to a problem. They do not understand how to write laws for the New Testament. This age is to begin the Generation of the FIG. That is the beginning of plan laws where all that is left is love. The church has faith and wait and all that is left is love. There is no future they define the congregation desires them to work for. You live in the Age of Accountability and they are responsible for their actions. You have to realize, they are in shackles. For example, if they take you on the road to hell, as they did in the year of Our Lord 2001 to 2004 and 2005 to 2008 AD, what will happen? For example, 1.4 million Americans went below the poverty level, without corrections and blowing the trumpet as you learn in the year of Our Lord 2004 AD. Then they will automatically lose John 3:16 because they have the wrong heart and did not use their hand to write just laws, if one person dies. Why would a politician in his right mind desire to be a politician when his soul is so at risk? What you are trying to do with a story of mystery and intrigue is end up with, there is nothing to fear, but fear itself. As long as they stay on course for what is designed in this plan, they will be without fear; however, they must resolve problems as they arise. If they fail to resolve the sorrows, the church must create and teach the meaning of fear led by the women, but developed at the Altar. When they get to the year of Our Lord 2050 AD, the politicians will give you a new plan for the year of Our Lord 2100 AD. You will proof read it, write the movie, play in it, get it out in the box offices, keep the money, and they have nothing to fear but fear itself as they achieve all that is defined. You must hold a vote to determine if you should release the shackles after there term in office. No one could vote to release the shackles on foolish George Bush. No one could release the shackles on the Dragon President Elect Barack Obama. May all future politicians be successful, but in the beginning that may not be possible. The Son of Perdition, the clergymen are killing them. You have certified the good deeds and you use the information to train the future politicians from the book of Timothy and book of Galatians. There is nothing to fear but fear itself, but still God helps those that helps themselves. That is a valuable lesson to learn. Still, you must judge them as saints because you love them. King Jesus Christ will use the Rod of Iron. Rod is the measure of success and iron is the Terrible Swift Sword.

We should finish the meeting with a prayer. In God's Kingdom, the requirement is God helps those that helps themselves. That is with the word helps with an "s", the actions of hope. When we pray to Our Gods, what we are doing is a call to action of ourselves to carry forward. Anything we tell King Jesus Christ to do is normally wrong. King Jesus Christ will meet us in Israel and work with the temple against the church. If you tell Him in a prayer to do your job, may the women of your congregation use their purses against you! So let us write a prayer.

Our Father, who art in Heaven, hallowed be Thy Name, Thy kingdom come is not included. What you do is your call to action. We will be reviewing the data as presented to us and adding our work of hope to the input for the next session. We are going to do this in King Jesus Christ's Name. Amen, may the above prayer come true. That is the new format as defined in the Holy Bible. Our Father, who art in Heaven, Hallowed be Thy Name. You grant Our Gods your call to action. What are we going to do? God helps those who helps themselves. Our call to action or the action of hope. We must have the faith of the unseen in His name King Jesus Christ, Amen. We do not have the power to see our call to action like the book of Revelation or I saw seven churches.

What Elijah has granted us is, first he has given us a chapter on the word lust. That is our work to get the hearts of the fathers back with the children and hearts of the children back with fathers. He has granted us the Seventh Trumpet Story, which is for the government to work on. King Jesus Christ has if you allow Him to manage the money in a kingdom, He will double the best Adam can do. He has given us the White Stone Story. That is part of the Stairway to Heaven. In there what is included? Everything required going from this meeting and carrying forward to all the nonaligned churches after we meet with the Catholics. What it takes us to get to the part of the Second Advent story, the Stairway to Heaven. We have what we should do with the economy right now, today. That is what is included in the chapter the Seventh Trumpet Story. Elijah started a new chapter with current changes. We have this presentation. Elijah through the work of King Jesus Christ's education has trained Elijah to achieve these items in His name. Elijah has given us the book of the Holy Bible that is missing on fear. Fear is the beginning of all wisdom (knowledge) and will be desired by the congregation as life grows to a life one thousand times better than the end.

What you do is your call to action. We will be reviewing the data, adding our work of hope to the input for the next session, and we are going to do this in His Name King Jesus Christ.

The book sixty-seventh book of the Holy Bible will be available. That is the book from Revelation 10:1 to 10:10.

End of presentation.

Reference to the chapters on "The Word Lust" and the "Seventh Trumpet Story" are included. The chapters are already part of this book and not covered here. The Holy Bible requirement is one thousand with five denominations. I, Elijah know what that means. When you go to the Vatican, you have one thousand signatures and only five denominations included.

After the first session, you return and review the chapters offered and create the Church Laws equivalent to ten Moses Laws or some number. Do not try to create a million laws. You decide what the sign of the times requires now and teach. Five laws can be better than one hundred, but you might decide on ten as better than five. The laws can change over time. You ask the members of your group to meet with twelve of their peers to do the same. You document the Church Laws or laws the clergymen must obey. You arrange for a meeting with the Icons of a denomination to provide the sermons you have to offer. Do not go to a Catholic Icon, but another of the seven names. Once your upper management has a chance to review, you take your material and reach the other denominations up to five. You go to the Catholics in the only Holy City and teach come on Archangel Michael, we cannot do it without you. They should reach the same ideas in knowledge of what God's Plan is all about and how the church becomes the most powerful organization in this world. Explain to the Catholics, the kingdom makes it easy for them to recruit brothers and sisters. Also, teach them the ultimate power corrupts ultimately and God requires seven churches, not one led by foolish ideas like Pro-life.

You require a powerful story to excite the churches all over the world and get them involved in creating God's Kingdom or implementing the Lord's Prayer. Just telling them without a story of great power would only result in many disagreeing and the useless deaths of many of your peers or people that presently run the church. The clergymen that work to save their lives will die and those that die will save their lives. The Holy Bible again is very clear. I am thankful to the Holy Bible for the answer or you would see many of your peers die for continuing their hell on earth sermons against the congregation by them continuing to be the man of sin, the lawless one, Prince of Darkness, and the Son of Perdition. Their gospel about Christ as grandmas will continue and not the gospel of Christ, which is the way, truth, and light. The Holy Bible is clear when it states the churches are doing one hundred per cent of everything wrong. Only a true God could make that penance real. Yet went they form the kingdom, they can learn the reality of scripture and the grace of God or they have to live by every word.

I heard the story from King Jesus Christ when He stated I am not going to turn stones into food; therefore, He gave the clergymen a great story to carry forward and demonstrate what can be done in the kingdom. It leads to the end if the church stays with the gospel about Christ and the book of Matthew 24:14 declares the end shall come. The usury laws destroy the economy of the United States like Hoover Ville, but the rest of the world refuses to help and the entire American economy fails like 1930s. Hoover Ville is a great story to understand the Mark of the Beast or review the book of Mark. In the book of Revelation you can read about the ships waiting off our coasts to deliver goods. Finally, the ships turn and do not return as the curse of God is upon us. We turn off the gas, electricity, water, and the poor shall inherit the earth by the guns the Republicans forced on America to win elections and receive campaign funding from organizations, like the National Rifle Association that claim guns do not kill. The United States cannot recover and all civilization as we know it today ends. Living in North Korea is a good place to be. When the church comes back to America, the land will be as it was in the year of Our Lord 1492 AD. King Jesus Christ again could meet us in Spain and show us the great land He has reserved for the Heartland of the world or the land to bring salvation back to the rest of the world.

The Holy Bible states the famine at the end is for the word of God. Many have stated as the Holy Bible defines the terms Lord of lords and King Jesus Christ is Lord. What has your church defined as the word lords? If they explain that it is for the Word of God, we should ask, "What are the Words to be learned?" The Holy Bible states it is not for daily bread. Should we shoot our clergymen in the head (literally) if he answers, "The solution is greater tithes for my church?" I will set up a soup kitchen that the Holy Bible states, you do not know who goes there. Is our religion down to we sing some songs, they reads some passages, they beg for all the money he can and we all leave? I have sat with many members of the church and they seem to agree the younger generations going to the church is missing. Do they say we need to be justified by law not by grace in getting children back to the church? If the church could only find Elias of this era to restoreth all things and Elijah, the prophet. They would teach it is time to convert from the gospel about Christ (the end shall come) to the gospel of Christ (heaven on earth).

I will start with the book of Daniel or the book the church does once. My first book, "Life of US (U.S.)" forms the kingdom and many other miracles. The book was added to the book "The Antichrist God's Version" and the true author's name was used or Elias of Mark 9:12. The book of Daniel stated that book would not sell, which I did not know at that time. As in the book of Daniel, my memos were set out to the real names from the book of Daniel. King Jesus Christ had to take the book of Daniel with names and create in the world today. The King of Babylon was President George W. Bush from his words in the year of Our Lord 2000 AD presidential debates. The three new names from the book of Daniel are Former President William

J. Clinton and Vice President Al Gore with the third is Pope John Paul II as covered in the book, "The Antichrist God's Version". The heat was created higher and higher as I tried to promote my book, but there was no smoke from the furnace because the heat is produced by a trial by fire or the Lake of Fire. Let us achieve something in His name, like we end all poverty for the congregation at a cost of less than zero dollars and zero cents. The Holy Bible tells you to take your inventions and turn it into gold.

What did the previous books cover in terms of the word lords? King Jesus Christ is Lord and His religious leaders of the church are lords over the court. I did not use that exact word but granted the congregation what is expected of them if they desire the story of salvation. They must go through the story of forty-two months or the story of resurrection. A judge in a court does not have a requirement to go to a church. Judges that attend churches should learn how to seek the gift of John 3:16. As being wicked in title, they have a higher order of responsibility to receive the gift or a friend in need is a friend in deed. A need is spiritual, not money. The gift is not granted lightly to the wicked, as they have to sweat out the details or no rest for the wicked. The priests must take their role very seriously because John 3:16 can be lost easily as an employee of King Jesus Christ. You must count on the meaning of a man called Paul from the Holy Bible. In America, there is no hell like a woman scorned because her children cannot get daily bread, health care, education, a bright future, or any other gift a child richly deserves. When a child is not only denied a gift, we can afford, but a gift of life is taken away by the government, there is hell to be paid by the clergymen. Stop telling the congregation, they will go to hell as that is the present state of mind, not a place. Their sins go all over the country called Cardinal Sins and Perdition cannot be far away for the men who give up and do not pick themselves up by the loincloth and walk like men. They must always walk a mile in King Jesus

Christ's footsteps. The only way they can correct the problem is to consider what the government must do. If the government does not change, ask them to leave the church as Eternal Death means you are still alive somewhere in God's Kingdom, but you wish you were dead every day of the rest of your life or until the penance is over. Satan cannot be saved. He is a real person or the one the clergymen worship and if the kingdom is formed, he will only be in penance for about a thousand years, maybe. If Elijah fails the world's penance is seven times longer than the last (two thousand years from Israel) or fourteen thousand years. The Battle of Armageddon will start before the year of Our Lord 2015 AD in the United States and I agree with King Jesus Christ in that I pity the women of suck when the church appears. Rather than they correct, they allow thirty thousand unnecessary deaths each day or over ten million a year. In the Battle of Armageddon, we can lose more of lives than in the Second World War or fifty million in one year. What a goal for the Antichrists that run the church. The church has the solution in the Lord's Prayer and they refuse to obey God, therefore no flesh is saved or no John 3:16. Only agreeing to implement the Lord's Prayer will the clergymen reach for the gift of salvation, which has to be earned like "I DO" at the Altar!

If we had a church and you were talking to the congregation about the fact of many millions of families falling below the poverty level, what would you tell the courts from the seven Holy Cities? The politicians can come like thieves in the night. Under Former President William J. Clinton, the poverty in the country was being reduced. I talk to many people like the clergymen should and asked an individual why he was working at night. He stated his family deserved me to have two jobs. Should the Holy Cities have heard the words from the poor boxes or equivalent in the United States? The poor boxes are where the women tell the church why they are living in hell, so the political leaders know what sorrows to overcome. We shall not want. The congregation poor writes and the government listens. If the poor women cannot do, they must teach. The poor women cannot write the laws of America, so she must teach. All seven Holy Cities love the input that all is getting better and reviewing the wondrous stories of living hell of sorrows, they have put to rest.

Here comes a new political man that we have heard the name before. In the Holy Bible, you have millstone (Perdition) two names and one name left or Ronald Reagan and George Bush and one name left George Bush (beast). As the Holy Bible describes him as a beast where the Scarlet of Babylon (former President William J. Clinton's girlfriend) is there and the King of Babylon. President George W. Bush rode into office by the Republican Party neutralizing former President William J. Clinton as available to campaign for Vice President Al Gore because of his girlfriend; however, the Holy Bible is clear as not one woman could vote for a mass murderer of children from Texas. Foolish George W. Bush promised to violate the book of Mark again by putting the money for education back in the treasuries. Many churches desired to blame the children in Pro-life instead of listening to the campaign and our promise keepers, the politicians. You are not as good as King Jesus Christ to be able to write prophecies for a country that did not exist when written and a man not born yet, but clear. So as a review in the Holy Cities in four years or less, what have you found? Governor George W. Bush a mass murder of children from Texas came like a thief in the night. He had almost no experience and as many untrained politicians, had a huge fortune, name recognition, and was in shackles while in office in Texas (one hour past midnight in the year of Our Lord January 1, 2000 AD). My other books describe what the church should do in Texas, but we have to overlook now because he is president. He would be better off if when President Elect Al Gore talked, he applied the millstone to his political career by doing what makes sense. I wrote previously, he should commit political suicide by describing his failure as a human being and becoming a beast from Texas. He resigns and changes the law in Texas. Not even his mother could vote for him if we had God's Kingdom. Does your mother desire you to go to Perdition?

You run a church and the statistical analysis of the country agrees with the knowledge all clergymen send to the Holy Cities when required as described in the Book Life of US (U.S.), where the first twelve chapters are local churches. The clergymen becomes our first line of defense against the tyranny of man where man fails himself as a man. As I wrote earlier, the only right you give up in God's Kingdom is the right to fail yourself. All other rights are enhanced. Where are the laws of liberty? We only have the laws of freedom or failure.

You ignore the work in Texas and start as president of the United States. You have read in my previous books on how to vote in the year of Our Lord 2004 AD. President George W. Bush in office has:

1. Spent money like a drunken sailor.
2. Started a war.
3. Went from a budget surplus of $232 billion to great indebtedness.
4. Created millions of job loses.
5. Created millions of people that fell below the poverty level.
6. Billions are required for hurricane relief, which should come from federal treasuries not waiting for donations.
7. Violated the book of Mark as God foretold as a beast and had a commitment to be a dragon and became the Red Dragon.
8. Created less than zero jobs in four years, just as President Herbert C. Hoover in the year of Our Lord 1929 AD. Job creation is a form of wealth creation. The clergymen should review the fishermen story.
9. Domestic violence did not soared to intolerable levels because of bad laws, yet.

10. Created a recession because of blessed are the rich.

As the Holy Bible states, the United States went from seven years of fat cows under President William J. Clinton to seven years of skinny cows eating up the fat cows. Where did the clergymen teach the politicians on how to divide the "Cows" wisely? Our Gods will stop the rain in the United States for the clergymen disobedience in the year of our Lord 2000 AD. The answer is the famine of Satan. All should bow down to Our King if the clergymen went through the penance of resurrection in the past before the Age of Accountability as scripture stated. What did they decide to do? The false prophet was in Jerusalem and they loved to blame our children for our young girls for not waiting to be women to bring in American children from women that are spiritually, physically and financially able to bear that child. The church desired to create more fallen angels. I will agree with God more penance is required. If you do not agree as a clergymen, may your future be one you richly deserve.

You can ask the congregation to summarize foolish George Bush's deeds including the politicians that worked with him like Senator Barack Obama and Hillary Clinton. King Jesus Christ has stated on how bad the laws where in Rome. Since you have recreated the Roman Empire in the United States as stated in the book of Romans (God is stating what the church is doing wrong). President George W. Bush wrote many bad laws. The church let him become Satan when he said, "Let me seek the vengeance.", not God. Since the congregation worships Satan, they have lost John 3:16. The clergymen as the Antichrist did not have John 3:16 at one hour past midnight in the year of the Lord 2000 AD. They came in an era of peace and prosperity. The new beginning is to form the kingdom or implement the Lord's Prayer.

Wait, I thought the title of this chapter was the Stairway to Heaven. What King Jesus Christ has invented so the church can recover easily from the second Bush is the White Stone Story. The story becomes so big that in three years you maybe able to stop thousands of people from dieing each day. I say maybe, because they should be the easy ones. You have ideas in place that may help the governments. What do you believe the pestilent is? The words of the clergymen are the answer. The words cannot seem to solve any problem since no flesh is saved except the angel from Revelation 10:9, Elijah, the prophet. You have to start using the gospel of christ and end the gospel about Christ only. You will learn how to teach the gospel from christ (son of man). King Jesus Christ will return with His christ in the seven Holy Cities.

The Four Horsemen are for communications within a kingdom and to use the rod of iron wisely. King Jesus Christ will return with His christ. Therefore, in the seven Holy Cities, you have your christ. You notice the number of divorces in the United States is over zero. You write to your Holy City. They return with their christ on a White Horse. They work with you to develop the sixth sense of the Holy Spirit words, "For the love of God's Children." The sermons are entered in a computerized system and you use the words wisely to meet the major prophecy or eliminating ninety percent of the divorces in twenty years and then try harder.

The Red Horse is when the kingdom starts a war. Foolish George Bush was a mass murderer of children from Texas or the beast of Revelation. The woman was former President William J. Clinton's girl friend. The seven Holy Cities start a war because they love foolish George Bush and do not desire him to continue to violate the book of Mark and become the Mark of the beast as president. The only right a person gives up in a kingdom is the right to fail themselves.

The Horse of a famine is used when the beasts create an environment where money disappears and results in a famine or the inability to buy daily bread. In the year of Our Lord 2004 AD, 1.4 million Americans fell below the poverty level and the government did not blow the trumpet, with the start of the correction laws. The sermons developed by the seven Holy Cities contain meat and great pain for the people that failed themselves or the politicians. The passage is, "If you fail to blow the trumpet and one person dies, I will take you by the hand. " The hand is writing laws or in this case to raise the minimum wage and wait to see if more is required. The congregation loves the joy, as their jeopardy is gone.

Foolish George Bush became a Red Dragon and desired to steal that woman's child. The congregation loves the fear created by the seven Holy Cities to cut off his ugly head. The Pale Horse will end killing wars. As I wrote in my literature, you may have to put Wal-Mart out of business for their failure, as they will not be able to sell a shoelace. The Passover story of King Jesus Christ is extremely powerful.

THE WHITE STONE STORY AS DEVELOPED BY THE CONCEPT OF CHRIST (SON OF MAN).

Below is a letter to my senator from Illinois.

12-04-the year of Our Lord 2005 AD

Senator Barack Obama

I believe you have an ally in Washington DC that you may or not be aware. See the enclosed email I am going to send to countless number of churches. I cannot afford to wait since our salvation is at stake.

If you read my book, you should realize through the Holy Bible, God has granted us an economy that never ends. I have copied the principals in my book and expanded on them. You should have heard of supply economics of Friedman from the

University in Chicago. The Holy Bible has that as near the end times (1992), we had abandoned buildings all over America. The theory was you give the money to the rich and we prosper. Well, that is just fools gold. Now, President George W. Bush is doing the same thing. If you know an economist like Alan Greenspan, you may give him a copy and ask his view. The United States through congress can end all poverty in our world. Since I copied it out of the Holy Bible, I know it works.

What the Holy Bible states is to create an economy that will never end or I have called Consumption Economics. You can trust the principal as you spend your way into prosperity, if it is done correctly. Therefore, as congress solves the social ills (sorrows) of the country the economy expands. You should remember the economy of the Democrats in the year of Our Lord 2000 AD, eliminate the government waste, and define a problem that I covered like health care. As you solve the problems in health care as I defined, you will achieve Universal Health Care for the entire country. What a glorious time to serve mankind or you can listen to foolish George Bush.

I know you were a man for peace like Howard Dean. I caught up with Governor Howard Dean in Wisconsin. If my publisher would have met the dates he maybe president today and the war never started. The rules to start the war or not was covered in the book Life of US (U.S.). I covered concepts from cheering his reelection of Hussein to total elimination of all human life in the country. The only answer any clergymen would try to hear is to cheer is reelection since they must represent the Prince of Peace. The Prince of Peace in God's Kingdom is the clergymen, the saints.

Try to get Senator Hillary Clinton involved since I was in contact with the Clintons and Former Vice President Al Gore. Former President Bill Clinton could still be invaluable to you.

email to many churches

The White Stone Story.

Email from Lawrence E Couch Office of Justice and Service Archdiocese of Washington 301-853-5343.

The House of Representatives will vote on a package of budget cuts tomorrow: Thursday, November 10, 2005. The bill is a compilation of budget-cutting proposals passed by several House committees over the past two weeks. The House bill could result in low-income and vulnerable people losing access to health care etc.

He is telling me to support his efforts to overcome the Republicans in the House of Representatives that will hurt our families by eliminating the money to overcome the social ills of the country. They do not have the money. He should just write "The White Stone" story and request all religious locations to teach. Yes, even the ones beyond the church like a temple. Congress is violating the book of Mark and the president will become the Mark of the beast like President Herbert C. Hoover.

You as a preacher may have agreed that we should start a war as conquers as stated in the book of Romans. As a teacher, you would develop the gospel stating the book of Romans is when the United States is run by another beast called a crown leader (Red Dragon). What happens is no flesh is saved (John 3:16), we worship Satan, and recreated the Roman Empire equivalent in the United States. The wars and Hollywood have made our children violent, as you believe Rome was. A big difference is swords, now are guns, wow. Any country that does not properly raise their children has no right to exist. Can you as a religious leader believe in a Hollywood movie where the women of the United States taught our men reality?

This memo describes a public opinion form that only women can be involved. They are King Jesus Christ's educators (woman of suck) and they should teach our foolish men. God states in the Holy Bible that in the new millennium, the Arabs will be hated above all others. You beat terrorism with hate and joy not hell of killing wars. You can read the news what happens and you should teach what happens, when you try to overcome terrorism with hell on earth. All we have accomplished is we made al Qaeda stronger. You teach that you represent the King of Peace and our story of salvation requires you to obey God. You make terrorist fools. What you are doing is from the Old Testament, where Our Father required Israel to do public opinion polls. That is still a requirement of the church. I believe waiting for the results is joy in the church. You can make a big difference if you are a grandmother to help your grandchildren.

Please teach not to let the dragon steal that woman's child (John 3:16 helps to understand the word "steal" that God used). You should use the words from your Holy Bible. Please remember that King Jesus Christ was the Prince of Peace you must obey. Now, He is King Jesus Christ and the clergyman becomes the Prince of Peace. Do not impose your will on the congregation or they may write a law against the clergymen like in the late sixties. A public opinion poll or did you lose due to a war and a law in the late 1960s. Please do not lose again. Use the power of our Gods wisely.

Why did King Jesus Christ use the word "stone"? In Israel, His Father used the power of creation to feed the children of Israel in their penance march. They learned but more lessons were required. Our Father used the power of creation to feed many. What did He promise the clergymen through the Devil? I will not when you forsaken my children, small and great, return with the food or turn stones into food.

What should be on the form when 1.4 million Americans fell below the poverty level in the year of Our Lord 2004? The politicians desire you to kill and only a penance man can get off this world alive. Damn, you mean you require the women to teach you reality. Mercy shall follow us all the days of our lives. Why not add to the public opinion form to add money to the impoverished at the rate of part of the saving of the war. I will state, for your convenience, all children below the poverty level receive $50.00 a month the first year and $100.00 the second. You allow a maximum of granting American children a gift for the first two only below nineteen years old. Congress will have to figure out the saving and you shall love, but not complain about the real numbers. You remember it is not your view as a clergymen but the women of your congregation and future voters. Women will not ever vote for a dragon and if he raises his ugly head their will should demand the church cut off his head by the Passover story and shove his body under the Altar. The Pale Horse Story or fear. You have turned stones into food. The Holy Spirit words or sixth sense is "Let us turn guns into food". Now, you are obeying King Jesus Christ in Joy by implementing a prophecy "The White Stone". Use the concept of the Last Supper, which in prophecy for you is "The Supper". Do not say you are too small to get twelve of your friends together to help the American children. Any church location with a telephone becomes very powerful.

Public Opinion Form

Column 1	Column 2
hell on earth	Money for our children for daily bread, schools, and health care or any other love (gift) children deserve

identification of the woman   identification of the woman

May a billion plus women take the poll! May women go to vote at the church and learn about the other miracles developed through the church.

You could put the poll on the web or make individual forms for your church and input the results. You remember your sermons are very important to create one view, one voice, one way.

Letter to Al Gore is below as I was trying to get him to be President of the United States in the year of Our Lord 2004 AD. You can read my analysis of the year of Our Lord 2000 AD debate in the book written by Elias or a man to restoreth all things.

June 1, 2004

The Office of the
Honorable Al Gore
2100 West End Avenue
Nashville, TN 37203

RE: Unconditional Surrender and the Children

If you read my book Life of US (U.S.), you have to realize a war with Iraq is only led by fools. God is waiting for a passage to come true. Peace on earth, good will towards man. What does that mean???????????

The leaders of the church are waiting for the politicians to provide a clue. They need to represent the Prince of Peace. The politicians provide the words peace on earth (the peace plan) and the clergymen are gatherers and do sermons on their discoveries until the will of the people understands.

Why would a planner need a great leader like Al Gore to commit to unconditional surrender in Iraq? Why would the Pope desire to teach all religious leaders of the church to listen and understand they represent God and His view is peace on earth? The clergymen only ponder. I can teach you how to do it, if you know how to do it or read my book Life of US (U.S.).

1. Some governments are taking US on the road to hell. Where is John 3:16 in the USA?
2. Many soldiers I call U.S. soldiers are soldiers of misfortune and will die.
3. A Puppet Government will form, will it last three days as before?
4. Cost of the war is $200 billion plus each year. Will ten years be short and three days later, all is lost?
5. Why were we so foolish to start the war, read Life of US (U.S.)?
6. If we put the original leader in place, stability in the region will occur.
7. Why would other governments decide to start a war, when penance is great?

How would the religious leaders find joy in the story of unconditional surrender? Since we destroyed over $600 billion of their valuable infrastructure, we should pay to replace. The church should love America in penance for hundreds of years for the foolishness of President George W. Bush and the politicians that felt compelled to go along for political reasons. I know Al Gore selected Howard Dean for president and he was against the war. If you read my book, God was against all wars like the First World War, the Second World War, etc.

How should the penance go forward? Well for each barrel of oil, we pay 1.75 times the price. Their government determines how it is to be spent like for an American style hospitals, GE power plants to replace what he lost for Americas foolishness, and do not forget the military to defend against the Turks and Iran. May the next power that starts a war go into penance for two hundred years even if their families suffer! The church should review and take John 3:16 very seriously. Only a penance man can get off this world alive.

What should Al Gore expect Pope John Paul II to do since he was against the war? The church should develop the twenty-five page book as described in my book Life of US (U.S.) which is a prophecy. Whenever a government official talks about peace like the peace dividend the clergymen as gatherers teach in all required locations and consider a rod of an Almond Tree as a tribulation to the king involved. The Dove Politicians win elections all over the world and the War Lords or Hawks and dragons like President George H. Bush we disregard. What they say is not heard of importance unless they have the words in my book and leaders of Iraq do all the terrible things, they have been accused.

What Pope John Paul II would be interested in is another prophecy. He should look up the words on the Rainbow from the Holy Bible and then my words on the Goldilocks Economy in my book. He should be interested in God's way, which is to consume to prosperity. The Republicans are a party of greed and hell and could not succeed. See the prophecy of Millstone and two names and in the year of Our Lord 2000 AD, there is one left, which is George Bush. God is against George Bush so the only man running in the year of Our Lord 2000 AD in

America was Al Gore. Not one woman can vote for a beast or a mass murderer of children from Texas.

An example of spend to prosperity is in my book under Double Tax on Dividends. The party of greed gave the money to the rich wicked and created very little consumption. Let us take the opposite view if we want to expand the economy. We give $25 billion to the poorest children in the United States. The family of $16,000 or less receives $2000.00 per child and someone close to $25,000 receives $200.00 per child. We ask the poor to spend the money as quickly as possible. They spend, their neighbors work overtime or are hired and they spend. It should be reviewed like what an economist uses for the banking industry or job creation theory. You end up with a multiplier effect and could be like the four to one multiplier as in the banking example. In this example, the growth of the economy could go by 60 to 100 billion dollars. At $100 billion, what did it cost the government? Maybe they made a profit or received more than $25 billion in return. So the prophecy is waste not want not. $25 billion given to the wicked is government waste, but satisfying the wants of the children is God's miracle and part of the Rainbow. Please joy. Vice President Al Gore through President William J. Clinton eliminating the sorrows of our land produced the greatest economy in modern times.

You and Pope John Paul II should propose a meeting between you two. You were God's choice in the year of Our Lord 2000 AD and still are the best-trained person the reestablish God's Economic Model. It is very critical to the survival of the world and the Church. No Icon has a greater calling than you, Al Gore. If we vote for the Republicans, we go back to penance for the clergymen not obeying God and two thousand years is very short. God comes back with the Seven Horns of the Eternal Temple or we start the story of Israel again.

The cost of health care. A question would arise if we eliminate the crime syndicates and the cost of caring for God's Children. Could the Pope receive a statement that we consider

95

the rights of our children not to bring Crack Babies into our country more important than the right of the crime syndicate leaders? Could Al Gore find some Supreme Courts judges that believe in no rest for the wicked? They have to leave our country or change led by the FBI. The prophecy is true and God asked us not to harm a hair on a child's head. I believe that children have all rights and the crime syndicates have none. No right to the true Heaven or no right to walk anywhere in this world.

President George W. Bush talked about a strong military. Well, God would call that government waste. The reason we start wars is we cannot talk. The world is still a cruel planet so our military has to continue. You might think about explaining a possible venture with Great Britain, Russia and the United States were we could reduce the cost but still have a powerful force. I know how to do that, as it is a prophecy. May we never use it unless there is no choice?

by Richard
Literary name Author of Life of US (U.S.)
And the next book Voice of Vengeance - Fear (now the sixty- seventh book of the Holy Bible)

Please do me a favor. I will continue sending out the letters until you let me know you receive the overview.
email me at comfortinGod@hotmail.com

END OF LETTER

I remember from a meeting Senator Barack Obama attended in Rockford that he taught law school. God calls our courts the land of chaos and confusion, the man with the gavel. In my books, I solve those apparent problems as copied from the Holy Bible. Our role in the world is to teach the courts how to judge or the requirements of the Holy Bible. In history, our founding fathers did not know how to write laws for the New Testament. If I succeed the way the Holy Bible states, you may end up designing a course on how to teach future and present attorneys how to be prepared to live in God's Kingdom or Thy Kingdom Come. All laws will be in the New Testament format. All that is left is love and seven year law plans. The Holy Bible calls that the beginning of the Generation of the FIG.

What my senator sent me was he could not represent religion. He could not take the above to the clergymen that represented the poor coalition from the year of Our Lord 2004 AD at the Democratic Convention. They left the convention to pray to God to stop the foolishness of the Democratic Party in terms of creating hell on earth or wars. They prayed for a miracle or telling God what to do. Since this was written, the government continued to violate the book of Mark in the years of the Lord 2005 to 2008 AD. What was part of the Mark of the Beast my senator allowed? In the year of Our Lord 2007 AD, the Domestic Violence as describe statistically became doubled the violence in one year. We have stagflation instead of a healthy economy and the stocks will fall as I wrote in the year of the Lord 2007 AD. I did not realize how much they would fall. The problem near the end times is the problem with the rich as defined in the Holy Bible. People who run for public office as even a mayor must understand how economies work. Now, before the election as a presidential hopeful, he still does not know. Senator John McCain is worse. The Holy Bible recommends Divine Intervention or the third power of eight.

I have a long history of trying to help the American children. Also in the Holy Bible, only a penance man can get off this world alive. We should know the eighth beast term would be over in the year of Our Lord 2016 AD. The problem is money or buyers and sellers remorse by the words in the book of Revelation. The answer is defined in the Old and New Testament. You must have the Mark of the Beast in your forehead so you understand what not to do and the voters recognize your picture as being trained by the church. If you do not understand, you will violate the book of Mark. I heard president elect Barack Obama state he will be looking at the entitlement programs or you should watch his hand at work and the mark of the beast. King Jesus Christ has written the feathers (Hawk and Dove) will eat up the flesh or where is John 3:16. The church forming the kingdom and working to end all poverty avoids the end and is the new beginning of heaven on earth. What a price the clergymen have to pay or become royalty and achieve from the Altar, God is amongst us. The clergymen become like Gods as describe from the Garden of Eden stories. Elias can make the clergymen like Gods as he can restoreth all things. I can turn what you say is bad into good like ending poverty. Actually, for me ending poverty with the Holy Bible is rather easy for anyone who desires to live without want or before the year of Our Lord 2050 AD for people who desire to try in the United States. Ending what is poor like bankruptcy courts will take from Here to Eternity or the effective use of God's Plan, or the words in the Holy Bible.

You remember may God not provide mercy to those clergymen that refuse to be involved. All clergymen that refuse to form the kingdom die a second death, go by the way of Satan, and cannot be saved.

Elias (from Mark 9:12)

Author of "The Antichrist God's Version": a book of God's miracles that people would say cannot be done like ending what we call poverty.

email comfortingod@mchsi.com

The book was published and listed on www.iuniverse.com and other locations.

As King Jesus Christ has written in the Holy Bible, my books contain great detail. I have listened to your view of what the Holy Bible states. You require Elias to train. I understand the Holy Bible better than anyone does. It took less than a minute to understand what the dragon story means.

The above is what I wrote to the Antichrists running the church locations. The church locations are so small that not even the Vatican can influence the congregation enough to end all killing wars or government waste. They do not even try. The Holy Bible states waste not want not and a house divided amongst itself always fails. To summarize today, what I said above is after the Vatican and others should even search the caves for church locations, as prophecy requires. Let us review what will be brought to all church locations.

1. You provided a presentation and received signatures.

2. You carried forward to the Icons of a denomination with many signatures.

3. You went to the Vatican with your knowledge.

4. The Vatican and others went to all other church locations to teach:

    A. Discussed a public opinion poll to end all killing wars or the White Stone Story and end millions of unnecessary deaths in a few years.

    B. Generalized on King Jesus Christ economic model to end all what is defined as poverty today where the Holy Bible will end all your money problems. The logic came from The Seventh Trumpet Story.

    C. Defined how to get the hearts of the fathers back with children and the hearts of the children back with the fathers by ending teenage babies and divorces, which came from the chapter "The Word Lust".

D. Fulfill a prophecy where King Jesus Christ has picked Elijah as the crown leader of America to accomplish what is covered in the thousand-year plan for the one world government of Israel for just the United States or the third power of eight.

E. Review the works in progress for the Seventh Trumpet Story movie and how the billion dollars plus will be used to build six Holy Cities and modernized the seventh.

F. Discuss in a kingdom, the clergymen becomes the campaign manager. Only cover the Watchman and Watchmen Elect for the United States and your prophecy on crimes.

G. Discuss you must even search the caves or unknown locations for potential religion and help the people. Have a means of data entry so you cover ninety-nine plus percent of all locations. One hundred percent is ideal.

H. The church has the beginning of heaven on earth, so the citizens receive John 3:16 back. You must discuss the eleven hundred and fifty days and twenty three hundred days from the book of Daniel and all clergymen that refuse will lose John 3:16, go with Satan, and cannot be saved.

5. You have many drawings of the Bird Of Peace and welcome the politicians desire to implement peace on earth and the church to provide good will towards men and you have made useless eighty two percent of the standing armies through King Jesus Christ's educators (the women).

6. All politicians realize if they desire to win elections King Jesus Christ's educators will only listen to peace on earth and dragons will be forced by the women to be shoved under the Altar and cannot be saved.

7. They the women will cry "Leave the church you foolish dragon that desires to steal our children. I do not want you to steal our children and we end up with bad health care, education, and daily bread for billions it seems. Let us keep fools from Perdition do to their failure as human beings." The older women will always be ready to teach the younger what is important to their children and their grandchildren. In Israel, a nation of priests was a man's world and in the church world the women are King Jesus Christ's educators; however, a woman must be subordinate to a man, as she cannot run a church and create fear. In both worlds, it is a child's world. In Israel, it was and shall be a land you promise your children. In the church world, you are to make God's angels special or double blessed by the clergymen at the Altar and the senators or equivalent. May our children demand all the gifts the children richly deserve and the clergymen and politicians learn the children shall not want or there is Perdition to pay led by the women living in hell or desiring nothing bad happens to any sister. All women are sisters.

Repeat of a letter from the book The Antichrist God's Version.

LETTER TO FOLLOW

07/05/2004

Feed The Children
PO BOX
Oklahoma City, OK 73101

Re: Heaven on earth

I have sent the pope this message as God's Comforter should. The latest I see on television is that many church locations seem to promote killing wars or hell on earth. The Holy Bible states God is against all killing wars. Now is a good time in the Age of Accountability to start.

How would you say the children should get involved? The Holy Bible states a child shall lead the way. The angel of your church should lead the way. That is a simple but powerful tool against the warlords or the Hearts from Perdition. You have a passage that states, peace on earth good will towards men. You represent the King of Peace who is King Jesus Christ. Based on what some churches are teaching, you need to bring out the big guns, OUR LITTLE CHILDREN.

In our country, the future Heartland of the planet or the location where God is going to make a stand, we have two birds, one is the White Dove or Bird of Peace and the second is the Hawk. The Hawk is applied incorrectly in our country but if you desire to know what is right just ask and I will answer. The Holy Bible states the feathers are eating up the flesh.

How will the child lead the way to peace is a simple question and great pleasure for the congregation? You should realize no religious leader can represent the Hawk and President Franklin D. Roosevelt is more like, how the church would need the political leaders to fight wars. If we obey God and learn how to talk even the resistance of President Franklin D. Roosevelt to get involved in the Second World War or as he called his war "a war to end all wars" as the Holy Bible states, becomes unnecessary. The country trying to beat hell with hell is useless. You beat hell with hate and/or Joy. You have Faith and wait and all that is left is love. The church must create the faith or the unseen and apply hope through the church to make that faith come true.

Since you can only represent politicians that represent the Bird of Peace the answer is easy now. You should also rely on peace on earth good will towards men. If you heard what Howard Dean stated, he was against the war. The politicians speak of peace on earth; you listen and be "gatherers". You should remember President William J. Clinton had the peace dividend in place. Certainly, the children of Rockford desire schools and former Vice-President Al Gore was there with President William J. Clinton and would be against wars. If you "gathered", you can be the good will ambassadors I made you in my book, "Life of US (U.S.)" by Richard my literary name at comfortingod@mchsi.com. You should think of why I needed in email to include the word comforter.

A child shall lead the way or start a contest in all church locations such as the Catholics, Baptist, Lutherans, etc as the children in ages two to twenty-one draw the Bird of Peace for the congregation. The title shall be "LET US TURN GUNS INTO FOOD" or six words of common sense (HOLY SPIRIT WORDS). King Jesus Christ is not going to turn stones into food, so how is the church going to get the food. King Jesus Christ is waiting for your answer. Each denomination has its own contest as they develop its gospel. The older eighteen and up do the pictures in oil. All denominations go to the Vatican to declare the victory for the children and you select the winner.

One day the leader of the United Nations (the church) may represent the Bird of Peace to the King of the king or the crown leader. May he be the President of the United States!

You should reform the church locations that need to represent the Hawks or create hell on earth. Those church locations are against God and the children that want food. The pope wanted a trillion dollars for food, may the money come from guns. If you read my book, you realize a trillion dollars is not much, but even my book takes time. My book of course is copied from the Holy Bible and the sign of the times. May you have forwarded all because I will make all additional attempts to get the information to the new leader of the United Nations! The present United Nations should change its name. The gospel of christ shall be taught in each nation, but a nation may not be the entire country.

LET US CREATE HEAVEN ON EARTH NOT THE END OF THE WORLD BY THE YEAR OF OUR LORD 2016 AD AS THE HOLY BIBLE STATES. THE ANSWER IS SOME GOVERNMENTS ARE TAKING US ON THE ROAD TO HELL OR THE FINANCIAL FAILURE OF THE WORLD. WE IN THE CHURCH OF THE UNITED STATES ARE THE GREATEST DEBTOR NATION IN THE WORLD. YOU HAVE HEARD OF PRESIDENT Herbert C. Hoover IN THE YEAR OF OUR LORD 1929 AD. THAT WAS GOOD DAYS IF THE CHURCH FAILS GOD. THE YEAR OF OUR LORD 2016 AD AND BEYOND IS WORSE!!!!!!!!!!!!!!!

The clergymen are to be in a war against wars or one of the four words for the next thousand years. If you believe, you can end all the problems of people of this world in jeopardy in one day, you are wrong. God asked you to work on the four words for one thousand years. Starting and promoting wars of killing is jeopardy for the clergymen or it may be considered fear for the entire congregation including the clergymen. God stated He would save the meek or people that learn how to inherit a future they desire to live in. Read my book.

Richard Cartwright
Literary name by Richard
Author of Life of US (U.S.)
email comfortingod@mchsi.com

END OF LETTER

All the oil paintings shall be put on display in the Holy Cities or the church locations. If the politician desire to talk about hell on earth again may the sermons be addressed to visit the success of our children to protect the chicken little running the church, retrain, and send yourself, and the politicians to the Holy Cities history museums in your Holy Cities to learn what happened last time. The angels came to the church and made useless eighty-two percent of the standing armies and all the nuclear bombs went by the way of the buggy whip industries or disappeared. Prophecy foretells about the three kingdoms that where put in penance of Russia from the Soviet Union days, Great Briton from the British Empire days, and the United States for recreating the Roman Empire as prophecy foretells.

What is left but to let the United States start the Seventh Trumpet story a chapter in this book and the movies we wrote! In the meantime, the aligned churches are closed until they can overcome the man of sin as prophecy foretells and address all questions. You shall know what you did before you die. King Jesus Christ's employees should read the Holy Bible on how long they should work to eliminate their Cardinal Sins like allowing greed to come into their land without sermons or meat to overcome. If a politician writes a bad law and the lords (church employees), training the courts to have the right heart fails to reverse, Our Gods will take them by the hand and the clergymen will again be sinners and not be saved. Do not think let Perdition be for the clergymen only as you try to sacrifice because it becomes you and them. When the church opens up again through their resurrection and a Vow of Silence, they have no questions to ask. All you have left is to incorporate the nonaligned, but what about the community church. You have seven names on the door in the Universal Church format granted in the year of Our Lord 1200 AD. The kingdom will live forever and ever Amen. What is required is to search the literature of Elias and Elijah in addition to the Holy Bible.

What you must do is give my writing to your people of challenge and determine what sermons and or procedures you must complete like becoming the financial planner for the lowest one third of income of each nation. Only the married men can earn the income to live above the poverty level in each country and live within their means. Teach the woman a man barely able to take care of her financially is quite a blessing. What if he earns a large income, will the children be well off? All your questions must be answered by your organization as the Seals are for communication and 666 beast books are documented Standing Historical written to biblical standards with your denomination on the cover.

King Jesus Christ did not forsaken you. He sent Elias and Elijah back from heaven to restoreth all things and to recreate prophecy as a way to run the church through mystery and intrigue. The man's profile is in the Holy Bible as I am proof that God knew me before I was born. As the four words of the millennium state or joy, war, jeopardy, and fear. We have not reached the title of the book Holy Bible or a perfect way of life. All we have are the four words of the millennium. Elias and Elijah are to complete the Holy Bible on how to restoreth all things and to teach the seven Holy Cities to run the world through the words inherit, judgment, and mystery and intrigue.

I will grant you the true Stairway to Heaven that must be in all churches when you are ready. When you pray, you raise your eyes to the Stairway to Heaven. You should take pride in the congregation for their achievements in His Name led by the Mother of Inspiration taking humility for King Jesus Christ and teaching through the Holy Spirit techniques.

The kingdom can resolve any problem in the world and will exist forever and ever. The church employees of King Jesus Christ must over come the end where the church and civilization as we know it disappears. The church has no questions to ask as our Gods have told us all things. The Second Advent story or King Jesus Christ can return to the temple or Israel and proceed to complete the work in Israel. All nations of the church against Israel. I already know the church does not have a chance.

In addition. Do not finalize the plans for any other government at this time. Let then learn in the UN and the church sermons and training classes for foreign governments. Have them start to finalize their commitments to their people, but do not rush. Always be ten years behind the Heartland of the world, the United States through all years like the year of Our Lord 2060 AD instead of the year of Our Lord 2050 AD. Give then a chance for America to bring the story of salvation across the world, as the Church of US (U.S.) becomes the research and development arm of the seven Holy Cities or the Heartland. You finalize their plan for each nation and present in the movies. We Americans desire to see many of them too. Your 666 beast books will produce many films and get ready to develop your own Hollywood or Los Angeles, California is the city of angels.

Elijah has provided the memo you use to talk to your peers to create heaven on earth. Your communication with your peers is a great requirement of a kingdom.

Memo for use to encourage others to become the chosen and faithful.

I was asked indirectly by a clergyman, what is the procedure necessary for King Jesus Christ to return. I have a chapter that covers the procedure as copied from the Holy Bible. The chapter title is called "Stairway to Heaven". I will summarize here how easy it is to start and actually to complete. God will never give us more to do than we can do.

King Jesus Christ will not return through our observation but good deeds.

From the book of Luke 17:20. And when He was demanded of the Pharisees, when the kingdom of God should come, He answered them and said, The kingdom of God cometh not with observation:

He will join us in the temple of Israel not church.

From the book of Malachi 3:1. Behold, I will send my messenger, and he shall prepare the way before me: and the LORD, whom ye seek, shall suddenly come to his temple, even the messenger of the covenant, whom ye delight in: behold, he shall come, saith the LORD of hosts.

Procedure:

Step one is we must first identify the Antichrist. The work is complete.

Step two is we must have a common ground to get together with the chosen ones. I have written the first meeting and the future work to review. What are included are the presentation material and the words. No additional work is required unless you desire to read some background material. If you can make a sermon, you can present the material. I can explain the seventh day He rests like His Father, so you require the material from the mysterious messiah for a thousand year plan from the Holy Bible. The church must be run like the temple of Israel in mystery and intrigue. The work is very detailed and is covered as a wall of hope for each church location. Do not try to add detail now, just read. Only God can provide hope. Hope is the actions required to fulfill faith through people like you. Forgiveness is provided after the social ill is resolved, not before. You cannot forgive people that have the power to change and refuse. You must think about it like deadly sins. They must repent to be forgiven. The Holy Bible is clear.

Step three is to start church laws like Moses laws that the clergymen must obey. I have covered a number of them and you should encourage others to think about what maybe required. An example is, "If the clergymen have a problem in their marriage, they must seek the marriage counselors of the church." The result will be the congregation will force you to end divorces in their marriages. Finalizing anything now is not to be tried, but the principles to be learned.

Step four is to get the signatures of the clergymen and ask them to try the same with others and get their signatures. When you are satisfied, you go to your upper management, make the same presentation, and show the wall of hope unfinished and some preliminary church laws. Have your upper management contact another denomination and do the same. Do not contact the Catholics.

Step five is to get five denominations and one thousand signatures. Now you are ready to carry forward to the only Holy City we have, the Catholics. You do the same thing.

Step six is you gather in a storage web site all the churches you can find all over the world. The Holy Bible states to even check the caves or places you would not expect to find what someone called a church. You are trying to contact all to do the same as above. In addition, you will ask them to do a public opinion poll and the sermons that are created. You will have to find someone in the five denominations to write the two to five sermons for the power of one voice. Now you have ended future killing wars. The existing ones of the United States will stop and killing wars will never come back. This is a requirement in the Holy Bible and will be joy to achieve. In addition, you will help millions of children with Daily Bread. You will go to the temples to ask them to take the public opinion poll in addition to the church. Upper management should be able to arrange that easily with the powerful voice of your God leading the way.

Step seven is the church opens up the Holy Bible and learns what tasks must be completed. Since my literature covers most and many answers, I would start there. For example, you must complete God's Covenants or the minimum requirement to run a church. You require a physical structure called an Altar to be used at all locations. You would design what education requirements are necessary. When you divide the tasks, you should get as many people as possible to get involved. If there is a sermon to be written, you do not desire one million plus men to all write that one. So you pick some people and the task and meet with the other denominations to agree as one voice. So think small and get as many as possible you can to develop the great tribulation (reward) or work on the return of King Jesus Christ. He does not expect you to be perfect as written, the first time you try something new it is not very good, but your work over the millenniums makes all your works appear perfect. The task is complete when you, not He has no questions to ask. So all clergymen must consider questions and have the taskmasters complete the work. Again, I repeat you should make each tasks small so many can be involved.

Elijah
Telephone 815.765.0161
Email comfortingod@mchsi.com

Chapter 3.   The Seventh Trumpet Story.

This opening paragraph was added on February 18, the year of Our Lord 2009 AD. The church has passed the Seventh Trumpet Story in the Holy Bible and I had to think why. I started writing this book before I started the book "The Antichrist God's Version". I realized I had to restoreth all things and the only name I knew was the name Elias. Later I learned the book by Elias would not sell as stated in the book of Daniel and I had to continue. I could have finished this story and all would be good as the third power of eight. I now think why the church is so reluctant to change. I go back to a passage that some of your stories are so great, if you can get to the very elect, all you would do is deceive. You cannot get the attention of the clergymen (the very elect). They all have invented their own form of religion and they are not setting any goals other than beg for money to keep their location open. Without any real requirements to achieve anything and their blasphemy mouth, they feel good about their future. They do not believe the hardest career to receive the gift of John 3:16 is the employees of King Jesus Christ. They must obey the Holy Bible like a slave and they are doing one hundred percent of everything wrong. The clergymen rely on the passage that the kingdom is not of this world, which is true. The first power of eight or Jacob, I guess my name is Israel, was not Adam but God. His only begotten Son is the second part of the power of eight and not of this world. The third power of eight is the watchman with thy kingdom come and is not of this world, but the work of Adam. The Holy Bible is not of this world, but the work of God and Adam as His representative.

Nostradamus 2012 has a writing that the end will come in the year of the Lord 2014 AD with 2012 AD as a political event. He states the book of life (Standing Historical) is empty and the banks fail. God granted the world a clear date and still the world does not believe the Holy Bible and Nostradamus 2012 that agree. When they are told the truth, they go by the way of Peter and become so afraid. They revert back to their believes rather than pick themselves up by the loin cloth and walk like men. God has added that being afraid is not a sin so He knew what would happen. Elijah, the true prophet must continue for the love of my grandchildren and their future. I know the worst people in the world are people you believe in that refuse to help anyone, including their own family. The story below would be in power had the church decided by anyone to find Elias. Since the church is failing, the United States banks will fail because of government bad laws, and it will be buyers and sellers remorse unless the church implements the Lord's Prayer. We go back to Hoover Ville of the year of Our Lord 1929 to 1933 A.D. The difference is the wax is cold and Adam has guns. The United States cannot recover and the United States is turned back to the land of before the white man showed up. All it would take is a clergyman to make a few telephone calls to reverse the course of human events. Elijah in the previous chapter has the plan from the Holy Bible in Chapter 2 of this book, as copied from the Holy Bible.

The use of the numbers in the Holy Bible is for planning, as this is a seven star world. We have seven days, seven seas and continents, we grow in the spine seven times, and have seven major organs. 666, 40 or 13 are planning numbers. We can start with the theory that the seven indicates an important plan of King Jesus Christ. Since the USA is the future Heartland of the world, you have to realize the story starts in the USA as King Jesus Christ will meet us in Spain. I know He desires to do the same story as His Father or the story of King David's child, where He will grant us a reprieve from all killing wars. We can make the people in what we call poverty today, wealthy, or they shall not want. The United States and other countries must work on the wealth creation, not foolish laws of more debt creation. The problem near the end times is the problem with the rich and is all about money and God's kingdom. By we the people implementing the Holy Bible, the wealth creation in the USA will be great as Senator John McCain or Barack Obama leads to the end. Neither are a qualified planner or tries to understand how economies work.

Think about the logic of the Republican Party. They desire to under tax the rich to win elections. They spend money like drunken sailors or heavy indebtedness. They sell the bonds to the rich. The congregation is paying the rich approximately two thousand dollars per person per year just for interest (in the year of Our Lord 2005 AD). Their view on how to run an economy is foolish, yet is used in most countries of the world. The United States is the greatest debtor nation and we do not have any reserves. We cannot afford Social Security. The politicians have been collecting the money from the thirties and spending it all as part of general revenue. If you use the Holy Bible and you believe a two per cent mortgage on a house is good, I would love to talk to you about investments in fantasyland. King Jesus Christ states no interest on consumer investments for a house, car, or furniture.

King Jesus Christ becomes the wall from the Old Testament. He will send our angels to protect the Chicken Little story where, the clergymen cry the sky is falling many times about wars and rumors about wars. When it really happens, no clergyman believes they can stop it. The real story is to implement the Lord's Prayer. The angels are our children or peacekeepers and the requirement is, "I do not want a hair on a child's head harmed." Yes, that means the hair on a child's head in a foreign country like Iraq, too. Are you glad the clergymen were involved to stop the war before it started? They as the Antichrists did not of course. The Antichrist came in an era of peace and prosperity. How can you get to God's plan of seven you ask? You have to review Standing Historical (history) and learn. The same Standing Historical all church locations must have.

Satan was a man where by appointing a Soul, Satan was granted much wealth and name recognition. He started with all the advantages most people in politics would desire in name and wealth. Satan as prophecy defined was in the only Holy City of our world. Many saw him in the Holy City of Rome on television. You have some passages that state, "Do not let that dragon steal that woman's child. If a man gains the whole world and loses his Soul, he gains nothing at all. In heaven on earth, do not send your policemen out to kill them because they will not go to school. If you fail to blow the trumpet and one person dies, I will take you by the hand. Some governments are taking you on the road to hell. Let God seek the vengeance said the Lord." The passages go on and on for what the saints in the Holy Cities of seven are to use to judge the politicians. Have you heard of the Mark of the Beast from the book of Mark? A politician must understand the book of Mark so he has the mark of the beast in his forehead. What that means is when you see him, you know they understand and were trained. The judgment of the saints covers all governments in the world where there is a church. The nations where they have a physical presence and politicians that claim to represent the church, the judgment of the clergymen (saints) shall be unbelievable in comparison with what anyone does today. In the United States, we do not even know the names on many ballots. President

Jimmy Carter had the best values in the laws for helping the poor of the United States in modern history. Even the best economy under President William J. Clinton could not match him because of the Republicans you granted him. Presidents Ronald Reagan and George H. W. Bush created gangs of one hundred thousand poor children and violated the book of Mark in big ways to satisfy the greed of the rich in America. Have you heard of the passage, "Do not let the government steal our houses?" Under former President George H. W. Bush, he steals over two hundred and fifty billion dollars worth of houses and the church would say nothing. Have you heard of the failure of Supply Economics or give the rich money that cannot use it wisely. The Holy Bible states the problem near the end times (in the year of Our Lord 2009 AD) is the problem with the rich. We had many abandon buildings do to the failure of Supply Economics. Are you glad the church did not send a beast like President Ronald Reagan to Heaven? Both presidents were great failures per the Holy Bible requirements.

Let us go back as the Holy Bible uses the number seventy-two (2000-72 equals 1928) for the United States, the future Heartland of the world and do the job of the saints of the seven Holy Cities.

- Year President
- 1929 -1933 Herbert Clark Hoover
- 1933 –death Franklin D. Roosevelt
- 1945 -1953 Harry S. Truman
- 1953 -1961 Dwight D. Eisenhower
- 1961 –death John F. Kennedy
- 1963 -1969 Linden Johnson
- 1969 - Impeachment Richard Nixon
- 1974 -1977 Gerald Ford
- 1977 –1981 Jimmy Carter
- 1981 -1989 Ronald Reagan
- 1989 –1993 George H. W. Bush

- 1993 –2001 William J. Clinton
- 2001 –2009 George W. Bush.

The saints of the seven Holy Cities have to judge the above leaders from the Holy Bible in terms of their achievements and campaign promises (promise keepers). The congregation shall vote after their term is over to determine if they desire to release the shackles. You should be able to determine if they are beasts or dragons. If they are violating the instructions for the clergymen (the Holy Bible), the clergymen are sinners. I have yet to hear a preacher whore that understands the Holy Bible and God's plan. The church is run by individuals taking God's name in vain, by false witness, or violating the Ten Commandments. They have pride in themselves not humility for King Jesus Christ. That means they are violating the Ten Commandments and all instructions in the Holy Bible. Have you heard of the Catholics stating they have done everything in the Holy Bible once? They are to live by all the words, not try to apply it once.

Email from Lawrence E Couch Office of Justice and Service Archdiocese of Washington 301-853-5343.

The House of Representatives will vote on a package of budget cuts tomorrow: Thursday, November 10, 2005. The bill is a compilation of budget-cutting proposals passed by several House committees over the past two weeks. The House bill could result in low-income and vulnerable people losing access to health care, etc.

Lawrence E Couch is telling me to support his efforts to overcome the Republicans in the House of Representatives that will increase the pain in our families by eliminating the money to overcome some of the social ills (sorrows) of the country. They do not have the money, as wars are more important than the pain in American family lives. He should just write how the Republicans are violating the Holy Bible and they should go to a church training session before they become politicians. Satan in the White House has his advisers trained to commit to making him bad as the Mark of the Beast is creating sins for all American clergymen. The clergymen are asleep at the Altar on Sunday as their services are not ready for milk let alone meat. The pain of the Mark of the Beast should be at all Altars in the world, not just emailed to a few people. Where is the training of the clergymen for the requirements of the Holy Bible?

What are the results of the Mark of the Beast caused in the year of Our Lord 2005 AD and 2006 AD? First, violating the book of Mark will make the economy worse. Second, with the United States with what is called Homeland Security in charge, Domestic Violence has been declared double the problem in the year of Our Lord 2007 AD and is necessary in Standing Historical. When you serve one master at the expense of the poor, what will happen? In this case, violence became worse as many people could not get the money required. The government went over four trillion dollars in debt under foolish George W. Bush. The inflation has increased and will continue with the foolish policies of the Bush administration and the Federal Reserve. Inflation is a tax on salaries and investment.

You as a preacher may have agreed that we should start a war as conquers as stated in the book of Romans. As a teacher, you would develop the gospel stating the book of Romans is when the United States is run by another beast called a crown leader and Red Dragon. In the book of Daniel, we are described as having metal teeth. What happens is no flesh is saved (John 3:16) because you have the wrong heart from the book of Luke, worship Satan, and recreated the Roman Empire equivalent in the United States. The wars and Hollywood have made our children violent, as you believe Rome was. A big difference is swords, now are guns, wow. Any country that does not properly raise their children has no right to exist. Can you as a religious leader believe in a Hollywood movie where the women of the United States taught our men reality? Let us send all men who talk about wars and rumors of wars to Perdition. Let the men learn the pen is mightier than the sword and use common sense to end the pain of lack of money (famine) in our families. The men have to learn, you cannot beat terrorism in America by creating hell on earth. Killing wars are hell. You do that through hate and joy. Before the war started, the Holy Bible instructed the clergymen to hate the Arabs above all others. When you hate, you love the Arabs less than the Muslins. You desire the terrorists to change. You also violate, "In heaven on earth, do not send your policemen out to kill them, because they will not go to school." We do not like our police officers of America, as we do not even desire to be jurors in court. Why would America desire to be the world police officers and get nothing but our society failure in return? King Jesus Christ told us not to even damage a blade of grass in Iraq when we bomb from the heavens (air).

Let us start with the presidents that violated the book of Mark and became beasts. We have Presidents Herbert C. Hoover, Richard Nixon, Ronald Reagan, George H. W. Bush and George W. Bush. The number only adds up to five. Let us look at the presidents that are dragons (warlords or hawks) and want to steal that woman's child. Since the soldier of misfortune did not die because of John 3:16, the warlord president steals that mother's child when the soldier of misfortune dies. The Holy Bible states you cannot put that child back in the womb. We would have to start from a time when the UN was formed and our presidents used the forum to violate the King of Peace instructions. Presidents Dwight D. Eisenhower, John F. Kennedy, Ronald Reagan, George H. W. Bush, and George W. Bush are dragons, which make them beasts. President Dwight D. Eisenhower started the cold war and nuclear weapons. The Holy Bible reads balls of fire that reach above the clouds and weapons where fire comes out of each end. My previous writings describe what America lost by allowing President Dwight D. Eisenhower to start a nuclear program and a cold war. You shall know the rest where trying to prove they were fools as America never won a war from the First World War on. Both countries had the church involved and the church lost both lands. That must be part of Standing Historical of Russia where the Soviet Union formed in a country where there once was a church. When the seven Holy Cities review our past presidents, they will notice the Republican Party never had a successful president in the last fifty years plus. Yet, the clergymen worked against the best economy in modern times under President William J. Clinton and he had the "peace dividend" in place. As the Holy Bible states, "The Antichrist came in an era of peace and prosperity" or one hour past midnight on January 1, the year of Our Lord 2000 AD. The clergymen allowed peace and prosperity to be lost. They were asleep as the Holy Bible proclaims at the Altar. King Jesus Christ judged you in the Holy Bible because He loved you. Where is the same type of love in the church? Where are the saints that obey the Ten Commandments and judge the world, but do not attack people in gospel armor like gays or children?

The United States is critical in prophecy, as the Heartland of the world or the location where Our Gods are going to make a stand. What do Our Gods stand for but every word of scripture? The Holy Bible states King Jesus Christ will meet us in Spain. He has granted us a beautiful land. We are the children of corn, etc. That makes our presidents more important than other countries as the future Heartland of the world and we should read the Holy Bible with comprehension. Let us look at millstone two names and one name left. Millstone means he would be better dieing than taking on the role he decided on and lost his Soul. The two names are Ronald Reagan and George H. W. Bush with one name left George Bush. Therefore, King Jesus Christ has told the clergymen the name of the presidents that will fail themselves long ago and the church cannot listen to an election or their values in office to learn. Preacher Whores are not ready for sermons about milk, let alone meat. We know for sure the names of three beasts. The clergymen should tell the congregation why they voted for them. Yes, I would agree. They will put that information in the seven books of Standing Historical of America, as we are the wax location of the world. Standing Historical is written in the book of life. One of the names of the seven books of life in America out of the 666 beast books will be Life of US (U.S.) Catholic.

Next, we should look at Satan and wonder why the first six beasts did not go to Perdition. The Holy Bible states King Jesus Christ has named the age as the "Age of Accountability". You are responsible for your actions. The Gates to Perdition are opened on January 1, the year of Our Lord 2000 AD at one hour past midnight. What beast number is Satan? The great depression should have taught the religious leaders something.

1. President Herbert Clark Hoover
2. President Dwight D. Eisenhower
3. President John F. Kennedy
4. President Richard Nixon
5. President Ronald Reagan
6. President George H. W. Bush
7. President George W. Bush

The Holy Bible says that the clergymen worship Satan, who was the King of Babylon from what was said in the year of Our Lord 2000 AD campaign and in office. Satan does not have two horns on his head, but the four horns, which will represent what he said. Governor George W. Bush was a beast as governor and he and the Republican Party used President William J. Clinton's girlfriend to ride into office. President George W. Bush became the Red Dragon not like President Franklin D. Roosevelt. You should remember, President Franklin D. Roosevelt desired to avoid the foolishness in Europe, but the Japanese would not allow it. With all the prophecies of scripture, the Antichrists I have heard in the year of Our Lord 2006 AD are still trying to teach about watching out for the King of Babylon. I know the clergymen are still calling the Prince of Peace, the prince, not King Jesus Christ. Therefore, the prince that runs the church in the kingdom is called the Prince of Peace. The true word of God would be how the Antichrists ended all wars as prophecy defines.

We still have a name to add in to get to the Seventh Trumpet Story. The Holy Bible asks a question, "Why did Satan react?" The answer was to win the future elections. In the year of Our Lord 2004 AD, a senator called Senator John F. Kerry opposed him. Satan's Darts or blame was used extensively in the campaign. What did Senator John F. Kerry try to teach? He could kill better than Satan could. Senator John F. Kerry becomes the False Messiah or the sixth dragon if he won. He is committed to allowing Satan to continue creating hell on earth like Hitler. He will go by the way of Satan. There is no hell like a woman scorned, when she sees her child die right in front of her eyes or they live in a hell hole of war in Iraq without end. You start with the Second World War is a war to end all military wars. Now, no dragon can appear in America (Heartland).

1. President Dwight D. Eisenhower Dragon
2. President John F. Kennedy Dragon
3. President Ronald Reagan Dragon
4. President George H. W. Bush Dragon
5. President George H. Bush Dragon
6. Senator John F. Kerry False Messiah Dragon
7. Watchman from the Holy Bible or peace on earth, good will towards men.

Please add the above titles to the people when you generate the books of the 666 beast books or Standing Historical. Instead of Elias and Elijah to be able to get the clergymen to form the kingdom the watchman or the seventh did not occur. Instead we the people of the United States elected the eighth beast. Senator John F. Kerry does not have the right title to be called the beast as these beasts are the crown leaders of America. The eighth beast is President Barack Obama as he represented President John F. Kennedy, not President Franklin D. Roosevelt as you would expect the Roman Empire to do. The major candidates cannot be saved and will go by the way of Satan. We will continue to use the title the Seventh Trumpet if America desires the story of creating heaven on earth, not perdition.

Seeing the names of our presidents makes the truth of Revelation 17:1 and up come alive. Revelation 17:10 And there are seven kings: five are fallen, and one is, and the other is not yet come; and when he cometh, he must continue a short space. Foolish George Bush in the year of Our Lord 2000 AD is the fifth from Revelation 17:8. The five are fallen and we can count. The one that is, and the other that is not yet come is trained by Satan. Anyone that voted for foolish George Bush or Senators John F. Kerry, John McCain or Barack Obama was wrong. Standing Historical as the book of life will explain in detail. The church will continue to be the Son of Perdition until they explain and train. They must do the story of Divine Intervention to help the politicians and the taxpayers. Therefore, Satan and his angels are the young Republicans and foolish George Bush. As I have written, we have to get rid of the Republican congress, their Political Action Committees, and do not forget the governors. Foolish George Bush was a beast as a governor, a mass murderer of children from Texas, and my literature has covered the rest. Prophecy is written that President Barack Obama must not win in the year of Our Lord 2012 AD and the Republican Party must disappear.

The clergymen are to find the Mysterious Messiah's representative or allow the eighth beast will destroy America. What Elijah, the prophet is to do is give the clergymen a thousand-year plan for the one world government to complement the clergymen granting King Jesus Christ His Kingdom. The truth of scripture is it was started approximately six thousand years ago or the seventh day He rests. The Holy Bible contains the truth to work for the next one thousand years. There is no reason for Our Gods to define anymore until the next millennium. The answers at that time are in the Holy Bible as God has continued to name the age and Adam should be able to do it himself. He will start to lose again because it will be too good. The clergymen must remember Satan can appear again if you fail yourself. King Jesus Christ has told us to get rid of all jeopardy and turn it into joy. He has told us how as the Holy Bible is written as no man can boast. As His watchman, he becomes the seventh or works for peace on earth, good will towards men. The clergymen can teach from the Altars many stories of mystery and intrigue. The Antichrists (clergymen) form the kingdom and end all killing wars. America starts planning through theology tremendous wealth creation in our country and uses the United Nations to teach the other countries. The government will grant our religious leaders a white paper on our plans. They can teach the American congregation on what is possible. The foreign congregations can learn and wonder what their politicians are doing. The one world government of the Old Testament or Israel shall be used if the people desire. The will of the people prevail. There will be one government in each political unit or country, which if there is a church becomes nation against nation plus kingdom against kingdom. In a foreign country like India, the church may not be large in congregation, but the politicians representing King Jesus Christ may win all the national elections until the temples gather the knowledge and train their congregations on economics.

The theory of theology or planning from the Holy Bible requires "Faith and wait with a little bit of fear". What we have learned from my previous works is Faith of an Olive Branch can move a mountain of despair, but without hope and the true actions of hope that faith will soon disappear. Therefore, the first part is to define what Faith of the unseen we have. We are challenged to do per the writings of scripture is to make all people in our country rich. We shall not want. Well to start, we should define a future we desire the citizens to start with, which is something rather easy for any citizen who desires to try. All who try end up beyond the poverty level that has the ability to work. We define the Faith of the unseen through the American citizens of Faith that through their efforts, they can be above the poverty level.

The last I heard a family of four must earn about nineteen thousand dollars a year to be above the poverty level. Many different costs of living prevail in America so I will define the standard now of twenty-four thousand in the higher cost of living areas. Trained planners may enhance the numbers for more meaning, but you have to start somewhere. The family of four is husband and wife. Let us change that to just husband, but he can work overtime or a part time job when available. We should have Faith that through trained politicians that all Americans that try and have the mental or physical abilities, can exceed that number. The clergymen seek politicians that believe the goal is realistic. Do not attack politicians like former President William J. Clinton in gospel armor. You are learning from the politicians their dramatic action plans and the congregation is to vote. The seven Holy Cities must judge all governments and teach the congregation where they are violating the Holy Bible or achieving good deeds by enhancing the way of life of the taxpayers. I believe living in America that number of twenty-four thousand dollars would not make the lower one third of the population rich today, but they would be above what is defined as the poverty level.

The next part is to define the hope through the church. When the system evolves beyond the church, we will change faith and wait with the actions of hope into a series of laws. The laws will be dynamic action plans led by the governors and the federal government and their ability to create work if they apply money correctly. They should not write bad laws. They must be written by the New Testament standards. Much government waste has been created. You listened to foolish George Bush that appears to be his only goal, but the goal for government is waste not want not. Well, ending all poverty is rather easy in the United States for the above goal as the laws start the Generation of the FIG. I will cover in detail later, but let us go to the church responsibility first as they maintain fear. The church cannot create wealth, but can train the politicians to succeed not fail themselves. Our God, King Jesus Christ has written; He shall double the best Adam can do in wealth. The Holy Bible is written so no man can boast. Therefore, the answers are already in the Holy Bible. Let us review scripture.

The Holy Bible has two versions that man can achieve. One is that Satan is the seventh beast. The end will come with buyers and sellers remorse with the eighth beast. If the eighth beast was a Republican that will destroy the American economy through the policy of the party or, "Read my lips no new taxes" and violating the book of Mark. I heard the education of Satan state, "I defy anyone to raise the taxes and improve the economy." The taxes at state and local levels are going up because of the policies in Washington DC and so is the burden on our grandchildren in terms of debts. Do not forget the burden of inflation on the wealth creation in our country. So as the Holy Bible states, "He is a beast, but not a beast, and yet a beast." That is because he has the wrong title to qualify as the eighth beast and he will violate the book of Mark and be a dragon. President Barack Obama campaign has promised he will continue his failure as not representing the God of Heart. You can read at the ending chapters why he can go past the year of Our Lord 2012 AD and why the United States will fail. The Battle of Armageddon will start with buyers and sellers remorse or the land King Jesus Christ has reserved as the Heartland of the world or the location where He will make a stand with the words of scripture. The Seventh Trumpet is where the clergymen and public put the best man qualified to understand and plan from the Holy Bible. He has to overcome the end of civilization in America and not lose his Soul through divine intervention or the third power of eight, which is eight years. A man becoming a beast in the White House or any government location is very dangerous on your future and easy, if you are not sure of what to do. Do not fall into a trap like Senator Barack Obama did where he might qualify for, "If you gain the whole world (United States presidency) and lose your Soul, you gain nothing at all." I have listened to him in the past and he has what I would call a "young mind" or no true understanding of planning and theology. I do not recommend he would accept the job of president even if the congregation votes for him. I would be concerned about his planning ability.

Therefore, the Seventh Trumpet Story comes from the mysterious messiah or the Holy Bible. I am a peace person as my first book published was written before the war in Iraq and it would end the war before it started. The book should have been accepted by the church and used to end the war before it started. It is part of my first book as defined in the book of Daniel, when it was combined in 'The Antichrist God's Version" written by Elias. This is the second book as defined in the book of Daniel. The Holy Bible states the Arabs shall be hated above all others, but King Jesus Christ told us not to damage even a blade of grass in Iraq when the bombs come from the heavens. There is a prophecy about the future two hundred million attacking Iraq led by the one third dead of our country. That is the USA that voted Republican. The Holy Bible is clear. There is no hell like a woman scorned and America is forcing her child to grow up in a hellhole defined by American foolishness. You beat the terrorism by America citizens by hate and joy, also. You can read the Seventh Trumpet Story as King Jesus Christ will give us a chance to end all killing wars by King Jesus Christ becoming the wall from the Old Testament. We are now past the Seventh Trumpet story and there is not much time left.

Where does King Jesus Christ get the information from to create the one world government of Israel, the church is to put in each nation? He gets the information to us from the Holy Bible or the source document. We can have nation against nation. You have to stop and study what happened in the standing historical of Israel. The Roman Empire came into Israel and imposed a fifty percent increase in tithing or taxes. Around the areas where the Romans did this, much hunger and problems occurred in other countries as history defines. As you read the Holy Bible, no such hunger occurred in Israel. The nation absorbed the cost and life went on. King Jesus Christ defined there was still a rich man to help build the first church; however, the fifty percent increase in tithing resulted in a woman being poor, but she could still be a giver. Therefore, the following is an update to modern times but you must use the Holy Bible in a training session for future politicians and judges to reach the final standards. Without the instructions from Israel of the Old Testament like, "Do not let the government steal your houses." the results would not be the same. Also think of tax increase in the beginning as, "Do not give money to people that cannot use it wisely" and other rules on investment where people were given money and they were afraid to invest it at all, because they may lose some. The playgirls or playboys shall not eat or they will go into penance. The book of Mark summarizes the laws that will result in the Mark of the Beast. Again, as the clergymen receive information from the courts and legislative branches take the words to the seminaries to develop the parables into teaching instructions for around the world for all of the nations to learn. The governments will work through the United Nations. The name should change to United Countries and wealth creation is the goal of all governments.

Memo issued to the Antichrists or clergymen who are not ready for milk, let alone meat.

11/2/ the year of Our Lord 2006 AD (Modified)

The Seventh Trumpet Story

King Jesus Christ's Thousand Year Plan for the One World Government of Israel for the United States from prophecy.

You remember you have to form the church with seven names on the door or I saw seven churches to make the Seventh Trumpet story real. You are living in fantasyland by believing the tribulation of the beginning of heaven on earth is bad. No flesh is saved is true (no John 3:16) as defined in the Holy Bible.

From the book of Matthew
Mat 24:21 For then shall be great tribulation, such as was not since the beginning of the world to this time, no, nor ever shall be.
Mat 24:22 And except those days should be shortened, there should no flesh be saved: but for the elect's sake those days shall be shortened.
The greatest tribulation is the clergymen granting King Jesus Christ His virgin bride back the kingdom and His return. Those days be shorten or the kingdom formed before the year of Our Lord 2000 AD no flesh is saved means no John 3:16. Unfortunately Elijah can prove from the Holy Bible all the clergymen can achieve without the kingdom or I saw seven churches are turning this world into perdition. Perdition is the land of eternal death or you live but wish you were dead every day the rest of your life. The story of Resurrection was forty-two months not seven years. For the sake of the very elect King Jesus Christ used forty-two months not seven years.

In the book of Galatians, the clergymen in His kingdom become the lords in the Lord of lords. You are to teach the judges of our country in a training course to be justified by grace and not by law. The laws are for the wicked, not the average man. Have you heard of a person getting a ticket for parking and being found guilty in court that must change or no traffic tickets. As you teach from the Holy Bible, you ask the judges of the court to send you a copy of how grace applied in reviewing the laws of America. Since all laws of importance are bad, all laws should be reviewed and altered to the New Testament requirements. You use the material to train the future Scripture Attorneys the reality of theology or planning from the Holy Bible. As an example as the judges correct the problems they caused by their rulings on Living Wills, you desire how and what was accomplished. Always rely on the courts to develop the concepts of the future training packages. As the government creates the laws of liberty and uses the format of the New Testament to write the laws, you will teach. If you cannot run the courts, you are to teach. The words are, "He who cannot do must teach." The watchman will use the concept that all Supreme Court Judges will have a term limitation of six years and will be granted a chance to go to a lower court, where they can review the knowledge that they developed.

In the book of Timothy, the clergymen are to train the future politicians in a course on how to coordinate the work of a governor or king as a bishop would coordinate the work of a clergymen. Age is work in the area not as a man without experience covering the role of a president like President Jimmy Carter without having the chance to grow into the position. My training and age is covered in the Holy Bible, so I do qualify. The government will develop the computerized planning technique, develop the training courses and turn future training in the one world government over to the seven Holy Cities. I would enjoy teaching the business design to the organizations of Social Security, US Post Office, and the IRS of the Holy

Bible. The Federal Government and others will pay the church to use the bottom up planning technique program in the Holy Bible or the path to the small door. The government will realize the program will be used by all people in business, as it is the business design of God and the work of Adam. For example, the computerized Holy Bible technique is invaluable to a doctor to help overcome malpractice and he will joy going to a training session and be taught by his denomination.

The angels are to be heard by our senators. The angels are God's special people or God's Children of 777 design. We are all children of God but when I use God's Children that means the age from born to twenty-one or the children to be special are double blessed. First they are blessed by the church as they can talk from the Altar, but not the president of the United States or any adult beyond clergymen. The senators are to listen to their special wishes as will be covered in a book of wants as generated by the church. When a senator learns to hear the church will call God's Children blessed. The senators like the clergymen are to have eyes to see and ears to hear. Today the knowledge is lacking by people asleep at the Altar that are grandmas. We shall not want, but may the government grant all of God's Children the gifts children richly deserve all over the world. Therefore, our federal senators are to work on special items like schools for our children for the country with the involvement of the state senators. We must listen to the children and learn. The House of Representatives Federal is to develop a strong balance sheet for all our citizens and businesses. God's Children will wish they had good parents that can afford to raise them properly. What a wish for all the people equivalent to a senator to learn and achieve. The State government is to issue business licenses for the state. If you want to start a restaurant, the state government working with your local governments can tell you where you can build or buy your business. Forty thousand businesses fail each month and zero is the only answer that is good. God's Children will not joy in their family business going into bankruptcy court, so we know we must eliminate. Churches, please grant the people a sign in the Wall of Hope. The state senators would focus on problems like hurricanes in your state. The environmental issues were covered in my original books.

In the example of a training course of the clergymen on the passage, "I do not want you to do a job you do not want to do.", make sure, you cover the technology from the Altar, so the politicians have a clue of what you are doing to complement their efforts.

As described in the Holy Bible, if the one world government (of Israel) in any nation writes bad laws, the sins (pain) of the clergymen will be all over the country. The problems will result in the rod of iron to be used. The officials of the government will be required to blow the trumpet. If they fail to do so and one person dies, King Jesus Christ will take them by their hand (fail to write laws to correct). The congregations are very interested when the government takes the country on the road to hell.

The clergymen are to end the pain in the lives of people. Under President George H. W. Bush of the year of Our Lord 1992 AD, there were forty million children in jeopardy. That is forty million Cardinal Sins of American clergymen. The problem near the end times is the problem with the rich as prophecy describes in scripture. Under President William J. Clinton before the end of his term, I heard the number of Cardinal Sins went down to twenty-seven million. Without the foolish Republicans sent to Congress, the number should have been much lower. As the politicians eliminate the jeopardy of famine (money), you desire to encourage them to continue by having them send you each of their efforts. We the congregation shall not want. The goal of the government can only be zero or the clergymen and government officials are in extreme jeopardy. Our Gods call it fear. All people one day will call that fear. You note why it has happened, when getting all people above the poverty level is so easy. Whatever we want, we can have as long as it does not impose pain on others. What an advantage to all citizens to live in God's Kingdom. In God's Kingdom of New Testament Laws, all laws must follow the rules of argument as trained and be veto proof. The New Testament Laws are dynamic action plans and begins the Generation of the FIG. The church staff will summarize their achievement as you take pride in the congregation. You review from the Altar, add to the local book of good deeds, and send to the right Holy City. The leader is granted knowledge to die and carry the message forward to the true heaven in His name King Jesus Christ. The word in the Holy Bible you are looking for is the word "Love" for writing laws.

Lawrence E. Couch of the Archdiocese of Washington, DC sent me emails in the year of Our Lord 2005 AD and the year of Our Lord 2006 AD where the Republicans were violating the Holy Bible in the book of Mark by eliminating the money to solve the social ills (sorrows) of the country. They did not use the Holy Bible to explain what they knew was wrong. That type of law violates the laws of King Jesus Christ and will make Cardinal Sins increase. If you understand King Jesus Christ's economic model, bad laws will reduce the economic growth of our country, thereby reducing the tax collection, and causing a famine (lack of money). The clergymen must identify the Mark of the Beast and train the politicians that your salvation is at stake as well as the clergymen. The rod of iron will be used, if the trumpet does not sound by clergymen that have eyes to see and ears to hear. The courts can help by reversing the bad laws before the social ills and the pain in the families cause the clergymen to have more Cardinal Sins. The Holy Bible is a way of life and always in time ends up with a life a thousand times better than the end.

The mentally or physically challenged in work is to help medical science as Mr. Reeve (the man that played superman) that died in the year of Our Lord 2006 AD, if that is all he can do. A child's job is education or joy, but an adult in an accident should try under Social Security to recover or help medical science with enlighten power in the Salvation Army Hospitals. All the rest of the men without jobs in our prisons are unemployed and a problem for the government to solve. Never say a challenged individual does not work and use the Holy Oil concept to enhance their productive lives until John 3:16 give them new arms and legs. Do not let them lose the way, truth, and light. You must teach or how can you turn their jeopardy of failure, for you must turn it into joy. Always remember the four words of the millennium or joy, jeopardy, war, and fear. The playboys and girls of today are in jeopardy. The passage, "A friend in need is a friend indeed." applies especially to the rich and certain politicians since they are in shackles. Only God can take care of your needs, as a need is spiritual. Poverty is a want for money as defined today and of course, the church cannot create greenbacks or dollar bills.

A movie to get the businessperson and their voter on your team is exciting. Therefore, you start with the challenge. The movie title will be The Seventh Trumpet. You can create an economy twice as good as former President William J. Clinton or the best economy in modern history of America. The Republicans will not con America to recreate a land of economic failure again. The goals below will satisfy ninety-seven percent of the voters. The remaining three percent are hard, but their hearts can be enlightened by the church teaching the truth about the rich, the Lord's Prayer (debtors), and reincarnation. Now, the church has a government plan where one hundred percent of the people of America demand.

You have to raise the taxes and use the money wisely without government waste. In the year of Our Lord 2008 AD, one percent of the people have more money than ninety percent of the people. To produce a climate for business, you never give money to people that cannot use it wisely. Today the consumer is greatly in debt and giving more money to the rich is insanity. We are slaves to the rich by the usury laws. See the Old Testament what happened under Our Father about interest baring investments like houses. The church must learn about interest baring loans on paychecks and car titles. The Holy Bible states America requires ten thousands seeds or ideas to correct America. Below is a list of projects we must under take to reestablish wealth creation in America. The ideas should be developed by congress and implemented through the procedure of New Testament law.

1. If you earn over one hundred thousand dollars a year, you will pay the first new dollar on income except in the area of capital gains and dividends.
2. Many corporations are cash cows. You go back to the old rates of the 1990s.
3. You have a strong commitment to the wealthy to review greed where a new 60% and 75% tax is added. It begins at three million dollars and over where the 75% starts at ten million dollars. All forms of income apply. Some people believe some Americans are over paid. The governors may consider a just change at the state level, which can be collected by federal.
4. Redo the Capital Gains and Dividend Taxes - all that happened is the treasury has less money in it. Profits on shorting stocks shall be raised to fifty percent. One per cent of the people have more money than ninety per cent and the Republicans desire to tax capitol gains at seven and one half percent. The one percent of the people could grow to one percent has more money than ninety nine percent of the people at current rates (like India and other countries) at the current rate. The economy will fail.
5. Review the inheritance tax laws since the courts may have made benefits that are not justified. Our

children require the money at their start of a family not dancing on our graves. Changes maybe required after a million dollars or higher in inheritance tax. You minimize giving large amounts of money to people who cannot use it wisely like playboys and girls.

6. Add a state tax collected by the Federal Government on corporate income of three percent. Use the money to reduce property taxes for schools and sales taxes. An example would be one percent for staffing the schools and one-half percent to eliminate all debt of the school districts. Start in the poorer areas first within a state. The results should be lower property taxes for schools and money to bring the poorer area education standards up. In a high tech world, America must use education to help the American businessperson with trained talent. The last review of our schools that I heard put us at eighteen out of twenty four. For the American industries that is bad. The sales tax money reduction shall be used in enterprising zones. Businesspersons should be encouraged to locate in selected areas where the business climate is lacking. In Illinois, downtown Rockford has many vacant buildings where a difference in sales tax costs could promote job and wealth creation to restore the area. One-half percent of the money should be used to reduce the city bonds. King Jesus Christ will make the economy grow and borrowing money must end. The future of our grandchildren depends on a good economy, not an economy run by fools.

7. You will have the government reduce its expenses when the economy is too big in growth as happen in the year of Our Lord 2000 AD. The small business sector can continue to expand because of lower

interest rates and use the savings to reduce the debts of the government; therefore, the big interest payments will be reduced and thereby reducing the taxes. An example is the growth is over three percent (real growth expansion minus indebtedness not Republican growth). The theory was proven in the past that a high growth in the no inflation growth economy cannot be sustained forever and yet grants you real earnings and pay raises. Today the Federal Reserve would raise the interest rates to slow it down. Interest is a tax. All governing bodies will project the tax revenue and save at least fifty percent for next year and buy its bonds back. In addition, money with real titles of projects that can be spent in the next quarter will be developed when the economy is weak and jobs are being lost. May the government not use the money but cancel all debt, thereby saving the taxpayers about two thousand dollars plus per person per year for government interest. Does it make sense to reduce the taxes on the wealthy and then have them buy our bonds and we pay interest? Let us save the cost by paying the debt not raising the cost of business by higher interest rates and greater loans. Our taxes will go down quickly. If the growth is very high, the government shall save one hundred percent of all new income. The Federal Reserve shall measure the cost of government in all-important areas as to what they spend. We shall understand government cost is decreasing when they are a smaller percent of the economy. Under the Republicans of the last seven years, the cost of government has grown tremendously.

8. In the year of Our Lord 2005 AD, we were receiving about a two percent pay raise and the cost of living

(inflation) was going up over four. The consumer is weakened and will require borrowed money to maintain his standard of living. We demand real cost of living increases like under the Democrats in the nineties where ten years in the future our standard of living should improved not become worse. We can live with our pay raises as long as the economy does not require additional spending and the politicians rely on us when it does (Consumption Economics). The United States greatest export is the greenbacks as our bonds disappear and foreign countries can do the same as us. Today we are like the Roman Empire where they brought the savings of the world into Rome to be wasted. Today America is bringing eighty percent of the savings of the world and keeping the taxes on the rich low by historical standards of the fifties under Republican President Dwight D. Eisenhower. The rich are living well and creating hell in many women lives with children. We pay interest on the money and give the tax break to the rich, which cannot use the money wisely (greed). If they could use it wisely, you would ask why poverty is so wide spread in America instead of good paying jobs that cannot be filled. In the beginning, one of the requirements of a good economy is job creation and a pay rises above inflation. Under foolish George Bush, both requirements have been violated. The Holy Bible requirement is a mind is a terrible thing to waste so the people in prison are consider underemployed or unemployed.

9. Develop the new economic system called Consumption Economics or consume your way into prosperity, so we can finish the Six-Day Creation Story. An example of spend your way to prosperity

is Double Tax on Dividends. The party of greed gave most of the money to the rich wicked and created very little consumption. Let us take the opposite view if we want to expand the economy. We give $25 billion to the poorest children in the United States (call it part of the White Stone Story). The family of $16,000 or less receives $2000.00 per child and someone close to $25,000 receives $200.00 per child. Only the first two children qualify. Now, we ask the poor to spend the money as quickly as possible. They spend, their neighbors work overtime or are hired, and they spend. It should be reviewed like what an economist uses for creating jobs. You end up with a multiplier effect and end up with a seven times multiplier (according to the economists of today). In this example, the growth of the economy could grow by about $175 billion. At $175 billion what did it cost the government. I will assume a low number like one-fourth goes back to the government and the federal government received more than $25 billion back, and tax revenue went to all state and local governments. So the prophecy is waste not want not. $25 billion given mostly to the rich (wicked) is government waste, but satisfying the desires of the children is God's miracle. Please joy. You should realize I copied Consumption Economics from the Holy Bible, so I have a very good authority that it will work. In theory, an economist that has a copy of the Holy Bible may have done parts of it or all as a work force. You wonder why it took from the year of Our Lord 1776 AD to now, to copy the answers for the politicians to implement. King Jesus Christ states in principle if you give Him the money He will double the best Adam can do. I can create an economy twice the best Adam can do or the "Goldie Locks" economy of former President William J. Clinton in the 1990s. The Goldie Locks economy was where the economists forecast the growth. No matter how optimistic the economists were the growth was better. The Holy Bible calls it the Rainbow or a pot of gold at the end of the rainbow by an Irish descent president. Many more decades would be required to create the wealth, we Americans deserve. The Republicans destroyed the wealth creation and turned it negative.

10. We had a problem with asbestos in our schools and businesses. Well, some companies were expected to pay billions to fix their problems. When the government allowed asbestos, all the companies were in conformance with the laws. When health specialists determined a health hazard exists, you ask yourself, why the companies were wrong. The job of the companies is to provide challenges for the people to satisfy the products of all, not to pay for government mistakes or lack of knowledge. Now, the attorneys determine the cost and solutions for their company and they present the information in the court. Congress pays the bills. Again, as we solve the social ills of the country (sorrows), you realize the government will collect taxes and the accountants can measure the costs. I have used examples in my books to represent the basic theories of Consumption Economics or spend your way to prosperity. Do not try to overcome the wisdom in spending of waste not, want not by foolish Republican ideas. Today the laws make it difficult for companies to survive, but tomorrow it may become another way of getting money in local government hands and solving the social ills of the country.

11. Some people that run a church claim King Jesus Christ causes all the hurricanes. They con the congregation to rise to the occasion in terms of money so the clergyman looks good. King Jesus Christ has written that we must restore nature. When you end poverty the government will pay, but what do they do to overcome the force of the unseen, wind and pay for the damage. As the Holy Bible states, you open up the treasuries of the taxpayers resources to help their fellow man. The Holy Bible desires you to protect yourself and return nature back to the old days of the year of Our Lord 1492 AD and includes Earthquake Divers. In California, you can smoke a pack of cigarettes a day, if you do not smoke before clean fuels. The wilderness must blossom like a rose. All takes time.

12. The Social Security tax should be reduced to only the first fifty thousand dollars of income. The theory should be the people above that category could take care of themselves, which would reduce the cost to government in the future. The business side should be kept the same until the system is considered solvent. The Social Security program should be defined as an entitlement program and be fully funded. Do not change the Medicare part, yet. The Federal government started the fund in the mid thirties and to date has spent one hundred percent of the money on something else. That something else was many hell machines. The money we wasted on war could have built a beautiful America. A land our children and families deserve and without the present high level of crime.

13. I heard a commercial that a Bristol Window installed in all the houses in the United States with three panes of glass in the energy efficiency as defined

in the year of Our Lord 1998 AD, could shut down the Alaskan Pipeline in concept. At that time, the windows met the government standards of the year of Our Lord 2009 AD in terms of energy efficiency. The commercial was if you bought the windows a lot of your natural gas and oil cost reduction will pay over time. The window had a real warranty when it defined years or 50-year warranty rather than lifetime. They would last like some of the older wooden windows, I saw in Chicago. Have you as a consumer heard that many house improvement centers have stopped the low cost windows you can buy from them? Why, was it you as a consumer purchased junk. Have you heard about the consumers that bought a new house and three years later are trying to replace all the windows? We Americans should demand quality products for all our houses. Is that an unalienable right? Should the real estate sales representatives recommend the difference and let us know? Some other companies have very high quality energy efficient windows, too.

14. We have learned something about blessed are the poor where if we can give them $25 billion worth of money the country would be ahead. In my example, our companies may book $175 billion in book sales. The stocks would go up and at the same time, the tax revenue would come in. Only the economist views where a new job multiplies the money should be used in the beginning, but my guess is over 25% of book sales are Federal Government taxes, the government would end up with over $25 billion in tax revenue today. That may be low or high depending on the economic factors over the years. That is just a guess though not a proven fact yet. If the economics are right, we already know we have the money. I

was discussing, we can shut down in concept the Alaskan Pipeline. Can you give the advantage to the poorest people? They would be the group least likely to upgrade and most likely to save us biggest dollars in fuel. It maybe that you take the money out of Social Security, zero percent interest rate loans for example to invest in only windows or products that meet a standard. We figure out what it is, but we put the money back in the Social Security Fund. The $25 billion should come from the government and/or consumer. You buy ten thousand dollars in windows and pay over ten years or about eighty-four dollars per month minus the energy cost saving minus the beauty of our neighborhood or the increase in value of our houses. Will they desire to invest in doors, siding or a new high tech furnace? Maybe as President William J. Clinton hired a Y2K Project Manager, we should hire a man like Bob Vila to promote through the government energy efficiency or finally the United States being a good neighbor. He could find the value in upgraded products, test them and promote which products qualify for special financing in Congress and advertise on television. We Americans should eliminate the junk we can buy as an unalienable right. At work, you add the eighty-four dollars to your Social Security withholding. Therefore, the fund is even, because in the beginning we are looking for ways of saving money. We get from the poor people twenty-five billion dollars worth of loans. We do this for many years in a row. The average person learns the advantage of windows like Bristol or Sears. They are the high-energy efficient window that meets the government's standards and we can have it tested to see which designs are best. We want the work.

Should we give the business personnel zero percent interest rate loans for research and production equipment for small businesses? What could our mayors promote if they pay our energy bills today and update as part of our good neighbor policy with Canada? Should European citizens have a chance to learn through the UN, from our marketing majors, and our clergymen? Next, the economy demands an expansion. We decide the environment is one area and we provide twenty-five billion dollars of gifts for energy saving products like furnaces. In addition, we suspend Social Security tax for the employee earning less than twenty-five thousand with children for a twenty-five billion dollar cost. The clergymen are promoting now is a good time to take a trip or buy new furniture. After a time, the government may have a problem in trying to slow down the economy. Over expansion can drive inflation to high and we would have to watch, but let them tell us about their problem which we Joy in. What an advantage we have in over funding Social Security. The average citizen should demand that Social Security becomes guaranteed under law as an entitlement program. We paid for the benefits and we should not let fools take it away.

15. I drive a Cadillac. If you see the ads on television you find out that, they have a tremendous amount of power. When I drive around during heavy traffic times, it would seem like you get a half mile per gallon. I wonder what I am going to do with that entire horsepower. It says one hundred and forty-five on the speedometer. I know Cadillac was testing four cylinders instead of their eights. Other cars have that now. If they could turn off four cylinders on the highway, we save fuel. Science

proves on the highways that you really do not use that much horsepower to cruise along at sixty-five miles an hour with cruise control. Have we heard of a Cadillac with thirty-five miles per gallon or better on the highway? If under extreme acceleration they had to turn off my air conditioner demand for power for a few seconds that could help the environment, I would be for it. We should test the cars at sixty-seven miles per hour or a speed we could use wisely. You can ask a doctor if he believes clean air produces less cancer. In Los Angeles before clean fuel, you smoked a pack of cigarettes a day in air quality, if you did not smoke. Let us set a goal of cutting our fuel consumption by fifty percent in twenty years and still keep the temperature in our houses as today. We Americans can prosper from the work. The government should set standards and educate. As an example, let the state government and vice president do all the government red tape work for wind farm generation of power. The businessperson should just provide the money and management expertise. Other business interests should be the same. We are working for the government to determine what type and where businesses shall be located. Do not forget the will of the businessperson shall prevail.

16. The IRS will be converted into a Quality Assurance auditing team for the advantages of American business. They will also start accounting and auditing public schools system and include Federal, State and local governments in their quest for knowledge. It will take time, as we desire to change from crime and punishment to law and order (laws of liberty) and apply money wisely. King Jesus Christ tells the church to get rid of prisons. Ninety percent of the crimes can be eliminated in twenty years and most

of the violent ones. The goal for the government is to develop the best accounting and auditing systems possible for government to compare costs and eliminate waste. Yes even the waste of prisons. I will explain later.

17. The new political party shall use the back of a Kennedy Half dollar eagle as its symbol and shall be called the party Health, Wealth, and Wisdom. No Republican from federal will be included. Now, we understand what we have to commit to save our Souls. The Republicans shall be considered where there is no Democrats, but not governors. In other countries, the party name shall be the same, but it shall be nation against nation. The challenge is what nation for example can make all people in their country rich. We shall not want. We will commit to listening to our children at federal, but no Political Action Committee will be heard except the ones that will not prosper from the change.

18. The word gambling is used in many churches for individuals. What does the Holy Bible cover? It covers gambling by our governments! In addition, promise keepers are big in some churches, but they are campaign promises. We have many gambling locations throughout the land. What is the age of full rights, but twenty-one? Have you heard of children gambling online in colleges? Are most losing their student loans chasing a rainbow that most cannot reach? All locations must change gambling to twenty-one. Also on web gambling, you do not know who is signing up. A betting organization states to call me on the phone. All on line gambling must end and be limited to government regulating casinos. All sports betting for student games must end. A card party at your house without a fee is

good, but not collecting a fee and earning a living or profit from it is not. In addition, we must judge charity events to determine if the charity is realistic. All gaming casinos must post on a freestanding sign the percent payouts for all games including cards. For example, slots shall have accounting results. The customer must have an easy view as he walks through.

19. For example, a person that cannot get insurance because of cancer should be able to purchase Social Security coverage at the cost to the taxpayers. If you go to a doctor and have standard coverage, the doctor should be able to explain what policy you require and make a change for Social Security. The costs of the policies must be judged by the Federal Reserve for inflation fighting techniques with the governors of each state providing solutions as discovered. Additional ideas through planning are always a requirement and doctors must be trained to help provide our citizens wants and solutions. When a family works and both have health insurance, only the best policy shall be used by that family. The other one will be informed and dropped, but cover supplementary expenses. The business saves the money so additional benefits can be invested in to retain workers in a shortage of workers economy. The doctors and hospitals shall post the costs of service as defined by Congress.

20. When people purchase health care, they cannot be sure of what they are paying for. Congress will develop a minimum of three policies that must be the only policies that can be sold, so competition between suppliers can be compared in your area like the automobile insurance of today. Universal health insurance requires defined policies.

A. First is the policy for the basic coverage or what a family of good health can purchase and save money.
B. Second is the standard policy or the minimum requirement for the average family or individual.
C. Third is the deluxe policy that individuals or a corporation purchases for the group that can afford what we term deluxe.

So by the year of Our Lord 2050 AD what is in place?

1. You started a war against crimes and destroyed the crime syndicates of the country long ago. The judges in the land became responsible for their actions. For a simple example, the man stole money. The judge sends him to a prison (now called a rehab center) on a six-month think about the joy you are missing. He returns to the judge and a work project is granted. He works for money and can spend some in prison and save. Once he has ten thousand dollars he is released to a half way house where more liberty is granted. His sentence (lack of joy) is over once he has twenty-five thousand dollars saved and many companies desire to hire him. You remember the Holy Bible requires the clergymen to turn all jeopardy into joy and mercy shall follow us all the days of our life. They should be one hundred percent on your side. You have a strong commitment to end poverty, which ends crime, and all that is left is love or a small number of people that refuse to work. You will hate (love less) the people that do not try.
2. At a governor's conference, you started a special project called Watchmen Elect. You commit to the choice of the people for determining three names to be the future vice-president based on a goal for the country like eliminating ninety percent of

the crimes in America in twenty years and we are still trying harder. The clergymen shall become the Watchmen Elect's campaign manager. The president becomes the Watchman and will commit to blowing the trumpet, whenever a major problem is encountered. When 1.4 million Americans fell below the poverty level in the year of Our Lord 2004 AD, the trumpet provides the solution. We will provide the information in a format that is understandable and not use money to deceive the voters.

3. The police have eliminated the people living in cardboard boxes and are in their new retirement houses called prisons (rehab centers) with opened doors. The street people are gone. The advantage of law and order versus crime and punishment is good for the taxpayers as well as the individuals.

4. The saving of the money for prisons was used for funding schools, providing health care for children, retiring government bonds and in the year of Our Lord 2050 AD, there is not one government agency in debt and taxes are a lower percentage of the economy. In the past, through pricing or taxes, a family was paying huge dollars just for interest on government debt plus their own debt. By the year of Our Lord 2050 AD, we will be satisfied if our families spent the money on something more important for our children than just government interest. How about the interest of our businessperson and our credit cards, housing, and major purchases like a car?

5. You score the jobs and I have scored the job of the waitress as like a truck driver that is a driver salesmen. The waitress will qualify for the real minimum wage or a two-dollar per hour increase over three years from three dollars and fifteen cent

to five dollars and fifteen cent prior to the year of Our Lord 2007 AD. Assuming she waits on eight people an hour that is a twenty-five cent increase per person in cost, but to her the money is good and the economy will start to increase by bringing money into poor neighborhoods. The governor shall review minimum wages like the Denver story, which I believe was seven dollars and fifty cent per hour in the late 1990s. Ideas like this are inexpensive, but will create a climate for business, since the consumer has money to spend. Note with the present high inflation the minimum wage was not increased from the year of Our Lord 1997 AD through April the year of Our Lord 2007 AD at federal, which is bad for the consumer therefore the businessman. I am saying you will raise the income of the waitress by over eight thousand dollars in four years (two because of scoring the job and two plus because of the minimum wage increase) and the government will collect an additional tax of over ten thousand dollars per waitress because of the multiplier effect. The result will be like hiring people in the poor neighborhoods. The stock market will be recovering from the Republican failure again where most of the money goes to the rich. Do not believe a rich man's stock market is good for America. The problem near the end times is the problem with the rich. The rich are living well and creating hell. Hell is a state of mind, not a place. The rich are the wicked and in shackles. The government will score all their jobs like the Post Office in comparison to Federal Express or Medicare in comparison to Blue Cross.

6. We started a project to determine who the American citizens are for tax reasons as they did in Israel from the Holy Bible or the Roman Empire census for tax

purposes. We have applied a quality improvement project at the Social Security offices for Social Security numbers backed up by the FBI. We used the information to find the cost of a Federal law. Health care used the Social Security numbers for identification and all children have been eliminated from being lost and on milk cartons. If a child were to run away identification is easy, but determining why is required. Illegal aliens are outdated and so is immigration. Our families prefer the jobs in our country rather than sending our children to a foreign country. The family may never see them again. King Jesus Christ's economic model creates surplus good paying jobs available in all nations has made immigration beyond its time.

7. You have created what shall be called "Consumption Economics", or spend your way into prosperity. Another example is the Federal Reserve determines the economy is slow, $50 billion is required extra to be spent within a short period, and they present Congress with a check of newly created money, which they could do. They may not be able to do it effectively (Germany high inflation) if the government is greatly in debt because that could cause heavy inflation and/or a weak dollar. Under the strong economy of former President William J. Clinton, it would be easy because our business leaders stated the currency was too strong; however, the idea would not be practical. The US Senate sends out debit cards to all high school and college students and asks them to spend the money quickly. The card expires in a defined period. The multiplier like the job creation takes over and the ripple effect happens. The economics have proven in the equations that a $350 billion additional consumption happens and

the taxing bodies receive a $100 billion bonus to pay off debts and spend to cure the social ills of their responsibilities. What was the cost? Make the answer big. Presently the Federal Reserve Governors would lower the interest rate (interest is a tax) and wait nine months to find out if they applied enough. You establish a business climate when the consumer has money to spend. What would happen if they gave Congress two hundred billion to spend over three months? You may wonder in some industries, when the overtime will end. Big paychecks are good, but some people in the end will desire time off for vacations.

8. To summarize Consumption Economics. In January, the Federal Reserve determines the economy has grown by two percent and will fall in the range of 2.5 plus and minus .5 percent. The inflation rate is between -0.2 and +1.0. The whole country like business is listening to determine what will happen in the last quarter and no change is expected. The government will not be forced to retire debt as the voters monitor. Next the number comes out at 3.3 percent and the people understand we have to watch the government budgets next year so they save money and retire the debt. We realize it is not a cost to us, because if they spent the money the economy would be worse. We again would rely on our pay raises again. The last is the economy grows by a negative one percent for the first three quarters. This is good news that the economy is bad. The economic might of Consumption Economics takes over to protect our jobs and business. The Federal Reserve brings $200 billion of newly created money for our children. All children under a family income of one hundred thousand dollars receive two thousand

dollars to spend or some amount. Daughter is telling mom I will see you on Monday (today is Friday) because the stores are having an open twenty-four hour weekend sale. Your wife is telling dad we have no choice but to buy new furniture for the family room because our grandchildren's jobs are at stake. How could women turn down a chance to shop to they drop. Did she tell dad to buy that new car he was promising the family? The politicians and corporations are implementing all the projects they have on the table like timing circuits for railroad crossings to end the impatient motorist that is hit by the train today. The projects were established to be spent in case the economy was bad. Your corporation has repainted all the employee rest areas and shopping centers have granted bonus dollars for the employees to buy. The Federal Reserve expected this but granted the money anyway. The price of failure is too great. The numbers come in at seven percent for the year. The government will save one hundred percent of the new tax revenue. The government and corporations have the money to put the projects back. The information on bond repurchase is exciting to some. Dad's boss has stated the overtime will last only two more weeks and dad is glad. The furniture is paid for but his new car makes his life good. Next year the number will be good and a disappointment in many will occur. All the country has left is to raise the poverty level to force a new wave, but do not count on it that often. We will make it through with better than expected results normally. What state will be entirely out of debt first or will the Federal Government prevail? If inflation is over 1.0 percent, a new income tax is added for people earning over one million dollars a year until it is resolved. Corporate executives are raising prices to fast and do not raise the corporate tax. If the cost of housing is on the rise, the governors will restrict the housing permits for some suppliers. Have you heard greed raised the prices of houses in Las Vegas by fifty percent in one year? You remember the real problem in paying off debt as history of the late 1800's states is inflation possibly will be negative, which is bad.

9. You started a new health care system, where you set a goal of health care cost of one seventh of the economy. The illegal drug problem (government, business, and church war on the crime syndicates) being behind made it easy for the governors to provide health care to the children of their state first. Malpractice was reduced by the year of Our Lord 2050 AD as medical problems where brought into the V. A. Hospitals and many new procedures were created. The governor judges the hospital and malpractice insurance is based on the hospital. A bad hospital you ask why. The health care increase cost has been low and you used as a commitment to business of one seventh of the economy and companies are finding the employees like health care benefits. Individuals that have health concerns like Aids or cancer are sometimes defined as uninsurable, so we granted Social Security at the same rate of the cost of benefits as the retirees. The doctors can judge our health insurance concerns and can sign us up for Social Security health insurance and other Social Security benefits on their office computer for disabilities. We desire all American citizens to have the advantage of health insurance in a country that has the unalienable right to receive the best health care treatment in the world. The

number of people on Social Security did double in twenty years but the cost of health care as a percent of the economy was the same. Since you are over the large increase in Social Security population and wars are a bad memory, you are ready to bring our people with expensive operations into our hospitals and Social Security pays in the Year of Our Lord 2050 AD or earlier. The way is planned like a free policy covering extra ordinary medical expenses. Bankruptcy Court is planned to be eliminated as not required for an individual, so the voter likes the children of the average family not to have that jeopardy of illness and cost. You will use federal money to encourage qualified students to receive one hundred percent of the education costs for doctors and nurses with a minor payback, as long as we are so short. The GP doctors have accept up to twenty percent of their patients as Social Security assignments. You have built three new hospital schools in the second biggest cities of the three poorest states. The locations train the doctors and nurses free as long as we are so short. In order to double the work force new schools were required and used to help children like the Danny Thomas Hospital and pregnant women with DNA problems. The technique is like the extra ordinary medical expenses for pregnant women and our children. The doctors with the correct web input can send our children to handle the most expensive procedures. Our CDC is working to eliminate the viruses and ideas have ended problems like Aids or Hong Kong Flu. When we donate a pint of blood we received a bracelet which states we are free of virus for that social illness and each decade Aids victims has gone down. A doctor, not an attorney decides who receives Social Security benefits before the right age. They are trained in school.

10. Long ago, you committed to publish when our Social Security System would be totally funded and raised the minimum benefit for millions that would fall far below the poverty level especially the women. You should talk about the bad income levels for some of our single women raising the future of America on bad paying jobs and the result on their benefits.

11. By the year of Our Lord 2050 AD, a college graduate man gets married at twenty-four years old and earns fifty thousand dollars a year for six months. Our Social Security Gold Mine (over funded) provides a three hundred thousand dollar house and twenty-five thousand for the furniture with no down payment on his income alone. We do not want our children to have a hard time in case a little one comes along so only the income of the husband is considered. We save our money in items like housing where a defined amount is granted the government each month through Social Security funding. Other saving techniques become hard to sell but healthy economy housing and other consumer commitments are good. The college graduate young man has worked for six months so he can prove he deserves the job. He pays zero down and zero financing cost. Over thirty years he pays less than one thousand dollars per month and at the end of his first year has a saving plan with ten thousand dollars equity and at the end of ten years that will be one hundred thousand dollars. His bride buys two cars at zero percent financing on the income of his wife or all interest payments have been eliminated thereby all consumer debt is gone. A citizens paying into the Social Security System has a new unalienable right

at not having a consumer loan, but an investment in America's future. The man pays for Social Security at the rate of approximately thirty-five hundred dollars per year. He actually is receiving a house and then Social Security benefits as if it is free. King Jesus Christ has promised a piece of land to all people and you may question why a person loves ten years of rent receipts and granting the rich the fruits of his labor. Others may not earn as much but a ninety thousand dollar house would cost two hundred and fifty dollars a month and at the end of the first year, he has an investment saving of three thousand dollars. Ending all poverty sounds like a rewarding challenge. As the Holy Bible states the church through the government absorbs all consumer debts. You do not have to be married to qualify. When does the person really pay for the inheritance per God's Instruction at the right age? The answer is obvious or at your death. The tax is called an inheritance tax and the number shall be presented to the congregation by the clergymen. When the average person demands to increase his inheritance tax on the first dollar to the number in the Holy Bible, the clergymen have eliminated the meaning of taxes. John 3:16 has taken care of the other or the two things man cannot do or eliminate the meaning of death and taxes. In God, all is possible, not in Adam.

12. You started the Social Security Job/Business Trust Fund by providing three percent housing loans to our educators in public and private schools. On average, most people believe they do not earn enough money in the year of Our Lord 2009 AD, but do not want to pay more taxes. As the economy expands without the new loans of three percent for housing and cars,

they will leave and seek other careers. They will become the first group of zero percent financing; therefore, they will be without a consumer loan but an investment in America.

13. You have received and work to continue a military with Great Briton and Russia. The other countries have decided to greatly reduce their military and rely on ours. Our state military is gone and security guards in many businesses are working on direct tools of production. Many teenagers or troubled children have been raised by a tough sergeant as determined by the court to bring the child to college potential or at least a good job. The orphanages are fully funded but the military is always on guard for reductions. The court judges have developed procedures so American families can adopt American children as babies not three years old and up as the Holy Bible demands. In addition, the judge has a commitment to not send out their police officers to kill us (turn us into three time losers) because we will not go to school. A judge stays with the losers of society, the person in prison and rehab is the answer. We grant them a chance for money. Terrorists, who killed 7,000 people in twenty years before the war started in Iraq is not that important. America had bodies (unnecessary deaths) all over the country. The people have learned if you solve the problem of bad laws (lawlessness or pen), the problem with terrorist disappears. You cannot end terrorists by starting wars, as they love good people to create hell of killing wars. Peace on earth is bad for the terrorists as they become foolish. The world ending over ten million unnecessary deaths per year due to bad laws (lawlessness or pen) is an exciting challenge.

14. Our courts have a new direction and their role is to train the world on how to run a court. Getting rid of the crime syndicates is a start with rehab for the poor as an unalienable right as America started out. Read my books on how to run a court. The laws of liberty must be created and finding a person guilty is against God's wisdom. Can you believe some judges find God's angel (777 design) guilty. Where are the churches and the Holy Bible used?

15. We will establish a shortage of labor as a job becomes an unalienable right along with a consumption pay raise above inflation. The requirement was established in the years the year of Our Lord 2000 AD under President William J. Clinton for unemployment. We had thirteen weeks of benefits and on the average, we found a new job within the goal of seven weeks. We still had six weeks of benefits to go. In addition, we can always try harder, but must maintain the minimum standard. Therefore, growth will be managed by starting with a target of two and one half percent plus or minus one-half. We will have to teach all government when to add spending or reduce. We will be closer to the goal of managing the fourth quarter (January through March) maybe easier to achieve. Governments will all be involved to the one party of the church. All laws have to be veto proof, justified by the advantage to America, and government deficit spending will not be allowed. Based on history, one problem we will have is trying to maintain inflation above a rate of less than zero. The lower one third-income group will be happy to try to help us keep inflation above zero by accepting minimum pay raises. Saving government money and stopping interest is a good inflation fighter. The

growth rate of each state is measured along with major population areas.

16. The schools have all been rebuilt in twenty-one years due to investment of fifteen billion plus a year. The federal government is still looking for new schools to experiment with new ideas for all American buildings. The schools will be rebuilt again in the year of Our Lord 2060 to 2080 AD at a cost of twenty billion dollars plus a year in purchasing power of the dollar of today. The project title was, "The peace dividend, Property Tax Relief". The property tax for schools is zero. Olympic type facilities were being developed for our grammar, high schools, and colleges during and after the end of the twenty years for all of our students. May the citizen demand we continue to build when the government can afford to spend more. In the year of Our Lord 2060 AD, we rebuild again and many major cities have the infrastructure where Olympic Games can be held. In rebuilding again in the year of Our Lord 2110 AD, all major cities can hold the true Olympics depending on weather factors. We have talked to the Olympic Committees and they have granted the world two new events of winter and summer for students only at twenty-five years old or less.

17. The Federal government fills out all small business and individual tax forms and must have it completed by April 15. I expect we will not make mistakes because many accountants will be our checkers. The IRS has become Quality Assurance for our corporations and governments like the federal budget. We have established a quality system on our Social Security numbers. If an individual has his identity stolen, he goes to a qualified attorney who

is paid by the FBI and they handle the discovery. If an illegal alien tries to work, the number will stop them. If a person steals a child without regard for life, the Social Security number will not allow that child health care, education, etc, so all lost children have been found. Terrorist cannot enter without numbers so that makes it hard. We make fools of countries that cannot take care of the children and the congregations have warned all politicians. The new system allows the politician to understand what an unalienable right will cost. The Holy Bible calls that new beginning the Generation of the FIG and we will try to receive a hawk from the seven Holy Cities for our work of waste not wants not. The new system allows all corporations and individuals to pay their taxes correctly. The attitude is that it is better to pay my percentage and spend what is left, than have no job and no future under bad politicians with false marketing plans.

18. We brought our economic discoveries into the UN and taught all governments the answers. Our problem was that most people will demand their government be importers. Now, we had to have eyes to see the shortages and ears to hear the problems. The American greenback and our training of politicians in the UN did create the greatest expansion of the economies of the world of any era. The economic tribulation of all income groups, take pride in the leaders, and is the greatest of all times. The thirty thousand unnecessary deaths a day around the world seem to be easily overcome, where there was a church. All countries were there was a church desired to care for the unneeded children in our orphanages and for them to be good parents. The world governments through their efforts at least

tripled the economies by now or as defined by the Holy Bible. Stock prices will force all companies to stop buying their stocks back through laws except in rare times. We the people desire lower highs and higher lows or the government creating orderly markets. Immigration has almost stopped. As good as, it is in America a shortage of labor in many countries like Mexico has stopped people from leaving the country they love and where they were born. A few executives came from overseas to take upper management jobs but why would the man from Mexico come here. That would be equivalent to the average American child telling their parents, "We are moving to Mexico and will not be seen by you again." That would not seem to be normal behavior that a parent desires.

19. Our children were heard in their demands for schools. We included fancy dining, food the doctors recommend like no candy bars but many apples, a health club in schools, and fancy offices for the educators including underground parking. In areas of hazards like hurricanes, one hundred percent of the students were safe and we accepted young children and mothers to ride out the storms. Our children in hurricanes were in school and party. Should the business community and government offices help care for the rest? Our development on building schools had a tremendous impact on the public sector construction, but much work is left.

20. One problem many poor women had with children is day care. All grammar schools paid for by the federal government were opened a minimum of six to six. The schools will be granted computers for homework and contain libraries. What were essential were the art, music and live play faculties

for our future actors. In order to support a nation of dance for teenagers many instruments and trainers to teach were required. Mother will not be there until six and the child had two or three hours of art or music to aid mother in her life. The computers make homework easy at school. Special education is featured like reading and math. Computers that can speak with games as how fast can you correctly answer the results of multiplying by seven are available. Computer programs with random test questions on math with detailed explanations are required. The new books came along with the outline of the course all instructors can add knowledge. The new techniques strengthen all educators. The computer automatically grades some papers and the results are posted in the educators files. Since the vice president is over seeing the schools of Washington DC, he should continue to grant money to develop the programs. Once tested all schools can use. If you are a private school and we pay no tax to continue your advantages, let them have the outlines, too. The programs can be sold but not used by foreign governments for no cost. A syllabus will be added for all new books and the educators will keep the information in the computerized system.

21. The lack of knowledge on what age a student should start kindergarten must be resolved. I see the professionals state it is four, five, or six. The answer should be yes. All students that are five in a year start kindergarten in August or September. The kindergarten instructors determine when they start first grade at the next year or stay in kindergarten for one more year. Mid schools of sixth, seventh, eight, and ninth are present. I ask why but cannot start out with what is known as to why. I went from eighth

grade to high school. Not all women are college graduates and can prepare a child the same. We need trained professionals, so all children start first grade with a confidence they can learn where possible. Do not let the women guess for their children, but learn from the professionals. In high school, the building opens at the latest six and stays open until at least nine. Open six days a week may be in the future as sports expand. The federal funding requires the Board of Education to consolidate. The Supreme Courts of the states resolved why Chicago has one Board of Education and Boone County of a smaller size has two and will continue. We started out with fifty states and fifty ways. We have discovered one way, which is the best way and the savings, went to learning not government waste. English is the only language used in schools.

22. We are making head way in hurricanes where the electricity never goes off or we considered that one of the sorrows. Poorly managed industries like airlines were forced to have strong balance sheets, so our children have good jobs. We do not need the executives to fail themselves by going into bankruptcy court. The House of Representatives has reversed the eighty percent failure of new business by providing the business license for the business to purchase and start. The new goal is for over ninety-seven percent of new businesses to be a success and over time to try harder. Where American industry is getting in trouble with losses a determination for consolidation or restructuring is planned.

23. The unnecessary deaths on our highways has been turned over to our high tech firms. Our police force (safety patrol) tests the new highway system to eliminate traffic tickets and causes. We

have developed a sound marketing plan to teach. On television, we present a race from somewhere to somewhere. Our fifty states have selected one policeman per state to represent we the people for the country to eliminate traffic tickets. The plan becomes a big marketing plan to eliminate the unnecessary deaths and injuries on our highways. They are granted a new American built car to test at cold, hot or any environment for handling mileage and to test our new high tech roads. The fifty cars are determined by a blind draw and the car is titled by the person chosen. Trucks were included. They present new laws and procedures and are testing the Civil engineers for safety designs. The regular police car is quality control for safety and they will be tested by Quality Assurance. They have demonstrated how they have tested the new highways and how we should drive. We are still trying to get all Americans involved in eliminating traffic tickets. Our children dieing on the highways is bad. A man losing his life by driving at the speed limit and being killed by a speeding car terrorist is not acceptable. The safety patrol has introduced the new driver education standards to reduce deaths of teenagers and grant them experience. Speed odometers are only to read seventy-five miles per hour and governors (computers) stop speed over that level. The safety patrol has challenged them to set speed limits. The safety patrol has review road construction sites to improve safety and limit the amount of time a construction firm takes to repair your road. New construction equipment was developed by the Federal government to allow all roads to be level so concrete can be applied with the help of lasers to add, let's guess eleven to thirteen inches. You drive your car where the shocks are not required on new roads, but an asset on old. Asphalt roads we would like to have the surface removed and chemicals added, then the surface replaced with the help of lasers at seven to five in the morning. Much work on new technology for road construction is still required. If possible, my road was requiring repairs yesterday, but today it is great. The government sells the patents to three American suppliers for the world and American industries to buy.

24. You have challenged the senators that represent our government to make the American Indians citizens of our country. They have kept their lands but were offered to care for Federal lands. We have offered ideas like our surplus horses, deers, and buffalo. They were offered jobs as qualified environmentalists, to fight fires, run our national parks, and to bring meat to our table as they care for the buffalo on Federal lands. Scholarships for their doctors and nurses will be granted. The prophecy for the American Indian is the cities shall surround their lands. We must meet their prophecies.

25. We have started a challenge to determine what our possessions will be and offered ideas like Social Security, good minimum wages with job security and good schools. By the year of Our Lord 2050 AD, we know the size of the United States of America. We have no possessions. See the Holy Bible or Holy Spirit possessions.

26. You have developed the concept in Washington, DC on how to rebuild all American cities. In your model, you have created a large shopping center with all underground parking. The condominiums raise at least ten stories above the shopping center and are for people over fifty years old or physically

challenged. You have handicapped access from the condominiums, which allowed many to be mobile from their units. They can range in price from ten times more for top units than the first floor. We have learned how to build from our commitment to provide new schools. The research and development for the school building allowed our government and business buildings to prosper. All politicians are required to live in Washington DC for federal by the year of Our Lord 2030 AD and after and belief in domestic tranquility was the answer. The vice president was assigned that task of domestic tranquility and one day will lead the country as president, health permitting. How to recover land in our cities by the government must be tested. For example, Lane Tech High School in Chicago for up to ten thousand students required more land by the year of Our Lord 2060 AD. All houses sold in the four blocks required are automatically purchased by the city of Chicago at a fair price. As high as the building for up to ten thousand students of Lane Tech in Chicago is, the churches will tower over the height of the schools and have a bright light (see the light) as the church is run by twenty-five individuals as the Holy Bible prophecy requires. Their building may hold more than ten thousand at a church dance but they will require land locations.

27. You have developed two concepts of high schools. The first is called high tech where the doctors, nurses, engineers and scientists go. In order to get in your seventh and eighth grade educators must agree. You go to a regular school, but you can go to the University of Illinois and still be trained as an engineer; therefore, so the parents do not complain we will grant all students at the end of one year of

high school to be granted a transfer, if qualified. The regular schools will focus on science but have to cover all other fields like electricians or carpenters. We will have a commitment to I do not want you to do a job you do not want to do. In the late 1990s I heard Allen Greenspan chairman of the Federal Reserve state ninety percent of our students do not get jobs in their field at graduation from college. Under foolish George Bush (the year of Our Lord 2008 AD, thank goodness for divine intervention), many may not get a good paying job at all. We had to restart the economy and change education to provide careers the student can use. Congress with required input from business and labor shall determine the class types. The colleges will continue to provide numbers from our schools. The goal was to reverse what is in place. Ninety percent do not use their careers from college to ninety percent do in the year of Our Lord 2050 AD. Can we do better than only a major change of only to ninety percent? Scholarships are not provided in areas of surplus college graduates, but the wealthy could still send their children to be lawyers in the year of Our Lord 2010 AD, but those requiring aid decided a doctor is a better career. America had to fill in the shortages. All the employers that hire will continue to be asked to determine their future hiring requirements. Pre-med can be finished in high schools at twenty or less. Young students learned the advantage of not going to a university to soon, but still get the education required. We should continue to save our families money, but support higher education.

28. You are using school buildings to develop construction ideas for commercial real estate. The school buildings will be run by DC with AC

converters to add electricity to the power grid. You desire all schools to be energy independent. Ideas like bringing sun light into the first floor hallways were created. Plants like real sun. Storing heat and cold were tried and tested. You tested to try to stop flu from going into each room. Air standards are very high. Even the soap is the right type. The top floor has the eating facilities. No half hour old food is allowed. The student can cook their own hamburgers, but must wash their hands before entering the eating areas. The educators are allowed to order from a menu and not be charged. To test the ways, Congress has established the eating areas in Washington DC. They have hired the chefs to cook, but were testing the ways of the schools. The calorie count is provided and the meals are good enough for our students, they are good enough for our Congressmen. The educators do not desire to leave their social environment and the benefits are good. Where else can a homemaker and mother be off school with her children for June, July, and August. The advantage to a married woman is June, July, and August. Married men can easily work in the school and other government commitments during the summer. Where else can a mother leave her child for nine hours and the child needed to talk about the piano lessons he started or the math contest all Illinois schools are involved in from the computer room. In high school, the sports are being filmed by students and the newspapers cover the good news of the day. Acting in high school is presenting parents with good entertainment. "A NATION OF ROMANCE FOR ALL" created by the church has granted all major cities with entertainment of live bands and plays all across the country. Television does not seen to be the first choice over the adventures in live entertainment granted. The church learned from the Old Testament about celebration.

29. Ross Perot talked about Bottom up Planning in the year of Our Lord 1992 AD election. Elijah, the prophet knew what that meant and how to achieve it for a corporation. A big problem is the corporations have to hire people to talk to their employees in the year of Our Lord 2008 AD. Elijah, the prophet trained the IRS, Post Office, and Social Security on how to do it. All developed material was turned over to the church training organizations for the world to use, as it is a requirement of the Holy Bible. The copyrighted planning technique of the Holy Bible was developed by the Federal Government and when added to government computers, the fees will be granted to the seven church names. We will except training politicians like bishops as required in the Holy Bible from the book of Timothy. The courts will be subject to the lords, which are from the Lord of lords or training from the book of Galatians. All federal and state attorneys will be justified by grace not by law as required. The politicians and attorneys representing King Jesus Christ must accept the way, truth and light or the congregation will be against them. All the major politicians are wicked and always look to the congregation to release the shackles.

30. The schools have internet for our students and the parents pay. The service is safe for our children. The sports are on the school system and we buy the rights to see. Your son has a golf outing against another school. When you come home from work,

you and he joy in the recording. How well did it go or is just watching it yourself better?

31. We understand the requirement of "earthquakes divers" from the Holy Bible. We are putting sensors under the sea to overcome the jeopardy of nature. Tornados are tracked through our high tech roads and NASA monitors from outer space the movements of heavy winds. NASA has provided the programming to get the phones, radio and television to warn the citizens. Many have seen the movie, The Wizard of Oz" and realize that Kansas has to protect its citizens with basement shelters. In the year of the Lord 2008 AD, the government allows houses on concrete slabs. The right to life of our citizens is too important for that foolishness. We are still working on guaranteeing no electricity goes off in our country for any reason.

32. The government started auditing the state and local government accounting systems, as they should audit the major corporations. First, they started creating cost effective programs developed once for all government agencies to use. The IRS even audited the Federal government as they would audit a corporation. We are working for saving the money of local tax collection and have the Federal government collect all funds and send to the governors for them to manage their state. The procedure for the corporations are as follows:

33. The IRS notifies they are going to audit your major firm.

34. The CFO is asked if he has any questions on accounting or tax law.

35. The tax law questions are reviewed and forwarded to the IRS officials where appropriate.

36. All asked questions are not covered in the audit.

37. The House of Representatives gives the IRS clear instructions as to the requirements if required.

38. The IRS sends all critical data to the SQC type-auditing firms of the corporations with implementation instructions.

39. The instructions could be in the way of a program if business desires.

40. The IRS will go out of its way to cover the new requirements in future IRS audit and note only future errors for two years.

41. After that point the House of Representatives feels they have overcome ignorance of the law is an excuse.

42. Any company can sue the IRS where they believe instructions are not clear and will be handled quietly in courts. The Federal government will pay the cost if a change is required.

The goal of America is no errors are built into our tax system. The American people have overcome tax as a concern, because they are too much of an advantage to the American children, business leaders and people who believe in eliminating jeopardy. If the church could only eliminate the meaning of death, we are to overcome the two things man says we cannot do or overcome death and taxes.

43. Society has developed accounting procedures when the price of a product is updated as higher or lower and the accounting numbers are granted to the Federal Reserve to aid in measuring inflation. The ideal concept would be America knows what one hundred percent of all products are sold for and what consumer groups are involved. Measuring inflation as an exact science is the accounting future to inherit in the theory of numbers. We have gone a long way from Joseph, son of Jacob days and are still trying harder. All pennies are desired to

be measured but much work in the future is still required. We are still down to dollars. The Holy Bible proclaims by the year of Our Lord 3600 AD, we should be down to the value of tin in the four hundred year plans.

44. May Americans grant us a list of unalienable rights they demand! No American citizen shall want but his or her IQ and work determines what he or she deserves, but blood is thicker than water. All takes time and life is like a circle, what comes around goes around. The old pain can return but the good life is what the citizen deserve, especially the children.

Goals for the year of Our Lord 3000 AD.

1. The goal for taxes (tithes) is ten percent of the economy. Today a six percent mortgage is a tax or cost to use money. If the mortgage is one third of your income, the six percent mortgage is an eighteen percent tax. The Federal Government collects all the money through income and business tax, today. Social Security is not a tax but a fund for investments in America like small business, housing, and enhanced future benefits. One third of the people will pay nothing for income tax, but must pay the Social Security System. The wealthy are charged the full ten percent for income tax. Long ago the business made it known in a loud voice they did not want their employees to pay the present rate for Social Security, so the corporate employer share went up and his employees went down to employer two thirds and employee one third. The business felt with the power of greed as a concern, the money would be taxed away.

2. We have a prison in Washington DC for the visitors to see all of Americans that failed themselves and the tours are conducted. Since no one is being held, the building describes all the unalienable right techniques that were used for rehab. At times, the reminder may be required, but not used.

3. Since the health care system of America is the finest, we live to over one hundred years and are approaching the theoretical limit of one hundred and twenty-years. Many are still playing golf over one hundred. American business has asked our politicians to remove the most expensive procedures to our Salvation Army Hospitals, so business or individuals are not burdened with unnecessary expense. The Salvation Army Hospitals take care of the extra ordinary medical expenses. The paramedics are equipped like a cameraman to get medical science to the first point of contact. We have changed the age of retirement to eighty but being poor can occur. A widowed woman from a small family can collect Social Security benefits at 60 years old. She must come from a small family. That is the goal for money as the rest can live in America without concern. The Holy Bible is proven true as it is better to give than receive. All can be givers is the ideal case and not one person must be a receiver. If a War Lord (dragon) wants to discuss his failure of committing to hell of War, our women have taught him the beauty of him going to Perdition before he dies. After we eliminated foolish Obama, we believed all military wars of country against country ended or humankind started a new beginning.

4. Our high tech highways allow trucking to go between cities without drivers. Accidents are rare but much work lies ahead. In driving from Chicago,

Illinois to Florida without touching a steering wheel except for fuel or planned stops, you are using your car computer to order tickets and learning of the food stops ahead. A man had a heart attack on the highway and the car brought the car to a stop and called for help. For a car that was far from the hospital, the car drove three hundred miles to the emergency room. We cannot put a hospital on every street corner.

5. Our churches and other religious nations became so wealthy, they took over education in the year of Our Lord 2800 AD in the USA as they helped us raise the children with their 777 design and all were faithful to a God. The angels of 777 design were proven God's Children and made special. The Jewish is before conception to 6, 7 to 13 and they added seven more years. The taxpayers decided to give the gift of new schools to the children first and rebuilt all including many sport complexes.

6. The economy is managed to a point, we find it easy to consume at the rate of 1% growth plus or minus 0.1. The economy at a high rate of $25 trillion in today's dollars with today's population is good. When we collect only 2.2 trillion in tax collection the Federal Reserve makes up the difference. In great years, they take the surplus away. The number appears low but the effect of interest and greed is gone and salaries are at least double of today in the great middle class and lower. The inflation is around zero since greed is gone. The people earning over $200,000 a year will cut back to manage growth that is too high. If you are less than $200,000 a year, we see no change. As an example, the richest man in the country suffers by only buying three of the ten new cars he desired. The other seven went to

satisfy the other consumption requirements. When the economy is falling short of growth gains, we can always count on our high school and college students to help the well off business leaders. An example of a truck driver is he starts at the bottom at $37,000 a year and in forty years, he earns double or a cap of $74,000. The labor union contract has become the main technique for a pay raise of rising in rank or we receive promotions. The labor unions are searching to establish no greed in labor. The minimum wage is about what we have of today for an income group called "Joe Six-pack". The economists know we cannot accept a rate of growth greater than 1.0 plus or minus 0.1. The accounting programming will be continually developed to test the true capabilities of an economy. As the Holy Bible states less than a small part of a penny is possible by the year of Our Lord 4000 AD or the value of tin. The year of Our Lord 3000 AD is a short time and much design and economic challenges are still ahead. It is good someone can understand the Holy Bible, because all listed came from our true Words of our Gods and translated into the grace of Adam.

7. What is always true is the continuing commitment to eliminate the unnecessary deaths to our citizens and the pain (sorrows) in people's lives through new solutions.

8. Our country has overcome environmental issues like those where the streams out East are stocked with fish. You can fish in downtown Chicago and eat the catch. The air quality is like air of the year of Our Lord 1492 AD as God told us to restore nature. Our sewer treatment plants are planned for one hundred percent rework each century or as required. We are still trying to recycle one hundred

percent of our waste products. The Holy Bible tells us to watch our waste areas. All the instructions from God are taken seriously by all. Packaging has been reduced to minimize waste. All packaging that cannot be recycled is marked in big letters, "Do not recycle". We have a continuing review to rebuild our cities and we desire the have the wilderness blossom like a rose.

9. Our sport players are representing our citizens in the major cities as warriors, since greed is gone. Many sports events from our students may displace professionals in many locations or student Olympics.

10. The ultimate in tax with representation has been achieved in America and all foreign countries are trying to match or if the citizens are poorer, the party in power will lose. Their resignation for causing 1.4 million people to go below the poverty level like in the year of Our Lord 2004 AD is not good and the trumpet is the battle cry for new ideas. In the year of Our Lord 2004 AD, the only answer was the Republican Party resignation. They refused to change. King Jesus Christ will take them by the hand if they fail to blow the trumpet to solve the problems. The Terrible Swift Sword (rod of iron) of the seven Holy Cities included the words of the women, "We can live without people who desire to create hell in our lives." The saints judge the world and American congregations love the words, "There is nothing to fear, but fear itself."

11. The CDC is working hard with the world doctors to end viruses. Aids is a faint memory but being a GP is a good career with the challenges on the table of ending illnesses like Aids or the Hong Kong Flu by killing the virus.

12. The American Indian has become our wilderness environmentalists and the streams flow as in the year of Our Lord 1492 AD. They run many of our National parks like the Grand Canyon and fight our forest fires. They decided to raise buffalo on federal lands and have done much to maintain fine dining at a reasonable cost. The American Indian has many universities to maintain their ways and challenges. The wilderness blossoms like a rose, but people keep finding more to do.

13. You started a project to rebuild America in the year of Our Lord 2009 AD and considered many times again. Do you desire to create all new roads, work environment, housing, etc? Is it time for the citizens to plan the rebuilding of our country again to enhance our standard of living?

14. Let us compare two jobs of today without the government waste of interest. First, a doctor is hired by the hospital for working five days in the trauma center at $100,000 a year. He is single but engaged. He works three months and opens his practice for one day a week on the North side of the hospital, which is reserved for private doctors only. The lease is zero if he maintains a connection with the hospital for at least one day at $20,000 a year in the trauma center. All office staff, medical supplies, x-rays, billing, etc is paid by him to the hospital. In other words, his cost to set up a practice is almost nothing. In six months, he works three days for the hospital and three days in his private practice. Other doctors vary from one day for the hospital and the rest on their private practice to all days as they continued their work in the hospital. Since the Social Security fund provides for expensive procedures, all United States citizens have ninety percent coverage with

one hundred percent for illnesses like cancer. His income has risen to about $150,000 a year when he works three days on private practice where the average doctor earns less than $200,000. A doctor will usually work forty hours once the practice is established. He desires to marry and buy a house. The question his bride has is, "Does she want to care for a $900,000 house and $75,000 she qualifies for furniture?" That price range demands a big house for two people. She is a nurse and they decide to save money through stocks and seek a smaller $500,000 house that cost approximately $2,000 a month, but you add for furniture. One problem they have is they must live within their means. In a few years, they must through religion determine what that means. You cannot earn big income and live in common areas. Some people will stop promotions so they can maintain their life style. All is good in their lives. You consider the man that becomes an assistant manager at McDonalds. He earns like Joe Six Pack of today or fifteen dollars an hour (minimum wage with time in grade) and higher at twenty-four. He gets married and he buys his wife a $160,000 house, where only his salary counts for about $600 a month. She buys him a wedding present of a three-year-old Cadillac and it looks brand new. Life is good and they know their financial security is sound living in America. He is looking for the next step up or a career change may be in order. We can reproduce in other countries as well. One thing Americans can afford to help other countries with is knowledge in the UN, which was changed to United Countries.

15. We Americans know the size of our country as all possessions had to make a decision on independence

or statehood. Many locations have become our escape of winter for our second house or beautiful vacation spots.

A goal is a modern day prophecy for Adam.

Once the goals are established for the government as I defined, you will experience the church will adopt the above as major prophecy. If a planner like me was involved, I would start with what our Gods describe as the Generation of the FIG, where we justify all laws that are veto proof to the happiness of the government monitors. Why did we invest the money and how do we measure the value of the laws. The church will request you combine all political leaders outside of Washington DC. No Republican can ever serve in the country again and must leave. To achieve it becomes easier to rename the party to Health, Wealth, and Wisdom to create one party in the United States with the name identifying the commitment. Since the church of US will have two hundred million people (Holy Spirit Possessions) in early 2000s, the church will represent the voters as in the beginning of our country. The requirement from the Holy Bible is, "Whoever is not written in the book of life (church congregation) shall be cast in the lake of fire (the laws of consuming flames that accomplish in His name)." I am sorry for other religions, but they may have their countries to represent their Gods. In our country, we must represent all the people, even though we came from the church. In the new beginning, we cannot commit to teaching the Holy Bible of religion in the public schools but our children can learn to be politicians from enlightened church locations. We desire all politicians we recruit to be trained like a bishop from the book of Timothy or responsible to represent our governors to develop the laws without arguments (evil spirits) that do not apply. Today, in the year of Our Lord 2008 AD, the voice of the powerful will drown out the voice of reason in that all laws are bad. The politicians are not the lawless ones, but all laws are bad. For example, what law would a governor state is the single best idea all governors agree to. The law should raise the money to solve the problem with the social ill of the state (sorrows) and yet minimize the impact on the consumer and businessmen.

Since I go to church, I represent King Jesus Christ in the King of kings (crown leaders). Our courts will learn the clergymen are the lords in Lord of lords. We must not let the church define the policies, but if they define a problem with unneeded children or taxpayer wants through the congregation, we will listen and help correct. The government must rely greatly on the book of wants. For example, no taxpayer should be against the instruction in the Holy Bible, where we do not let the government steal our houses. King Jesus Christ will judge our politicians through the saints. Any gifts we can afford, we should provide such as health, wealth and wisdom to the children and then the parents. There are thirty thousand unnecessary deaths of people each day and through our Washington, DC commitment and education that must go to zero. The only limitations will be how foreign governments can learn to manage their economies in the UN. May religious people of the world seek knowledge, which is what America can afford! As Americans, we desire to eliminate the unnecessary deaths in America and train foreign governments. May America lead the challenge of overcoming ten million deaths each year do to the pen!

The other nations in our country like the Israeli man (Jewish) will determine a land in America like certain cities and run them like a Promise Land or a land you promise your children. He must abide by in Rome do as the Romans.

In the year of Our Lord 2050 AD, we will rewrite the movie. May the change of the year of Our Lord 3000 AD not be changed, except for enhanced unalienable rights? The schedule will be as follows:

YEAR COVERING
1. 2050---2100 and 3000.
2. 2100 --2300 and 3000.

3. 2300---2500 and 3000.
4. 2500---2800 and 3000.
5. 2800---3000 and beginning of 4000.

If you have any questions on how to do this, I can easily answer.

Richard Cartwright
430 Pembroke Rd SW
Poplar Grove, IL 61065
Email comfortinGod@mchsi.com
1-815-765-0161
Author of "Life of US (U.S.)": a book that forms God's Kingdom (Lord's Prayer).

Author of "The Antichrist God's Version": a book of God's miracles that people would say cannot be done like ending all poverty. Author's name Elias and sold through www.iuniverse. com and other stores.

Present writing the Sixty-Seventh Book of the Holy Bible, author's name is Elijah, which will get fathers and children back together again or reestablish the families, without divorce. We must get children back with fathers or reestablish marriage the church has lost. Where are we in the Holy Bible but back in the book of Genesis or a new beginning.

What shall we do with the money generated by the movie? I estimate the profit would exceed a billion dollars. You get Hollywood to bid on the job and they will receive cost plus. The writing and acting can be done by volunteers from the church or actors. I believe many actors would volunteer their time for the love of God's Kingdom.

We require six more Holy Cities in the approximate location of where the religion started. If you buy one thousand acres, put up a church and office building to house the staff, computers, and your own email and computer network, you may not have money left over. Do not forget the Catholics. This is only one movie and you are in many countries. You can understand the reward money to the church is great. The reward to the USA in material wealth is unbelievable. All the politicians representing the church will have a movie to represent the future they inherit of that country. You will ask the political leaders to grant you the parables you should teach. The future politicians and judges shall pay the church like any other class at a university. The cost at Notre Dame University should be the cost of one more course, but only one course may not be enough. The course for accreditation should be developed for ongoing requirements for beyond a PhD. How could you be a Scripture Attorney and not have the required religious training courses? An attorney representing the local mayors will have the attorney review all the laws to see if it meets the New Testament requirements. Go back to the laws of liberty and create many new ones. One day all businessmen will seek the training of the Holy Bible computerized planning or a path to a small door. We cannot recognize religion of today with the true religion of the Holy Bible. As the Holy Bible states, it is a new beginning or the end.

You have various passages to judge our politicians and courts. As they are creating the laws, they are presenting you with the opportunity to share their achievements with all the seven denominations. A review prior to the church vote to release the shackles on your television stations probably would aid the congregation. Do not bore them with hundreds of hours for each party to review, but make that available where interest is required.

Let us start with Satan.

1. He was a beast of Revelation with a woman riding on its back before the presidential election.
2. He became the King of Babylon during the presidential debates.
3. He created less than zero jobs during his first four years in office.
4. He created a negative wealth creation environment.
5. He was the Red Dragon from prophecy.
6. He became Satan by blowing his horn (speaking or using his mouth).
7. He started in an era of peace and prosperity.
8. He continually violated the book of Mark and other passages in the Holy Bible.
9. Do not forget his angels or the young Republicans.
10. Only one third of the country is Republican despite the Catholics, but they vote.
11. The Holy Bible states not one woman could vote for George W. Bush in the year of Our Lord 2000 AD as he was a mass murder of children from Texas and was against her child's education.
12. He went four trillion dollars plus in debt in less than eight years. He started with a budget surplus of two hundred thirty two billion dollars.

Some of the passages would classify his failure as a nonhuman being that continued as the seventh beast. He cannot be saved. In the year of Our Lord 2002 AD, the Republican Party increased their leadership role in the Federal and many state governments. Many clergymen would vote for Satan again and President Herbert C. Hoover from the year of Our Lord 1932 AD.

Some minor summaries may be as easy as he started with the best economy in the history of modern America in an era of peace and prosperity. Our pay raises prior to his administration was above inflation and the unemployment number was defined as less than four percent. The prior president talked about using the surplus money to fund our Social Security system, the inflation number was about zero overall, and about four percent inflation in health care. The Republicans blamed the change in the economy on Allen Greenspan, but it was their bad laws and the lack of confidence of their mouths that caused the problem; however, an organization of His Kingdom may have more information than the above to start with. Much data can be derived from the senators and house members of your congregations. I would not go to the newspapers or television today for information at local news. You talk about at the end of eight years all the measurement of the desires of humankind where the economy has improved. The Holy Bible would call the politicians grandpa, not the Father of Perspiration. The answer is nothing is better. Satan George W. Bush made everything in the United States worse and was training Senator John McCain. They made everything in the economy worse. His father's results of the year of Our Lord 1992 AD should have given the church the answer. He and his Republican Party should have resigned by doing the millstone story variation where they state, "We cannot beat the Democrats financial success under President William J. Clinton and all should vote Democrat." We ended up with one party and they should eliminate the government waste built into the Republican laws. The financial rewards of our country would have been great. Good money in the hands of our families will aid the church greatly to improve morality. Morality should be taught in the church. All must be trained to be reborn again at the age of King Jesus Christ. That requirement will require the church to get the teenagers back. The government must support religion, but cannot listen to blame like Pro-life or the churches war against our children.

At this point, I go back to scripture. We have a theory of economics to explore the cows. The Holy Bible commands the clergymen and government to split up the cows wisely in the year of Our Lord 2000 AD. Jacob from the Old Testament was to be justified when he walk past the people begging for money and did not sell all his gold and give it away. The government not the individuals should pay. In America, we pay taxes. President elect Al Gore was talking about Republican government waste. During President William J. Clinton's administration in the United States, we had seven years of "Fat Cows" being developed. During the seven years, Europe was in a recession or allowing the fat cows to be eaten by the skinny cows. Mexico came to America to borrow money and Republican Gingrich did not desire to help them. In Asia, a billion people were under serious distress as in South Korea, the people were selling their gold to buy food. The joke was that billionaire Bill Gates could buy all of the Korean stocks for petty cash or a small part of his monies. The rich of Korea still had big fortunes. In Argentina, the government went into bankruptcy. What did I hear the Catholics say on January 1, the year of Our Lord 2000 AD? The French had twelve per cent unemployment. You may be wrong but it appears that the Catholics believe good economies happen by accident. The Holy Bible states the problem near the end times is with the rich. All good economies happen through planning. A country can develop a good economy despite what the fools in other countries are doing. While the church in the United States was begging for more Ames for the poor, the Holy Bible states that Jacob should be justified. The church should believe in the politicians to eliminate poverty through laws not fantasyland of the clergymen. The church should simply tell the government they are out of the General Welfare. The congregation should believe that collecting our tax money from the good people is enough. You could read that Jacob saw the people begging for money and he did not sell all his gold and give it all away. They were still demanding immigration not training politicians on the American laws under President William J. Clinton. Once the church let the women defined the hell in their lives, the new political party should correct. The poor women of the United States have a moral responsibility to teach the future presidents of the United States on why they are living in hell, so the government could learn to plan.

All the church has to do is double what we believe a party of one hundred percent Democrats could do. By the religious leaders reading my one thousand year plan copied from the Holy Bible, "We would state King Jesus Christ is right as He can double the best Adam can do." King Jesus Christ's economic plan will eliminate greed and make all American citizens rich. Rich will mean we shall not want, but our IQ and desires will determine our income. A truck driver at twenty-four years old in the year of Our Lord 3000 AD is more financially secure than a new doctor of today at the same age. We have to have faith and wait for the church to declare that victory for the United States. What if another country has a victory of economics declared first? Should we cheer or wonder what are past politicians have done wrong? I believe despite our government being fifty three trillion dollars in debt as described by Tomorrow's World on television, our American citizens should all be rich by their words first in comparison to Asia or South America. We will have two views of rich. One is as a truck driver, I shall not want and one as a man that created an idea like Bill Gates, I am in shackles. In Israel, it was proclaim do not seek to be rich by money, but I shall not want is a gift of God, not Adam. You remember a Bill Gates or rich man was in Israel. Someone must hold the money despite the problems of their children becoming play boys and girls. If that happens the clergymen must teach them not to eat or die.

Let me grant you a requirement to over come the book of Mark. We have food stamps for many below the poverty level. As twenty-five percent do not qualify, what shall we do with the money for food stamps? Many would say to reduce the cost by twenty five percent. We should spend more money per person on food stamps and define what is left to reduce the number of people below the poverty level. At the end all the money for food stamps will not go for food stamps, but may be used to pay the Social Security tax for a temporary dynamic action plan. Another way is you use the money as direct payments knowing only a widowed woman of sixty from a small family receives the gift of being a receiver. Therefore, you must account for all the money. One day, we have a problem when we reduce the budgets, but they can be defined as eliminating sales tax for all. Do not just reduce the number but also define a dynamic action plan to enhance the economy. If you reduce, many politicians already know what will happen as campaigns and the American people will increase the faith and wait. The politicians have to follow the Holy Bible in the Generation of the FIG or Perdition may be your inheritance. You will go from the high rate of over fifty percent if you include the tax of interest down to ten percent of the total economy. Many enlighten plans are required, but over coming the book of Mark without Perdition must be done or why would a man desire to be a politician.

Chapter 4.   Addition to the Seventh Trumpet Story

The Seventh Trumpet Story is words of great prophecies as defined in the Holy Bible. This chapter is in addition to the original as the knowledge became great and I decided to continue in an additional chapter. You must believe in blessed are the poor, they shall inherit the earth. The poor are the people involved in the sorrows of your country like the hurricanes and the negative impact on people lives for a country unprepared to resolve. The Seventh Trumpet story will add hundreds of trillions of dollars to the world economies, led by the church. They must create the gospel of Christ and end the gospel about Christ.

To summarize what can before is the many miracles that God has promised the church will train the politicians on. Chapter 3 defined what a beast is, a dragon and how God used the Holy Bible, and the signs to grant us the number seven. Since we have to live by every word of the Holy Bible and God will return when the church has no questions to ask, any item the God said He would do the clergymen as His employees must do. What are some of the additional items?

1. God will make you rich, therefore no man worries about money in a kingdom. You shall not want. No church location would beg you for money if the kingdom was formed.

2. God will take care of the virus. Easy to plan, but the time to complete will draw the story very old.

3. Restore nature. Have you heard of global warming?

4. Waste areas.

5. The war to end all wars was the Second World War, so the church can end all killing wars.

6. One world government as many church locations talk about, so I have developed the plan.

7. God will take care of the wicked, so that plan or theology is written until the year of Our Lord 3000 AD.

8. The church is to absorb all debts, so no person, government, or company is in debt.

9. Consumer loans for housing, cars, furniture, or any other want must end and be replaced by interest free investments in America. Owning a piece of land is a requirement for all citizens, as an investment in the future of America and all other countries.

10. Tithes are to be only ten percent. If you know any government that is collecting more than ten percent of the economy to spend, that is one of the miracles run through the church. In Israel, the government received ten percent for Our Father to help the people. Read the Holy Bible. Today some countries like the United States collect more than ten percent. A loan for one third of your income at six percent interest rate is an eighteen percent tax just for interest. The only people that could proper from interest are the wealthy.

11. The Holy Bible requires the politicians to write laws from the New Testament and we still are writing laws the way of the Old Testament. That would be exciting for the churches to teach.

12. There is nothing to fear but fear itself. Today, you should not seek public office because the politicians are achieving, if you gain the whole world and lose your soul, you gained nothing at all. Satan, the Red Dragon, the false messiah, the eighth beast are all dead spiritually and cannot be saved in this lifetime. They will go by the way of Perdition or eternal death. The church must train how they will be judged and the information is completed for the main items, as copied out of the Holy Bible.

The book of Timothy must be used to train the politicians in a seminary setting like a course on Physics. The chapter before covered most but I will cover Standing Historical of the politician of the United State in the year of Our Lord 1820 AD or the laws of liberty. The way the United States started is gone and God tells the church to get back to the laws of liberty as today we have the laws of freedom, not liberty. The Holy Bible states to take our inventions and turn it into gold.

In the year of Our Lord 1820 AD, we had a new idea call a train to explore. The politicians looked in the Holy Bible and found they were to create interest free loans. They granted lands, so the railroads would have value and issued a piece of paper to investors for ownership. We would call them stocks. The railroads were not to go into debt. President Abraham Lincoln stated in the year of Our Lord 1860 AD that the wealth creation in our country was great. The government did not sit around and wait for the businessman to think railroads were to be built. They establish a technique from scripture to force the wealth creation. Under the communists governments, one of the great advantages was they could plan and force the railroads to be developed. Under the laws of liberty, the government could plan and motivate. Today under the laws of freedom, they wait for the businessman to create wind farms and actually work against them. In the year of the Lord 1896 AD, the United States created the New York Stock Exchange and the Holy Bible requires Standing Historical of the church to cover. I will cover other ways the church will use in their training course included with the book of Timothy. The plan comes from give me a sign and the church to teach how to live by every word.

The only chance the world has is for God's Kingdom to form and the clergymen to become the saints to judge the world. King Jesus Christ will meet us in Israel not the church world (temple not church per Malachi 3:1). We were seeing the seventh beast with the eighth beast campaigning in the year of Our Lord 2008 AD. At that time, he had the wrong title to be the eighth beast. The famine at the end is for the word of God and is all about the usury laws and money. Check the Old Testament why Our Gods told the church to absorb all debts. The true Lord's Prayer does read to forgive the debtors or what was done by the rich like in the Old Testament. The church must find Elijah, the prophet. He can restore the economy to King Jesus Christ demands and get the hearts of the fathers back with children. The best way is for the rich to accept the tax on greed to forgive the debtors or American taxpayers at least in the new beginning. Do not say that will be the only way. The requirement for jobs is a mind is a terrible thing to waste or zero unemployment. If someone said the plans are too expensive think about zero property tax, sales tax, and interest payments for the consumer. The businessman will and must understand the potential markets in America to satisfy the taxpayers. We shall not want. What taxpayers want is zero tax on property for schools not a one percent tax reduction on income. The project title shall be the peace dividend, property tax relief. Next they would desire sales tax relief. The government must be out of debt and zero property or sales tax charge to any one. The change must occur as soon as possible. All is possible in God.

Update on January 26, the year of Our Lord 2008 AD.

Since I have written the Seventh Trumpet Story based on the Holy Bible, what I said in my first book "Life of US (U.S.)" of the year of Our Lord 2002 AD is coming true. I stated if you desired to understand the economy of President George W. Bush, all you have to do is study the economy of his father. Many social ills (sorrows) of the country have had the funding removed; thereby, violating the book of Mark. I wrote eight years of Bush is twelve years too many. The first four years (the year of Our Lord 1989 to 1993 AD) was four years too many. The church can find great sorrows all over the country and it will become worse. The Mark of the Beast is the beginning of the end. The church never taught the meaning of the Mark of the Beast in the forehead of politicians to the taxpayers. Senator Barack Obama and John McCain do not have the knowledge. A trumpet is what a president would use to explain important economic or other type issues. The seven is an important plan of God.

First, the economists on market analysis television were blaming the Federal Reserve for not lowering the interest rates as quickly as possible. The Bush administration is going to use the old theme of money to avoid the recession in the early to mid Year of Our Lord 2008 AD. I hear a number like one trillion dollars of borrowed money. In an environment where citizens are greatly in debt and their jobs are possibly affected, we will have a tendency to save. Even some professionals on television are telling people to do that. A greater decline will occur if you issue tax cuts, which further causes the dollar to decline. Inflation at the present high rate could expand and many economists are waiting for that to happen. What that is called is stagflation or high inflation without good growth. The last time the Bush administration lower the taxes (the year of Our Lord 2003 AD), the layoffs continued at three hundred and fifty thousand a month for the next year. The tax money going to people above one hundred thousand dollars a year was government waste. Ninety percent of the money of the tax cuts went to that income group. The change did not work. If you lower the interest rates, the professionals are stating, "What are you going to do to get the banks to borrow money and put the money to work?" If you give people that are rich, fifty billion more dollars and they already have twenty five trillion, after rounding you wondered why you bothered. Using the same amount of money on the roads, you will create new jobs and good tax revenue goes back to the government treasuries.

What would King Jesus Christ representative teach you to do or explain? First, you have to start out with what is known or the Sign of the Times. You must define a future you desire to inherit or lower inflation, strengthen the American dollar, and take care of an important social ill of the country. A possible recession is over and consumer confidence soars. What is known? Give me a sign.

1. 1. Much greed is found in the United States. The Holy Bible states the problem near the end times is the problem with the rich.
2. 2. A greater budget deficit will devalue the dollar further and increase inflation. A fall in oil prices can occur for a short time, but cars and other products will rise again.
3. 3. We should not take a chance and do nothing.
4. 4. If you give the money to the consumer, he may not spend it.
5. 5. Consumer confidence or the ability to spend may not increase.
6. 6. Many construction workers are without jobs caused by housing.
7. 7. One percent of the richest people have more money than ninety percent of the people.

8. 8. A major social ill of America is the country is 1.6
trillion dollars behind on their roads.

A new tax on greed must be imposed on people earning
over three million dollars a year. Some people state our sports
players earn a lot of money. Have you heard about the Exxon
Mobil executives earning four hundred million dollars per year?
Now, we collect one hundred billion in new tax revenue from
greed. Congress uses the tax money to fix the roads. We are 1.6
trillion dollars behind. In California, I heard sixty per cent of the
roads are bad in one county. You must build confidence, define
a long-term project, but it must be an important social ill of the
country. If you use borrowed money to give to the consumers
that will weaken the dollar and inflation will consume most of
the money. Have you heard of one hundred and fifty dollar oil
or higher if you further weaken the dollar and the associated
inflation? Even oil over one hundred dollars a barrel is not
socially acceptable. You can see a short-term drop because of
a bad economy. Inflation and the rich will make it rise again.
Recessions in many countries are just a result of bad laws
or granting people money that cannot use it wisely to win
elections. You will find they love to give money to the wealthy
not to the people that can use it wisely.

The construction commitment creates many millions
of new jobs and a commitment to add more tax revenue by
reversing the Bush tax cuts for people earning over one hundred
thousand dollars a year. Again, the money is added to road
construction absorbing the construction workers. They spend
and buy items like trucks, housing, and food. The governments
all over the United States are collecting additional tax revenue.
Our government at our present tax rates will collect almost
twice the monies spent on roads and must save the money
for Social Security benefits. The value of the dollar soars and
causes a corresponding decline in the cost of oil. A higher
value of the dollar will cost Americans less for imported oil.
As oil prices decline all products delivered and many produced

will decline lowering inflation. The decline in oil cost will be permanent far into the future. Electricity and natural gas costs decline along with oil causing inflation to continue dropping. The house owner may end up with over five hundred dollar in less cost between gasoline and utilities. The saving may be much higher. Today the price of oil declined because of bad economies. In a kingdom, bad economies are not possible and the politicians stay in office.

You review what you desired to inherit in the future. Inflation is way down, the American dollar increases in value. You are starting to fund Social Security with new tax dollars from the new tax rates. People who receive pay raises will actually receive real consumption dollars not inflation dollars. You must get many non-inflation taxed dollars in the hands of the consumers. We shall not want. You create millions of jobs and the word recession is behind you. The consumer confidence soared, which by itself helps the economy. The last time a president raised taxes on the wealthy or on the group over one hundred thousand dollars a year, you were starting to hear the stocks going up in the year of Our Lord 1993 to 2001 AD and the wealth creation in the country was being restored. In a few years, we may hear the rich complaining again like in the late 1990's, "I made so much money, do I have to pay taxes?" The answer is to get the governments out of debt as the word of God is, "Do not give people money that cannot use it wisely". You think about the rich have ten trillions dollars to buy stocks, but the rich are not using the money to create jobs. Job creation will overcome the present abandon buildings as described in scripture. The Consumption Economics will be trained in the United Nations for all countries to prosper from the enlightened power. There are zero reasons for a recession in Europe or anywhere if God's Kingdom forms.

Road construction is so far behind, you should try to get the labor unions to get people from hot areas in the summer to go north and in cold climates months to go south. You offer the people work for forty-eight hours a week if they move, weather permitting. America can put the story of recession and bad roads behind us and fund Social Security at the same time.

What has happened to oil by the beginning of the year of Our Lord 2009 AD? The economy became so bad that oil dropped. If you check the records you could learn the prices are still distorted. If the economy became good the wealthy would just drive up the price to poor levels, through greed.

This memo will be added to the Seventh Trumpet Story, which is a thousand year plan for the United States government as copied from the Holy Bible from the economy of the Old Testament, Israel. The story is mostly about money. The Holy Bible states if you let the view of King Jesus Christ on the economy, He wills double the best Adam can do. Doubling the best Adam can do is easy if you use the Holy Bible. Have you ever met a person that claims to be Elijah, the prophet and has a thousand year plan you can verify from the Holy Bible? King Jesus Christ has stated for the church to absorb all debts. That will mean no consumer loans. I know how to achieve the results required. The seventh day He rests as He has given you the answers in the church world for the next thousand years.

Without the church, correcting the bad roads cannot be done and the millions of jobs created. What a surprise for the people that run or goes to church. Have you heard of the passage, "Some governments are taking you on the road to hell?" King Jesus Christ judged the world many centuries ago because He loved you. What are you doing to judge the world so your love can shine on the congregation? You must be the saints that judge the world. I can teach you how to do that. Please deliver to other church locations so we can avoid a government taking us on the road to hell. Make your sermons count!

Tuesday, the year of Our Lord May 20, 2008 AD.

When you read this book, you will realize the church must teach us on how to apply a date to writing. I will leave many versions in my book until they decide.

I desire to update what is required for the economy at this time. You have heard the politicians and you can judge. Above I have developed a plan for millions of jobs, funded Social Security, and reduce inflation for example on oil. What to do in addition is further reduce our dependence on foreign energy supplies and maintain the temperature in our houses the same. I have heard fools state, we should expand the supply. I am not waiting in a line at the gas pumps as I have in the past and America is consuming twenty-five percent of the world production. Other industrialized countries like Germany consume one-tenth the oil of America. Even Germany will have to greatly reduce what they consume because there will be none left. Now is the time not a hundred years from now. We would prefer to leave vast resources in the ground and not require it used in this era. Also before winter, the gas industry stated there were adequate supplies of natural gas. We did consume some or our vast coal supplies. The major problem was the cost based on the American dollar as caused by the foolish Republican Party and their campaign of "Read my lips, no new taxes." The taxes are increasing or borrowed money spent at local levels and through inflation. Inflation and interest is a tax.

Part of the price at the American pump is because the rich trading oil futures and the value of the dollar. The decrease is temporary since it was based on bad economies. The world will pay a tremendous price for reduced oil costs this way because of bad economies. The value of the dollar is because of bad laws and decisions in Washington DC. I see some people say our dollar will soar again because of the failure of the politicians in Europe. That is not acceptable to the families and certainly should not be acceptable to the churches. They should look up lawlessness ones and realize the Holy Bible is discussing the politicians that are in shackles, but the church allows weak economies, which promotes crimes and are the lawless ones that refuse to end bad laws and prisons. We are having an impact on the world like President Herbert C. Hoover of the year of Our Lord 1932 AD. You change the commodities trading and the value of the dollar, inflation will go negative in America. Dollars will flow into our country not out and our stocks will go up, yet when the government pays off our bonds, the greatest export will be the American greenback. You must establish a climate for business. Two new plans are required or prophecies. A prophecy is a plan in the world of today because of teaching theology. It has always been for Adam. If he plans, he is prophesying. Many countries that have tied the value of their currency to America have raised inflation because of oil. Saudi Arabia told us the price of oil will go higher if America devalues their currency. Part of the cost of food is because of energy and option trading of commodities. Do not believe a drop in oil prices because of recessions and depressions are good. Both values in economies will disappear in God's Kingdom as the Holy Bible is written so Adam can finish the six-day creation story or see what country can create the best life for all its citizens. That is to become the greatest goal of the government and business.

I will start on how to reduce the dependency on foreign oil and allow the economy to expand. That expansion will require more energy and if done incorrectly will pollute and tax our production standards globally. How can Adam expand the global economy and reduce its dependence on oil. We heard about wind farms but how about cars. A fool like Bush would talk about technology that is not available today or I heard it would cost a million dollars to buy a hydrogen car. I realize through volume we can reduce the price, but where would we get the hydrogen? If you generate it in the car, the cost is high today. Where are the refueling stations required? What can America do to reduce its six hundred billion dollar cost of imported fuel? If we raise the value of the dollar back to the year of Our Lord 2000 AD, we still have about a four hundred billion dollar import cost but gas only runs about two dollars a gallon or less. To pay for our high tech roads, we must increase the gas tax, but the future will require new techniques. Since we must consume less fuel we should change the cost down to zero and replace with taxes on people that I have stated in the past that have more money than brains or greed.

What shall we do with the technology we learned from hydrogen fuel cars? We should use that type of technology to fill our pipelines with hydrogen gas. One day the natural gas will be gone. Now is the time to invest, not wait until it is very late. We should set up a pilot program. We maybe better off saving our coal resources for a possible Ice Age to return. We may desire to heat our atmosphere at the expense of the environment.

For our car savings of fuel, what should we demand of our governments? I wrote about my Cadillac earlier. We must establish a change even though what was written before is good. Now, we have to apply what America did in the year of Our Lord 1820 AD as we opened up the Holy Bible to create wealth and we had new technology to apply or railroads. I will not cover all areas where the newfound knowledge of the past can be applied. The Holy Bible states to turn inventions into gold. We did the theory for Chrysler in the year of Our Lord 1978 AD.

We will offer our two automobile companies that have their corporate headquarters in America a deal. We desire all their cars to get a minimum of thirty miles per gallon in the cities by a decade away. The federal government will define what cars they desire to buy and to provide a market. The state and local governments will do the same. The government will only buy hybrids or electric. We will test the cars for highway mileage at sixty-seven miles per hour, at low temperatures, and any way to uncover wasted fuel. Presently when we increased the speed limit on the highways, we never changed our test results. The manufactures look at fifty-five and when I am on the highway, the speeds are higher. My Cadillac has achieved better results at fifty-five and I cannot turn off four cylinders. The hybrid cars can be recharged to help achieve the thirty miles per gallon requirement in the city. In the city of Chicago, a person may not have the gasoline engine start until thirty-two miles per hour and the car will be like an electric car. If the battery gets low or speed increases the batteries will charge and gasoline will be consumed. Some that commute on local roads to the downtown areas may not use any gas at all, yet a total electric car may not be his answer for the weekends, yet. The next generation we should call electric hybrids.

To pay for the conversion, the Federal government will offer the corporations Ford and GM zero percent financing sponsored by the Federal Reserve as in the year of Our Lord 1820 AD except the Federal Reserve buys the stocks. They can sell us stocks at fifty percent or higher over the market price. We will price before the sales are made. The company can pay off all their bonds, can use the money for research and new factory equipment, or offer the Americans financing for the new products at four percent interest or lower. We will put the stocks in our Social Security Job/Business Trust Fund and not sell the stocks for less than what we paid or more than a thousand shares a day. The day we receive the stocks, we might already have a profit, but the cost of foreign oil is our main goal. Since the world will run out of fuel someday, our goal must be zero, but do not rush that day. We will replace with electricity for gasoline. The car companies can no longer sell bonds. The Federal Reserve will be available to provide funding directly by buying stocks, but maybe not at a fifty percent level over price. Our Social Security trust fund is to help the businessman and the consumer with investment money ideas. One day GM and Ford will keep their employees paychecks in the company treasuries and act like a banker with debit cards. The cash must be used for the advantage of the employees and consumers of their products. We will raise the price of stamps by two cents and all other deliveries to convert the fleet of US Post Office to electric hybrids. The employees of other firms should convince their management to do the same. Congress state and federal can review the others and determine where technology should be developed. All conversion equipment must be made in America down to the smallest screw.

What about car tires? Many run in a range about thirty to thirty-five pounds. I remember you raised the pressure for gas mileage and high speed runs. We should test our tires at much higher pressure as a joint venture between American tire companies and our car manufactures. A small change in mileage can add to the reduction. Do not forget about the health hazards in polluted air on our children and seniors.

We will offer people on Social Security a free new refrigerator under income of twenty five thousand a year. The new ones cost about forty dollars a year to run. The manufactures will be asked, what they have left after their regular sales to deliver to the people. The people on welfare will be next. In addition, the firemen will install free CO_2 detectors and grant a dozen new light bulbs. The old technology light bulbs cannot be manufactured in the United States or sold here one year after the law is passed. Some fancy light bulbs will continue until replacement can be found. The electricity will be used for our cars. Apartment buildings may be granted new refrigerators.

The local transit authorities will be contacted to modify the existing buses to run on electric hybrid technology. The federal government will pay for the conversion and the cost of developing the new technology if required. All future transit buses will run on electricity and the clean fuel made from farm products. Our cities clean air standards make that a natural change.

All electric meters shall be able to run backwards as demanded by many consumers. The farmers claim they are burning gas that could be used to produce electricity. Many people will invest in solar panels, which will expand the market and help drive down the cost. Some people will invest in solar panels even if the numbers do not justify it, just to help. All they may require is a new meter to protect the network, if required.

All the projects shall have their costs defined and the savings to the country on imported fuel measured as the Generation of the Fig. Some projects we will do anyway even if the cost is not justified. Government waste must be limited and proven to the taxpayers. America is working hard to have the seven Holy Cities grant America a Hawk or a bird of minimize government waste (waste not, want not). If we do receive, America will declare the fourth of July as a day of the laws of liberty and encourage celebration. The fifth of July will be a day of rest. May Americans play on the fourth in celebration! The world may explore our love of Our Gods and the seven Holy Cities certify our good deeds all over the world. May no other country try to be ahead of us! If they do, America must go further ahead. May all other church nations compete and America must stay ahead or the church may declare the other country the land that King Jesus Christ will make a stand or the new Heartland. What does He stand for but every word of the Holy Bible? You better read my literature.

What shall we do with our farms? King Jesus Christ will eliminate the money problems of our farmers. Commodities are a problem in America. Hedge Funds have and could drive the prices to unrealistic costs, for the consumers. Back in approximately the year of Our Lord 1850 AD, we started posting the buying price for wheat. Many decades the system appeared to work, but the middleman made big profits. Back around ten years ago, the farmers complained when Canada dumped wheat in America at two dollars a bushel, today it is more than twice as high. The Federal Reserve will become our bankers of natural and other resources. We will establish a web location where the farmers can sell and the buyers can buy. In a bad crop year, the farmer would have stated what he wanted to produce. He develops a plan. If the only factor were the weather or something beyond his control, he would be paid on his plan. In big crop years, he still will only get his plan. The Federal Reserve, not the farmer will take the risk. The Federal Reserve shall be our treasuries and will handle all items in storage as required. The commodities shall be part of our trust fund. That technique will be used for all other commodities. The rich man should not seek wealth as a goal, but if it happens, he will pay in his future as described in scripture. May people like billionaires Warren Buffet and Bill Gates make more money, but love to pay taxes to help their other members of the congregations! When they die, we can add stocks for inheritance to the Social Security Job/Business Trust Fund and will sell a little at a time.

The United States airline industry has through pure competition, caused a hard time on employees with the bad balance sheets, and has a fleet of planes older than Europe and Asia. Are we a third world nation? Our planes should be the state of the art and its employees not in jeopardy of losing their jobs because of bad management. Now is the time to use the story of GM and Ford above, but we desire more. First, we will force certain routes to maintain a fixed price. Scheduling of routes shall be redesigned to maintain a minimum passenger load required like ninety percent, but cannot be an inconvenience to their customers. America should force reduced cost consolidation in the industry with the strong carriers buying up others and using only stocks to complete. No more bonds that drive up costs and hurt the balance sheets. Airline should buy, not lease the planes. New model airplanes save approximately thirty percent of fuel costs. May new technology bring that cost down further! The military can afford new planes as a big contract was released.

Our soldiers of misfortune will fly in new planes and our citizen will get a ticket on old technology. The airlines cannot afford a modern fleet. Electric machines for moving airplanes around airports should be developed. America must end consumer, business, and government loans. America should desire their families to fly on modern fleets and establish good paying jobs for their children. US government will buy stocks for carriers that desire to modernize their fleet and get our producers to meet that demand with expansion plans but not greed.

What should the country do with credit cards? The rich bankers have the borrowed money cost over twenty percent in many cases. They are sending out literature to sell you more. The profits from credit cards should be high when the banks can borrow at low rates and give to us at high rates. They have convinced many people to borrow beyond their means and King Jesus Christ is going to eliminate the strain in money issues. We have a clue from above as written. The Seventh Trumpet Story told us about zero consumer loans by the year of Our Lord 2050 AD in the USA. What is required now? First, you should lower the maximum interest to be charged to eight percent. Next within two years change the number to, not more than two percent over what they can get money from the Federal Reserve. Think that the Lord's Prayer says to forgive the debtors as happened in the Old Testament. We desire the great economy of Israel, where a fifty percent increase in taxes caused a woman to be poor, but she could still afford to give to the church. The hunger as you review Israel and compare with the world today, you can ask, "How could a person compete with God?"

We have the potential for generating power in Yellowstone National Park. We know we have generated power with this type of energy source. We must merge the two thoughts into a big trial plant. For three and one half years, the design shall go forward and use three and one half years to build and start operations. The tourist shall not see from the normal tours. The transmission lines must be underground. A second plant will create hydrogen gas to heat our houses and run our cars. We may drop the electric part one day as two far from consumers, but the technology may be used in other locations.

The second generation shall start when you create the first generation, you must stop the development in order to complete the project. The research and further deployment for the next generation shall continue. We must continue until the profit in terms of technology from the next generation is small. American companies will be allowed to license and manufacture for the world. All parts must be manufactured in America.

I have seen a water non-typical dam to generate electric power plant. We must explore and possible redesign what we did in our Salmon streams. I believe the fish may be desired by Americas. We have streams out east that used to produce good fishing. The new dam possibilities may make both enjoyments. The Mississippi River may use the new dam format to generate electricity. The America government can only lead to peace on earth and happiness for American citizens. Much technology other than hell machines are required by the world.

On July 18, in the year of Our Lord 2008 AD, I taught about trees. Our forests are a good way to absorb carbon. We shall plant fine woods along our federal roads. In what would be a short time, we can start to cut down fine woods to enjoy in house construction. Where leaves can be a problem, we can use pine tree. May billions of trees be planted along our roads and teach the world the advantage of beauty and carbon reduction. We require Mother of Inspiration, Father of Perspiration as Holy Spirit words.

I had experience in house remodeling industrials and a big cost is the companies to get a contract. For our firemen and police department, we desire to grant cameras that can show energy lost in the winter. They can film a neighborhood, get the contractors to provide insulation on a neighborhood bid, and past out contracts. The contractors work, but the people in the neighborhood can look at the pictures and determine what is to be done. It may cost half as much if they have most of a block to do. They can take pictures in the same houses next year to see if the desired results are there. The house owners can sign up for three percent loans through Social Security. We should not care if it takes ten years to pay off. Do we desire to grant three percent loans for student loans in the new beginning? The interest goes to our Social Security System or Americas new gold mine, not the rich through the bankers.

In the counties where the hospital schools are, the governors must define laws for alcohol. Only restaurants can serve beer or wine, no bars. Alcohol can only be sold as in Canada or controlled stores, but limited to beer and wine. Surrounding areas shall be limited to where bars can be placed. We send our children to learn the meanings of life, not life in a bottle. Doctors or churches can teach, "What is wrong with alcohol like Israel?" Doctors that love John 3:16, can go to a church to learn and teach beyond the school. We should buy stocks and develop new hospitals for our doubling of senior citizens. They will require more beds. After the load is normal the old locations should be removed.

We have more projects to define, but do we have the time or people to work. The unalienable right we reach for is a mind is a terrible thing to waste. Once we run out of workers, we must stop. America has a moral obligation to train in the United Nations and give a copy of the results and projects to our religious leaders. They should publish in their book of wants and they train at the Altar wherever there is a church. The temples will be granted the love of American politicians for its citizens also. The church must believe in jobs as a right as God's view and Adam must learn all over the world.

As scripture describes, America requires ten thousand new ideas to run the country, as all fields appear to be losing our advantages. We must go back to the beginning of the Unites States and recreate the laws of liberty. To become the

Heartland, where King Jesus Christ is our King in the King of kings and Lord in the Lord of lords, ideas and knowledge must be developed. He asked the Jewish Rabbis, "Are you not the seeds of Abraham." which means idea men. Shall America follow Israel into the Battle of Armageddon? To go to a church and believe in Our God's and have people fully understand the trees stories is great. The tree stories are the Grace of God. By the Grace of God, you are saved. He has done the work and provided the wisdom. Now is the time for Adam to learn, how to grow up and learn how to live by every word of the Holy Bible. The title is bible or a way of life and holy is perfect. God has promised us a perfect way of life. If you know someone who does not have a perfect way of life, the church, government, and business have to change. All going to a church has been granted a right to achieve a perfect way of life, if the clergymen obey God. Any difference between a perfect way of life and reality is cause by the men of little faith or the church run by the Antichrists. A good paying job in America must become an unalienable right. May the desires of man of government send wars as the way of the buggy whip industries and lead by happiness all over the world. Adam should always understand what he desires to create in Our Gods names.

A brief summary of the above is the church can:

1. End all killing wars.
2. Train politicians through the book of Timothy.
3. Train the courts through the book of Galatians.
4. End what we call poverty today.
5. End prisons and crime syndicates.
6. End viruses.
7. The most important is for America to bring salvation back to the rest of the world as the Heartland or the land King Jesus Christ will make a stand. What does He stand for but every word of the Holy Bible!
8. Last is any idea man can think of to finish the Six Day Creation Story, which will take from Here to

Eternity. Eternity is a measure of time where one thousand zeros of time is short to utilize the love in the Holy Bible from Our Gods.

Chapter 5.   The Beasts

Across the world the party representing the rich as the Holy Bible defined, "the problem near the end times is with the rich" is a major problem. In the United States, I have listed the beasts, that prophecy covers as the year of Our Lord 2000 AD minus 72 or you start with President Herbert C. Hoover.

The Seals cover the famine or a man that resulted in a bad economy or lack of money to solve the social ills of the country like food. The famine is lack of money and the church must provide the words. Why is a famine a lack of money not growing crops. All countries are to have surplus food. If your country does have a bad crop year and your storage is gone, why would the people be hungry. It is because your government does not have the money to go on the open markets and buy surplus food. Now lack of daily bread is a famine in your country. The Pale Horse or death is for the war lords where you cut off his ugly head for being a dragon and preparing to steal that woman's child by the death of the child as a soldier of misfortune. The body of the church, the women declare him dead and the church must do the pass over story, when they cut off his ugly head for anyone like Wal-Mart that will not understand.

Since we have never had a successful president from the Republican Party in seventy-two years, the church should have no problem getting rid of them as defined in my first book if they were the church of God. What do we do with the greatest of failure where a man gains the whole world and loses his Soul? The whole world in this case is the United States and its influence on his world, the United States of America.

The church requires the information to stand forever and ever. In the year of Our Lord one thousands zeros, what will the church do if America hires a Bush and the planets we have discovered are not as friendly as we believe. We hear wars and rumors of wars start. What the church desires is to have the beast failures of the United States not be forgotten, as their presidential locations still exist. Some locations of our presidential libraries have disappeared. They were in power so long ago, but the failures defined in the Holy Bible still have the American Flag flying at half mass and upside down. Never lose the meaning of hell on earth and the Mark of the Beast. The church will have to bring out the old wounds so the future we have designed to inherit is good. Never lose the meaning of the words of scripture. The Holy Bible is required in its final form from here to eternity, where eternity is a measure of time. May one thousands zeros of perfect life always be the goal until we reach one thousand zeros of time and we desire to continue. We will never be able to see that far in the future except by Scripture but we must find Elijah and Elias. The time left is very short or Matthew 24:14 will come true.

Now is the time for the churches to revisit history and record the failures as described in the Holy Bible. Many words will be covered in the seven books of standing historical (666 beast books) for America, but you will not be able to include all old news, movies of hidden failure, and other items, so we do not lose the wisdom of the Holy Bible. Place the rest in a museum in your Holy City.

In addition, much literature written by Christians must be saved for future young men to follow in the footsteps of King Jesus Christ and yours. I will use an example of Pastor Murray on television five days a week, plus. He qualifies for some of his stories are so great that if he could get to the other clergymen (God's Elect) all he would do is deceive. Others like Pastor Murray should have the literature saved. Gerald Flurry is defined in Revelation 3:9. Do not lose his television recordings of time on WGN. He is a man that believes he is right when he teaches the sword is mightier than the pen, but the pen kills faster and in more countries than the sword. He would make a good Nazi in the Second World War time or "Chicken Little" today. He claims as "Chicken Little" the sky is falling because of weapons and King Jesus Christ desires to be the wall. TBN is included in my book; therefore, you desire to keep those recordings and others.

The beasts can destroy the men of the cross, where the clergymen cross to bear is the Holy Bible; therefore, a must is to save the back round information for Standing Historical now. Do not lose the future by not saving the past now. Also, keep copies of the numerous bibles written by man without understanding.

The 666 beast books are Standing Historical. Life of US (U.S.) Catholic is one of the seven in the United States. Life of Mexico or Russia would be a separate kingdom, as it has to be kingdom against kingdom. The reason is a challenge as to what country through a nation can satisfy the wants of the people. A want is a demand the government must satisfy like ending poverty, problems in schools, health care, or anything else that people state is bad or a sorrow. Do not forget the needs as only God can take care of your needs or that is spiritual.

The format of the Standing Historical is the same as the Holy Bible, where the history of the Church of the United States to the time of implementing the Lord's Prayer is like the Old Testament. The Holy Bible tells us what to write like King Jesus

Christ will meet us in Spain (Christopher Columbus). Winston Salem or how we started out and ended with a witch-hunt. The children of corn is the story we joy in the American Indians teaching our pilgrims how to plant corn and America ending with Thanksgiving. A war brother against brother and sister against sister is the Civil War. Do not forget the laws of liberty where twelve of your best friends where trying to minimize the penance to get you back to be a productive member of society. Today the judges in court desire to be hanging judges and judge without mercy. Great writing will be required on how the seven churches formed, as we are the wax location of the world. Modern life will include who Satan and his angels were or foolish George Bush and the young Republicans. Much of my writing will be reviewed for use in the Standing Historical books. Do not lack for efforts to save invaluable information now as in one thousand zeros, it will be too late.

Chapter 6.   The Word "Lust"

Elijah, the prophet is to get the hearts of the fathers back with children and the hearts of the children back with fathers. Have you heard of a single woman raising a boy? Have you heard of a boy being raised without a father in a divorced area where the father has abandoned the child? There are one half million children in orphanages. Where are their fathers and mothers? A child cannot be born without at least a mother, but should be raised by a mother and father. The prophecy in the Holy Bible is the fallen angels are with the women. The angels are the children raised without fathers. Boys are harder to rise and many end in prison. The girls today think good dads are not important and many end up raising boys without a thought of a husband. Many are too young to even get a job and raise the future of America on welfare. How could the prophet of King Jesus Christ be expected to achieve what a million plus employees of King Jesus Christ has given up on or marriage as a way of life? Fear is the beginning of all wisdom (knowledge). Fear is one of the four words for the millennium story. A possible location of a church without fear is not a church. It is run by a man or women taking God's Name in vain.

In Israel, Our Father had instructions on fear to enhance the development of man to a better way of life. If the parents abused a child, the religious order had a moral responsibility to kill them or Death Penalty. The hunter from prophecy are the Jewish Rabbis or the judges in Israel. Israel had rules on divorces that required a man to make a decision and make it work. He did not meet a woman, run out to Las Vegas, come back married, and three months later seek Adam in the court to resolve his mistake. That was the end of married life. The "Death Penalty" (child abuse) does not apply in the church world for the congregation the requirement is, "In Heaven on earth, do not send your policemen out to kill them because they do not desire to go to school." The lawless one the church is looking for are themselves.

In Israel, they had the religious teachers training the younger generations to become good or great adults at the right age. The Ten Commandments were designed to promote a life one thousand times better than the end and raise a nation of priests. The environment was design to keep the religion pure and managed to achieve very quick results.

You learned King Jesus Christ protected a woman created by Roman standards of the church world when He said, "Let the man without sin cast the first stone." Now, He in His Kingdom teaches not to attack a teenager or a couple without a plan where they attack you, the clergymen. They have gospel armor. Since the clergymen are the sinners, that passage becomes very important to them. In the church world, the clergymen are to live by the Ten Commandments and thereby become the saints to run the seven Holy Cities and judge the world. If you hear a clergymen blaming the congregation on anything like lust or being a sinner, he had better review that passage. If he casts the first stone (blame), he is not without sin. In Israel, a woman or man was not attacked but at times, Our Father imposed His will. Did you find in the Holy Bible where the congregation worked against Him for forty years like Pro-Life? If they did, they went into penance. Penance of Pro-life is the failure of the clergymen. You may ask a Catholic Priest, how the women could be against hearing from a new mother with the victory of a desired child from a woman that is financially, spiritually, and physically able to bear that child. Israel learned what was proclaimed was best. Eighty percent of the USA teenager mothers that keep the child go on welfare. As the Holy Bible states the fallen angels, (children in trouble) are with the women and the Catholics are trying to make it worse. In the United States, do we have the fallen angels of sons to be raise without a father. Children (angels) rose by a husband and wife is better than the view of the Catholic leaders; however, when Our Father reluctantly gave us a king, it took time before Israel learned to obey. In Israel, the man was the one to pay for lust and he had to learn. Have you heard the government of Mexico was trying to give America its undesired children because of Pro-life and failure to teach marriage and living within your means in the church.

I remember where a United States president came out and explained he lusted over a woman. Many today would hear him and maybe laugh at the foolish statement. Life in America has deteriorated so quickly in the last thirty years. That was President Jimmy Carter back around the year of Our Lord 1980 AD. In the church world, what are the clergymen to develop or children of 777 design to become good or great adults at the beginning of their adult life. How are they handling lust of a teenager or woman today? Why would I use the words of female rather than male? To my knowledge, the clergymen are forgiving something that cannot happen or sins for the clergymen and still violating the Ten Commandments. King Jesus Christ said he would take care of the sinners, which are the church employees of King Jesus Christ. The words of the millennium explain jeopardy to joy. The Antichrists (clergymen) sins go up to the heavens. I have to agree with the Holy Bible as the experiences I have had with the clergymen their sins go up to far away or solar systems.

King Jesus Christ has made the women His educators and they become the Body of the Church; however, have you heard of the controversy in the church on the word "obey" in the marriage vows. The women are refusing to obey their husbands in the marriage vows. I do not know what the Antichrists are doing exactly, but I assume they are ignoring that wisdom. If the women are Our God's educators, who do you believe they should obey? They should obey God. The clergymen teach what moral responsibility the women are expected to learn over their lifetime as the women demand, what knowledge the clergymen are to create. Why would a woman not desire to learn what the older women believe is best for the educators to learn to enhance their lives? The only desire of the men running the church is for all women to live a life one thousand times better than the end. For example, in "Spare the rod, spoil the child", they learn how to teach their husbands never to say no to their children. If a rod of pain is tried, the educators have learn that is called child abuse and in Israel, they would die. In the church world, the women are trained to use the words "good job" and in schools, the Catholics have given up on giving demerits to children as that is child abuse. We measure through the rod of desire to measure the success of a child. The rod is love and love conquers all pain in women lives in raising a child that man can understand. We cannot overcome the fury of angels, but we will try. We must judge our angels (children) so at twenty-one they become good or great adults. How will the children desire to be judged? Well, it is up to Adam to listen and learn. He should not impose his judgment on others but learn what judgment is required by others, like the value of education and techniques used in schools. What responsibility should the clergymen teach the women to make them demand, what is printed in the Holy Bible? King Jesus Christ has published you cannot go to Israel and learn how to raise a child. The wisdom becomes a great quest for knowledge for His teachers to rediscover. The procedures worked in Israel, but are learned in the church. If the religious leaders only had a book that explained reality, maybe they could learn something about religion to rekindle their desires of mankind to try to achieve a life one thousand times better than the end, the clergymen are seeking. Once the gospel about Christ is all over the world, the end shall come as defined in Matthew 24:14. Why? It is not the word of God, but His plan. A clergymen teaching a child to grow up in their land is the true word of God or the gospel of Christ.

How could the religious leaders handle this Faith and wait and a little bit of fear or the word lust in the church world? The greatest gift a man will desire in the adult world is a woman. You should notice even divorced men seek a woman and many divorced women will encounter through lust many times a new relationship. Even the gays have one as the female and male role. How far do you believe President Jimmy Carter could get without the woman loving the mystery of the affair? How about President William J. Clinton's girl friend? Would he get in jeopardy without the lust of a woman? How should the church teach this without attacking President William J. Clinton's girlfriend?

Let us go back in time to a better life in America or the year of Our Lord 1900 AD. Life is like a circle, what comes around goes around. At that time, we had a nation (religious order of church) that believed in love and marriage. What if the clergymen got together in the year of Our Lord 1900 AD and had to review the Holy Bible about a new trend of divorces. They first realized they had to become the marriage counselors. The Holy Bible states, "What God put together let no man tear asunder." So now, the seven Holy Cities developed the following instructions through Christ the Son of Man. They put a training package together and some sample sermons for the seven denominations to use. All was sent to the leaders (the very elect) of the church that held the Holy Bible for all at that location. They sent horsemen out on white horses to proclaim the new living word. Today we could use computers of white horse emails. All knowledge should be stored in the computers for possible reuse in the year of Our Lord 100,000,000,000,00 0,000,000,000,000 AD or earlier or later. The outline letter the seven Holy Cities received was like the following as I sent to many locations:

07/31/ the year of Our Lord 2004 AD

RE. William Wakefield Card. Baum
Via Rusticucci
00193, Rome Italy
OR PLEASE CHANGE THE HEADING AND SEND TO THE RIGHT PERSON OF YOUR DENOMINATION

Re: Gay Marriage and Divorce.

I have seemed the problem developing in the USA. As I read and heard the words in the Holy Bible, God has given us the answer. The passage, "What God puts together let no man tear asunder." Why not:

a. Issue a marriage license from the Vatican and define the training required.
b. Verify if the gays are saved.
c. Force you to disobey God (marriage vows say man and woman).
d. Will they hurt the children in the future through teaching?
e. Teach a confessional is:
f. The only place to allow a divorce as God provided the instructions in the Holy Bible.
g. Save ninety percent of the divorces in twenty years and then try harder by becoming the marriage counselors.

h. Divorce court.
i. A land of chaos and confusion, the man with the gavel.
j. A place where Catholics resolve marriage issues.
k. A court should only handle money issues for the church congregation.

I know God has demanded, "I do not want a hair on a child's head harmed. " You and I should believe a divorce is worst than harming a hair on a child's head. You may use the same technique Pope John Paul II used by forgiving all that came before and commit to the new way for the present married couples to get married again in the church. God's forgiveness is important to us by committing to a new beginning. Help God help the children. The church should teach jeopardy to joy or become the marriage counselors not the divorce courts.

Richard Cartwright
430 Pembroke Rd SW
Poplar Grove, Il 61065
email comfortinGod@mchsi.com
author of Life of US (U.S.) at www.iuniverse.com (at that time)
FAITH HEALING IS ENDING DIVORCES OR THE PAIN IN FAMILIES LIVES.

Any clergymen who does not try is taking God's name in vain or committing a Cardinal Sin. In the book of Luke, it states if you believe in John 3:16, but you must have the right Heart to eliminate the pain.

The sixth sense in prophecy is six words of common sense. The theme is "For the love of God's children" or the words of the Holy Spirit.

The above is already in my book, "The Antichrist God's Version" written by Elias with the technique to get the older women to demand the clergymen resolve marriage issues not Adam or a man in a divorce court. You can understand how well the Antichrist have eyes to see and ears to hear as this was issued to the Antichrist at the Vatican and many other locations of various denominations back in the year of Our Lord 2004 AD. If there had been a true church of God, the above would be in favor. Had the church developed the above in the year of Our Lord 1900 AD, divorces would not be common as today or possibly non-existent in the USA. How well has the church progressed over the last one hundred plus years? The Holy Bible states for the United States 1776 plus 124 equal the year of Our Lord 1900 AD. In the year of Our Lord 1900 AD in New York City to today the church has gone backwards and the wax is cold. The nation of the year of Our Lord 1900 AD was a land of love and marriage and the federal government was zero dollars in debt. Gone backwards means the clergymen have made love and marriage and everything else worse. They will tell you if you ask that they are doing a great job, but God told them the truth.

The senators of the United States and equivalent in other countries are to listen to our angels. Well the fallen angels are children with the women or women trying to raise children without the advantage of a husband and usually in poverty. Do you believe our senators are listening to the children in the orphanages? Do you believe the Pro-life churches are listening to the children in our orphanages? The children are to be special or doubled blessed by the government and church. Many children of divorced parents will react against society and yet the divorce rate of the American family is the same, whether you go to a church or not. Where in the congregations of America, do you have a strong commitment of father raising good sons? Boys are harder to rise than girls and the boys fill our prisons from poorhouse holds led by women. President

William J. Clinton wrote a law that the Federal Government could find the men for child support in the late nineties. If you have to ask the average American church to be involved, you should believe in your blasphemy mouth of the clergymen as defined by God in the Holy Bible. How well do you believe our politicians are helping the children avoid the jeopardy of divorce and avoid becoming fallen angels? Have you heard of one hundred thousand gang members of our poor American children under the foolishness of Presidents Ronald Reagan and George H. W. Bush? They took money and jobs out of the poor neighborhoods. That will result in a great number of divorces without money and the challenge of mankind. How will the clergymen make the congregation rich? Well that is another chapter. How should the religious leaders teach the politicians to create laws that avoid penance (reincarnation or Perdition) of lust and the words stepchildren in government and business? In the church environment, the word stepchild is extremely bad for their workers unless there is a death. The clergymen can read the requirements of Israel and must obey. Therefore, the instructions of Israel apply for the church employees. They must be saints. The instructions for the congregation must be updated for John 3:16. Only a penance man can get off this world alive.

When you send an idea to a politician as a wish, they better put that in practice or they could lose their careers or worse. If the idea is wrong, they should explain why. The politicians of governors and kings with their senators and house members are in shackles. If the children tell the politicians to try to end divorces, they had better listen. Do not avoid the meaning in courts. The congregation will desire them to leave not become president of the United States for being against the wishes of the congregation. We the people of the United States desire the ultimate in taxation with representation. The following is an example, I created for this book of fear.

The Word Lust.

If I become the Watchman as prophecy foretells, the policy for the minimum standard of romance in the government locations shall be:

1. If a single man or woman starts a romantic relationship with a married person, the single person shall be fired for cause.

2. If two married people start a relationship, they shall be transferred and never be considered for a promotion within the next ten years. If the romance continues to a divorce, the employees must be downgraded.

3. Human Resources shall be involved with money of newly divorced children of parents to protect the children, even to the point of a commitment through college.

4. If a single person goes out with a peer, all is good unless a transfer is required.

5. If a single person goes out with a single boss, upper management shall report the relationship. A transfer should be required.

All work locations shall train their workforce, develop the follow up procedures for their location, and send a memo to congress to summarize. Do not allow the employees to be put in jeopardy. The government shall support marriage as a way of life. Sexual harassment shall result in down grade and transfer only, for the love of the children. The transfer may not be close to where the present job location is.

my signature

Email comfortinGod@mchsi.com

The above concept was sent to my Senator Barack Obama from the State of Illinois. The above would result in former

President William J. Clinton being required to fire his girl friend. The woman should just tell President William J. Clinton, "Do you believe I am an idiot?" President William J. Clinton's daughter would gain her dad and mom, without change. Mrs. Hillary Clinton would say nothing, because nothing ever happened. As the clergymen know, sexual harassment is confusion in the American courts. The clergymen are the lords in Lord of lords. To correct the problem I sent it to Senator Barack Obama. No reply was returned for the many ideas I gave him, except he stated he could not represent religion because of separation of church and state. Apparently as a legal professor, he did not know what that meant. The clergymen must study MOTHER OF INSPIRATION, FATHER OF PERSPIRATION. That means back in the days of Abraham Lincoln, only as president could he invite the Jewish religion into the United States, not congress. He can represent the one world government of the Holy Bible, as I know from scripture. The future politicians representing King Jesus Christ shall be trained and put in office by the clergymen and congregation. They cannot put demands of the clergymen in power through laws because the will of the people prevails. If the clergymen writes a book of the congregation desires called "wants" government must address the desires of the congregation and the will of the people prevail. The politicians will be taught by the church not to let the government steal our houses as Presidents Ronald Reagan and George H. W. Bush did under Supply Economics (bad for marriages); however, if the congregation wants the government to steal their house, it would be all right. No congregation member should desire a person to lose a house through bad government laws. Now God's will and the people's will agree. To date the senator has not tried to help American people with divorces. Should we consider a marriage only for the religions or do we allow a judge to marry people? Start with the view that the first marriage is in the best interest of our children, so define the public policies as such. In the church, they should promote the Holy Bible view only.

If they disobey the above, which could end with a divorce, they go into reincarnation penance. Only Our Gods on Judgment Day (the day you die) will you know when your penance is over. Our Gods will use reincarnation. The clergymen are to determine if the married man and single woman are saved and the answer for all is no. Now, no church in any land can marry the couple. Upon death, Our Gods will impose fear. The clergymen are to teach fear on the great and dreadful Day of the Lord or Good Friday. Only adults can attend. Children of 777 design are God's Children and cannot be judged with fear, but are granted mercy. They are the angels that shall be judged by spare the rod, spoil the child.

The above is much information, so a summary is required:

1. The clergymen are to determine if the couple is saved before the marriage. During the engagement period, a training course is to be developed by the million plus that represent the church. If a single man or single woman desire to marry the person they caused a divorce by the women in lust, the church leader must explain they are not saved and will end up with at best reincarnation. As the Holy Bible states, "Only a penance man can get off this world alive." Unless they are rich, they will not go the way of Satan. I will not cover all the variations.

2. The Italian Mafia cannot be married in a church as they are not saved.

3. The clergymen must set up a program to train the couples on the pitfalls of marriage, financial planning, and other topics before the wedding covering what the Body of the Church (the older women) feel is necessary.

4. The marriage license issued by the seven Holy Cities has across the top "What God put together, let no man tear asunder."

5. Much work is put into the sermons for the Holy Spirit Words, "For the love of God's Children" on how to avoid the Holy Bible view of divorce in marriage.

6. The clergymen become the marriage counselors.

7. On the great and dreadful Day of the Lord (Good Friday), the women learn about the fear of lust. Since all women are sisters, they do not desire to harm a hair on the head of their child or others. Even Hollywood makes the single women in lust foolish, when they murder them to get rid of them. The women should be trained a man committed is "Forbidden Fruit" not their new toy. No child of 777 design can attend on Good Friday, the great and dreadful Day of the Lord.

8. The couple should answer the question for Our Gods, "Are you ready for this union and are confident you are saved at this time?" The saints must judge the world. If the answer is no, they had better try harder. You wonder if the saints are saved if the answer is "no". The clergymen must not ask a question where the answer is no. Do not ask the question I wrote, but learn how to question without the answer being no. You could add , "Or is there more education required."

9. The people in government and business that love John 3:16 have developed procedures that enhance married life like above.

What is the role of our children prior to becoming an adult? Their number one challenge is through education to maximize their knowledge to make their future what they desire to work to achieve (inherit). The church has the 777 design and the Holy Spirit Words on, "A Nation of Dance for Teenagers." The church has created great songs like "I Should Have Danced All Night" and "Sweet Eighteen and Never Been Kissed -----------Seriously". The highly trained counselors have learned to get the top ten songs in America to be like sermons of meat where the Words of dance are meaningful to the teenagers and yet the songs are praise to Our Gods.

As the children dance the counselor may be asked by a sixteen-year-old girl, "My boyfriend appears to be applying his temptation my way. What should I do?" The counselor directs her to get the sheet music from the book store on "Sweet Eighteen and Never Been Kissed -------------Seriously", where she learned the advantage to her not to have a bundle of joy being raised to become a Fallen Angel of her future or to be less than what King Jesus Christ desires for her child. At the next church dance, the counselor sees the young girl talking too many of her friends to educate. He finally sees her alone to talk and the praises are to Our Gods is her view of her calling and calling beyond her calling.

The church dance for teenagers at the college level could be started as "Speed Dating" or a chance for a teenager to interview her classmates, the boys. The age is too soon to get married as teenagers, but the young adult women will desire a chance to pick from the men. On Sunday, the local church will have sermons for the teenage and college men only. The young men learn what it takes to be a man. Only the teenagers and men can go and they are granted a pass to the dance. The women have to pay. The favorite question the young women have is, "What have you learned?" Many older women would love their teenage boys to start college and graduate as engaged happy future leaders of America. Should their grand children be what they live for to see their future success?

The Ten Commandments covers lust, which explains the views of the clergymen, which they cannot violate. They will be judged by their Gods and since they seem to walk on water in comparison with the average family, they will qualify to populate as saints in the Holy Cities. They become a living example of a family in the church world. A man should understand the virtues of the Ten Commandments on his life before being ordained. Make sure he is fully trained in Church Laws (Moses laws equivalent in the church world) also. The price of failure for the future employee of King Jesus Christ should be well understood. Do not apply a list of must do for anything man can consider, because the price of failure is Eternal Death if the Holy Spirit Words cannot be taught through you. Do not make it impossible.

The Holy Bible states, if you are not reborn, you probably will not see the kingdom of God. That means the church has not formed. A person shall be reborn at the age of King Jesus Christ with the wisdom of the age in his mind. The women shall promote their biblical wisdom on lust is essential in the present environment. The congregation shall learn life is like a circle, but the word lust in woman is endearing for Here to Eternity. In the year of Our Lord "now" our King Jesus Christ stated I pity the women of suck and so do I. So, without religion of desire, the children cause the women to live a living nightmare or there is no hell like a woman scorned as no one cares for her child. Where are the fathers and children in Pro-life or divorces?

The prophecy for the church in creating the kingdom is to eliminate ninety percent of the divorces in twenty years and try harder. On the great and dreadful Day of the Lord (Good Friday), you teach your failure of only ninety percent. Once the kingdom is formed and you use the technique of the book, "The Antichrist God's Version" half the divorces will disappear over night. The Word of God and yours on lust and twenty years makes the goal of prophecy rather too easy to eliminate ninety percent of the divorces, but invaluable to all mankind.

Why should we get to a point where fear is only a word? The future to achieve great Grace is not one single woman would consider going out with a divorced man. If the clergymen only had a book, the penance of reincarnation of pain would not be our present future as we would have learned from Israel. As King Jesus Christ has stated there is no reason to change a word of the Old Testament. There is nothing to fear but fear itself, once Adam learns the evidence of his conviction and the truth will set us free, once we learn and understand our truths. The saints running the seven Holy Cities are to judge the world and as marriage counselors, may divorces by the year of Our Lord 2500 AD as a prophecy just disappear. Think and understand life is like a circle. Just because it disappeared does not mean it cannot reappear. Do not again sleep at the Altar as an employee of King Jesus Christ.

The religious organizations appear to have a problem with the above when they find a passage that states the will of the people prevail. Is it the will of the older women that a daughter of the church goes into penance because of temptation of the word lust? Is it grandmas will that her grand children live without a father or she never sees them again, because of her sons temptation. How could Our Gods impose their will on us when we do not like fear? On the great and dreadful Day of the Lord, the teachings are terrible, for the short run or thousands of years. Do you as a woman challenge all I have written above or what is in the Holy Bible as you have learned Satan cannot be saved and Pope John Paul II (Archangel Michael) was condemned to this world through reincarnation. No penance can be great enough for Pope John Paul II for what he did against our children. His penance is the fact he will never live in the true Heaven.

What are the religious organizations to do as King Jesus Christ was discussing the Sabbath and all the rules mankind made without totally understanding the future? In America we have heart attacks on Saturday and the people like having a new chance for more life. Should the clergymen address only virgin brides are saved or stay with the wisdom of Paul? You have to think of the will of the people and the people's will prevails. The beginning sermons should be what the desire of the mothers of the clergymen are for their grandchildren. Do not just create words without a foundation of truth. You open it up to women and ask what the ideal case should be through memos. Ask their views on what you have to teach to achieve their ideal views or a life one thousand times better than the end. I pity the women of suck and so should the Antichrists. With the questions in mind how can you justify fear and the will of the people prevail?

First you have the older women discuss what they need for their grandchildren. In the beginning, some may agree that divorces are good, but they do not desire their grandchildren to be raised as stepchildren unless their original parent or parents die. They should not believe orphanages are good in America. Parents of two are better. You are writing sermons of "For the Love of God's Children" and incorporating the view of grandma (Godmother) into your truths that are self-evident. The self-evident truths are reality that set us free from jeopardy in life. What if you just state your views and they disagree? If God is for you who could stand against you?

On the great and dreadful Day of the Lord (Good Friday), you learn about fear. Fear is the beginning of all wisdom (knowledge). Did you make them so afraid that they ran away? There is nothing to fear but fear itself. If the church develops the concepts and takes responsibility for being the sinners, you will find all that is left is love. If you do it correctly you should believe by the year of Our Lord 2500 AD, no single woman would go out with a married or divorced man. Life is like a circle where what goes around comes around. If you find the problem coming back, you had better review your works on the Holy Spirit words, "For the Love of God's Children".

What are the terrible concepts you have to teach on the great and dreadful Day of the Lord? In my previous writings, you forgave everything that came before in divorces in the

Age of Accountability. When you eliminated ninety percent of the divorces in twenty years or less your congregation, may through your works avoid the penance of divorces in the future and have a chance to go to the true Heaven. If we have a number of twenty million divorces in the United States and eighteen million will not begetting a divorce in the future, you can do the math in that only two million of the people will get a divorce. The eighteen million in penance will have a good life through reincarnation as you believe they are your congregation of the church. If you did not form the kingdom the clergymen would be responsible for the death of a trillion children plus as the Battle of Armageddon starts in the United States. Which world do you desire to live in?

What is the penance for the people that accept the new marriage license and procedures as I have written? When the church fulfills the prophecy of ending ninety percent of the divorces and try harder, the ninety percent through reincarnation go through good penance. Only a penance man can get off this world alive. So the penance you must explain is they are coming through a womb and they will have to have a good life. The penance is they will not get a divorce, the children (God's children 777 design) will be like good angels, they must have profitable careers, and will live in joy or a life must be better than the end or one thousand times better to go. A lot will depend on how the clergymen can inspire and how well the congregation desires to get the pain out of their lives. God's love conquers all and He will be the same today and all the days of our life. All that is required is His employees to eliminate their pride and teach by having the imagination of a two-year-old child or a great idea man. Have you watched a two year old playing with his toys and the imagination he has? You must create the stories of mystery and intrigue. My role is to copy the story of salvation out of the Holy Bible and grant you the wisdom of the seven thunders. Seven means an important plan from God; however, He has told us all things and when you read you will understand scripture you can achieve many miracles.

Chapter 7.   Developing the Words of the Holy Spirit.

The Holy Bible is very clear in its meaning to me of the words to be created for the Holy Spirit to speak through a church leader. In the book from Elias, "The Antichrist God's Version", Elias has used the technique from the Holy Bible to resolve my problem areas. Any church location could start to define an issue, create the sixth sense technique from prophecy and reform the other church locations on how to achieve. The information goes to the Holy City before you start the coordinated efforts when required. In addition, you can send to the Holy Cities and they will come to you with a man that has the words King of kings and Lord of lords or King Jesus Christ's christ. In a kingdom, that technique would be simple, as you talk to your peers in the church or love against all jeopardy. The church is required to turn all jeopardy into joy. Then when the story is behind you, you put the story to rest. In the present church environment, what stories have they defined is behind them. I have not heard of one.

What is the greatest failure of the church from the year of Our Lord 1900 to 2000 AD in the USA? They simply refuse to talk to each other as they did before the year of Our Lord 1900 AD. At that time, they were teaching about starting schools, and involved in the community. They worked in themes. They even had trained the rich women to teach their children about greed. Today, it is Baptist location against Baptist location as no one needs to seek help from the outside or can get total agreement as to what to teach. They appear to be jealous of the same denomination down the street. Since they are so smart, they have as the Antichrist failed themselves. They will not learn or listen except for their vision of religion, despite the entire USA and the world falling apart. I am like Paul in the Holy Bible and can understand reality and fantasyland. The clergymen are in denial as the Holy Bible states because of their blasphemous mouth, they worship Satan. That statement is true and all would say I have overcome Satan. Should the congregation ask them how? Will they just lie to cover up the shortcomings? One Antichrist, I have heard said King Jesus Christ will fight Satan in the state of Alaska. You have to think, what would be the purpose be for the words? Then you should ask why that is in the Holy Bible in the first place, if it is not important. If it will not affect us, you question why it is in the Holy Bible?

What does the Holy Bible state about the Adam that runs your church location? Some of the stories are so great, that if you could get to the very elect, all you would do is deceive. So all the preaching he does to convince you he knows it all, if he would develop a story to help people it would be wrong. Let us say in the year of Our Lord 2000 AD, he asks you for money for food in the United States. The Holy Bible with the shortage of labor, what should he teach? If you give the man the fish, he eats for a day. If you teach him how to fish, he eats for a lifetime. In addition, Jacob was justified for not selling his gold and giving it away for Ames for the poor; therefore, if we hired the right man in the White House, your preacher whore clergymen should not beg you for money. He never should beg you for money for anything. If he did, all he did was deceive you. The goal through job creation is one hundred percent employment for all people that can work and good paying jobs. In the year of Our Lord 2000 AD had the church formed God's Kingdom, you should close or sell all locations that distribute food! The federal government had two hundred and thirty two billion dollars surplus and seven years of "fat cows" at the beginning of the year. The government should divide the cows up for food wisely until we reach a mind is a terrible thing to waste. The church should give up the soup kitchens as the Holy Bible states you do not even know who is going there. That is the role of the government not church. Why is the Antichrist allowing all the deaths or children because of a famine (money)? It is because he refuses to form God's Kingdom and learn how to talk; therefore, any story he would teach you other than how he is going to implement the Lord's Prayer will always be wrong. Therefore, no matter what he tried to teach you, he is wrong. King Jesus Christ put the church in penance when they disobeyed in Israel. Adam without God is incapable of doing anything right. So one hundred percent of everything Adam is doing is wrong. The only thing that is right is the Holy Bible and it does not have to change if you translated into the right words for the first sixty-six books once we figure out what words shall be used. The Holy Bible is without error and our Gods have told you all things. Since the end is before the year of Our Lord 2016 AD or it all happens in one generation. One thing the clergyman has proven is the Noah's Ark Story is kind. God killed most of mankind and that story is kind in comparison to what Adam will achieve by his own failure again. You are not alive at Noah's Ark time; therefore, you would not have to live through the Battle of Armageddon. The end is close because of the pen.

I was at a conference at the North Love Baptist Church in Rockford, Illinois. They were having training on some of the most foolish ideas you can have, but it showed the mentality of Adam. I already had the solutions to the problems they discussed on food, gambling, drugs and other items in my book, "The Antichrist God's Version" or a book of miracles the church could implement if they form the kingdom and used the technique of the Holy Spirit to speak through them. He was a nonaligned part of the Baptist church, so he could not go to his upper management, state what program he had, and have the instructions send out to all Baptist and other denominations as in a kingdom. In addition, he did not have Christ (the Son of man) in the seven Holy Cities to develop one hundred percent of all he needed to teach. For a church except for collecting money, this was unusual. I will go through only one part of the program. I picked the one I did not have the Holy Spirit Words created to resolve. The one is on alcohol.

One item he started with was to beg for money and not develop the exorcist story, which grants the church the money. He stated at the meeting that twenty-five million Americans were in trouble with drugs and alcohol. As I wrote, my books give you a plan to over come drugs as the Holy Bible states drugs should only be taken for medical reasons only. Since that was already covered in my literature, let me describe alcohol only.

His plan and the others were to wait for the man to lose his job, lose his family, and his health so he could identify himself as having a problem or feel guilty. The Holy Bible already described the technique as life in Israel. If he only had a copy of the Holy Bible, he may have read what our Father and King Jesus Christ told us to teach. He is to serve wine in the church; therefore, since his story violated all the teachings in the Holy Bible, they would only fail. Once the man had nothing left, how would that church location achieve a life one thousand times better than the end?

You know what the Holy Bible reads for a man that refuses to let the Holy Spirit speak through him. If you go back to that location, he would still be failing himself and others. He would not change. I even granted him a copy of the first book from the book of Daniel written by Elias. What did I try but to send knowledge all over the USA? The memo describes the true action.

To all Church College Locations please forward.
DO NOT FAIL TO LET THE TRUE HOLY SPIRIT SPEAK THROUGH YOU.

A message from the true Elijah, the prophet. Elias is the man that King Jesus Christ sent to establish His Kingdom or Thy Kingdom Come in the Lord's Prayer.

I was at a conference at the North Love Baptist Church in Rockford, IL. Being the man from the true King Jesus Christ, I will give you information that Elias can do easily or the power of the Holy Spirit. My book "The Antichrist God's Version" will give you the true meaning in Chapter 17.

If you are still interested in being involved in learning from Elias, I will give you the secret of turning America into a form of Israel in terms of alcohol. You require the power of the Holy Spirit to be developed by the "Architect of the Future" or it is just me. Once the true church forms and the technique maybe can be taught through King Jesus Christ's christ.

HERE IS THE SEVEN-STEP PROGRAM OR SEVEN IS THE MOST IMPORTANT NUMBER IN THE HOLY BIBLE.

Step 1 First you define a problem. We do not use alcohol like the ones we read about of people in Israel. King Jesus Christ's mother requested He make wine before the right day to start. Can you believe that in America, King Jesus Christ has a requirement to have the criminals go through a wine party

235

at the church? Most Baptist clergymen would state we have enough problems with alcohol without starting more. Did the Baptist church lose the Holy Bible for the prophecy of alcohol in the conference? They desired to use the word guilty against people after they totally failed. The Baptist Church is to change jeopardy to joy as two of the words of the millennium.

Step 2 Have a very good idea man come up with a marketing idea or sixth sense. In my book, you have many words from the Holy Spirit in the use of sixth sense. There is a critical sense or common sense in six words. "Don't let Drink, Take the Drink." It is the same as "spare the rod, spoil the child" King Jesus Christ has given as an example. That example is defined in my book and it is not the Catholics Sisters using a ruler on our children or a father deriving pleasure from a spanking. Both of those examples are child abuse.

DON'T LET DRINK, TAKE THE DRINK.

Step 3 Find some clergymen that may be close and ask them to develop sermons for the Altar and test them in their environment.

Step 4 Have them work through the back room (not Altar, yes capitalize Altar) and develop the way. Before you find that the pleasure of a glass of wine is lost, you seek our Savior's solution.

Step 5 Provide the story of the Last Supper but as prophecy would state not to make your first one the last or call it Supper and use the technique in the Holy Bible as the format.

Step 6 Have all proven works sent to the students of a Baptist College to summarize like a graduate project.

Step 7 Have the Baptist College teach the ways of the Holy Spirit to talk through the clergymen until twenty-five million (legal and illegal) is down to none or you have the beer and wine of Israel. Do not forget gin (God's secret) for the right use.

During the seven-step program start a contest for the songwriters to give our Gods a gift of a song. The words must be written like the songs in the Holy Bible in modern terms being a song that can achieve for a new beginning. Start the opening with the drink to think of taking the drink. Next, you sing for the congregation where beer or wine for a wedding or conference is our way. Follow with the pleasure of the New Testament to give us a view of the church world. The last is the many tribulations (rewards) for the joy overcoming the jeopardy of losing for you the advantage of a drink in God's Kingdom and the meaning of His Kingdom. You know a drink is good for the tummy, but too much of anything, can ruin all good things.

The rest of the addictions are in the book, "The Antichrist God's Version" like food, illegal drugs, etc. As the Holy Bible states if you could get to the very elect (people that determine what is taught in the church) you would deceive. You had to wait for Elias, unless you shorten the days, which you did not. With your help in theory, one hundred percent of the Baptist leaders will be involved, but you should not ignore the other six church types.

You have the seven steps to develop the wisdom of the Holy Spirit. Should you joy in living in the true Kingdom of God forever and ever?

ARE YOU SURE YOU DESIRE TO ASK ELIAS WHO THE PRINCE OF PEACE IS in the year of Our Lord 2005 AD, if you form the kingdom? Elias needs to work for God is amongst us. Once you understand good and evil, you will be like Gods. Check the Garden of Eden to determine how all flesh must die or your Baptist leaders can be like Gods. Elias's book will make you like Gods or the saints to judge the world.

Chapter 8. The White Stone Story.

New hope for our families and the joy is for Our Gods to be thankful to you for the millions of children's lives, you can change. Today there are thirty thousand unnecessary deaths a day in the world. With your help, ten thousand or more a day could end in a few years. God states to stop sending Him little ones small and great.

I sent the following to my senator or Senator Barack Obama in the year of Our Lord 2005 AD. What he sent back was he could not represent religion. Later in his campaign, he stated there was no cry from the people to end the war. He could not bring what is below to the leaders of religion for them to pursue or the clergymen that represented the poor at the Democratic Convention in the year of Our Lord 2004 AD. They desired to end the war. Talk to Rev Jesse Jackson or a person that gave foolish Obama a chance for eternal death and he desired to win the presidency as scripture defined as the eighth beast. He should have been trained by God through the church and develop the right heart, but he would not listen to Elias or Elijah. As a senator, he can achieve some governments are taking us on the road to hell. He is in shackles and allowed the following to happen without understanding of how economies work.

Senator Barack Obama just came back from his review of the wars America started. He did not do well in Iraq as I saw in July 22, the year of Our Lord 2008 AD. His views on Afghanistan are he must become a dragon and killer like Senator John F. Kerry. They are for political, not spiritual views. Since Senator John F. Kerry was and is like the False Messiah, he cannot be saved. Senator Barack Obama will go the way of Senator Kerry and he and his wife cannot be saved. The church must stop their continuance of being the Son of Perdition. They must tell the people the truth. You cannot end the terrorism in Washington, DC, where the politicians refuse to live in the city, by going to foreign countries. American selling drugs to Americans is funding the war. You beat terrorism with hate and joy as defined by Our Gods. All I can do is fire the Republican party of Washington, DC and Senator John F. Kerry and Barack Obama. Maybe Senator Hillary Clinton was blessed when she lost. God save the Queen of the South.

Senator Barack Obama

I believe you have an ally in Washington DC that you may not be aware. See the enclosed email I am going to send to countless number of churches. I cannot afford to wait since our salvation is at stake.

If you read my book, you should realize through the Holy Bible, God has granted us an economy that never ends. I have copied the principals in my book and expanded on them. You should have heard of Supply Economics of Friedman from the University in Chicago. The Holy Bible has that as near the end times (the year of Our Lord 1992 AD), we had abandoned buildings all over America. The theory was you give the money to the rich and we prosper. Well, that is just fools gold. Now, President George W. Bush is doing the same thing. If you know an economist like Alan Greenspan, you may give him a copy and ask his view. The United States through congress can end all poverty in the church world and other religions. Since I copied it out of the Holy Bible, I know it works.

What the Holy Bible states is to create an economy that will never end or I have called Consumption Economics. You can trust the principal as you spend your way into prosperity if the laws are good; therefore, as congress solves the social ills of the country the economy expands. You should remember the Democrats' economy of the year of Our Lord 2000 AD, eliminate the government waste, and define a problem that I covered like health care. As you solve the problems in health care as I defined you will achieve Universal Health Care for the entire country. What a glorious time to serve humanity or you can listen to foolish George Bush.

I believed you were a man for peace like Howard Dean. I caught up with Governor Howard Dean in Wisconsin. If my publisher would have met the dates he maybe president today and the war never started. The rules to start the war or not was covered in the book Life of US (U.S.). I covered the concepts from cheering his reelection of Hussein to total elimination of all human life in the country. The only answer any church leader would try to hear is to cheer is reelection since they must represent the Prince of Peace, themselves.

Try to get Senator Hillary Clinton involved since I was in contact with the Clintons and former Vice President Al Gore. Former President William J. Clinton could still be invaluable to you.

---

email to many churches and attachment to above. The Holy Bible states to repeat important issues so I made the below a separate chapter.

The following was sent to Senator Barack Obama, so he cannot deny, he did not know. This is exactly what Reverend Jesse Jackson and the poor churches were looking for in the campaign of the year of Our Lord 2004 AD. You remember Rev Jesse Jackson and probably the others representing the poor where disappointed when foolish Barack Obama explained his foolish ideas on how to create peace. Former President William J. Clinton had the peace dividend in place, but when he became rich, my opinion of him changed greatly.

The White Stone Story.

Email from Lawrence E Couch Office of Justice and Service Archdiocese of Washington 301-853-5343.

The House of Representatives will vote on a package of budget cuts tomorrow: Thursday, November 10, 2005. The bill is a compilation of budget-cutting proposals passed by several House committees over the past two weeks. The House bill could result in low-income and vulnerable people losing access to health care, etc.

He is telling me to support his efforts to overcome the Republicans in the House of Representatives that will hurt our families by eliminating the money to overcome the social ills of the country. They do not have the money. He should just write "The White Stone" story and request all religious locations to teach. Yes, even the ones beyond the church like a temple.

You as a preacher may have agreed that we should start a war as conquers as stated in the book of Romans. As a teacher, you would develop the gospel stating the book of Romans is when the United States is run by another beast called a crown leader (Red Dragon). What happens is no flesh is saved (John 3:16), we worship Satan, and recreated the Roman Empire equivalent in the United States. The wars and Hollywood have made our children violent as you believe Rome was. A big difference is swords, now are guns, wow. Any country that does not properly raise their children has no right to exist. Can you as a religious leader believe in a Hollywood movie where the women of the United States taught our men reality?

This memo describes a public opinion form that only women can be involved. They are King Jesus Christ's Educators (woman of suck) and they should teach our foolish men. God states in the Holy Bible that in the new millennium, the Arabs will be hated above all others. You beat terrorism with hate and joy, not hell of killing wars. You can read the news what happens and you should teach what happens, when you try to overcome terrorism with hell on earth. All we have accomplished is we made al Qaeda stronger. You teach that you represent the King of Peace and our story of salvation requires you to obey God. You make terrorist fools. What you are doing is from the Old Testament, where Our Father required Israel to do public opinion polls. When the church doing public opinion polls, the congregation learns of their will. That is still a requirement of the church. I believe waiting for the results is Joy in the church. You can make a big difference if you are a grandmother to help your grandchildren.

Please teach not to let the dragon steal that woman's child (John 3:16 helps to understand the word "steal" that God used). You should use the words from your Holy Bible. Please remember that King Jesus Christ was the Prince of Peace you must obey. Now, He is King Jesus Christ and the clergymen become the Prince of Peace. Do not impose your will on the congregation or they may write a law against you like in the late sixties. A public opinion poll or did you lose due to a war and a law in the late 1960s. Please do not lose again. Use the power of our Gods wisely.

Why did King Jesus Christ use the word "stone"? In Israel, His Father used the power of creation to feed the children of Israel in their penance march. They learned but more lessons were required. Our Father used the power of creation to feed many. What did He promise the clergymen through the Devil? The meaning is when I will not when you forsaken my children, small and great, return with the food or turnstones into food.

What should be on the form when 1.4 million Americans fell below the poverty level in the year of Our Lord 2004? Can you get the congregation to stop the parents that the Republicans are forsaking? They need you to kill and only a penance man can get off this world alive. Damn, you mean you require the women to teach you reality. Mercy shall follow us all the days of our lives. Why not add to the public opinion form to add money to the impoverished at the rate of part of the saving of the war. I will state, for your convenience, all children below the poverty level receive $50.00 a month the first year and $100.00 the second. You allow a maximum of granting American children a gift for the first two only below nineteen years old. Congress will have to figure out the saving and you shall love, but not complain about the real numbers. You remember it is not your view as a clergyman but the women of your congregation and future voters. A woman will not ever vote for a dragon and if he raises his ugly head, the will demand the church cut off his head by the Angel of Death and shove his body under the Altar. You have turned stones into food. The Holy Spirit words or sixth sense is "Let us turn stones into food". Now, you are obeying King Jesus Christ in Joy by implementing a prophecy "The White Stone". Use the concept of the Last Supper, which in prophecy for you is "The Supper". Do not say you are too small to get twelve of your friends together to help the American children.

243

PAGE 2

Public Opinion Form

Column 1
hell on earth

Column 2
Money for
daily bread, schools, and health care

identification of the woman   identification of the woman

May a billion plus women take the poll! May women never want in a church and learn about the other miracles being run through a church.

You could put the poll on the web or make individual forms for your church and input the results. You remember your sermons are very important to create one view, one voice, one way.

Letter to Al Gore is below as I was trying to get him to be President of the United States in the year of Our Lord 2004 AD. You can read my analysis of the year of Our Lord 2000 AD debate in my books.

June 1, 2004

The Office of the
Honorable Al Gore
2100 West End Avenue
Nashville, TN 37203

RE: Unconditional Surrender and the Children

If you read my book Life of US (U.S.), you have to realize a war with Iraq is only led by fools. God is waiting for a passage to come true. Peace on earth, good will towards man. What does that mean???????????

The leaders of the church are waiting for the politicians to provide a clue. They need to represent the Prince of Peace. The politicians provide the words peace on earth (the peace plan) and the clergymen are gatherers and do sermons on their discoveries until the will of the people understands.

Why would a planner need a great leader like Al Gore to commit to unconditional surrender in Iraq? Why would the Pope desire to teach all religious leaders of the church to listen and understand they represent God and His view is peace on earth? The clergymen only ponder. I can teach you how to do it, if you know how to do it or read my book Life of US (U.S.).

1. Some governments are taking US on the road to hell. Where is John 3:16 in the USA?
2. Many soldiers I call U.S. soldiers are soldiers of misfortune and will die.
3. A Puppet Government will form, will it last three days as before?
4. Cost of the war is $200 billion plus each year. Will ten years be short and three days later, all is lost?
5. Why were we so foolish to start the war, read Life of US (U.S.)?
6. If we put the original leader in place, stability in the region will occur.
7. Why would other governments decide to start a war, when penance is great?

How would the religious leaders find joy in the story of unconditional surrender? Since we destroyed over $600 billion of their valuable infrastructure, we should pay to replace. The church should love America in penance for hundreds of years for the foolishness of President George W. Bush and the politicians that felt compelled to go along for political reasons. I know Al Gore selected Howard Dean for president and he was against the war. If you read my book, God was against all wars like the First World War, the Second World War, etc.

How should the penance go forward? Well for each barrel of oil, we pay 1.75 times the price. Their government determines how it is to be spent like for an American style hospitals, GE power plants to replace what he lost for Americas foolishness, and do not forget the military to defend against the Turks and Iran. May the next power that starts a war go into penance for two hundred years even if their families suffer! The church should review and take John 3:16 very seriously. Only a penance man can get off this world alive.

What should Al Gore expect Pope John Paul II to do since he was against the war? The church should develop the twenty-five page book as described in my book Life of US (U.S.) which is a prophecy. Whenever government official talks about peace like the peace dividend the clergymen as gatherers teach in all required locations and consider a rod of an Almond Tree as a tribulation to the king involved. The Dove Politicians win elections all over the world and the War Lords or Hawks and dragons like President George H. Bush we disregard. What they say is not heard of importance unless they have the words in my book and leaders of Iraq do all the terrible things, they have been accused.

What Pope John Paul II would be interested in is another prophecy. He should look up the words on the Rainbow from the Holy Bible and then my words on the Goldilocks Economy in my book. He should be interested in God's way, which is to consume to prosperity. The Republicans are a party of greed and hell and could not succeed. See the prophecy of Millstone and two names and in the year of Our Lord 2000 AD, there is one left, which is George Bush. God is against George Bush so the only man running in the year of Our Lord 2000 AD in America was Al Gore. Not one woman can vote for a beast or a mass murderer of children from Texas.

An example of spend to prosperity is in my book under Double Tax on Dividends. The party of greed gave the money to the rich wicked and created very little consumption. Let us take the opposite view if we want to expand the economy. We give $25 billion to the poorest children in the United States. The family of $16,000 or less receives $2000.00 per child and someone close to $25,000 receives $200.00 per child. We ask the poor to spend the money as quickly as possible. They spend, their neighbors work overtime or are hired and they spend. It should be reviewed like what an economist uses for the banking industry or job creation theory. You end up with a multiplier effect and could be like the four to one multiplier as in the banking example. In this example, the growth of the economy could go by 60 to 100 billion dollars. At $100 billion, what did it cost the government? Maybe they made a profit or received more than $25 billion in return. So the prophecy is waste not want not. $25 billion given to the wicked is government waste, but satisfying the wants of the children is God's miracle and part of the Rainbow. Please joy. Vice President Al Gore through President William J. Clinton eliminating the sorrows of our land produced the greatest economy in modern times.

You and Pope John Paul II should propose a meeting between you two. You were God's choice in the year of Our Lord 2000 AD and still are the best-trained person the reestablish God's Economic Model. It is very critical to the survival of the world and the Church. No Icon has a greater calling than you, Al Gore. If we vote for the Republicans, we go back to penance for the clergymen not obeying God and two thousand years is very short. God comes back with the Seven Horns of the Eternal Temple or we start the story of Israel again.

The cost of health care. A question would arise if we eliminate the crime syndicates and the cost of caring for God's Children. Could the Pope receive a statement that we consider the rights of our children not to bring Crack Babies into our country more important than the right of the crime syndicate leaders? Could Al Gore find some Supreme Courts judges that believe in no rest for the wicked? They have to leave our country or change led by the FBI. The prophecy is true and God asked us not to harm a hair on a child's head. I believe that children have all rights and the crime syndicates have none. No right to the true Heaven or no right to walk anywhere is this world.

President George W. Bush talked about a strong military. Well, God would call that government waste. The reason we start wars is we cannot talk. The world is still a cruel planet so our military has to continue. You might think about explaining a possible venture with Great Britain, Russia and the United States were we could reduce the cost but still have a powerful force. I know how to do that, as it is a prophecy. May we never use it unless there is no choice?

by Richard
Literary name Author of Life of US (U.S.)
And the next book Voice of Vengeance - Fear (now the sixty- seventh book of the Holy Bible)

Please do me a favor. I will continue sending out the letters until you let me know you receive the overview.
email me at comfortinGod@hotmail.com
END OF LETTER

I remember from a meeting you (Senator Barack Obama) attended in Rockford that you taught law school. God calls our courts the land of chaos and confusion, the man with the gavel. In my books, I solve those obvious problems. Our role in the whole world is to teach the courts how to judge. In history, our Founding Fathers did not know how to write laws for the New Testament. If you do not know, you can read how to do it. If I succeed the way, the Holy Bible states, you may end up designing a course on how to teach future and present attorneys how to be prepared to live in God's Kingdom or Thy Kingdom Come.

I have a long history of trying to help American children.

Elias (like from Mark 9:12)

Author of "Life of US (U.S.)": a book that forms God's Kingdom (Lord's Prayer)

Author of "The Antichrist God's Version": a book of God's miracles that people would say cannot be done like ending all poverty. (ADDED)

Present writing Voice of Vengeance – Fear: a book that takes books like the book of Revelation and turns it into present day reality.

email comfortinGod@hotmail.com

First two books published listed on www.iuniverse.com and other locations.

As King Jesus Christ has written in the Holy Bible that my books contain good detail.

What has happened in America since our elected officials did not understand how economies work and the Republicans only chance to win is "Read my lips, no new taxes." as their marketing plan from the year of Our Lord 1992 AD. President George H. W. Bush used those words. His son used, "I defy anyone to raise the taxes and improve the economy" in the year of Our Lord 2004 AD. In the year of Our Lord 2008 AD, the words are let us reduce the taxes on corporations, etc as the standard of living decreases and the wealth creation of the country falls.

In the year of Our Lord 2006 AD, again they removed more money to help solve the social ills of the country and spent more money overseas, which does little for our economy in comparison for example of fixing our roads. We end up with high inflation, more problems overseas, our friends turn against us here and abroad. Can you believe politicians have the right heart, when they cannot agree to provide American children with health, wealth, and education (wisdom)? The answer is more bombs and failure to represent the God of Heart. I believe in more penance for Americans unless we reform.

The political leaders left great Marks of the Beast by violating the book of Mark. The one example I will use is Domestic Tranquility was reversed tremendously as violent crimes doubled in one year, in the year of Our Lord 2007 AD. I heard that on television but cannot verify. Now more prisons and more taxes are the answer. I cannot hear any plans that will work. The Holy Bible has the only answers.

What shall we do, but let the women's voice be heard above all others. I heard the women of Russia state they would not have followed the foolish paths of man before the year of Our Lord 1989 AD. I believe the documents of history may be part of the movie. The women are King Jesus Christ's educators to teach the younger women that their sons are not for Adam to kill in worthless works of man. The movie profits shall be used to create a wing in the Holy Cities museums and more. Above the door must be, "A War to End All Wars". Inside you see the beautiful painting and libraries so the young men in the year one thousand zeros can understand the background and reason for Adams and Eve's good works in God's name. May Adam learn the power of true Gods! Without God, Adam is just a fool.

Chapter 9.   The Terrible Swift Sword.

In the year of Our Lord 2900 AD, the most terrible of all events that could happen actually happened. The police of a country found a child that died in the mud of despair. One child is dead in a country of this world. One child is dead and the police department is so afraid. We do not run out to the news. We love the Vow of Silence for respect of the view of the families as first concern. There is no advantage to the blame to come back on the five o'clock news, as there is no hope in that view. So the religious leaders have convinced the world, the love for the family in mourning is more important than the foolishness of this news as an item for all to hear; however, the police have troubled looks upon their faces as they report to their religious leaders. The blood of a just man to end the Black Plague, the word blame has resulted in the Vow of Silence to be in power. Can you as a loving human being see the unnecessary death of one child somewhere in the church world as the greatest tragedy of the time? King Jesus Christ has taught us through the church, "I do not want a hair on a child's head harmed." The child is dead. How? You use your imagination. What should the church do?

One version is to immediately create fear in the world by demanding all safety procedures are retested because one has waken up the concerns for the year of Our Lord 2008 AD to reoccur, where the people do not give a damn. It is just one child among the millions that die unnecessary deaths. The leaders of the Holy Cities, do not need to go backwards again as they did in America from the year of Our Lord 1900 AD to the year of the "Age of Accountability" in the year of Our Lord 2000 AD. If they try this technique, what will happen? The will of the people may not prevail as they question the blame on the congregation. So how can the seven Holy Cities go forward if that procedure is not in favor? You should review the laws for the lawless ones, the clergymen.

The church should start the six words of common sense for the congregation to learn. I will use words from old or "For the love of God's Children". You address all the good as gifts the children have received in church such as education and others. The clergymen question the news to review the glad tidings of your world today. Get the public opinion to be to address the future they desire to inherit. You state the leaders of the seven Holy Cities are to address the congregation in thirty days and question all as to what the tidings could be. Ask them to use the words like Jacob where he said, "I guess my name is Israel." The leaders take the writing of good tiding of guesses as a view of where they stand in terms of society in general. You hear good deeds and quote "no bad, maybe", but you are gatherers of the news and have your young students in the ministry to summarize the tidings.

The day of fear comes out as the governments did nothing of importance. The seven leaders bring out the "Terrible Swift Sword". They report to the adults what occurred that a child died in the church world somewhere in the mud of despair and tell the government officials what to do. The women are demanding it once they learn. The government officials put their heads together and some have a great concern for cost. To review and strengthen all may cost the world three quarters of a trillion dollars. They desire to meet with the church heads.

The meeting is set as a world news event. The leaders of the seven Holy Cities are granted their rightful place in the conference center of the United Countries. They are announced and properly presented. Government representatives ask the questions of cost and wants of the women. All seven arise and state, "DO IT!" and leave without talking. Three quarters of a trillion dollars is just money, but a child's life is lost.

Back in the various church locations, the congregation is hearing all the glad tidings over the year of Our Lord 2000 AD. They recognize the differences and the women understand they do not desire to take one-step backwards, when it comes to a woman's child. The Holy Bible will be reviewed on the passages and what was achieved on the great and dreadful Day of the Lord, next year. The passage is, "If you (government) fail to blow the trumpet and one person dies, I will take you by the hand."

What else shall the congregation provide in information of interest to the clergymen? How about the example of a secret military build up in one hundred thousand years or back in the Second World War. The Germans were preparing for war. The new soldiers were trained to report all the secret military build up to the kingdom of God and shouted from the highest rooftops. The words would flow back to the seven Holy Cities. The church prepared for the Terrible Swift Sword. All information of the secret build up was released to the public at the Altars and to all news that was interested in presenting. The Holy Bible states the people shall shout the information from the highest rooftops. Many sermons were developed. No, it did not happen in the past, but let us go to the future and life is like a circle. War of hell on earth will become fantasyland, not reality, because killing wars cannot happen. The hostilities are discussed as to why the build up and the politicians become fools. All the people of that country are out to seek new direction and the start of a new bad beginning is ended. Can you believe secret information on taxes or marketing plans, just to win elections?

Can you believe in an organization out to change the views of the people because the politicians do not learn or listen? All secret organization like PAC (Political Action Committees) or terrorists that desire to use power to persuade people to do what is bad for their societies shall learn from the voice of logic. Where are the effective organizations like the Chief Financial Officer or a man with a gun of a crime syndicate trying to make his life worse upon his death? Their potential bad deeds shall be shouted from the highest rooftop and do not let those people leave. National television, FBI, IRS, or other correct voices are necessary.

A possible war between India and Pakistan was in the news. If we had a kingdom, all-military information would flow to the church and temples. The soldiers of misfortune that will kill or be killed have reported all information to the religious order. A day of declaring the start of the war occurs by the political leaders. Instead, the military personnel of the Red Dragon abandon their stations and go to church or temples. The news is released and all responsible like President George W. Bush and the Republican Party in Washington DC as being the same were arrested and replaced. We as a country did not need them to lose their Souls. The clergymen are to write a book of twenty-five pages on the Rules on Stealing Land. They will continue to teach as they go through "Holy Spirit Possessions" or Chapter 9 of my first book. A war is impossible to start in a land where the nation of the church has formed, as the children (the angels) are the peace keepers, not the military.

How about cigarettes being sold to minors? The children have been trained to report illegal incidences to the church personnel, so the children do not get hurt. They cannot sell drugs, cigarettes, alcohol, and illegal legal drugs like steroids. The Terrible Swift Sword is not used for smaller items, but in a city like Chicago, the Passover Story of the Holy Bible may put a gas station or other types of businesses in bankruptcy court when illegal operations are granted our children and pain is started in our families. Even Wal-Mart will not be able to sell a shoelace if they try to overcome the educators of our church the women. Do not let the old ways of ignoring come back in the locations that are to have eyes to see and ears to hear. You train the children, when they let you know they are not "Rats", but people helping people to a better way of life. You can appreciate the Supper Story when it comes to items like above, where the clergymen can call on their peers to develop the strategies. Have you heard of members of the congregations getting a bargain on auto parts that maybe stolen or people offered jobs to steal cars for parts? The Holy Cities are always informed. We the people must use knowledge of what is bad to convert into good. How could a world function without a kingdom? We have the Noah Ark story and the story of penance of Adam. Adam without God is just a fool. The world requires the church employees to take God seriously and not invent their own or Adam's view of religion. Religion is a way of life and the Holy Bible in a kingdom will always result in a perfect way of life. May a thousand zeros of life in God's Kingdom be a short time!

The church must develop parables where they find the government trying to serve two masters. The rich (Republicans) are serving the rich at the expense of the poor. Now is a time to document and add to the Standing Historical. You should not serve a master at the expense of another. The Holy Bible states the problem near the end times is the problem with the rich. If you serve the poor, the results could be like in the late 1990s where the rich stated, "I made so much money. Do I have to pay taxes?" The answer from the Holy Bible is, "You never give people money that cannot use it wisely."

I will bow to the religious leaders to be gatherers of parables for the Whistle Blowers as defined. May any wicked person not lose their rights over what the church will define as foolish logic or the lawless ones are the clergymen that cannot end crimes. The FBI should be allowed to enhance the Italian Mafia's lives to a better way of life or may the Catholic priests help defend through the use of the Terrible Swift Sword the God Fathers, children lives, and their futures as eternal death of the clergymen.

Chapter 10. Greed

With the wealth of the rich that are living well and creating hell in countless families, how could you understand the judgment of the rich and the word greed? The rich are in shackles (wicked) and cannot go to heaven. The best the rich can achieve is reincarnation to become poorest child in that country. Therefore, you can look forward to the poorest children in your country and see the rich man of the past. King Jesus Christ gave the example back in Israel when the rich man requested to be a disciple. First, you must sell all your gold. The average rich man of today would not desire to become poor. Now the clergymen must sell all their gold before becoming an employee of God. Today the clergymen would teach sell all your gold, but not let Jacob be justified. Back in the era before the year of Our Lord 1900 AD, the rich children were in general trained by their mother to share his gifts. The church worked in themes.

Many opportunities are gone in the United States as we have created corporate structures that have great financial strengths to develop technology and produce product. The individual creating a General Motors or a food chain like the Jewel food stores is hard. The vast majority of people would be better off living in dynamic corporate structures or small businesses where intelligence and hard work are to be rewarded.

Humanity places value on the stocks of corporations. In the year of Our Lord 2008 AD, it is possible for a man to earn a billion dollars in one day by the fruits of the labor of the workers of a corporation. Much work is still required by the interest free loans individuals can make to corporations to raise money through selling stocks. In the year of Our Lord 1820 AD, we read the Holy Bible and developed the technique in the United States. In the year of Our Lord 1860 AD, President Lincoln talked about the tremendous wealth creation in the United States because of interest free loans or stocks. That period must be defined in Standing Historical as the potential of the Holy Bible and the laws of liberty. The clergymen have to teach the power of greed to over come the shackles of the rich man. We have been granted a starting point in my literature of a definition of the dollars required to be rich. We will learn the new supply and demand curves based on Consumption Economics, where greed will reduce supply. The future will teach the average person to demand the government tax inheritance money, as the Holy Bible defines. King Jesus Christ has promised to take care of the greed. We have the beginning of tax laws against greed in salaries and stocks in King Jesus Christ's plan for the one World Government of Israel that you can copy out of the Holy Bible. The country must understand the value of a new tax to control inflation is important. I have given you the concept of reduced expenditures on the people by the year of Our Lord 3000 AD of income or over two hundred thousand dollars a year. The concept of the reduction in government consumption in the beginning is new. The rich man will be very interested in the sacrifices required when the advantage to his future through reincarnation is understood.

The above sounds simple, as I have granted you the salary of a doctor in the year of Our Lord 3000 AD; however, it is not that easy for man to achieve. Much work in reviewing the present, past and future is required. You have many interesting examples in the past of technology replacing workers. Much work is required to achieve this as a goal without the worker losing the value and challenge of his calling. He will define the problem if displaced by technology and you must expect the government and industry to respond (react) if the problem seems to occur over night. You cannot let the unions run into greed, as their executives are in shackles. The parable about General Motors or the steel industries of America are essential to learn and understand. May the politicians not fall asleep at the creation of seven year law plans (laws of liberty again).

Let us start with a labor/management problem of union workers versus a strong balance sheet of all corporations. What should be the role of a union in a society where a shortage of labor is a constant threat to the salaries of the workers, their bosses, and the consumers (congregation) that rely on them? We should all be interested in our future for a new beginning of life at the end of our present life, so we desire to learn. Today a union may come in with demands that exceed what the corporations can do and the corporation offers something they might believe the union will not agree to. Sometimes we stand in picket lines and our families and the economy can suffer. The Holy Bible had King Jesus Christ go to a court, so we learned how to run a court. He who cannot do must teach, so the Scripture Attorneys go to a court to resolve the issues. That is not today, but the words "Scripture Attorney" sounds exciting.

In our example, I will repeat what former Vice President Al Gore stated in the year of Our Lord 2000 AD election that Canada was scoring jobs in the courts. The labor agreements have expired and the money and benefit issue is up. In the Chapter "The Seventh Trumpet Story", we may have learned the clergymen are the lords in the Lord of lords. The judges are trained per the Holy Bible to be justified by grace, not law. I will stop, as the future has not been defined as well as we would like, so this is harder than what we say it should be. The labor union believes they are under paid and the company is making to little money. The prices are to low. The company and union have a real problem on their hands. The judge is ready for the information.

He decides he wants to listen to the Scripture Attorneys on the labor union first. He starts with a question, "You teach me about the financial strength of the corporation and how it compares to similar industries." One of the major roles of a union is to monitor the corporate books to guarantee the corporation is financially secure and the workers are not to pay a tremendous price to bail out the corporation. We started with our desires and we do not need management to fail us. The role of the employees is to satisfy the customer demands. The customer is to satisfy the corporate leaders in terms of money. The corporate leaders have learned from the Holy Bible, we think more of the paycheck then the sheep or the product we make. Once money is good, then the customers are more important than our bosses financial reward or stocks. The stockholders like the House of Representatives like strong balance sheets.

The next issue is for the corporation to present their employees demands for workers and is there any potential surpluses or shortages to satisfy the customer demand. They learn the demand is higher than they can satisfy and the amount of workers they can attract is less than supply demands. The judge desires to hear the status of similar industries in the country. He calls in the House of Representatives and the Scripture Attorneys define the problems. The House of Representatives is in charge of a strong balance sheet for all industries, but the judge sees this problem starting to be like the Airlines of old. The House of Representatives, Federal does a total review, forced raising prices and salaries are put into law, and justice prevails as new laws of liberty are developed. We the people love the price increase as explained because the future children of ours will have a life they love and more products will be available.

King Jesus Christ has built judgment into scripture. Who would qualify for, "He who judges shall be judged." The judge did judge. The executives fail to use the money to expand production. They knew the market was there. The labor union in the future takes demands and raises the workers income too high. The House of Representatives did not write a dynamic action plan law to review seven years later, the trust they gave to the story. Sometimes being a religious leader, you must guarantee you have taught the future politicians and judges the gift of trust in, "He who judges shall be judged."

You ponder the second way where money is not enough to add the desired production. The labor union within seven years files the case where the additional income will attract the workers, but no production factory is there. The judge will judge the House of Representatives, the executives, but not the labor union unless just cause can be understood. We must get to the root of the problem. Watch the word greed and remember, "A friend in need is a friend indeed" or the rich in this story are in shackles. The laws are for the executives and congress. The people in shackles are the labor union upper management possibly until retired, the rich running the corporations, and the government. The House of Representatives planned a million more units of production. The company may file the case if a strong balance sheet will not occur. Greed can come from many sources and education would appear to overcome fear. The House had to add a minor amount and all was good.

The company in a mind is a terrible thing to waste and infinite demand can find temptation easy to consider, but do not even let go of the labor union that arranges a bigger union if labor costs are too low. Without the education of the church, an economy like the one the Holy Bible can produce is not possible. A mind is a terrible thing to waste and a person doing a job he does not want to do is stopping a country from creating a life one thousand times better than the end. The only difference is religion. Adam will always create a hellhole of his creation to live in without God. Through the Holy Bible, we can have a perfect way of life through worship of God. You understand the importance of worshipping God and why the Holy Bible states it the way it does.

The government can have assurance the dynamic action plan of New Testament law will work. The only statement we should understand is the company and the workers are beyond the curse of the law. Why would the company not want to expand production and pay additional salaries required to attract the right talent in a shortage of labor. The court should plan a follow up. The politicians have used this example for the religious leaders to train future politicians. All is good. Well, that is not true yet. There is nothing to fear except fear itself. Adam is to smart to fail himself, but Adam will continue to try to fail. Until the one million additional units are being produced, the society is suffering for lack of consumption. Consumption Economics is not as easy as it seems. The individual states have to get involved to issue the various building permits and review the training for the schools. To reach the goal of I do not want you to do a job, you do not want to do many forces of society may come into play. Also new technology may be purchased for greater efficiencies and the number of new workers may be negative. The existing work force has to be presented with choices that enhances their lives not detract. Living and creating what we desire for all humanity or heaven on earth is a lot harder than writing a law like lowering the interest rates by three percent, see if the economy expands to absorb surplus people, and encourages the right production.

Do not fail to recognize what is required on the great and dreadful Day of the Lord if the above become something the rich do not take seriously. Without a call to action, a leader of the Holy City made find Archangel Michael as a theory to learn. As you accept responsibility, your reward can be great for society, but your failure is not what you desire. Living by grace is the greatest challenge man can seek. Man does not live by bread alone.

What is required on Easter Sunday is to learn the meaning of the word mourning. Grandma new arms and legs are thoughtful, but meat must include what the rich (wicked) are doing to return to this world through reincarnation through their preparing to become the poorest child in the country. The church is trying to define the greatness of the poorest child's life in your country because of the rich man's good deeds and sacrifices. The clergymen must study the Lord's Prayer and the reality of forgive the debtors or the American children are the greatest debtors in the entire world.

Chapter 11. The Seven Deadly Sins

Many individuals have been trained to memorize the Seven Deadly Sins. King Jesus Christ will take care of the sinners. How can a man reach for greed and end up with a deadly sin? If he is rich like the people running Exxon Mobil and earning four hundred million dollars a year, is that greed? The answer is yes but only the clergymen can have Cardinals and become sinners. Israel was a nation of priests; therefore, in the church world the clergymen are the sinners that must repent. They must have the heart of King Jesus Christ as clergymen to become saints to judge the world because they love the congregation. The Holy Bible states the clergymen have not identified the man of sin. As you read in the Holy Bible, King Jesus Christ will take care of the wicked, which is the rich by their personal fortune, today. The Exxon Mobil executives are rich, wicked, in shackles, and cannot go to the true Heaven. They are in jeopardy. The best they can achieve through reincarnation (new arms and legs) is to become the poorest children in their country. They are the friends in need are friends indeed and in jeopardy. What good deeds are they doing? I would say none. Why did King Jesus Christ develop the story this way? You can read and state when He told His friend to sell all the gold, the rich will not do that and that is not a good idea for all mankind. King Jesus Christ knows someone has to sacrifice for the good of mankind to have enough money that he cannot go to the true Heaven, but even in Israel, someone had to run the tools of production.

The Federal Senate had the executives of Exxon Mobil in their environment. Many people heard the words and deeds. The Democrats where trying to make a difference and the Republicans laughed at the Democrats. I heard people taking both sides. We the people ended up having to except the fact the executives could take any salary they wanted, up to a point. How is the church through the teachings of the Holy Bible going to make a change?

The rich cannot go to the true Heaven so at the end of their life at the best they will become the poorest child through reincarnation. King Jesus Christ made a point in Israel that the rich would not sell all their gold and give it to the poor. In Israel despite the greatness of Our Father's economy, some people where poor. The Roman Empire imposed a fifty percent increase in taxes (tithes) and that actually caused a woman to be poor but she could still afford to be a giver. If the Japanese of the Second World War won the war in concept in the year of Our Lord 2008 AD, could American business and individuals pay the fifty percent increase in tithing? You are earning forty two thousand dollars and have to send twenty one thousand dollars to Japan. The American economy would be destroyed. Many countries beyond Israel you found extensive lack of money under the rich of Rome.

We the people of world earth should take the government of Israel seriously. King Jesus Christ has promised to double the best economy Adam can create and I do not believe He hid it very well. It is the government of Israel, but they still had people that were rich. Did you hear of the Israeli man as being like the American executives and in greed? The answer is no.

What must the church start in the One World Government plan that I wrote from the Holy Bible? I will start a greed tax like Europe. The governments will stop spending new tax revenue if the economy grows to quickly, so the American families can continue to prosper from the economy of the Holy Bible. When the government cannot stop the inflation, a tax will be placed on the people of one million dollars of income and higher until the inflation and prices are good. A new economic model will have to be developed by the church to teach economics where you have infinite demand and what limits supply is the ability to produce. You get to increased prices without supply when greed takes over. For example, I heard the prices on houses in Las Vegas went up fifty percent in one year. You should realize the costs did not go up that fast.

When a clergyman reads to this point, he should realize King Jesus Christ needs the church to develop the Holy Spirit Words and if not done you can read what happens to the church leader. There is nothing to fear but fear itself, so I started the plan for you. In order to make the government work it requires you to be supportive and teach the congregation reality. We the people have to stop using fantasyland views in campaigning, where we blame and never learn. Why did Satan react? He did to win the American election in the year of Our Lord 2004 AD by Satan's Darts or the word blame. The clergymen will go by the way of Satan if they do not develop sermons that will end greed; therefore, they will not be able to overcome their deadly sins.

At the end of the Mysterious Messiah's thousand-year plan or of the year of Our Lord 3000 AD, the people earning over two hundred thousand dollars should be trained to cut back on consumption if the economy is too strong. A man like Bill Gates may buy ten new cars a year. Now, he will have to cut back to only three and keep the others for at least one more year; however, you can go buy the cars he did not. Today with that environment, the prices of cars would soar. That is why the doctors in the year of Our Lord 3000 AD desire to only earn two hundred thousand dollars a year, so the consumption of their family does not have to change. Money above that level has little value in their lives. The government has rules on inflation and a voluntary compliance avoids fear. There is nothing to fear but fear itself. If the Holy Cities must get involved, it is possible a large tax above two hundred thousand dollars will be imposed for your world to recognize the failure of your country. The Holy Spirit must and will speak; therefore, the Seven Deadly Sins are for the clergymen that must become the saints to judge the world. If they accept greed, they will go to Perdition with those in greed. We the congregation will realize all is lost and the end of civilization could occur; therefore, the clergymen must respond to the seven deadly sins of them for God's Plan to work.

In the church education centers, you will learn how to be a saint and how you are to judge the world. Much written instructions before you are ordained must be completed. Your continuing education by the clergymen you report through is ongoing. One day you may hold the book for your location. You should never be deceived. I have defined the seven steps in previous works to develop the Holy Spirit works as a new beginning. I will provide that memo in this chapter. If you fail yourself, you should resign and you sell shoelaces as a concept. You are waiting for your end.

An example of the Seven Deadly Sins of the church employees of King Jesus Christ is you are doing financial planning with the lower one-third income of the nation. May the women learn the advantage of a man that barely can take care of his wife and children! Along comes a new law you believe may improve the economy as far as the courts are concerned. Now, you find many in the congregation that cannot live within their means. It is apparent the government is taking you on the road to hell. There is no hell like a woman scorned. She cannot get daily bread, health care for her children, or education is from bad schools as define by her children. She believes her children's future is not one she desires her children to inherit. You as a clergyman will die of the deadly sins as life of your congregation became worse. You must send the information to your Holy City. You should not ignore the problem instead of becoming the Mother of Inspiration to retrain or replace the Fathers of Perspiration. It will become you versus them and may end with fear if you have to go that far with the politicians. Again, to repeat, if King Jesus Christ's employees refuse to help, their future as trained in the seminaries is their own failure. There is only one path if you fail to allow the Holy Spirit to speak through you to define a future the congregation would state is good or they desire to inherit. You must speak a future to inherit through prophecy.

An essential element of money is for the clergymen to teach what money means. Money (compensation) is a medium of exchange for the consumption you deserve. If you earn fifty thousand dollars a year for fifty years, you will earn two and one half million dollars. How does the average person compare with published salaries of greed? You buying a share of stock are a consumption item. The salary of Exxon Mobile executives was four hundred million dollars and that did not take into account investment money. If your consumption violates the rights of others within your society, it will be called greed. If the labor unions or executives develop a salary that is not justified by skill, the salary shall be called greed. Yes, the executives of the labor unions are in shackles and can go to Perdition if they have the power to make a big difference. Small associations should never consider holding their world up for more money than the job richly deserves.

I developed this story before Tiger Woods had a problem. I will retain. Let us grant ourselves a parable or a story that means the same. A story the congregation would love to hear on the day of learning mourning or Easter is the gift of John 3:16. Tiger Woods is rich because he will earn well over a hundred million dollars per year. Rich by my previous definition possesses a hundred million dollars or more, today in the United States. He can afford a house and a staff his wife will manage. As we learned, he cannot go to heaven for good deeds because of his wealth. He and his wife will become the poorest children at the time of their reincarnation as decided by Our Gods. He is rethinking his works within the United States and the older woman may decide on greed and train the younger like his wife. She is listening to her mother maybe, but the older women are teaching the younger what they should ponder in fear. Women cannot run the church and create fear. They must be secondary to a man in fear. They can run the Holy Family Hospital and schools, but not the church. They are to seek the men of the cross or the Holy Bible.

The clergymen have taught the older women about reincarnation of people like the super rich. They think about what they need for their children and ask themselves how the rich daughter would ever find the right man to marry as a daughter of a billionaire. A playgirl is bad, but a billionaire's husband. How would the man feel adequate? His wife is talking to her man about the future of their daughter and themselves. She asks the man in charge of their financial security, what will happen when he dies. The rich feel they need a good life in his next life, even if their parents are what we call poor today.

I will not finish the entire story but just the money. I will use what a man like Tiger Woods could do. If I am to continue my life as a golfer, we will be rich. Let me go to our companies and see what I can do to reduce my earnings, but increase my chances of playing golf in my next lifetime. I will get Buick and myself in joint ventures of supplying scholarships for golf through tournaments or leagues, a gift card for playing a thousand rounds of golf, and other ideas they may promote through commercials. The television time will try to deal with greed and promote golf all around the country. They state to get the executives to sponsor more golf events from their incomes that Buick and I can see. If I can get more executives involved. I believe, even the poorest child in the United States can have a chance. Can the executives invite the grammar, high school, or college students to their country club and hold a tournament?

The Antichrist or clergymen have proven the passage, "Some of the stories are so great if you can get to the very elect all you will do is deceive." That is one hundred percent of all literature written on religion except for the work of Our Gods and the two books from the book of Daniel. Many I see have the deadly sin of pride like Tomorrow's World and Gerald Flurry.

TO ALL CHURCH ORGANIZATIONS, PLEASE FORWARD TO YOUR FRIENDS.

Do not kill the messenger Elias in your life. Elijah is writing this book so the clergymen can learn what they must teach on the great and dreadful Day of the Lord or Good Friday and prophecy or planning from the Holy Bible. Easter Sunday, we learn about John 3:16 and today some believe the Easter Bunny or the egg the bunny brings as described in prophecy is taking over. The Easter Bunny is more important to children than what happens to grandma when she gets old or new arms and legs.

Some clergymen believe in Daniel and Paul in the Holy Bible, but a true God cannot create a man called Elias in the year of Our Lord 2005 AD. A true God can do all wisdom, but it is up to you to live in heaven on earth or as a foolish man do you place the planet's future on a man that takes pride in himself and not humility for King Jesus Christ, the Antichrist.

King Jesus Christ has promised you a book in Mark 9:12. King Jesus Christ stated, "Elias will cometh first and restoreth all things." You remember or learn your fore fathers of the church disobeyed King Jesus Christ nearly 2000 years ago and He put you in penance.

What does the book achieve?

1. Forms God's Kingdom to over turn what God calls our present whoredom. Matthew 24:14, "And this gospel of all the kingdom shall be preached in all the world for a witness unto all nations and the end shall come." The mystery is in the word this. God does not need the gospel about Christ, but the gospel of Christ. You must develop the gospel on divorces in each nation or the gospel of Christ. God is stating the whoredom technique in our present church is bad and will end civilization, as we know it. You shall form the kingdom and learn how to talk. The church has gone backwards. The church will worship Satan and it has happened. God will not save the preacher whore but the meek. Elias has copied some of the instructions from the Holy Bible and the book is very detailed. What happens to religious people from the book of Daniel in eleven hundred and fifty and twenty three hundred days that do not return King Jesus Christ's Virgin Bride to Him is they all go to Perdition or the way of Satan. The book of Daniel is a lot about fear for the clergymen and how King Jesus Christ will train His representatives. You ask yourself why our Gods used the Word Virgin. If you fail to form the kingdom, the Battle of Armageddon starts in America in less than a decade. You will live through penance seven times longer. You through reincarnation will be born again as eternal death. In eternal death, the pain is great and death is the reward, but you will not die but be born again in pain. God never promised you everlasting life, but eternal life. King Jesus Christ will come back with the Seven Horns of the Eternal Temple. You have to work for the gift of ending the meaning of all death in the church world just like ending all divorces. The word virgin means you have nothing correct

and the animal the ass and oxen make a clergymen look bad. At least they know their own crib.

2. The book will grant you the computerized system from the Holy Bible, Four Horses, the Seals from the Book of Revelations, and more. I have a memo on it. Please email to comfortinGod@mchsi.com for more information.

3. Grants you God's Economic Model, which is better than the Rainbow economy. In the book, you form the one world government representing the church. You train the politicians from the book of Timothy. You will truly bless the congregation and beyond when you end all what you define as poverty today; therefore, you should not believe that for a true God ending what you call poverty is hard. A miracle, yes, but impossible to do, no. The answer you can read in the Holy Bible and Elias defined for you. No clergymen could refuse to end all poverty and die with the view he represented God. He would fail himself and receive eternal death. The Holy Bible states the famine in the end times is not for daily bread but the word of God, which is about real money.

4. Teaches you how to use the concept of Sixth Sense to develop the technique of the Holy Spirit to talk through you to end ninety percent of the divorces in twenty years and then try harder. Half the divorces will end quickly once you start with the wisdom from Elias copied from the Holy Bible.

5. Grace ends a nation of abortion not by law, but by the Word of God and your hard work. Joy is a companion to happiness in Israel. In America, Joy is church and happiness for example in a court is government. Where is the Joy in blaming our teenagers? Elias will get the teenagers back for

you. You remember there is a requirement to count the faithful because once the congregation taxes your ability to teach, you cannot take on more congregation. That will happen if you form the true Kingdom. In the United States, you will have 200 million people in gospel armor.

6. Grace ends all killing wars.

7. There is more in the book like crimes, children on milk cartons, etc. If you can name the major problem where there is a church, the book "The Antichrist God's Version" which contains the Word of God will with the Holy Bible restoreth all things. The Holy Bible is written so no man can boast. All of the above subjects are contained within the gospel to be taught in each nation. Whoredom is, "The road to hell is paved with good intentions."

Archangel Michael was condemned to our world for his war of 777 design or against the children. He was the false prophet who was drunk with power and God does not respect a title. Pope John Paul II was Archangel Michael. He is dependent on the Catholics to create heaven on earth not turn our world into planet hell. The six other church types should work for heaven on earth or the Lord's Prayer. King Jesus Christ will return when you have no questions to ask.

In reading the Holy Bible, a clergymen should look in the mirror and realize where the problem lies. God compares His clergymen with the animal the ass and I know who lost between the animal the ass and the Antichrist. I have not heard of one church that has the twelve days (real time) where God's angels our children talk from the Altar and the congregation learns of the importance of a birthday from the children. Why would you change that in the year one thousand zeros and the memory of the Holy Ghost is old but the importance of a needed child's birthday is still new in our hearts.

The answers are at www.iuniverse.com and you can buy a book (206,000 words but little in comparison to the total religious books). In your mind that should be the best investment, you ever spent to read a representative of the true God called Elias that you have read about for many centuries, waiting for him to fulfill his commitment to you. The Holy Bible was finished at that time. With the help of Elias you will reach, God is amongst us. We will have a new prince of peace or the clergymen. He becomes a prince as the Son of God was.

Elias from Mark 9:12 King Jesus Christ stated, "Elias will cometh first, and restoreth all things." All will happen in the one generation. It started the end of the millennium (2999) minus a strange number in the Holy Bible or 1007 equals the year of Our Lord 1992 AD. We have the King of the North and the King of the South in a debate over money in the United States.

Of all the sons you women (My Educators) have produced, there is not one man that can take a woman by the hand (wrote anything that makes sense). You remember the wax is cold and the hand is writing laws.

I will write more on the book of Daniel or the book the church does once. You start out with a book of life, "Life of US (U.S.)". The book formed the kingdom but also was an attempt to restore the USA to its calling and its calling beyond its calling. The book contained three names or the King of Babylon, Pope John Paul II and former Vice President Al Gore. The USA is the greatest debtor nation in the world according to the Holy Bible and reality. The wisdom you can learn in this country. What the taxpayers would joy in is Archangel Michael to shower our planet with gold. So you would expect it would define the number one problem of the government is thirty thousand children of God dieing of unnecessary deaths due to poverty. Therefore, the first book in the book of Daniel would define real people and real solutions. What happen was the church did not have eyes to see and ears to hear or be gathers of all possible solutions. Since all judgment from our God's is already in the Holy Bible, you are to teach theology or planning to every man, woman, and child in your world.

Since the church did not need to learn as prophecy foretold it did not sell; however, I did not know about the prophecy until the year of Our Lord 2005 AD. As the Book of Daniel states, the three were thrown into a furnace and the heat became extremely hot, but there was no smoke. No smoke means not an fire of oxygen, but a consuming fire of trial by fire in modern times. The lake of fire where God is going to burn down our cities with kindling of our desires or trial by fire of good deeds not intentions. In addition, my first Book only had three names and one was the King of Babylon who I was working against, as the religious leaders should have. If you read the second book, "The Antichrist God's Version" you learn about the third name of former President William J. Clinton who is the King of the South. God stated to the Catholics to save the Queen of the South or his wife from a divorce and his daughter from disgrace led by the Catholics. The Southern Baptist Church should have gone to Rome in force, but why does a clergymen work against divorces when as a preacher whore you have no goals except as God states failure. You have the three names instead of the concept names in scripture but the King of Babylon, King Jesus Christ is against and so should the clergymen. The first book was added to the second book and it will be the first book in the book of Daniel.

You have created the sixth trump in the election of the year of Our Lord 2004 AD and worship Satan. All is covered in the book, "The Antichrist God's Version". This memo is going to be in my next book, the sixty-seventh book of the Holy Bible, which is the second book from the book of Daniel.

If you desire to compete with Elias, reread the above. I have recorded (not typed) about ten chapters before I realized I had to write, "The Antichrist God's Version". By the year of Our Lord 2900 AD, you have not found a death of a child in the mud of despair for a century. Today it is thirty thousand a day. You bring out the Terrible Swift Swords in the Seven Holy Cities and are working for, "If you fail to blow the trumpet and one person dies, I will take you by the hand." Hand is you failed to write the new laws. The power of the church is great but you ask through your teaching why would that occur. There is nothing to fear but fear itself.

Please do not kill the messenger yourself by trying to say God is wrong in His choice of Elias. My life is in the Holy Bible and He knew me before I was born; however, how about Satan, the King of Babylon, Archangel Michael (Pope John Paul II), Former President William J. Clinton and former Vice President Al Gore. I believe Elias could for the members of the church teach the Holy Bible and prove because of the election in the year of Our Lord 2004 AD that God is real and all knowledgeable.

I will define the penance for Satan and grant you a story where committing suicide through the millstone story will reduce the penance. Satan cannot be saved but with the help of Elias, the hell will be restricted to only the year of Our Lord 3000 AD. If he fights me as the clergymen did with the book Life of US (U.S.) and thereby lost the right to shorten the days, then his penance as he creates a world of Hell is greater. Only through the concept of Satan losing, will Satan truly gain. He cannot be saved.

I know the first book was to be called "The Antichrist God's Version" The next one by Elijah I must sell with the first to fulfill the book of Daniel.

Not even the education centers can be taught the procedures they should follow. Letter to follow but first is the letter to the Baptist Church that I gave a copy of my book too.

10/30/the year of Our Lord 2005 AD

Dr Paul Kingsbury, Pastor
North Love Baptist Church
5301 E Riverside Blvd
Rockford, IL
To all Baptist Church Locations please forward.
DON'T FAIL TO LET THE TRUE HOLY SPIRIT SPEAK THROUGH YOU.

A message from the true Elias the man that King Jesus Christ sent to establish His Kingdom or Thy Kingdom Come in the Lord's Prayer.

I was at a conference at the North Love Baptist Church in Rockford, IL. Being the man from the true King Jesus Christ I will give you information that Elias can do easily or the power of the Holy Spirit. My book "The Antichrist God's Version" will give you the true meaning in Chapter 17.

If you are still interested in being involved in learning from Elias, I will give you the secret of turning America into a form of Israel in terms of alcohol. You require the power of the Holy Spirit to be developed by the "Architect of the Future" or it is just me now until the true church forms and the technique maybe can be taught through you.

HERE IS THE SEVEN STEP PROGRAM OR SEVEN IS THE MOST IMPORTANT NUMBER IN THE HOLY BIBLE.

Step 1 First you define a problem. We do not use alcohol like we read of people in Israel. The King's mother requested He make wine before the right day to start. Can you believe that in America the King has a requirement to have the criminals go through a wine party at the church? Most Baptist Church Leaders would state we have enough problems with alcohol without starting more. Did the Baptist church lose the Holy Bible for the prophecy of alcohol in the conference? They desire to use the word guilty against people after they totally fail. The Baptist Church is to change jeopardy to joy as two of the words of the millennium.

Step 2 Have a very good idea man come up with a marketing idea or sixth sense. In my book you have many words from the Holy Spirit in the use of sixth sense. There is a critical sense or common sense in six words. "Don't let Drink Take the Drink." It is the same as "Spare the rod Spoil the child" King Jesus Christ has given as an example. That example is defined in my book and it is not the Catholics Sisters using a ruler on our children or a father deriving pleasure from a spanking. Both of those examples are child abuse.

DON'T LET DRINK TAKE THE DRINK

Step 3 Find some church leaders that may be close and ask them to develop sermons for the Altar and test them in their environment.

Step 4 Have them work through the back room (not Altar, yes capitalize Altar) and develop the way. Before you find that the pleasure of a glass of wine is lost to you seek our Savior's solution.

Step 5 Provide the story of the Last Supper but as prophecy would state not to make your first one the last or call it Supper and use the technique in the Holy Bible as the format.

Step 6 Have all proven works sent to the students of a Baptist College to summarize like a graduate project.

Step 7 Have the Baptist College teach the ways of the Holy Spirit to talk through the church leaders until 25,000,000 (legal and illegal) is still down to none or you have the beer and wine of Israel.

During the seven step program start a contest for the song writers to give our Gods a gift of a song. The words must be written like the book of ECCLESIASTES in modern terms being a song that can achieve for a new beginning possibly above just a sermon. Start the opening with the drink to think of taking the drink. Next you sing for the congregation where beer or wine for a wedding or conference is our way. Follow with the pleasure of the New Testament to give us a view of the Gentile world. The last is the many tribulations (rewards) for the Joy overcoming the jeopardy of losing for you the advantage of a drink in God's Kingdom and the meaning of His Kingdom. You require the physical structure of the Altar in the Gentile World where you place our True Holy Spirits work in the church called the Holy Bible.

The rest of the addictions are in the book The Antichrist God's Version like food, illegal drugs, etc. As the Holy Bible states if you could get to the very elect (people that determine what is taught in the church) you could deceive. You had to wait for Elias, unless you shorten the days which you didn't. With your help in theory 100 % of the Baptist leaders will be involved, but are you going to ignore the other six church types.

You now have the seven steps to develop the wisdom of the Holy Spirit. Should you joy in living in the true Kingdom of God forever and ever?

ARE YOU SURE YOU WANT TO ASK ELIAS WHO THE PRINCE OF PEACE IS IN THE YEAR 2005 if you form the kingdom? Elias wants to work for God is amongst us. Once you understand good and evil, you will be like Gods. Check the Garden of Eden to determine how all flesh can die or your Baptist leaders can be like Gods. Elias's book will make you like Gods.

Elias
Email comfortinGod@hotmail.com

MEMO

RE: The End Shall Come.

Not to blame the churches but a review of what King Jesus Christ states in the Holy Bible is true. King Jesus Christ judged you because He loved you. I copied what God stated in the Holy Bible. The clergymen are to judge the world because they love the congregation.

Many states Jesus saves but have you granted King Jesus Christ His virgin bride through the Lord's Prayer or His Kingdom. Why would your God use the word virgin?

The Holy Bible states you have gone backwards in the United States. If you compare New York City in the year 1900 and today the year 2005, what has changed? The wax is cold.

The teenagers have left the church. They have become a nation of abortion.

The divorce rate of couples going to a church or not is about the same or three out of five. They have become a nation of divorce.

I went to your Baptist conference on addictions and found what King Jesus Christ stated, "That of all the sons that the women have produced, there is not one man that can take a woman by the hand (wrote anything that makes sense)." The Reformers Unanimous 2005 International Training Conference was at North Love Baptist Church in Rockford, IL on October 24 to 28.

It is very sad when King Jesus Christ has given you the answers and you fail yourself. You tried to convince the Baptist Leaders you have the answer to illegal drugs. What is missing is the true answer from the Holy Bible. You have to remember the Holy Bible is written so no man can boast. If applied properly you end up with the title of the book or a perfect way of life for the people you help. The conference proves by reacting instead of using theology or planning from the Holy Bible, you create pain for the families. As defined in the book by Elias, you have to rely on you only to use legal drugs as you teach the Baptist teenagers. Now you should reform the Catholic Church. You have a Biblical requirement to teach the Catholics, I do not want a hair on a child's head harmed as defined in Scripture. So the Italian Mafia has to go. The project run by the Catholics and Baptists is there is no rest for the wicked or American Crime Syndicates should be conquered. You should reform the Catholic Church by letting them understand they cannot tell God what to do unless He asked and the Godfathers of the Italian Mafia die the day they are born. Now you can end the pain in all the Baptist children lives. I believe the Catholic woman would appreciate you reforming the Catholic Church. The answer is in a book King Jesus Christ has promised you or "The Antichrist God's Version". You should not believe that our true King should waste His time reading you the Holy Bible and resolve the issue of pain in the Catholic and Baptist women lives for your call to inaction or be against common sense.

The second part is legal addiction for AA or alcohol. You wait until the man has lost his job, his family is gone and his health is poor and now you react. The book "The Antichrist God's Version" has the beginning of the end of AA which should be run in a church. What is missing in the book is the sixth sense the Holy Spirit can talk through you or the theme "Don't let Drink Take the Drink". The sixth sense is six words of common sense like love is patient love is kind and spare the rod spoil the child (turn him into a drug mind). From the Altar you teach the advantage of a drink for the tummy but if you feel you are failing yourself come to our program to stop the disadvantage of the drink taking the drink. You in the Baptist world can develop the sermons from the Altar and with the talent do the work in the back room. The first time you try the program it will not be very good, but as the millennium continues with your new Gospel to be taught in each Nation the AA program involves to what you believe Israel was like with beer or wine. I believe King Jesus Christ would love you to accomplish what His Father did in His name. You remember all call to action prayers are in His name King Jesus Christ and you becoming with the help of Elias, God is amongst us.

I will cover gambling which I have heard the church leaders do not have a program for those involved. The book from Elias covers the answer. If you want to understand it now, it is through the church the congregation learns financial planning or theology. For the few that desire to "bet the farm", you pay special attention to or end the pain in the family.

In the year 2005 Elias can easily read the Holy Bible and the Church of Philadelphia many leaders are desperately trying to prove, is a good church run by liars and they worship Satan. Only Elias could make Revelations 3:9 real. The rest of the churches that come before are worse and not saved. God states you have to experience death. You shall know what you did before you die.

When I talk to church leaders and state I am Elias sent from King Jesus Christ from Mark 9:12, they do not believe. They read about Daniel and others like Paul, but do not believe that a true God could create a man called Elias in the year 2005. The Holy Bible is the story of God and man or in the Garden of Eden, Adam stating, "God, I demand I want to do it myself." So, what you would expect God would give you a man, so you can do it yourself or you become through Elias, God is amongst us.

You could buy the book King Jesus Christ has promised you that restoreth all of the above and everything else at www.iuniverse.com titled "The Antichrist God's Version" and sort on the author's name Elias. I am not taking God's name in vain. Are you?

I have a grandson born on 9/23/2005 that deserves a chance at life not living in a country where the Battle of Armageddon starts in less than ten years as scripture defines. The penance for you not implementing the Lord's Prayer and becoming royalty (prince) is seven times longer. Since the church failed God in Israel, the penance is to end now through Elias. If you fail to try the penance is seven times longer or fourteen thousand years. Elias wants your help to help my grandchildren avoid fourteen thousand years of additional penance. With Elias you can achieve God is amongst us.

You should realize any Baptist or Catholic location that fails to get involved to help the congregation is working against God and you must question the church leaders' story of salvation. If a loser states you are saved because you go to my church, you should just leave. Please buy the book from Elias that will restoreth America to the glory you should believe American children richly deserve.

What must be taught is the technique of the Supper or King Jesus Christ requirement for the church "The Last Supper". Do not call your enlightenment through the Supper, your last unless your career is over.

I will go on the web and email Baptist Church locations to help you let the Holy Spirit talk through you and for you to develop the Gospel to be taught in each nation. Please check Mark 9:12.

Send your comments to email comfortinGod@mchsi.com. Think why I would use comfort in God. The book, "The Antichrist God's Version" contains the true wisdom of "Holy Spirit Possessions". You will love that reality. The answer is granted through Chapter 17 and subchapter 9 of Chapter 24.

DO NOT KILL THE MESSENGER. ALL I CAN DO IS USE MY INCREDIBLE IQ TO COPY THE ANSWERS OUT OF THE HOLY BIBLE.

Chapter 12. By the Grace
of God You Are Saved

With the Antichrists running the churches, what shall we learn on the great and dreadful Day of the Lord or Good Friday where only adults can attend? The reality is all adults must attend if they joy in the meaning of the end of all death or John 3:16; however, God did not promise everlasting life, but eternal life. There is a big difference. Do not be deceived! The four words of the millennium story must be understood which are war, jeopardy, joy and fear. For one thousand years, you will be learning the true meaning of the four words and how the words apply. If your church is not perfect and you do not understand the computerized teaching of the tree stories (door), your clergymen are inadequate to be saved.

We must have the clergymen go back to the Garden of Eden and think of why the Flaming Swords were guarding the Tree of Life and the Tree of Knowledge. Adam told God, "God, I need to do it myself." Adam started much penance of pain such as the pain of childbirth and the pain of many tongues. We know the Antichrist speaks many tongues, as the language of the church is to be English. How else, can the most powerful organization the world will ever experience, the church, communicate through language and computers? The only reason the Son of Perdition desires to keep the church ineffective is so as a nobody, he can do it himself. The Antichrist takes pride in himself, not humility for King Jesus Christ. Pride is a deadly sin of the clergymen. Working together for common goals to overcome the social ills of his world is the problem and the solution. Now, you should understand the importance of the Tree of Knowledge and the Tree of Life. The Holy Bible and God's Plan evolves around Adam learning how to work together to achieve common goals like no child is hungry, without health care, receives a good education, and has a bright future. There is no hell like a woman scorned when her children are denied a chance at life and all gifts a child richly deserves. In God's Kingdom, children are not dieing due to bad laws. If you heard Senator Hillary Clinton speak, she said. "The Republicans and Democrats have opposing views." What that will achieve is the voice of the powerful drowning out the voice of reason or a house divided amongst itself always fails. That is how Adam desires to be in the church as well. What does the Holy Bible say about life in the year of Our Lord 2008 AD? Adam was put in penance back in Israel for disobeying and Our Gods refused to help us. In the year of Our Lord 2008 AD, you find great social ills all over America and we cannot work together to resolve. Adam after 2000 years without God's help is doing one hundred percent of everything wrong. Adam without God is just a fool. The Holy Bible is clear. You write down in column A what the church, government, and businesses are doing today. In column B, you write down the opposite. That is a summary of what the Holy Bible states. You work to resolve the social ills (sorrows) of any nation by working on column B. That is exactly what the Holy Bible states as the animal the ass and oxen makes our religious leaders look bad. You can write what is good and what is bad in two separate columns. When the column of good only contains the Holy Bible and you get tired of writing down what is bad, take something that is bad and put that story to rest once what was bad can be put under the column of good. You must work to change and put stories to rest. You do that with all other social ills or what is poor. You have a church with seven names on the door with the Universal Church format granted in the year of Our Lord 1200 AD. "Why is all bad?" you say. It is because Adam never learned the meaning of the two trees. Yet the Holy Bible defines them clearly. To achieve the above, you will have to teach the true tree stories. By the grace of God, the tree stories, you are saved. Do not listen to a man that states, "You know you are saved." Why because you attend his church and you are a crime syndicate boss or divorced three times.

I have originated memos like the ones the church should communicate by and sent to the people that Americans and beyond are very dependent on. What have they written me when I explain and copy the Holy Bible for them to understand? They write I believe in John 3:16 and therefore I am saved. In the book of Luke is where they should quote from and believe they have a heart of Our God of Heart. The Holy Bible states that because of their blasphemous mouth they worship Satan. They should explain what terrible knowledge they have relied on and teach on the great and dreadful Day of the Lord or Good Friday. The road to hell is paved with good intensions. Cover what procedures they are going to use in the future to become saints to judge the world. You will guard against repeating evil spirits; they have created in man's mind to deceive the congregation and themselves. The church employees do not even know what the word evil means. As a church of enlightened power, you never admit defeat, but rely on pending victories. Can you teach the congregation to do the same?

Now, you should teach what the Grace of God is. Fear is the beginning of all wisdom (knowledge). The church will go through extreme fear when they realized what they did before they died. The Holy Bible proclaimed the church personnel should experience death, and go through the story of resurrection. If they did not get involved on the first great and dreadful Day of the Lord after seven years, you explain what locations are staffed with people that cannot be saved. Now, you are developing and have in the last forty-two months and seven years, the techniques of Paul from the New Testament and review what the Holy Bible states. Paul is like a Quality Assurance person that comes from the seven Holy Cities and saves people of the other six names. You can explain that your fear is your quest for knowledge to avoid hell on earth and your calling beyond your calling or your true death (unpardonable sins). Do not go too far and try to cover too much. Next year you know you will be better and have new areas you are going to explore like, "Some governments are taking you on the road to hell" or you will try to send the Italian Mafia to Heaven with only one eye. You may have to keep the congregation for more than one hour and ask them to use a Vow of Silence for the love of God's Children or 777 design.

What is happening right now? Antichrist Ken Copeland on TBN states there is no fear in me. I will state the truth about his show in that no knowledge is coming from his mouth. All he states is a deception on his viewers to get them to love him for all the skills he possesses, yet he never accomplished anything for the children of 777 design (born to twenty-one). What can he tell you about what he thought about the government taking you on the road to hell, which has happen all over the world? Famines (money) are killing millions of children each year due to the pen. The Holy Bible states, "I do not care what they eat but stop sending me little ones small and great." Fear in politicians could end hunger in America over night. Now, you suffer for what you have faith in the unseen and the actions of Hope. The children will get food from the politicians all over the world. All you had to do was teach that is fear. The "White Stone Story" I have copied out of the Holy Bible will end hunger where there is a kingdom of the church. Antichrist Ken Copeland has no fear and therefore no knowledge. The Antichrist can stop wars in eighty-two percent of the standing armies. The angels (children 777 design) are King Jesus Christ's peacekeepers. The requirement is, "I do not desire a hair on a child's head harm." Yes, that means a child in Iraq, too. Killing his father is worst than harming a hair on his head. The Antichrists running the church could have ended wars centuries ago. You must learn that the Second World War was a war to end all wars. The clergyman did not record what President Roosevelt stated and train future presidents or crown leaders. I covered the subject clearly in the book "The Antichrist God's Version". The clergymen must become the meek that inherit the earth. The meek are very powerful in correcting social ills like unnecessary deaths of children with hair on their heads.

Have you gone to a church that teaches, by the Grace of God you are saved? There is nothing you have to do. How about the churches that only teaches the New Testament? In those types of churches, they require you do nothing. Yet when a man told King Jesus Christ, "I can barely take care of my wife and child." What did King Jesus Christ say, "You are doing all that I asked." What do you do if a dad abandons his family? Is that individual doing what King Jesus Christ stated? All should say, "You must take care of your wife and child." Is that doing something more than nothing? You have nothing to do because King Jesus Christ has planned all the church must do like end with' "I do not want you to do a job you do not want to do." One hundred percent of all members of the church must only do jobs, they want to do. If you took a public opinion poll today, the church would be falling far short of the Glory of God. Some would ask, "How can I get a job?" If a clergyman asks how can he do that or any question, King Jesus Christ will not return.

In the book of Luke, it is written you must have the right heart for John 3:16. You can ask the Catholic priest if the Italian Mafia has the heart of the God of Heart or King Jesus Christ. If they answer, you must be baptized at eight days, is that more than nothing? In addition, the Holy Bible states the crime syndicates can go to heaven with one eye. In the church world, it is an eye for an eye or fear. The religious leaders are to teach that is legal businesses only. So generation after generation of Italian Mafia children die at eight days because their fathers teach them to live in the wrong world of success for themselves.

Now, you should learn from a clergyman what the Grace of God is and what that passage means. First, you can start with the saints that run a church. King Jesus Christ judged the world long ago, because He loved you. The saints are to judge the world or do they have the right heart? Before the clergymen are ordained and lose their citizenship in the country they live in, they should start learning what it means to live by the written instructions the seminaries have for King Jesus Christ's employees on the Ten Commandments and how they apply. Israel was a nation of priests, so the priests in a church must obey. Once they officially are part of the church, they receive real life experience training from their peers and bosses. Once they reach the age of King Jesus Christ where He started the concept of His kingdom, they are reborn again and should reach the total sainthood commitment and be prepare to judge parts of life because of their love of the congregation. Now, they are the right age to judge on their own merits. Many in the church should love the celebration of their ministries being reborn again, but their own family members being reborn again will make other celebrations seem small. What becomes the hardest to judge? It will be themselves and what function they should perform for the enlighten power of all humanity or inheritance. The man that holds the book and is the very elect in God's election on how the church is to be run is his challenge. The best man to run the church must always be the best man to run the church. If you go to a church of a one-man show, you must realize one person cannot run a church. The requirement is twenty-five or the clergyman and twelve and twelve. Today the Holy Bible states the clergymen are stealing tithes and offerings from God. What happens if a man has a stroke and does not recover one hundred percent of all he had? How can those below him judge? What if he was in perfect health and someone is better? Should the new man say, "God, how come you have forsaken me?" Now, he has the responsibility for all souls before him and the challenge becomes great. He must have a perfect church and when a stranger enters that does not know the tree stories, do not drive him away. The church employees must develop the ways. How can you teach the politicians something you have not learned yourself? Are people like George H. W. Bush (King of the North) capable of judging himself in comparison to William J. Clinton (King of the South) to manage the wealth creation in the United States in the year of Our Lord 1992 AD? President George H. W. Bush stated, "We have to watch out for Governor William J. Clinton, because he is good." prophecy defined the pot of gold at the end of an Irishman's administration or tremendous wealth creation (rainbow). The Holy Bible requires the church to divide up the fat cows of President William J. Clinton and not allow the skinny cows of President George W. Bush to do what his father did to the economy. In addition, you were to learn Jacob was to be justified in the year of Our Lord 2000 AD. You can read about him walking through Egypt without selling all his gold and giving it to the poor. Did you hear Allen Greenspan (Federal Reserve Governor and accountant), when he stated it normally takes three months to count the money and in the year of Our Lord 1999 AD, it will take six months longer? That was wealth creation. They must learn and lead the way. Who are they going to send to the Holy Cities to judge the world and select the right people to lead the way? You have a young child or teenagers. Are they willing to move or are you going to put God's work above your children? You must find the creative minds to become King Jesus Christ's christ in the Holy Cities. He must have the innocence and imagination of a two-year-old child. So much for the saints to learn and teach us how we can judge ourselves and the future we desire to inherit. Does the unskilled mind of two foolish George Bush's minds desire to take a critical role in judgment? The best they could achieve is, "If a man gains the whole world and loses his soul, he gains nothing at all." Millstone two names George Bush and Ronald Reagan and one name left George Bush. God warned you long ago and now Satan cannot be saved in this lifetime. Watch out for his angels or young Republicans. Do not let them go by the teachings of Satan and becoming a beast in their future is the church failure.

We started out with, there was nothing to do. All the answers to the above are available in the Holy Bible. You have to reach for a perfect way of life as saints and become the role models for those without your extreme training. Over many millenniums let all that follow King Jesus Christ ways in the kingdom gain until all reach a perfect way of life. That challenge may take a hundred thousand years or longer, but will it be lost again to divorce. Life is like a circle, what comes around goes around. The true saints will find one person requesting a divorce will have to start a new beginning or the end may return. Now, you should realize King Jesus Christ has told you all things. So your judgment on your organizations becomes essential. They even provided Paul to keep you informed and provide mercy in reform the church, when you go astray. Paul can save only because he will work for the church employees only and reform the church.

What is the next part of it is one hundred percent theology? We should take a passage like, "I do not want you to do a job, you do not want to do." Since a want is a demand the government must satisfy, how would the Grace of God qualify. You must understand King Jesus Christ is the trunk of the Tree of Knowledge. Presently, King Jesus Christ admits the trunk and even the roots are dead. One branch off that tree is the above passage or a path to a small door. You cannot create lives one thousand times better than the end unless all people in His kingdom are doing jobs, they desire to do. In America, I heard half the people do not like their jobs. A large percent do not even have a job to dislike. How are the parents of the children dieing due to a famine (lack of money) love their jobs all across the world? They are back to the old saying, "Hey buddy, do you have a dime, I cannot buy a job." The one hundred percent theology requires the men to be able to care for their families with a job they desire to do. You may ask the Catholic priest in Mexico, "Why do the Mexicans come to America, when the Catholic Church is to teach all the people to love their jobs? The church, government, and businesses are the branch and the seeds of knowledge are the leaves. Each passage that applies has a branch and the fruit of our labor is the success of the congregation. Anything short of perfect is short of the glory of God and must be considered poor until corrected. By the Grace of God, you are saved. How can a politician fail himself when he is working to produce happiness? All the people of his nation will get the right education in schools and churches and the businessperson will help provide the information and feed back as to the success of the theology. The businessperson has a great part in the jobs and wisdom on the branch or the path to the small door. All the children are working their way to a small door where their paycheck is more important than the sheep (product), yet their loyalty to the business is well accepted as the way, truth, and light. A billion plus jobs to go and all jobs the people must shine in. Where is the Grace of God in the year of Our Lord 2008 AD? It is in the Holy Bible as each church location works against their success.

Where is the information to be stored on the Tree of Knowledge? In the Garden of Eden, it is stated that once you are responsible for good and evil you will surely die. The existing poor format of people stating they represent King Jesus Christ has created no flesh is saved from a spiritual view. One hour past midnight in the year of Our Lord 2000 AD, became the Age of "Accountability" or you are responsible for your actions. Once you know how to manage good and evil, you will be like Gods of saints as the Holy Bible defines. The Catholic Church is good at storing data as they where hired by the United States government to straighten out our records; however, the Holy Bible defines the true way, which has been hidden since the beginning of time. The answer is in programming a computer. The Holy Bible grants the way to be created in the church and held in trust for the love of our children, so the church can afford to grow to satisfy the demands of the congregation. The procedure was covered in my first book, "Life of US (U.S.)". A reprint is included in, "The Antichrist God's Version" as part of chapter 24 or subchapter 13 of chapter 24. The program has been committed by me to be developed by the Federal Government of the United States and put on their computers with the fees granted to the church. All businesses, universities, associations, and all the rest will demand training through the church seminaries and fees applied. The church will become well off as they train the world on theology or planning from the Holy Bible.

In the Garden of Eden, we were denied the Tree of Knowledge and Tree of Life and King Jesus Christ has the wisdom already in the Holy Bible. I have heard Antichrists trying to teach me the table in front of them is not there. I suggest they sit on it so it will not disappear. The desktop is just what you normally put as the first screen on a computer. Now, we have one tree left or the Tree of Life.

The purpose of life is life not unnecessary deaths because of bad laws that kill millions of children each year. The prophecy is, "The problem near the end times is the problem with the rich." Which party represents the rich in the USA? Normally it is due to the rich being elected and serving the rich at the expense of the poor (social ills of the country). The Tree of Life is the temptations, we encounter like a clergyman hires a beautiful secretary and she is richly endowed. He looks at her and sees more than he should. A blessing is coming forward and the temptation was too great. The types of temptation like discussed is to be developed and through fear to be overcome. Fear is the beginning of all wisdom (knowledge). You never fear an American soldier but a God that can cut off the dragon's (warlord) ugly head is powerful. Through the church, the Tree of Life must be taught and the reality of our decisions noted in the book of life (666 beast books). Today, we require many millenniums of work to overcome the lack of wisdom in our example. Temptation must be delivered from evil and the consequences of our decision through fear must be understood. For example, the clergymen are to teach what their mothers need for their grandchildren. Does she desire her son as a clergyman not to understand the emotions of man? Penance is desired, when her grandchildren are affected. The clergyman can teach what his wife desires from the Tree of Life for her grandchildren. Does the average mother desire less for her children? The will of the people will prevail. When God's will and the people's will agree, no penance is required and the clergymen have effectively taught the Tree of Life. The divorces in a church environment are the same as the Old Testament, but you must update for John 3:16. I have covered the answers in other works, so the church can get fathers back with sons and not create fallen angels or boys in prison. The fallen angels are in general with the single mothers. The clergymen can easily develop the teaching for the Tree of Life as they are responsible for the deadly sins and must live by the Ten Commandments as saints and role models.

I wrote a definition of a need or want in my book "Life of US (U.S.). A need is a new beginning of life that ends with a desire for a new beginning of life. Only Our Gods can take care of our needs or spiritual view. A want is a demand the government must satisfy. We in the congregation shall not want or the congregation will demand the government make them rich. I have covered how to achieve in past writing. We learn the Tree of Life is a need. The Tree of Knowledge is a desire. There is overlapping in the two. I covered how the church is to determine whether a desire is a want or need in chapter 2 of the book of life titled "Life of US (U.S.). Whoever is not written in the book of life will be cast in the lake of fire and prosper from the trials by fire started by Adam. All Adams will proper in the tribulations of joy.

The end of this chapter should include, we have to live by every word and the Holy Bible is a planning book where through theology, you plan the future you desire to inherit. As an example, fear is the children teaching the religious leaders what information they must learn to achieve their success or spare the rod, spoil the child will be the failure of the clergymen. The senators are to hear what is required from the children (angels) to meet that demand of the child to reach happiness in his career and God helps those who helps themselves. All God's Children (777 design) are to be doubled blessed or special. Do not let the wicked senator ignore the wishes of our most important citizens or the children! A country that does not properly raise its children has no right to exist. The United States has gone the way of the Roman Empire with our children.

Chapter 13. Petition the Church.

In the Holy Bible, the congregation is to be able to Petition the Church. Many of us are aware of a petition in a court, but the Holy Bible states a church, yet the church has what they define as petitioners. You can ask yourself why the Antichrists never developed a system to petition themselves to train the courts, but that is obvious. The clergymen did not even develop the training course for the judges that desired John 3:16. The judges should desire to have the right heart and represent King Jesus Christ as he lives by grace not by law (book of Galatians).

We should look back in history and consider times where the old saying came true in that you cannot fight city hall. There are many times when even city hall could not fight city hall. Let us start with an example. Mayor Daley of Chicago, Illinois set up what is termed a sting operation in a nearby county of DuPage. A sting is a plan to uncover what is bad by trying to accomplish what his internal forces should enlighten. The forces of good take over and correct the problem. In DuPage, many guns were easily sold and used to kill people in Chicago; therefore, you go to another county to obtain a weapon of terrorism called a gun. After the sting, the Republican Party of Illinois went out of their way to discredit the belief of Mayor Daley that killing Chicagoans was bad. The Illinois Legislative

Branch had Republicans bringing guns into the State Capitol building. The mayor had overwhelming evidence and could not beat city hall as the killing procedures of laws were continued. Many years later no change in laws are expected. Their common sense words were people kill, not guns. You ask yourself how many people would die because of guns if the guns were not available to kill people.

Former President William J. Clinton tried to get military weapons out of the hands of some of our less fortunate citizens to stop the terrorism of American citizens killing American people; however, Americans gave the president many Republicans and no one wanted to continue the fight. He came in front of Americans and that was the end. The clergymen continued to be the lawless ones. So today, the laws have resulted in many incidences of terrorism such as drive by shoot bys and the police officers trying to survive. My personal opinion is, "If I were the policemen, I would not even desire to stop motorists violating the laws, since it is not safe." You could find other cases of city hall not able to overcome city hall; therefore, how would you overcome, "A house divided amongst itself always fails"? The voice of the powerful will drown out the voice of reason (common sense). Do not say petitioning the courts are effective, when the Holy Bible calls the man with the gavel working in a land of chaos and confusion; therefore, the church allows that situation. They are to lord over the courts. Would you say a drive by shoot bys or the land of chaos and confusion is good? The knowledge of this book contains the word fear. Is it today fear for the police, courts, or the Antichrists? Let us decide if we truly live in the Kingdom of God and all take their responsibilities seriously. We could develop a story or parable that makes sense.

We would have an unusual situation in congress, if we had a kingdom. We had one party for military type weapons in people's hands that did not have jobs. Second, we had a party that did not believe that was a good situation of people killing Americans with military guns. We had an example of a house divided amongst itself. When did that occur in biblical history? When we formed the United States, we had the work of the thirteen or thirteen colonies into one unified nation of one religion. Later, we had an example of thirteen Free States versus thirteen Slave States or a house divided amongst itself. The house divided amongst itself could not teach the Holy Bible or what Abram stated, "I do not care what it costs I have to free the slave." That became a war of brother against brother and sister against sister or a war of greed. In America, the church can only represent the King of Peace or King Jesus Christ. The clergymen (Antichrists) were wrong; therefore, a war was started. The killing of Americans through terrorism continued in the Civil War. The war of terrorism in the year of Our Lord 2008 AD on our streets continues because Americans did not have a chance to decide.

In Thy Kingdom Come, what option did President William J. Clinton or Mayor Richard Daley have? He was a member of a church in Washington, DC or Chicago; therefore, he arranged to talk to the man that held the Holy Bible for that church location. Any of the seven names on the door are to treat the petition the same. The instructions were well developed and agreed by the saints in the Holy Cities of proper title. The saints in the church are to judge the world, but they cannot attack a person in gospel armor. The congregation welcomes the petitions and votes so the will of the people prevails even in government. The kingdom would result in the ultimate of taxation with representation, the world will ever experience. Let us go through a small story to cover the words. After the review is completed in America (pro or con), the concept could be turned into a play to be recreated all over the church world. Since President William J. Clinton cannot write the laws, he has a moral responsibility to teach. The clergymen learn of the problems (or in this case watch the news).

William J. Clinton, the man walks into his church location in Washington, DC and fills out the correct papers and requests an audience. The audience is granted and the following conversation starts.

William J. Clinton: It has come to my attention that the people of America and our government have a commitment to Domestic Tranquility as an unalienable right. In our country, we have a Constitutional Amendment for Americans to bear arms. The problems that persist is our police force is dieing due to gun shots, many murders have annually been recorded, some younger generations commit to drive by shoot bys, many gangs sell drugs which rely on guns to protect their gains, and the crime syndicates rely on their guns and courts to keep law enforcement away. I do not believe crime syndicates could be as effective without the right of having guns. If you look at our prisons, you find many Americans found guilty of Armed Robbery. Guilty is against the Holy Bible. If a man walked into a bank with bare hands, I do not believe he would attempt unarmed robbery. The handgun appears statistically to be the weapon of choice to kill our citizens through the terrorism of Domestic Violence. If in America no person could walk into our stores and demand money with a gun, I know armed robbery and the ten-year prison sentence for the victims of poverty would be over. Domestic Tranquility at the work place and our streets would be above all other countries.

The reason guns in America are a constitutional right is long past. We started the country using weapons for food and protection. America did not have a large standing army to protect our shores. If an armed conflict were to be on American land of the original forty-eight states, I do not believe weapons of guns would be effective to keep an Army of Great Briton out, as we were able to do in the year of Our Lord 1776 AD. If our regular army fell all should surrender. Many may add the evil spirits of we could go like the French under ground, but without a country like America, all that will happen on our lands will be useless deaths. The Holy Bible does state the Antichrists are to end all wars and in God's Kingdom, King Jesus Christ becomes the wall. The Antichrists could neutralize eighty two percent of the standing armies, as the Second World War was the war to end all wars. Now, we the people of the United States are required to protect our citizens from making the mistake of armed conflict. I realize the project will take many years of slow removal and I am willing to manage the project until my death or completion. One problem we have is many stores use guns to protect. If we eliminated the guns in the stores, they would say, only the bad people have guns. When the police officers are willing to walk around without guns our store owners will understand, but not today. The police officers could provide guns where hunting may be allowed like Alaska. My peers will be available to take over my project management role, if required.

This is not a simple petition and the will of the people prevail. When God's will and the people's will agree, we are getting closer to the title of the book or Holy Bible. Many other petitions may not be this big, but citizens can fight city hall.

Clergyman: I agree and I will send your information through the seven Holy Cities and the Constitution will automatically be changed.

What has just happened? The church has taken over writing the laws and the will of the people is gone. The clergyman has promised one hundred percent fear. Where are the words of the Holy Bible? The only way the church can fail us is if they rush forward and declare what is to be done. Here they are violating all that is in the Holy Bible. You do not create fear except by getting the congregation to demand it. I have explained in earlier writings on how to do that. If the above procedure of telling the congregation where adopted, the people would give up and tell the church to do it themselves. The will of the people did not prevail. All is lost and the people will end up working against the church. Maybe some of us understand what is happening in Pro-Life where the will of the people is not considered by the Antichrist.

We have to do a second version. Let us believe the clergyman is convinced the petition is the right way to go. He believes the Constitution should be changed to improve the moral character of the country. He should not provide his own opinion of what will happen. That would lead to confusion on the part of the congregations. No clergyman can vote. This is not God's Elect for church procedures. The church becomes the voice of the congregation, even if they believe the congregation will be wrong. If it is a valid petition and he happens to be against that view, he must continue. When it gets into the seven Holy Cities, they will continue or stop the idea. If they stop it, they must be beyond the shadow of a doubt, sure they are correct. Most petitions should be major in the beginning and training available for pursuing.

Clergyman: You have presented the material completely and I guarantee the petition shall be consider for adding sermons with meat all across the land. In this case, the Holy Cities would let the petition go through. I may be mistaken for something that we do not know, but if all is available, the issue will be addressed. A vote will be taken as a public opinion poll and Congress will have a clear understanding of the will of the people. If by chance, the will goes your way, your closing agreement to be the country's Project Manager is one of the first questions I believe the seven Holy Cities would need addressed. They will call you a missionary and give you a rod. In addition, any statistics you can have developed would be a requirement in this case. That would make you a missionary, but not paid by the church. We will present your progress (white papers) at the Altars if accepted by the congregation. This project would possibly take decades to complete since the question of protection will be discussed. The deeds are writing the law plan and careful decisions of implementation. The Holy Cities will create the Words of the Holy Spirit. Christ (Son of man) will go to a city to have the beginning sermons started as a review of scripture and the intent of the United States in terms of Domestic Tranquility. The views of the National Rifle Association and our Vice President of the Republican Party in the year of Our Lord 2004 AD trying to get assault rifles in the hands of our poor, has to be covered. How the out come will be will be apparent as the newspapers and other sources are involved, but you will have a clear answer. If it goes as today, future works may be available.

Do not express your view but get the congregation to demand the intent of the United States in terms of Domestic Tranquility. From the year of Our Lord 1776 AD to today, there are too many unnecessary deaths and people in poverty given very few options. The Petition the Church maybe used extensively by businesspersons to overcome "Red Tape"

The plays created as to how America provided an unalienable right will be a success in other countries. Sermons of meat with the call to action must be the way. As the Holy Bible states something that takes less time than the story of resurrection is probably not worth doing. Should the plays cover many subjects and not be limited to petitions?

What if there is another man in the White House and he loves guns? The will of the people is to provide Domestic Tranquility and he refuses. Fear states as the seven Holy Cities write sermons and the people question their voting judgment and the judgment of the president. He should be trained on, "If he fails to blow the trumpet, which could happen and one person dies, King Jesus Christ will take him by the hand." He goes to Perdition like Satan and cannot be saved. You should teach not to let a man gain the whole world (United States) as the president and lose his Soul, as he has gained nothing at all. The church may have to do the Passover story if a company like

Wal-Mart fails to understand. The store shall not be allowed to sell even a shoelace. Since management is trained that should not happen, but will if necessary.

If the petition goes through, what choice does the man of heart have that runs the Supreme Court of the state or federal. Through the book of Galatians, the judges are to be justified by grace, not law. The courts will be trained and whether the new Constitution will be by State Supreme Courts or just Federal is not important to the average American. The work will possibly go by state in the beginning. Which states will be first to change. A Vow of Silence will be in order. We must start an individual has the right to privacy. What can be released is best done through a white paper to the church, possibly for the first Sunday of each month on status or as required. As developed the other states courts will be trained. The knowledge can be presented in the United Nations and the church summarizing across the world. Many citizens are questioning their politicians as to their progress across the world. May the American unalienable right to Domestic Tranquility go as a wild fire in man's trial by fire! Whomever is not written in the book of life or Life of US (U.S.) Catholic for example will be cast in the lake of fire of the wild fire or trial by fire. A child walking safely down a street of our lands is critical to the clergymen and judges of our courts.

An older mother of America comes into her church. She is telling the women there what happened. She got behind on her heart medicine money and did not pay her property taxes on time. The amount was large but small in comparison to the value of mercy shall follow us all the days of our life. She received some legal papers and did not understand. Maybe she should have brought the problem to her friend, but she did not. She could have hired an attorney or just pay the tax, but just understand, not blame and prove you are foolish. She learned someone new owns her house through a tax sale. The women state, we must petition the church. The women help with the paper work and it goes right to the seminary and then the Holy

City. A training course of new ideas is presented to the men or women seeking John 3:16 in her church type. Many attorneys are eager to present a case in front of the State Supreme Court and are over desirous to seek a solution. The Holy Bible states it will take ten thousand ideas to straighten out America. You can read the problem King Jesus Christ had to try to get the Israeli man to be like the Greeks.

The court of her state developed a plan for the governor to send out an attorney from his office to offer a reverse mortgage to his world. The women are there when the governor makes the announcement and she is asking for forgiveness for the government on their foolish actions. The congregation is waiting to forgive the other states for their wrong hearts and time and action is short for achievement. The procedures are just copied and Federal law changed as mandatory.

What a beautiful world we live in when city hall can overcome city hall and an older woman can make a big difference in God's Kingdom. If you cannot do, you must teach. We the citizens and especially the businessperson long for God's Dream for us, His Kingdom shall last forever and ever. My God teach us the glory of true Gods through living by every word.

Through Petition the Courts, we can learn why a clergyman can have deadly sins or unpardonable sins. He studies the Holy Bible and learns he cannot let the government steal a woman's house. The government has a plan for tax sales and he does not accept a petition. The church employees of King Jesus Christ lords over the court for the people that love John 3:16. The clergymen fail to train and the governors create bad laws or the clergymen become the lawless ones. The unpardonable sins of the church employees go all over the world where grandma or others are losing their houses. How could a person forgive him for his failure to overcome unpardonable sins? We cannot, as we desire to shoot him in the head, as he will be hated above all others for My name's sake. King Jesus Christ certifies the politician through the book of Timothy and courts through the book of Galatians. King of kings and Lord of lords. We must call the president king not president as King Jesus Christ gave him his title. Only in the nation, use the title king and one day the country and all other countries, the title will be the same.

Chapter 14. The Power of Forgiveness

When you arrive at your first choice to worship our Gods, you may hear a lot about forgiveness and the word mercy shall follow you all the days of our lives. Another item of importance is to teach you to pray. The number one prayer is for King Jesus Christ to resolve all issues in your friend or family members lives. You may be like the woman King Jesus Christ met in Samaria. You had five husbands or five men you seriously lusted over and some you divorced, but your prayer is for others to change. King Jesus Christ put you in penance back in Israel for disobeying, yet the average church prayer is for Him to do everything. Now, the clergymen do not have to put any story to rest. They can write sermons where they are not ready for milk, let alone meat. They can sleep at the Altar.

Have they convinced you, they will forgive you for everything?

The Italian Mafia is attacking your grammar school children to have their workforce sell your children, drugs. Your children have more than a hair on their head affected. Did the Catholic priests do a public opinion poll to see if the women whose children died of drugs should forgive them? The Italian Mafia does not have to change. What should the Catholic priests do, if the public opinion poll does not agree with them? The will of the people prevails and may not believe the Italian Mafia should go to the true Heaven for good deeds. They have the wrong heart; however, they were baptized at eight days. They can go to church every day for the rest of their life, but they cannot reverse the jeopardy of the Catholic priests' unpardonable sins. The Catholic priests believe they can tell their boss anything and He must do it. They are teaching false witness and reach for pride in themselves in what they say is the word of God. The clergymen are the sinners to repent and the Son of Perdition.

The Republican Party through Vice President Richard B. Cheney desired to give people that did not have jobs assault rifles in the year of Our Lord 2004 AD campaign. A problem in the United States is guns killing American teenagers. What if a public opinion poll to provide assault rifles to certain people goes against the Republicans? How can we forgive the clergymen that allowed the guns in our children's hands? Why are they so ineffective on important issues? Many clergymen were boasting about the Republicans winning the elections and fighting against common sense in the year of Our Lord 2004 AD. The Republicans like the campaign money from the National Rifle Association. The Democrats were against guns in the hands of people without jobs and assault weapons.

The judges in American courts had a public opinion poll and they desired to be hanging judges. Do the clergymen desire the Death Penalty? Finding a person guilty in the church world is against God. Where is the mercy in the courts? The requirement is "In heaven on earth, do not send your policeman out to kill them because they do not want to go to school." Only the president of our country can end crimes. Where are the clergymen teaching the laws of liberty as the United States started out? We have lost the way. Do the clergymen desire the president to fail because of their words against God?

A committee was formed in the late 1990s. They reviewed why crime had gone down from President George H. W. Bush to President William J. Clinton. First the church should understand that committees are ineffective and not the way in scripture. The committee determined there was no reason why the results should be different. President Ronald Reagan and George H. W. Bush took the money out of the poor neighborhoods and gave it to the wealthy. President William J. Clinton gave the states one hundred thousand new police officers and created wealth in the poor neighborhoods. The committee could not notice a difference. If all children were born of fathers that were not in want of money, our lives could be blessed. The prisons should disappear. Should we forgive all the people who vote for fools like the clergymen? Money in the poor neighborhoods is a deterrent to crime.

What should the clergymen do to a man who desires the feathers to eat up the flesh (Hawks and Doves)? Should the clergymen teach the politicians that a warlord is not a Hawk, but a dragon that desires to steal that woman's child? I heard a woman state that President George W. Bush killed her child. We would love to hear that through reincarnation, that the child was granted new arms and legs; however not hearing of the death would be better. King Jesus Christ states we cannot put that child back in her womb. Do the women state they do not mind a Red Dragon stealing that child from her? Is that the opinion and the will of the people? The Holy Bible asks the clergymen why Satan (Red Dragon) attacked. The answer was because he needed to win the presidential election. Is the clergymen forgiving the dragons and allowing them to kill that woman's children? Should the clergymen be forgiven that desire to be conquers as defined in the book of Romans? Does he have the right heart? The book of Romans is when the United States recreates the Roman Empire or what America is doing wrong. The church still teaches us King Jesus Christ is still only a prince and does he believe that as a clergyman, he can have the wrong heart. There is no hell like a woman scorned. She cannot get health care, daily bread, a good education, and/or a bright future for her children or the children of the land the government desires to conquer. The Preacher Whores running the church desire to help the government to kill her child and they forgive the Red Dragon.

President George W. Bush was doing what he did in Texas. In Texas, he took the money set aside for health care for children of Texas and gave the money to the rich. He violated the book of Mark. Should we forgive him for being a beast or a mass murderer of children from Texas? He is the beast of Revelation many clergymen Preacher Whores talk about and the woman is former President William J. Clinton's girl friend. Now, he is against children getting health care in the year of Our Lord 2008 AD. How many children will die because of him and yet many will say he is saved? Does he have the heart as Our God of Heart and we should forgive him? The Antichrist running the church would forgive. The congregation should question what heart the clergymen have. I say, the clergymen cannot be forgiven by the congregation or King Jesus Christ for their ideas of foolish religion. The church is disobeying one hundred percent of all instructions. They must obey the Holy Bible as slaves or as a prince. Their cross to bear is the Holy Bible and they must teach us how to live by every word.

If you understand the above maybe, there is more to forgiveness than we have been taught.

I desire to document what I have learned on December 15, the year of Our Lord 2007 AD. I realize I am the best biblical scholar in the entire world. It took me thirty seconds to understand what I heard on the radio back in about the year of Our Lord 1998 AD. Do not let that dragon steal that woman's child. A dragon is a warlord and the soul does not die, but through reincarnation is reborn again, goes to the true

Heaven, or somewhere else. The solution to understanding the words is the word "steal" and understanding John 3:16. You can ask the clergymen, which of the Four Horsemen are to cut off his ugly head. I have been studying the Holy Bible with great intensity, because I desire to stop the Battle of Armageddon from starting in the United States. My family and the future of my grandchildren are at stake. The only people that can reverse the course of human events to the end shall come, are the clergymen. Many agree the end is near. As the Holy Bible states, I am to handicapped to do it myself. In the past, I have written to try to understand when the clergymen of the United States failed three times like Israel. Today I know, on January 1 in the year of Our Lord 2000 AD, the Antichrist came in an era of peace and prosperity. President William J. Clinton had the peace dividend in place and the federal government was approximately two hundred and sixty-seven billion dollars ahead in the future Heartland of the world. The final number turned out to be two hundred and thirty-two billion ahead that he granted a beast from Texas to accept the title of President of the United States. The Holy Bible states that unless you shorten the days (formed the kingdom) no flesh is saved (no John 3:16). In the Garden of Eden, it is written that once you are responsible for good and evil, you will surely die. The new beginning was the employees of King Jesus Christ to form the kingdom with seven names on the door, as this generation becomes the Age of Accountability.

What did I learn, today? I knew the Antichrist is the clergymen or employees of King Jesus Christ. They do not even understand what the definition of the word evil is. The church has created the definition as morally bad: profoundly immoral or wrong. The root of all evil is money; therefore, that has been translated into the "bad guys". On television, you may hear references to we also have crimes of passion. If they had to apply knowledge, they should learn the definition is wrong. I know evil means lack of knowledge and it takes money through time to discover. A passage states if you are not in a quest for knowledge, you are not priests of mine. Some say look we can go to outer space to prove that is what we are doing. King Jesus Christ states you talk like little children. We must learn the tree stories.

I use a story for me to understand about antilock brakes. When we focused on brakes over the last century for our cars, we developed great knowledge, but what does that have to do with driving on our highways safely as the government has lost control. The people say, we can all drive too fast because everyone does it. In addition, we have an accident every six seconds and our children learn from the adults, but do not have the experience. When you go to a hospital or see some television shows of reality in turns of technology, you see wonders. Yet, children die in the world because their families cannot afford health insurance. King Jesus Christ did say in prophecies, we cannot go to Israel to learn how to raise a child, yet some churches state we require a law to teach the Holy Bible to the children. The reason is the children do not like organized religion or the clergymen have driven the children away. A country that does not properly raise its children has no right to exist. The children of 777 design (God's Children) should be great women at twenty-one or good men. I have heard the women state there is not enough good men to go around. They are either gay or married. Where is the quest for knowledge in the church like Israel? You must keep in mind that the Rabbis are to be the hunters and the church personnel are gatherers.

The above shows the church employees of King Jesus Christ were not saved on January 1, the year of Our Lord 2000 AD at one hour passed midnight. King Jesus Christ has named the Age of Accountability. The Gates to Perdition were opened at that time and they are the Son of Perdition. The religious leaders take pride in themselves, not humility for King Jesus Christ. All locations I have gone to use words like Jesus saves and they do not use His title. Read Luke 17:21 neither shall they say, Lo here! or, Lo there! for, behold, the kingdom of God is within you. Have you heard, I am the only one that understands this, but they have not formed the kingdom so they can learn how to talk.

When the Red Dragon went around to many kings in other nations, he convinced many others to join by using intimidation to start the war in Iraq, but first he said, "Let me seek the vengeance." not let God seek the vengeance. Once the Antichrist allowed the war to start in the Age of Accountability, their entire congregation lost John 3:16. As the Holy Bible states the Second World War is a war to end all wars and we start another war. The Holy Bible states King Jesus Christ's employees shall be hated above all others. The answer is obvious. What heart does the Red Dragon or Satan have? He does not have the Heart of Our King. Satan or the Red Dragon and his wife cannot be saved and will die without having the possibility of salvation in this lifetime. King Jesus Christ will save the meek, not the preacher whore. You may have heard of a church without shackles or similar foolish ideas from the Son of Perdition, the clergymen. Have you heard about the saying, there is no fear in me? The words of the Holy Bible would mean there is no knowledge in you. Fear is the beginning of all wisdom (knowledge). A very foolish idea is King Jesus Christ is responsible for all divorces and a church law like the saints who run the church say, "If I have a problem in my marriage, I must seek the marriage counselors of the church." They can create a song like the Songs of Moses and sing in church and create sermons. The congregation would demand they handle their marriage problems too and the divorce rate would fall. King Jesus Christ does not create the divorces of church families, but the wrong heart of the clergymen and their unpardonable Cardinal Sins do. Many state come to my church, I can save anyone; however, the only one he can save is himself or his peers. Paul from the Holy Bible is out to help the clergymen maintain their story of salvation, not the congregation. King Jesus Christ saves, not the clergymen; however, through the actions of reform the church you can save others of His employees. The meek can end all killing wars, stop the drug lords, and many other miracles, if they form the kingdom and learn how to talk. Once they start to form the kingdom, the congregation gets John 3:16 back and the Battle of Armageddon will not start. If we live by the sword, we will die by the sword (guns) of our own citizens of the United States.

So what have I learned? The worst career to get John 3:16 through work is being the Pope in the year of our Lord now or the future. Unless he forms the kingdom as soon as a person joins the church, they will die. The congregation should realize King Jesus Christ saves souls, not the clergymen. King Jesus Christ judged you long ago because He loved you. The clergymen are to be the saints and they refuse to judge. Do they desire the congregation to forgive them for stealing John 3:16 from the entire world and letting the end come because they take pride in themselves and not humility for King Jesus Christ? They will never get John 3:16 back. The next step is the penance continues for seven times longer and King Jesus Christ returns with the Seven Horns of the Eternal Temple or Israel. One day the new clergymen again will be granted a chance to form the kingdom and learn how to talk, but in the mean time, they killed one trillion children because they refuse to obey King Jesus Christ by becoming royalty and wearing the color purple. Learn King Jesus Christ has told you all things and the church has a book that always ends up with a life one thousand times better than the end, called the Holy Bible.

Can you forgive them for their total failure as human beings? The Holy Bible states the congregation shall shoot them in the head (spiritually). They must experience death as King Jesus Christ did. They will not die physically but spiritually. They shall know what they did before they die. They died as stated in the Garden of Eden and must go through the story of resurrection of eleven hundred and fifty (42 months) or twenty three hundred (seven years) days.

Next, have you heard the clergymen stating, "I will forgive all your sins"? Do you believe in the foolish ideas about the Italian Mafia and forgiving? If the God Father from the Italian Mafia has a heart attack on the highway and he is taken to the hospital where the Catholic priest is there, he goes to the true Heaven for good deeds and forgiveness. Next time as he survived the first heart attack, he is driven to the hospital and is dead on arrival, before he sees the Catholic priest. Now, he goes by the way of Satan. What does the Holy Bible state to do with criminals like the Italian Mafia? They are to go to the true Heaven with one eye. What does "we the people" desire in return for that forgiveness? They must only have legal businesses and work hard to destroy the crime syndicates of your country. What does that mean work hard? Did the FBI receive all possible knowledge to stop illegal drugs (for example) from coming into our country and destroy all their ties with other drug lords? On the great and dreadful Day of the Lord, Good Friday, what do you cover for adults only? Their good deeds and desires give them a chance for them to go to heaven. Judgment Day is the day we die and death is beyond the scope of the saints. The clergymen have to teach the terrible reality that we have to forgive them for killing our children (what came before), because of their good deeds. All illegal drugs in the United States are planned to be over. Will the women understand or go after the clergymen for them to seek vengeance? You do not desire to explain to the congregation, yet forgiveness is a powerful tool to resolve problems. The Holy Bible states only a penance man can get off this world alive. You have to think about a rich crime boss and realize he will go through penance, but the pain in the future family lives ends with that generation.

I have written the judges in the courts are to correct the foolishness of items like property tax sales, living wills, being defined as hanging judges in courts. What will happen without the congregation learning to forgive? Have you seen people showing up at pardon review sessions to guarantee the courts maintain vengeance? How can a young man who killed your husband with a gun or on the highway be forgiven? The clergymen will have to learn how to convince people to let God seek the vengeance as I defined in the chapter on Dr Martin Luther King. The questions to explore are why the courts gave him a gun and why they lost control of our highways. Once the judge corrects the problem, we will forgive or blame will rise to overcome the ability of man to correct problems. Check my writings about Mayor Daily of Chicago and what blame can do. We must learn the correct use of the power of forgiveness or correcting and defining problems becomes impossible. The Holy Bible defines America requires ten thousand ideas to straighten out their country. The voice of the powerful drowning out the voice of reason can destroy even America, which started out designed by the Holy Bible. A land of freedom is a land of failure or "LAND OF FREEDOM LAND OF FAILURE" and a land of liberty to return as the laws of liberty. A land of liberty is a land you give up the right to fail yourself and all other rights are enhanced. The sermon to compare should develop LAND OF FREEDOM LAND OF FAILURE to LAND OF LIBERTY LAND OF SUCCESS.

I did not comment on their words or "I will forgive all their sins." Israel was a nation of priests. Priests have to obey the Ten Commandments and become the man of sin to repent. The clergyman that states you should obey the Ten Commandments and is critical of you, is wrong. Have you heard in the year of Our Lord 2000 AD where the Catholics stated I have a man that can really dig out your sins? He was blaming you and should not be forgiven. Only through the end of those foolish words can he repent. The Holy Bible states the clergymen must identify the man of sin. When King Jesus Christ stopped the Jewish man from killing that woman developed by Roman standards He said, "Let the man without sin cast the first stone." They knew if they cast the first stone, they would not be without sin. They were a nation of priests. How can you be blamed as a sinner and the Catholics are casting the stones? The Catholic priests are failing themselves as the congregation is in jeopardy. King Jesus Christ was too intelligent to call the people in the church world, who were not priests, sinners. The clergymen cannot be forgiven if they call the congregation sinners. That has a tendency to drive the congregation away at this time.

What should be the case where the Antichrists are out to kill the messengers? As the volumes of religious materials are great many would state my literature is the true living word. I say the Catholic library, TBN, Pastor Murray, Gerald Flurry, Tomorrow's World and others all boasting their material is the true word are wrong. They have not formed the kingdom and learned how to talk. You should realize the Holy Bible states everything is one hundred and eighty degrees off or just the opposite of what should be done. All laws and religious material are wrong. Why would all important works of man be wrong, when we can invent antilock brakes? The answer is Adam is always trying to prove he is right. The Holy Bible gives all clergymen the answer to one hundred percent of all problems in the world. When Adam is faced with someone smarter than himself, he will argue and try to kill the messenger. I have a number of experiences with the Antichrist and their pride in themselves. One told me after I asked if he needed to end divorces, he said no. I believe a woman that is beaten up by her husband should have a divorce. When his congregation members are beating up their wives, he cannot be like King Jesus Christ and walk a mile in His footsteps; therefore, he does not have a heart for change to love the congregation. With that type of attitude, he is failing himself. He should just resign after he said those words and just sell shoelaces (Passover story). Adam only needs to do what Adam needs to do to take pride in himself, so he always believes if he is challenged, he must defend. He will always try to kill the messenger. When a teenager hears her parents arguing, he does not desire to hear from the child (the messenger) and for him to correct the marriage issues; therefore, Adam let the voice of the powerful drown out the voice of reason (common sense). The only answer is for the church to invent sixth sense or six words of common sense to let the Holy Spirit speak through them; however, they are all trying to prove their church location is the best without achievements or goals to work for. They must develop the stories to the small doors and that can only be achieved with the innocence and imagination of a small child. The tree stories are the quest for knowledge that strangers must learn in the perfect church environment. We cannot as the congregations forgive them. Only through them changing can we forgive them for all good intentions without good deeds that came before.

We had a public opinion poll that states the clergymen were the most believable and the attorneys were tenth. I can trust in the Italian Mafia's attorneys better than the clergymen. The Italian Mafia's attorneys, we should know stand for their own failures in turns of which heart they have. The clergymen are rejecters of all knowledge, do not know how to talk, but when a woman is being beaten up by her husband of their congregation, they have no solutions other than a divorce through Adam. When you petition a church, you would see a look of failure as the man does not even listen in the year of Our Lord 2000 AD to do a public opinion poll from our children to see if they desire good schools from President elect Al Gore. They allow a debate and let a beast violate the book of Mark. The Holy Bible states not one woman could vote for a mass murder of children from Texas who desires to steal the money required for schools and give it to the rich. His mother should not vote for him as he was about to gain the whole world and lose his soul. The clergymen do not learn because they tell you are to have eyes to see and ears to hear and they cannot learn. They do not desire to learn and are not priests of King Jesus Christ. It must be all heard in a church. How worse than foolish are they? I will go through a real conversation.

I go to many churches trying to get one to realize his responsibilities to King Jesus Christ. I am King Jesus Christ's representative and I am like Paul in the Holy Bible or a man that can improve the church. So I go to a Baptist Church, tell the clergyman who I am and what I need to do and naturally, with his pride in himself, he kills the messenger. He states, "You know, I have to wait for Jesus to return." Now, I intent to go back and teach; however, the church is locked (not open twenty-four hours a day) so I leave. He was to start on Wednesday night at 6:30 PM, but was not there in the afternoon that I could see. I had received the following letter from him to discuss. He apparently needs me to tell him how great he is. The Holy Bible compares him with the animal the ass or oxen, which know their own crib. I already knew by listening to him and understanding the Holy Bible, he is asleep on Sunday at the Altar. He could not tell me about the stories, he has put to rest, like he through the kingdom has eliminated ninety percent of the divorces in twenty years and is trying harder. The Holy Bible states he has gone backwards in the United States from the year of Our Lord 1900 AD to today and the wax is cold. Now, you have a background you can judge by as copied from the book he claims to represent. The book is called the Holy Bible. He cannot judge himself, but he can kill the messenger.

His letter to follow dated December 10, the year of Our Lord 2007 AD.

Mr. Richard Cartwright
430 Pembroke Road
Poplar Grove, IL 61065

Dear Richard

We were honored to have you with us at First Baptist Church last Sunday. I trust you felt welcome and enjoyed the service.

Because we seem to live in such a fast-paced society, we need a special time on Sunday to regroup. It is for this reason we strive to provide a service, which inspires and motivates us to establish and grow in a personal relationship with God.

We think people really feel comfortable in a church where
The people are friendly and helpful,
The music is uplifting and encouraging,
There is a meaningful and inspiring message, and
A special time for the children is provided.

We are trying very hard at First Baptist to meet these objectives. You can help us by letting us know how we are doing. While your visit is still fresh in your mind, would you kindly write down your first impressions of us on the enclosed card and drop it in the mail? Your opinion is important to us.

If at any time I can personally be of help to you, please call upon me. I am delighted that you chose to worship with us Sunday, and I hope you will do so again soon. Our service times are:

Sunday School 8:45 - 9:30 Coffee Time 9:30 - 10:00
Worship 10:00 - 11:00

Your Friend;

original signed by Pastor Rex. A. Rogers
1255 W. Jackson
Belvidere, IL 61008

I finally was able to contact him on the telephone. I state I am answering his request to judge him. I ask if he needs to end all divorces and he states no. I hear he desires to blame King Jesus Christ for his own failure as he states King Jesus Christ is causing all the divorces. Next, I ask if he needs to end the unnecessary deaths of children all over the world. I state, "Do you need to make all the people in the United States rich?" All people of the world shall not want or be rich. He claims there is nothing he can do, because King Jesus Christ is causing all the unnecessary deaths and all that is bad, he implies. He is telling me that God is in charge and no matter what he would do, he could not change anything. The Holy Bible is clear as God will return to Israel when the clergymen have no questions to ask. Where is the love from the clergyman as all they have is good intentions but no good deeds? I tell him I am Elijah. He calls me a liar and refuses to meet with me to test if what I say I can do is true. He is required to be a gatherer and in a quest for knowledge and he refuses to learn. He just needed to kill the messenger. Is that what the congregation desires? A teenage child hears his mother and father yelling at each other. If he came to him, he would just kill the messenger. He like all others have accomplished less than nothing in the last one hundred years and the congregation can now learn why. If I am successful in creating heaven on earth, what he told me becomes part of Standing Historical as it is the way of all churches. They are required to be the Mother of Inspiration and all they desire to achieve is grandma (little old ladies writing sermons). They have not put a story to rest but have made life in our country worse. Have you heard those supporting wars, beasts, criminals, illegal aliens, bad schools, false witness and more unpardonable sins than man can count or a God would say? The Cardinal Sins go up to the heavens. They are the men of sin that must repent and obey the Ten Commandments. The most you will hear is they call you sinners and you must repent. They will imply they are perfect, but only one beast away from destroying the entire United States in the year of Our Lord 2008 AD due to the pen. Can you believe a clergymen would call a member of God's congregation a liar? That is blame and he requires the blood of a just man to end the "Black Plague" or the word blame. I believe if someone can reach for we shall not want (money or anything else) a clergymen should take time to listen. They are to take public opinion polls as well as except petitions. They are the only ones that can offer a divorce, not a judge in court one day. A judge should only divide the money.

He called me a liar and never called to apologize.

Let the man without sin cast the first stone. He throws a rock and now he should know he is not a man without sin. The Holy Bible states for a man to get the lost sheep, so I will try again with the letter I have sent. The letter to follow.

December 26, the year of Our Lord 2007 AD

First Baptist Church
Appleton Road & W. Jackson St
PO Box 276
Belvidere, IL 61008-5800

Rev. Rex A. Rogers

Regarding your letter dated December 10, the year of Our Lord 2007 AD, you asked me to judge you. You stated, "Would you write down your first impression of us". King Jesus Christ has judged you in the Holy Bible long ago and I agree with the Holy Bible. He did it because He loved you. The book states for you to form the kingdom and learn how to talk. You like all your peers cannot tell anyone what stories you have put to rest.

Your defense is for example, King Jesus Christ is responsible for all divorces; however, the Holy Bible states for you to find Elijah to return fathers and children back together. If you form the kingdom, the Holy Spirit words for you to use to learn how to talk is "FOR THE LOVE OF GOD'S CHILDREN". We are all children of God, but God's Children (Thy Children) are the angels and the ones you are to make special. When you create Church Laws (Moses Laws), one should be if the saints running the churches have a problem in their marriage, they must seek the marriage counselors of the church. The clergymen are the saints to judge the world. The older women that are to teach the younger women will force you to do the same for their daughters. I have invented a prophecy for the church and teachings in my literature for you to end ninety percent of the divorces in the United States in twenty years (777 design) and then try harder. I say you should be able to achieve the prophecy easily. King Jesus Christ has defined the answers. The Antichrist running the church would say, King Jesus Christ is responsible for all the divorces and there is nothing I can do in a kingdom. A prophecy is a future, the congregation will desire to inherit. Blind faith is the future you desire to create in His name, but you cannot see the results in our future like individuals have quoted in the Holy Bible like Daniel. You must create hope to make your commitment to the congregation come through.

King Jesus Christ has a requirement for you to stop sending Him little ones small and great. You say and all Antichrist states King Jesus Christ is responsible for all the unnecessary deaths and there is nothing I can do. If you trained the politicians and through a little bit of fear to recognize that daily bread is their responsibility, I say they would work hard to eliminate hunger. If you formed the kingdom in the year of Our Lord 1900 AD and made that a requirement for all politicians that represented

King Jesus Christ, hunger as you know it would be gone or greatly reduced.

You can check the Holy Bible. If you abandon "THY" children of 777 design (born to twenty-one) I will abandon you and the penance will continue for seven times longer or He comes back with the Seven Horns of the Eternal Temple. You are in penance as the Holy Bible is clear and you do not even know it. The children do not like organized religion.

Since you believe you are a greater biblical scholar than I am, you can finish the chapter on "The Word Forgiveness" that must be used by all church locations without exception. If you do not desire to learn from me, please leave the church and go sell shoelaces (Passover Story). All clergymen that refuse to form the kingdom or seven churches with the Universal Church format granted in the year of Our Lord 1200 AD, have the wrong heart. The Holy Bible states you worship Satan, which I can prove. You do not have the right heart for John 3:16.

The last statement for now is the Holy Bible always ends up with a life one thousand times better than the end. The eighth beast is next as you have failed and the end shall come. You will be responsible for a trillion unnecessary deaths in the future. Why, you refuse to create the greatest tribulation the world will ever experience by forming the kingdom and you become royalty.

NOW FINISH THE CHAPTER ON THE POWER OF FORGIVENESS WITHOUT ELIJAH. IF YOU CANNOT COMPLETE PLEASE APPLY THE MILLSTONE STORY TO YOU AND YOUR WIFE. THAT WOULD BE KIND FOR YOUR WIFE OR YOU COULD SEEK King Jesus Christ's TRUE MESSENGER ELIJAH.

Richard Cartwright
430 Pembroke Rd SW

Poplar Grove, Il 61065
Telephone 815-765-0161

Elijah is located at Candlewick Lake
Any major problem you can define, I can solve through planning or what the Holy Bible calls theology. The world must be developed through one hundred percent theology, which is planning from the Holy Bible.

I told him about the one world government of Israel of over 20,000 words. If he calls, I will give him this new part of the chapter on forgiveness and the documents so he can start to create heaven on earth or implement the Lord's Prayer. The start is he would be required to reproduce some papers, make a few telephone calls, read my book "The Antichrist- God's Version", and have his friends listen to a voice file on the presentation. The beginning of heaven on earth can be a reality.

Well, I did not wait. I wrote a new letter to him and copied the chapter I wrote on the Grace of God you are saved. He being the Antichrist, he must work with all clergymen to reverse the course of human events that leads to the Battle of Armageddon (biblical battle between good and evil: in the Holy Bible, the battle between the forces of good and evil that is predicted to mark the end of the world and precede the Day of Judgment per Revelation 16:16 in the USA.) Below is a copy of the letter. I will send similar letters to other Antichrists I have met.

January 6, the year of Our Lord 2008 AD

First Baptist Church

Appleton Road & W. Jackson St
PO Box 276
Belvidere, IL 61008-5800

Antichrist Rev. Rex A. Rogers

RE: Kill the Messenger

Now, you know whom the Antichrist is that is creating all that you see and hear as bad or as the Holy Bible states, Adam. What is good is nothing or the Noah's Ark story from God is kind. That I can prove. The new beginning can be only a few years away with your help. As Elias, I can form the kingdom and the book is complete or, "The Antichrist- God's Version". You should realize why the book has that title. As Elijah, I can end ninety percent of the divorces in a kingdom in twenty years and the prophecy will be found to be easy. You must get fathers back with sons or the fallen angels (boys) will be with the women. Also babies will be having babies. You cannot believe you will not reach for the greatest tribulation a clergymen can see or the return of King Jesus Christ, once you have no questions to ask. I have copied King Jesus Christ thousand-year plan for the government from the Holy Bible and you can prove it from scripture. Can you allow all the people you see to die in the Battle of Armageddon, which starts in the United States because you do not need to hold a meeting?

You are responsible to find Elijah if you believe you cannot form God's Kingdom by yourself. The Universal Church format, which was granted in the year of Our Lord 1200 AD, has seven names on the door and seven Holy Cities. If you understand reality because of your blasphemous mouth, you worship Satan. If you stay with the gospel about Christ as defined in the year 31 AD, as the book of Matthew states the end shall come. It is not the word of God. The Holy Bible is His plan. I have contacted you in the past and all you desired to do is kill the messenger.

The teenagers of America do not like organized religion so you believe that is not your problem. Let me kill the messenger. The teenagers do not like their parents getting divorces and you say I do not give a damn. I will kill the messenger. I am perfect. Why would I desire to change? All I have to do is con the congregation out of their money and I can tell them how great I am. The Holy Bible states, you are taking pride in yourself and not humility for King Jesus Christ. The Holy Bible states you are asleep at the altar. Why would you desire to change when you judge yourself as perfect? You must judge the world as saints. The Holy Bible states you have the wrong heart for John 3:16 as you worship Satan. I can prove that statement. Can you prove King Jesus Christ's messenger is wrong?

I am Elijah to teach you how to end divorces so you can get the heart of the fathers back with children or teenagers back to the church. I am a prophet that can end the millions of children dieing each year due to a famine (money). Do you desire to kill the messenger? A great amount of money is required and King Jesus Christ states I will double the best Adam can do. I have King Jesus Christ's thousand-year plan for the one world government of Israel for the United States. Do you need to kill His messenger and tell the congregation, "You know I have to wait for King Jesus Christ to return?" The Holy Bible states He has told you all things, so you should know all the answers. Are you lying to the congregation and yourself? May you die without any possibility for John 3:16 as you desire to kill the teenagers that have a message or Elijah!

Are you killing the messengers of the Italian Mafia and lying to the men that are failing themselves? They are in shackles and as failures cannot be saved. Are you killing the messenger of the families whose children die of drugs? The Italian Mafia has the wrong heart and the church does not care or are the Son of Perdition. Do you judge the politicians violating the book of Mark and become the Mark of the Beast? No, you are the Son of Perdition.

King Jesus Christ has judged you long ago. The Holy Bible is clear. Do you have seven churches with the Universal Church format? Where is your Holy City? You are just the sinner that must repent and the Son of Perdition.

I have asked you and your peers to check the chapter you must teach on the great and dreadful Day of the Lord or Good Friday. If you desire to check, you can correct and send to me. If you agree you should ask Elijah, "What should I do next?" If you take no action, just resign from the church or do the Millstone Story. You will find it impossible to be saved. You have a heart that is different from your God of Heart as you have the heart of Satan or heart of failure of yourself.

What is required of you? I have created the presentation and a voice file. You must read, listen, learn, reproduce some papers and set up a meeting. The rest I have done for you. You will learn more about religion in less than one hour than you have learned in your entire lifetime. It is time for Adam to grow up and learn how to talk. King Jesus Christ will not return until you have no questions to ask. The seals are for communication within a kingdom. The 666 beasts are books of Standing Historical or the history of your denomination in each nation where you have a presence. The beasts are the politicians you start a war against to avoid their failures as human beings. The 666 beast books are to last longer than heaven and earth or from Here to Eternity a measure of time. May a thousand zeros of time be short in terms of the effective use of the Holy Bible to resolve any problem in this world through one hundred percent theology!

Elijah

Richard Cartwright
430 Pembroke Rd SW
Poplar Grove' IL 61065

Tel # 815-765-0161

Elijah lives at Candlewick Lake, has a daughter and grand children living in Elk Grove Village, and can prove all that he has written.

The four words of the millennium are fear, war, jeopardy, and joy. I have not heard your understanding of how they apply for the next thousand years.

Rev Rex Rogers cannot be forgiven and will go by the way of Satan. His advantage if he works to help the children the penance will only last one thousand years for him and if married his wife. If the kingdom does not form a thousand years is very short.

The letters went to many other church locations.
January 8, the year of Our Lord 2008 AD

Immanuel Lutheran Church
1045 Belvidere Rd
Belvidere IL

Antichrist Rev Allen Buss Sr Pastor

January 6, the year of Our Lord 2008 AD

Cross and Crown Lutheran Church
7404 Elevator Rd
Roscoe, IL

Antichrist Pastor John L. Heins

January 7, the year of Our Lord 2008 AD

Poplar Grove United Methodist Church

105 E Grove
Poplar Grove, Il 61065

Antichrist Senior Pastor Lisa Kruse-Safford
(She told me you called me the Antichrist and you cannot learn from me and that is true. I have sent countless emails to her and the best she can answer is she is not capable or required to learn.).

I think about his sermon for the day I heard from the Baptist Rev Rex A. Rogers. He stated it was strange that the Rabbis of Israel did not go to Bethlehem (God's World) to witness the birth of King Jesus Christ. I was at the Bethel Church. Where was the commitment from the clergymen to find me? I wrote a book as the name Elias that is required per Mark 9:12. I am Elijah as defined to bring the hearts of the fathers back with children and being the watchman for the United States. I being the watchman can only happen if the church is formed. The Holy Bible is clear. I must seek through Devine Intervention the presidency of the United States or the third power of eight.

I arrived at his church with great excitement in the belief he would be willing to learn. I just walk in and he runs to greet me. He states he does not desire to learn the teaching of Elijah despite the Holy Bible and knowing I can end divorces and what we call poverty today in the millions of children lives all over the world. All he needed from me is to state how great his sermons are. The Holy Bible has his judgment well defined, where King Jesus Christ compared him with the animal the ass or oxen and he lost.

What should the congregation expect God to do with men that can reach for such greatness by implementing the Lord's Prayer and all they desire to hear is how great they are? He is taking pride in himself, not humility for King Jesus Christ. Our God will meet us in the temple, not church. We cannot sit around and expect Him to return through our observation. The Antichrist reaction is what made the world of ours achieve one hundred percent of everything wrong. False witness of reality will cause the world to go into penance seven times longer and the Antichrists running the church will be responsible for the unnecessary deaths of a trillion children. What do you expect God to do to seek vengeance on Adam? All he has to do is continue the divorce from Israel and let Adam create a greater Hell or earth. He will return with the Seven Horns (what is said) of the Eternal Temple or Israel. One day the clergymen will be asked to create the beginning of heaven on earth again. The Lord's Prayer with seven names on the door and seven Holy Cities will be the answer. The answer is the same and shall always be the same. The greatest tribulation the world will ever see will be the church formed and the return of King Jesus Christ. What is required? The clergymen to obey King Jesus Christ, live by the Ten Commandments to become saints to judge the world, and commit to end the pain in the families lives like divorces. See the Chapter The Stairway to Heaven.

Going back to Antichrist Rev. Rex A. Rogers. The letter stated he desires to kill the messengers. He has another man that works with the young, but when the children do not like organized religion, he would say there is nothing I can do. When the children send a messenger they do not like divorces, he ignores. When the women see their children dieing all over the world, he cannot listen to the hunger of the messengers. How should God judge him? When he dies, he can judge himself as to what he believes and how he should be judged. If he lies to himself may the judgment be worst than Satan.

I have to go back to an old story. The clergymen where considered better than the attorneys in truth in a public opinion poll. I trust in the Italian Mafia attorneys more than the clergymen. We can easily believe they are not achieving anything other than their own failure. The clergymen were judged by God long ago, as Antichrists and they will lie to your face to prove they can be trusted with your inheritance or future. Many claim that King Jesus Christ caused all that is bad all over the world and there is nothing they can do in a kingdom as defined in scripture to resolve all problems. The Holy Bible states I have told you all things, so as a kingdom they can correct any social ills within any society. All they do is commit to false witness (sins) to prove they are justified to beg for your money to keep their church open.

We must include the Lord's Prayer in defining the word forgiveness. In the church side of the book of judges, the church shall include all the logic and wisdom defining the meaning of forgiveness as life evolves. What I am doing here is the foundation of truth, not the entire truth. I can use the judge in the court that stole your grandmother's house through a tax sale as an example. The answer was simple in the governor sending an attorney to grant a reverse mortgage to your mother. Countless number of people could have prospered from the new instruction; however, instead of blaming the court, the church must teach forgiveness. I can relate to my own family where under President Herbert C. Hoover. My father's family had two houses and money in the bank. The family was large and many men could work in the year of Our Lord 1928 AD. The local bank forecloses on the house and the family loses two houses yet they had the money in the bank. Many people have qualified for houses and under President Ronald Reagan and George H. W. Bush lost their houses and farms. We should not forgive them. They did not attempt to avoid stealing our houses. Under Ronald Reagan, he had interest rates to twenty-one percent and the carpenters could not buy the house they are building for the government. If they built the exact house for sale, they could not afford a loan at twenty-one percent and many desirable houses for Americans where not built. There is zero reason for creating a depression or a recession type environment in our country. If you understand the Holy Bible, you should state neither condition could occur unless we had a large number of people retiring or other major reason for the number of workers decreasing (not unemployment). We cannot forgive losing our houses or the fools running government allowing a recession or worse. Now in the year of Our Lord 2007 AD, the parties and economists are debating and millions of lives are at stake. The answer is to raise the tax on greed and use the money to fix the roads and other sorrows. One social ill in our country is the roads are bad and we cannot forgive the politicians. With the tax rate so high today, the governments would receive more tax revenue than they spent on the roads. The value of the dollar would soar if the additional tax revenue were saved; thereby, the cost of gasoline could go down to half from the highs and inflation could go negative. Do not think of lower prices because of a bad economy is good. We should restrict the future spending of new tax revenue to fund Social Security as I have defined. Once the businessman understands the Holy Bible economic plan, they should say, "What are we going to fix next?" The problem arises only when you cannot define a social ill to fix. We shall not want. Once the congregation has their wants satisfied, they are rich. They must try to define more wants so the challenge can continue.

Only through the elimination of the social ills can the congregation forgive. Only through continual change will the clergymen reach the power of God.

The Tree of Knowledge and Tree of Life with the meaning of Good and Evil are covered in another chapter and you require a true understanding for the word forgive. The Holy Bible is the most complicated book in the world and only through a kingdom can be understood. The reason I can understand it is because I have created the requirements to form a kingdom years ago and my literature has evolved beyond just a new beginning. I know no one else in this world could do it without millions of men working together to learn how to talk. Since the church refuses to work together or hear from the messengers, King Jesus Christ had to send His representative back and he became the voice in the wilderness. He does not even have a secretary. He must rely on his memory and logic to write the companions and the sixty-seventh book of the Holy Bible.

What shall be added to the books of Standing Historical for the United States with the thousands of memos I have originated to the Antichrist all over America. I have email through their web sites and email addresses countless number of solutions to mankind problems. The only hope I have left is the fact I did not learn of the name Elijah from Gerald Flurry of the book of Revelations liars of the Church of Philadelphia until about December of the year of Our Lord 2007 AD. That one item will keep me going. The Holy Bible states, I can be broken if I cannot use my hand. Hand in a colorful language of scripture means writing laws or being the president of the United States through divine intervention or the third power of eight. I must continue for the love of my grandchildren. On July 28, the year of Our Lord 2008 AD, you have two men that desire to be dragons as the eighth beast. Just like the year of Our Lord 2004 AD, if you voted for Satan or the False Messiah in the United States, you were wrong. Do not let the congregation make that mistake again. The end shall come.

I believe in the words of the Holy Bible. I would not try to save the Preacher Whores running the church. I would save the meek, which can end wars, stop crime syndicates and conquers the beasts that desire to rule and not satisfy the demands of people of their country in the want of health, wealth, and wisdom.

What are the church employees of King Jesus Christ to do with the Elders and the anointing oil? As written before, they are to do the Exorcist story. King Jesus Christ took the Demons out of the man's mind and cast them into the pigs. He who judges shall be judged and no one is judging the psychiatrist. How can we forgive them when they have turned American children from A and B students into D and E through drugs? In the year of Our Lord 1939 AD, the number one problem in school was gum. Today the children are not the same. What has America done but ruin countless numbers of children by bad deeds? King Jesus Christ shows the church employees to be board certified by the state and take over that role. The Demons that will come back in the minds of our soldiers of misfortune from Iraq. Our children through the church may through their medical science be better off and may we not have to forgive them for unkind medical views. King Jesus Christ on their side makes the church strong to do the exorcist story of the Demons in our minds. A person hurts a child by accident. May the Demons be removed and the power of forgiveness be effective! A child dies and mom has to work to continue life. Maybe an adopted child to replace like the Garden of Eden is the answer. Please clergymen have people certified by your area and end the pain of grieving as today and learn the power of mourning. Only through your change can the congregation forgive you. Easter Sunday is for teaching the meaning of the end of all death. Teach our children about the pain in grandma and she is waiting for the true Heaven to get new arms and legs. We can only forgive the clergymen when the congregation truly believes in John 3:16 and the cross was to show you the new beginning, the meaning of John 3:16, and a transfer of power. Please teach the people the meaning of caring for children and having the right heart. The clergymen cross to bear is the Holy Bible. We must through the church teach to learn how to live by the words, not just read them with foolish concepts. We can start to forgive the clergymen only through their creating the one hundred percent theology.

When I say a clergymen cannot be forgiven, I mean it. They are the worse examples of human beings in the entire world. Only through their death can the clergymen be saved and thereby be saved by King Jesus Christ.

Chapter 15. Dr. Martin Luther King

This is a book on fear as the sixty-seventh book of the Holy Bible. Many would say it should include Dr. Martin Luther King. How could the church teach that King Jesus Christ has forgiven all your sins and a great leader falls for what should be the view of all Americans? The next thing the Antichrists would say is, "I forgive all the sins of the Ku Klux Klan and all the white trash that support it." The sinners that should repent are the clergymen and their management. The congregation is in jeopardy. The Holy Bible states all men are created equal and the blacks should have been free through the church long ago. They should have the same rights as all others as they have a soul. As the Holy Bible states in the seeds of all knowledge or the book of Genesis, Abram stated, "I do not care what it cost, I have to free the slave." If you study the Holy Bible, it would appear that Americans that failed themselves in the Civil War or war of brother against brother and sister against sister would be impossible to start. The Southern clergymen should copy the answers out of the Holy Bible. In the book of Genesis, it states, "I do not care what it costs, I have to free the slave." Any other answer is wrong.

Let me go through a story of old. I was working for my degree in Electrical Engineering back in the 1960s. A friend told me a story of a woman he knew from work at Western Electric. The company was forced to be dynamic in applying government policies, as our executives were to appear before the United States Senate. We tried to over conform to government hiring policies. I was labeled an Engineering Associate progressing up the corporate ladder to success. A woman had just received her engineering degree; therefore, at that time she was over qualified to be my level, but qualified through education for a level higher. In the progressive company, she could not earn the right to do my job, because she was a woman.

What did Congress under the Democrats do, but solved many social ills of the country. Many only understand the blacks had been granted an advantage, but now a white woman could get a credit card, be an engineer, start a business, or be the Chairman of the Board at a corporation. One statistic that many left out in disagreement with the laws was the white people still had a lower unemployment number than the blacks decades later. February should be Black History Month, but the white female and all minorities should love his birthday. President Linden Johnson had a chance to free the slaves that President Abraham Lincoln died before he could make free completely. President Thomas Jefferson had a choice to be president or no political career. Many great solutions of the unfair labor practices have come from the Democrats; however, the Holy Bible states we require ten thousand new ideas (seeds) to bring America back to establish the laws of liberty. America like Israel of old is asleep as far as love and understanding. No one in their right mind would desire to live in America and its future if the Lord's Prayer is not implemented.

What should be addressed in the life of Dr Martin Luther King, is his wife. For thirty years as I heard, she was suffering for the fact the attacker was not found. The Holy Bible states with John 3:16, we should mourn not grieve. The church still preaches mourning as the technique of grieving; however they do not even use the techniques of Israel to get the grieving behind in a year. The reality of mourning in the case of an older woman should be I am in joy to receive my just reward of new arms and legs. The choice is our Gods, but renewal of life through John 3:16 is a great reward. John 3:16 is the end of all death for those that have the right heart.

What went wrong in Dr Martin Luther King's wife is she lost nearly thirty years of joy due to false preaching at the church. Have you heard of people going back to a court ten years later to guarantee the penance of Adam's foolishness is continued? What the exorcist story should display is the virtue of God seeking the vengeance, not man. You lost all as clergymen, when you allowed a fool to use his horn (mouth) that as president, I will seek the vengeance on the terrorists. The vengeance on terrorists of God would be the penance, "In Heaven on earth, do not send your policemen out to kill them because they will not go to school (UN education, where we get oil and they get money from Iraq not killing wars). The peacekeepers are the children of America and Iraq, not the soldiers of misfortunes or United States military. What happen is the United States became the fourth empire as prophecy foretold. The first was Rome, second Great Britain, the third was the Soviet Union and the fourth does not have an animal. The book of Daniels states the United States will be the fourth. The book of Romans is what King Jesus Christ has judged you and the Antichrists reading the book of Romans are trying to make part of the judgment on us seem good. The church will tell you as a violation of the Ten Commandments, they have over come Satan through their great teaching about the gospel about Christ. As the Holy Bible states their way will result in the end or the Battle of Armageddon starting in the United States.

What are some of the procedures the clergymen are to use? One is they should shove Satan's body under the Altar. If you ask them they would say all you have to do is believe in King Jesus Christ and I can save anybody. They have not saved themselves. King Jesus Christ states I will not save the Preacher Whores. The clergymen take pride in themselves as they state, "I can tell King Jesus Christ what to do." They are to obey King Jesus Christ and have humility for Him. You obey a king, not a king obey you. Their cross to bear is the Holy Bible. They are in penance and they do not even know it or confess it. How could a clergyman believe in King Jesus Christ when he allows the president to seek vengeance and thereby become the Red Dragon and Satan? The courts of the United States are run by hanging judges and mercy is to follow all of us all the days of our life. The church is to train the courts on the procedures of the Holy Bible and my books to believeth in Him not the version of religion developed by the clergymen. The judges are to have the right heart.

How many times have you heard the clergymen doing King Jesus Christ version of the Passover story. If Wal-Mart did not learn (exploiting the workers), they could not even sell a shoelace. When have you heard of them where they brought out the Terrible Swift Sword (Rod of Iron) in the seven Holy Cities, so the world earth shakes in concept? As the Holy Bible states, there is no fear in the church and all God's instructions are violated.

Many minorities have gained advantages in college because of color. If I were to start, I would plan the same way; however, I see many blacks and minorities in various jobs today. I believe the voice of common sense maybe as we build new schools in the cities and create a shortage of labor, we should review the laws to eliminate the advantage. It should be slowly over time not quickly. Money should be available to the minds not race. In some occurrences, a student should go to a fine junior college to catch up before going into the universities. In the end that is the only way. In other countries where similar problems exist, we might review what happened in America. Our laws today should express challenge rather than color, since the black man has gained entrance to all schools.

We should think about Dr Martin Luther King's wife. She believed if they did not find her husband's killer that all was lost. She did not believe in let God seek the vengeance said the Lord. All I can say is for the wife of a great man; she had a life that she denied her husband the right to go to heaven, because she was deceived in mourning, where she was trained to grieve. She ended up with a bad life.

Chapter 16. Are Clergymen
Easily Deceived?

God has an interesting passage in the Holy Bible that states, "Some of the stories are so great, if you could get to the very elect, all you would do is deceive." First, you have to analyze the word "some". Many churches have many stories and you have to determine their best of their best. You ask yourself as a member of the church, "Are the clergymen nothing more than people that at best they would be deceived?" If that does not occur is the rest of the Holy Bible nothing more than a con on all mankind? You have others that I covered like for your blasphemy mouth, you will worship Satan. Again another statement that you should tell your clergymen, I want that proved. Are they easily deceived? How can that happen to over a million men that state they understand the Holy Bible enough to run a church location? Does your clergyman state his proof is, "You know, I have to wait for Jesus to return?" He does not even use His correct title and Name. What does the Holy Bible state but form the kingdom first and learn how to talk. King Jesus Christ will return when the clergymen have no questions to ask because the Holy Bible states, I have told you all things. King Jesus Christ put the clergymen in penance back in Israel for they disobeyed three times and He refused to help them.

He states you cannot go to Israel to learn how to raise a child. Check if you abandon thy children (777 design) with millions dieing each year due to lack of daily bread, I will abandon you and the penance shall continue for seven times longer (fourteen thousand more years). Have you heard American teenagers do not like organized religion? The church has abandoned the children of 777 design. At that time, He stated it is not the right generation. After January 1, the year of Our Lord 2000 AD is the right generation or the Age of Accountability. The clergymen are in denial, about themselves being the sinners that have to repent. Any statement of false doctrine is blasphemy and violates the Ten Commandments. In the church, you should realize by starting wars of killing and the clergymen supporting the action of the Red Dragon is a story of deception.

I went to a conference where as Elias or Paul; I am to judge all mankind, on all subjects (restoreth all things). Any topics you say are bad that I can learn I will turn into good. The theory of theology or planning from the Holy Bible is you start out with what is known.

I will start out with the back round of a great story that is total failure or the clergymen are deceived. The Love Baptist Church had a conference on the wall. I go to many locations. When I read about the Reformers Conference in my neighborhood, I called and gave my credit card. Mr. Lay and I talk about casting not written in the book of life is to be cast in the lake of fire and he thought that was bad. I attended the first session expecting the meeting to be small so I prepared what I would say. I already knew the answers to addictions since it is a small part of the miracles in my book, "The Antichrist God's Version". I did not add the words that should be developed by Christ (son of man) for alcohol addiction, so I developed the sixth sense or "DON'T LET DRINK TAKE THE DRINK" and was ready to introduce myself. What the religious leader did was he advertised throughout the country and I learned he was a nonaligned Baptist Church or independent. He could not go to the President of the Baptist Church and proclaim a pending victory over addictions.

You have to realize many Baptist Church locations were contacted and many decided not to be involved. As an outsider of the employees of the church, you wonder to help our fellow man on drugs, food, gambling, and other addictions all should have shown up; however, the Holy Bible states you cannot get to the very elect or the man that runs the church. The story on the surface was great but like Paul I judged the entire story wrong. The technique was to make the people feel guilty after for example on alcohol they lost their job, health, and possibly the family. You say, "What can we do?" I have written memos on the subject and I promise the answers came from the Holy Bible, which not one person there used as God intended. Guilty is against God and man should not use that technique in court or church. The words were the words of man not God. The solution to alcohol addiction is to teach how to drink beer and wine like Israel of the Holy Bible. They do not drink wine in a church as the Holy Bible defines which would find alcohol problems. A drink is good for the tummy, but excesses are bad for all humanity.

I have judged the television station TBN in my book, "The Antichrist God's Version". After six hours of reviewing the recordings and analyzing what is being preached not one story met the requirements of the Holy Bible. The station is a composite of small religious men who covered richer people to enable them to afford to go on television or had money themselves. All church locations, I have visited are not ready for sermons on milk, let alone meat. The reason they are not successful is they refuse to work together to create any story you can use to resolve what is bad. All are trying to gain your listening time and money to stay on television. They will tell you almost anything by violating the Ten Commandments to get your interest in their false teachings. In Chapter seventeen of the book, "The Antichrist God's Version" you can use to judge any church location if you have good skills.

I wrote to preacher whore and Antichrist Ken Copeland of the television station TBN. I asked what he is doing to implement the Lord's Prayer and he writes back that King Jesus Christ has forgiven all my sins. I wrote back and asked what that had to do with implementing the Lord's Prayer. He was lying, as Our God King Jesus Christ will take care of the sinners or the clergymen. The Holy Bible reads, we require a new story of John the Baptist. He likes his story of con to convince the viewers he knows what he is doing is good, but it is the way to the end. I know the Holy Bible states that the Antichrist (clergymen) sins go up into the heavens. The clergymen are the ones that must repent. They are called Cardinal Sins and he does not even have a Cardinal or equivalent in his organization. The television station is not using the Universal Church format that was used to form the United States government. He like many is trying to build a congregation without hope and he writes he has overcome Satan, which again he is lying. His whole show is against the development of the true Word of God, but to get you to take pride in him. I would only guess his greatest story would be his conferences. The one in Washington DC he states that whatever party you represent, you should vote. I sent him a question long ago asking, "Why do we have two parties which violate the Holy Bible?" He sent me to another source to seek the answer, but he never tried to learn himself. The Holy Bible states, "A house divided amongst itself always fails." The clergymen should teach the hell created by thirteen Slave States versus thirteen Free States or half Democrats and half Republicans. I sent Keith Moore of his show a questionnaire on the Holy Bible when he stated, "I am the best biblical scholar around." I am sorry because I am. The test is in the Chapter "Bible Answer Man Test". He did not contact me for the answers or write me with any correct answer. The test is the Word of God on the written Standing Historical all church locations are to have.

If you asked him for his Standing Historical or stories on the twelve days of Christmas, it would be a waste of time. The man is not even saved because he believeth in Ken Copeland and himself through pride not the words required to implement the Holy Bible or humility for King Jesus Christ.

One thing you can count on is Preacher Whore Ken Copeland sending out as a beggar for money. Many proclaim that tithing is a way of life. The beggars are to make the poorest child in the country rich (we shall not want). If the child's family is without want, he still is the poorest. So the beggars continue and he includes many passages so he can con the people out of their money. Tithing is what an individual does to live within a government, so they can provide for the common good like roads and business licenses not to provide money for Preacher Whores to sleep at the Altar. King Jesus Christ stated you denied me the tithes or money the government will receive. When the church eliminates what they today call poverty, the church becomes extremely well off financially. They are not to be beggars.

I have watched Pastor Murray on television five days a week and he like many others sell the ideas to maintain television time. Many viewers watch and try to learn. Back in the early 1990s I started by recording his television show each day, working my job, and listening to the Holy Bible. It was not very long and I soon learned he was wrong on almost all he added. The only part he added to the word was like the word hate. He had a definition that made sense or the meaning is love less. He read the Holy Bible on how a man once married had to hate his parents. He did not talk with any conviction that he understood. I listen to a religious radio station and the question on the new bible was, "Did it include the word hate?" In my first book, "Life of US (U.S.)", I showed how to use the word hate for a law the congregation desires changed. Pastor Murray states all laws are good. In truth, all laws of importance are bad and not written to the New Testament standards. You will not find in this world a law of importance, you would define as good. If all laws were good, this law the congregation should hate would not exist. The word hate is so the government realizes they must change it; therefore, you love that law less. Before the fools started the war in Iraq, the Holy Bible stated, "The Arabs were to be hated above all others." which come from the book of Genesis that would happen. As the church taught the government on how to divide the "Cows" up wisely and the Muslins would as a good religious order get the terrorism to end by making the terrorists fools. That was the instruction from King Jesus Christ; therefore, the church cannot teach that love conquers all and the word hate is crucial to learn with understanding. The stories you have heard with the word hate are wrong. Have you heard of hate crimes? Do you love those crimes less?

I have heard long ago Pastor Murray believes the Mark of the Beast is the people that go to the Psychiatrists. He may have changed it now. The Psychiatrists are not teaching the people to define what future they desire to inherit and is very expensive in their failure; however, the Mark of the Beast is the government violating the instructions in the book of Mark. When the government under foolish George Bush from the year of Our Lord 2001 to 2004 AD was continually violating the book of Mark, you wonder why all the pain in the millions of American lives did not change the results of the Republican Party not presenting foolish George Bush's name again. The first four years was too much pain. The Republicans did not care. All they desired was to win the elections. Pastor Murray like all other clergymen cannot sit down and through a kingdom discover the instructions in the book of Mark. Your violation will result in increased pain in the country or state and the pain is the Mark of the Beast, like Hoover Ville. Pastor Murray stated he finally had a good Republican governor. The governor stated his biggest problem was he did not have enough prisons. King Jesus Christ states to get rid of prisons, which is easy to start. All courts do in criminal action is under crime and punishment is find people guilty. They are violating the Holy Bible. The Holy Bible defines the Republicans as Beasts and the lawless ones are the clergymen that vote for them. Pastor Murray is so easily deceived. After nearly two thousand years of Holy Bible study by men that claim they can understand the written word, they could not learn. In a kingdom if one person noticed the connection, the answer should be understood. What he has created are stories where he does not have to work with his peers to achieve. His blasphemy mouth is the result or becoming a man worse than a fool. So any story written by anyone that does not discover the book of Mark to identify the Mark of the Beast qualifies for the passage, "Some of the stories are so great, that if you can get to the very elect, all you will do is deceive." The very elect is the clergymen that vote in God's election. The church should vote on God's Covenants or the minimum requirement to run a church. The Universal Church format granted in the year of Our Lord 1200 AD was used to form the United States government. The clergymen should realize that format is the only acceptable structure available for them to use with seven names on the door or I saw seven churches.

What is a summary of a man on television five days a week? Pastor Murray claims the Holy Bible is so easy to understand a child can understand it. He claims his role is to read the book and King Jesus Christ is to do everything else. If that was true, King Jesus Christ sure wasted much effort in creating the Holy Bible for Pastor Murray to teach his entire congregation to live by every word. All he does is read without understanding. The Holy Bible states all judgment is already covered in the Holy Bible. The saints from the church are to judge the entire world. Anyone who teaches, "He who judges shall be judged." and states as a member of the church not to judge all those stories are wrong. Pastor Murray does not teach what it takes to believe in King Jesus Christ like teaching one hundred percent of the children that Our Gods do not want them to do a job they do not want to do. When any church raised a child and he graduates from college, the clergymen have taught him how to maximize his life in work for the advantage of all America. No ninety percent of the American children take the wrong courses in college. Pastor Murray like all others on television is doing nothing to teach the children of 777 design. The Holy Bible tells Pastor Murray to stay at the Altar. Once he beams the gospel about Christ all over the world, the end shall come as Matthew 24:14 defines. Why? It is because it is not the Word of God. The clergymen teaching our children how to take the right courses in school is the Word of God. He is trying to teach God's Plan not the true Word of God. All of his tapes and television shows are wrong. The only question of importance he can answer is the type like, "What year was the war of 1812?" after that he is lost. What he is doing is taking pride in himself for the number of listeners. After all that time you would have to ask him in a country where life is deteriorating so quickly over the last thirty years, "What have you accomplished in taking humility for King Jesus Christ?" Why are you denying the requirement of the Lord's Prayer? Is it because you cannot get the other clergymen to understand and order your literature. You would only deceive.

What shall we do with all the deceptive literature? The information shall be sorted and stored, so in the year one thousand zeros, the new teachers can learn the meaning of the passages on penance and deception. The answer has always been to form the kingdom and learn how to talk. Do not lose that invaluable search of learning of the deception of Adam on Adam. The usual reason is the voice of the powerful drowning out the voice of reason or man adding their view by evil spirits or false witness to hear themselves speak.

Let me review another television show called Tomorrow's World on Sunday. I have been writing to them for weeks and they have requested no knowledge. Their show is a total deception.

The first thing they will try to teach you is the greatest problem in the world is killing wars as they read the Holy Bible. They cannot learn the pen is mightier than the sword. You solve the problem with the pen and the killing wars end through the kingdom. All men are brothers and the Holy Bible already teaches in a kingdom, how to end all terrorism and killing wars. They represent some person named Armstrong whose stories qualify for if you could get to the very elect all you would do is deceive. I have kept a copy of most correspondence with that church location and I will share with you my memos to them. The Holy Bible states you cannot get to the very elect, so you would expect them to reject all knowledge. They only desire to maintain pride in their false doctrine. The Holy Bible states not to write prophecies for yourself. The true prophets are dead. That is all they do and try to gather a small audience of people who can pay to continue their failure. If they desired to write prophecies, they should bring them to the organized religions. If you asked, they probably would say you cannot get others to listen, so they violate the Holy Bible and go to the public. Most of my literature is directed to the Antichrists that run the church. I realize they will not listen. The chance I have is they shall know what they did before they die. They die when they realize, they must create the kingdom. The Holy Bible states, they have to experience death; therefore, I try to prove to them they are worse than fools and yet they are the only chance the world has. The Battle of Armageddon starting in the United States because of the pen is only one beast away. The Antichrists do not know that a beast is a human being that lost his way and cannot be saved like Satan.

Emails to follow

Tomorrows World (WGN on Television)

You talked about the eighth Beast. Since you are trying to foretell the future, you should know the past. What are the names of the first seven and what did they do to become Beasts? Since that is just Standing Historical of a church, all clergymen should know the answer. I certainly do.

I will grant you my definition of a Beast. A Beast is a nonhuman being that believes more about winning a political race than serving the taxpayers. You have a chance. You state we will have a famine or lack of daily bread at the end, but a famine is all about money. You should read the Old Testament. Therefore, a Beast can create a famine or in our country be a Hawk if he becomes a dragon.

Instead of guessing, you could ask of King Jesus Christ's Representative like Paul in the Holy Bible the answer to that simple question. If you desire to become a group of importance and make up for your lack of knowledge, you should do what I asked of you.

Ask your listeners to go to as many church locations and types to ask the Antichrist (clergymen) what they are doing to form God's Kingdom (Lord's Prayer) and create heaven on earth. Ask them for you to summarize. If they learn, all is good. The Holy Bible states the church has gone backwards from the year of Our Lord 1900 AD (1776 plus 124 equals 1900) in New York City until today. They have created a nation of abortion, divorce and became the greatest debtor nation of our world. They desire to be justified by law not Grace (King Jesus Christ's Words or when you live by all the words of the entire Holy Bible that is the Grace of God). The Holy Bible states you have gone backwards and the wax is cold.

I desire you to help my grandson who will be one year old on September 23, the year of Our Lord 2006 AD avoid the Battle of Armageddon, which will start in the next presidential term according to the Holy Bible. My daughter told my grandson, his job is to love his mother. Women greatest desire is for a child to understand a great woman greatest desire. The church failure will be the penance is seven times longer and the answer is form the kingdom and for the clergymen to become royalty (start heaven on earth). I fail to see the disadvantage to the congregation and that becomes the greatest tribulation the world will ever go through. The clergymen as they learn about today in the year 27,000,000,000 would desire a chance to accomplish as you have. The book of Daniel we do once to establish the kingdom as required by His Father and to be completed through the Lord's Prayer.

Your basic understanding is you become what Armstrong warned you about. He said the Nazis will rise again or teach the sword is mightier than the pen. The Holy Bible states the pen is mightier than the sword. In two thousand years, you can imagine the money and lives King Jesus Christ allowed you to lose in penance to achieve. Today I heard you kill thirty thousand people each day due to the pen. Before the foolishness of the war, what was the Chicken Little teaching about the sky is falling? Terrorism as you defined killed seven thousand people in twenty years and you can identify thirty thousand each day due to the pen. King Jesus Christ is going to grant you Angels to protect the Chicken Little that runs a church or God's Children of 777 design. You are waiting for two-year-old type children to protect Chicken Little from the Communist of the year of Our Lord 1952 AD under every rock and now terrorists that have massive invasion forces greater than the Japanese of the year of Our Lord 1941 AD in terms of a problem. You stop and think about all the bodies all over America due to the pen. You become the Nazis that Armstrong warned you about as you help Satan. Think about the terrorism in Washington,

DC where the politicians refuse to live in the city because terrorism is great by American citizens learning to resolve discussions with the sword. Do you desire greater assault rifles in Washington, DC for greater Domestic Tranquility?

After the Second World War or a War to end all Wars, the Holy Bible defines one third of the world was dead. I believe you know about the ungodly of the Communists. On January 1, the year of Our Lord 2000 AD at one hour past midnight (no Y2K), you became responsible for good and evil. I have never met a religious person that knows what evil means as your definition is the "bad guys". The clergymen are the greatest evil on this world not the "bad guys". In the Garden of Eden, once you are responsible for good and evil you will surely die and you did. No flesh is saved and the Lord's Prayer is the only solution. The Holy Bible recommends you get to the congregation's leaders.

Elias (like from Mark 9:12) is like CHRIST (son of man) since King Jesus Christ divorced you.

You will know the true Word of God by the representative of King Jesus Christ not the preacher whore who reads without understanding, cannot site the many miracles of stories he has put to rest, and must be justified by law not Grace.

Author of "Life of US (U.S.)": a book that forms God's Kingdom (Lord's Prayer).

Author of "The Antichrist God's Version": a book of God's miracles that people would say cannot be done like ending all poverty. Author's name Elias.

Present writing: author's name is Elijah, a book that takes books like the book of Revelation and turns it into a present day reality. No man of today could avoid the wrath of God without penance. I have gone to many different types of churches like Paul from scripture and I guarantee the Holy Bible is correct.

The church of today went backwards from New York, NY in the year of Our Lord 1900 AD to today and the wax is cold. The church must be justified by law because grace is gone. Have you heard of a nation of divorce or abortion and the church desires to be justified by law not grace?

Email comfortinGod@hotmail.com

First two books published listed on www.iuniverse.com and other locations.

I have King Jesus Christ patented planning technique knowledge on how to get to a small door. Check the door story of Revelations on Armstrong's lack of any understanding or run by liars. Restoring all things is implementing the Lord's Prayer with the numerous miracles the church can create like ending all poverty but not all that is poor. Ending all that is poor takes an Eternity of time. Eleven hundred and fifty and twenty three hundred are real time or are forty-two months or seven year planning (theology) cycles. Ponder or you consider 777 design for children to become adults at twenty-one that the church helps raise like in Israel. King Jesus Christ states you lost the most critical knowledge the world had from Israel or the ability for a child to grow up with the proper understanding of how the child can serve himself best. As I have written in my book and King Jesus Christ has in the Holy Bible, you do not attack the child. I wrote possessing the IQ that I possess, how can I serve myself best? Yes I said, can serve myself best.

I have changed the author's name to the biblical requirement or Elijah.

Tomorrow's World

I read your article on Genuine Financial Security. The reason we have poor people on Feed the Children is that the Antichrist (clergymen) refuse to obey King Jesus Christ. In your future writing, please use His correct name and title. The

Holy Bible states to form the kingdom first. It is a simple matter to end the money (famine) in people's lives. I have a thousand year plan, which is copied from the Holy Bible, and a recession is almost impossible to achieve. A depression is only caused by total and absolute fools. I have asked clergymen (Antichrists) if they desire to end poverty and one said no and another said it is not possible for the two that answered. The only problem is there are seven names on the door and seven Holy Cities from the book of Daniel. My thousand-year plan for America I want to turn into a movie.

King Jesus Christ economic model as defined in the Holy Bible is required. The Holy Bible is written so no man can boast, so I just copied it out of scripture.

Richard Cartwright
430 Pembroke Rd SW
Poplar Grove, IL 61065
815-765-0161
Email comfortinGod@hotmail.com

Ask and I will send you a copy or ask and you shall receive. I am sorry but I would have to rewrite your entire magazine.

Tomorrow's World

I saw your show on 11-26-the year of Our Lord 2006 AD. You asked a question of, "What lies ahead for the USA?" You think of a King that divorced the church (put you in penance), how much He would help you?

Without the clergymen (Antichrists), forming His Kingdom the answer is the famine would happen. The famine is not for daily bread but the Word of God. The Word of God is the usury laws story from the Old Testament or a collapse of the value of the dollar that leads to buyer and seller remorse. The Battle of Armageddon starts and King Jesus Christ returns in seven times longer for penance, so about the year of Our Lord 22,000 the clergymen have a chance to form the kingdom or do the book of Daniel you do once.

The second answer is the Antichrists (clergymen) implement the book of Daniel you do once, forms the kingdom, and creates the one world government of Israel. The USA becomes the Heartland of the world.

Author of the book The Antichrist God's Version at www. iuniverse.com

---

Tomorrow's World

The great and dreadful Day of the Lord is Good Friday where the adults only learn about Fear. King Jesus Christ will not return until the church does the book of Daniel once or implements the Lord's Prayer. All flesh is dead because you failed to implement the Lord's Prayer and you worship Satan. The Battle of Armageddon starts in the USA due to the Famine, which is lack of money.

Why not just ask for my presentation on how to start the Lord's Prayer in any location. I will provide the voice file.

Think of what is the biggest problem on the planet. The church has a book that always ends up with a life for all citizens of one thousand times better than the end. You and I agree that Adam is about to create the end. What Adam has proved is Noah's Ark is a kind story from Our Gods. If Adam is going to create the end, what is he doing right? The answer as defined in the Holy Bible and I can prove is nothing.

Ask for the presentation. Someone that has a connection to the church must form God's Kingdom. That is the greatest tribulation Adam can work on. You can start the beginning of heaven on earth and the Second Advent or King Jesus Christ's return will be after forming the kingdom and the one world government of the Old Testament.

12/11/the year of Our Lord 2006 AD

Tomorrow's World

I received your literature on the Scarlet of Babylon riding the Beast. Your booklet misses the point. Just like the Antichrist comes in an era of peace and prosperity so does this Beast. Therefore, one hour past midnight on January 1 in the year of Our Lord 2000 AD, you are as a kingdom watching for a beast that violated the book of Mark. He becomes the Mark of the Beast.

Did you listen to President elect Al Gore talk about Governor George W. Bush becoming a Beast when he had money to provide health care for the children of Texas? He becomes a mass murderer of children from Texas when he puts the money in the treasury by violating the book of Mark. As the Holy Bible states, "Not one woman could vote for foolish Bush as a Beast." He promises to take the money designed for the school system and give most to the people that earn over $100,000 a year. They received 90% of the money or it became government waste. You think of what happen to President William J. Clinton campaigning for Al Gore. He was a non-event because of his girl friend or the Scarlet of Babylon. Many Antichrists thought more about Pro-life than the lives of children of America. What does the Holy Bible state or you abandon Thy children and I will abandon you. The USA lost John 3:16. We are the country where the Battle of Armageddon starts.

Why not ask for my presentation on how to start "the new beginning" in creating the kingdom? You can become great people the world will remember for your good deeds not just intentions.

Email comfortinGod@hotmail.com

12/14/06

You stated on one of your shows that Adam was deceived on the day of worship. Actually, Adam is deceived on one hundred percent of everything he has done. That is in government, church and business. I can prove it. King Jesus Christ put the world in penance back when they disobeyed in Israel. Adam without God is just a fool. The end is about to come and Adam has a book that always ends up with a life one thousand times better than the end called the Holy Bible. The answer is to form the Lord's Prayer and do the book of Daniel once. I have created the thousand-year plan for the one world government of the United States. Why do not you just ask for a copy or are you against a quest for knowledge.

12/17/the year of Our Lord 2006 AD

Tomorrow's World

Please read and tell me or yourself where we are wrong.

All flesh is dead, since you worship Satan. Satan is a real person that became a beast and cannot be saved. He is the seventh beast and the eighth beast is the end or the Battle of Armageddon starts in the USA due to the famine (lack of money). As in the Garden of Eden once you are responsible for good and evil, you will surely die. All flesh is dead due to John 3:16 being gone. Where do you find the clergymen obeying King Jesus Christ? I have gone to countless church locations by visits or writing and they are useless. The clergymen is the Antichrist as they are trying to get the congregation to worship them and ignoring any goals. A good goal is to get the pain out of the family's life like divorces and achieve spiritual bodies. Have you gone to a church where they have the twelve days of Christmas and the children (angels) are teaching the congregation the importance of a birthday or the 777 design to become good adults? The greatest knowledge I am aware of is the church helping the woman train the children to become good adults. In reality the clergymen (Antichrist) has abandoned the children of 777 design or to twenty-one.

The Holy Bible always ends up with a life one thousand times better. Any difference between one thousand times better and the end is the clergymen's sins that reach the Heavens. The clergymen is required to do the book of Daniel once and form the kingdom as seven names on the door and the Universal Church as granted in the year of Our Lord 1200 AD.

The four kingdoms you are looking for are not as Armstrong stated but starts with the Roman Empire and ends with the recreation of the Roman Empire as King Jesus Christ has defined in the book of Romans. The second is the British Empire or check the shield of Richard the Lion Heart. The third is the Russian Bear or the Soviet Union. The fourth is without an animal. I live in a country without an animal. You are looking for the greatest debtor nation in the world whose currency is green. Do we speak English? The United States has recreated the book of Romans as you were judged long ago. We allowed the Red Dragon to steal that woman's child and steal John 3:16 from the entire world.

The church does not even know what the word evil means. They say it is the bad guys. Actually, the clergymen is the most evil or lack of knowledge. I have not found a location that is a gatherer of all knowledge. Like if I sent a letter to you, you would read and respond by seeking the knowledge I have to offer. How many people have offered you a thousand year plan for the one world government of the United States based on the Old Testament format and updated to include the New Testament. If you do not desire to learn, you are not a priest of King Jesus Christ.

A beast is a person that turned into a wild animal once he becomes a politician like President Herbert C. Hoover by violating the book of Mark.

I have not even gone to one church location that uses His correct title or King Jesus Christ. All locations say come to my church and I will save your Soul. The only Soul he can save is his own unless he is like Paul to help the clergymen. All your Paul can do is help the employees of King Jesus Christ. All judgment is in the Holy Bible and he must teach the people how King Jesus Christ will judge or he has created his own religion and is the Antichrist.

You keep teaching the sword is mightier than the pen and the Holy Bible states the pen is mightier than the sword. If you form the kingdom, ending killing wars is easy. Read my thousand-year plan that I say should be turned into a movie. The sales would reach a billion people plus and the money should be used from the box-office and copies to start the six other Holy Cities and purchase the computers required for the kingdom. A quest for knowledge at the church locations will require great storage and email for the seals.

The angels are the children and Archangels are adults.

The famine at the end is not for daily bread as you state, but the Word of God and is all about money. Check the Old Testament.

Why not ask for the presentation and become a hero in God's Kingdom instead of a voice that cannot achieve. I have the presentation and the voice file that all a church location is required to do to start is make some telephone calls. I also have a thousand year plan for government that you can prove from the Holy Bible. You have never met a man that can create a thousand year plan and I could not without the Holy Bible.

Just ask and you shall receive. Do not continue with fantasyland.

Richard Cartwright
430 Pembroke Rd SW
Poplar Grove, IL 61065
1-815-765-0161
Email comfortinGod@hotmail.com

Ask for the presentation and voice files, which you can air. You will become great Icons of the church instead of a voice of nobody.

12/21/the year of Our Lord 2006 AD

Tomorrow's World

You stated that financial security is easy if you join the kingdom. If you study history, you could not overcome a fool like President Herbert C. Hoover. What the Holy Bible states is for you to implement the Lord's Prayer or the book of Daniel you do once. You should form the one world government and grant King Jesus Christ the advantage through the one political party of the church as trained by the church to state, "If you want to represent King Jesus Christ through the church, you must end all poverty as you define it today." You have achieved the beginning of, you shall not want through government. Without the power of the kingdom, you are just violating the Ten Commandments.

12/24/the year of Our Lord 2006 AD

Tomorrow's World

In December, you talked about God's Plan. Why not just ask for the presentation to start the beginning of Heaven on earth by implementing the Lord's Prayer? I can guarantee you will learn from it. You are to be in a quest for knowledge if you represent King Jesus Christ. All your literature should reflect His correct title. That would have meant that in a kingdom all clergymen would be the Prince of Peace.

The beast is a politician that violates the book of Mark. See the laws. Please check "The Beast of Revelation" you sent me for correction.

Send your request to comfortinGod@hotmail.com.

Have you heard of any church location where the people learn the importance of the twelve days of Christmas where the children run the church and teach the importance of a birthday? The angels in prophecy are children. The fallen angels are with the women as they have a good chance to go to prison or come from single women. The sins of the clergymen (Antichrist) go

361

to the Heavens. The number is equivalent to anything that is bad because if you apply the Holy Bible correctly you always end up with a life one thousand times better than the end. The Lord's Prayer is the new beginning and failure to implement the book of Daniel with seven names on the door is the end.

I am like Paul in the Holy Bible. I have audited many church locations and I understand the planning in the Holy Bible. When you said we have to live by every word, where do you believe any church location has tried? Our Gods have put us in penance in Israel when we disobeyed three times. The only answer is to implement the Lord's Prayer and form the one world government. I can do both and end the pain in people's lives like poverty. My one thousand year plan for the one world government of the US ends poverty so quickly in the United States; you wonder why anyone ever worked on it.

IS IT WORTH ASKING FOR ANSWERS OR DO YOU DESIRE TO CONTINUE LIVING IN THE DARK?

1/1/the year of Our Lord 2007 AD

Tomorrow's World

Try reading the Holy Bible where the angels are the children. Archangels are adults. God is going to send the angels to protect the church from wars by, "I do not want a hair on a child's head harmed." The wealth you talked about cannot be protected simply by the church when the congregation votes for a beast like President Herbert C. Hoover in the year of Our Lord 1928 AD and 1932 AD.

The answer is to implement the book of Daniel once by the Lord's Prayer.

Tomorrow's World

You still define problems and your small ideas to the masses. Try forming the kingdom and trying to solve an easy problem like global hunger. The answers are so easy you wonder why anyone worked on it for two thousand years without success. The end is near as we agree but the only solution is the Lord's Prayer and the book of Daniel you do once.

The famine at the end is for the Word of God and the end is all about money (government).

You seem to desire to teach me but what happens to a teacher that cannot learn.

The above are typical of all clergymen. The Holy Bible states they are to have eyes to see and ears to hear. Since they never listen to the congregation, they only guess. For example for all the years Tomorrow's World has been on television, have they changed their answers to what scripture means? The same words are quoted and more guesses are presented that are wrong. Tomorrow's World does at times state to continue tithing.

We should address the church types that have a chance to be one of the seven names on the door. This is a seven star planet where seven is the most important number in the Holy Bible for planning. We should just go to the only name on the door that you can guarantee will survive, if the kingdom is formed now. The name is Catholic as they have a "Holy City" location. The Catholics will tell you there is only one name on the door and that is Catholic. Our Father needed His son to create seven names on the door so the ultimate power does not corrupt ultimately. The saints are to run the Holy Cities and use the Holy Bible to judge the world. King Jesus Christ stated in the Holy Bible that He pities the women of suck of today and so do I.

The Catholics have distorted religion so bad and claim such merits in their way it is unbelievable. I saw a television view of the Priests standing in front of their religious literature and it is huge. The Holy Bible states if they could get to the very elect the clergymen in God's election all they would do is deceive; therefore, you are possibly aware of Pro-life in the year of Our Lord 2000 AD. They needed the future Republican who was a Beast. In the campaign, he became the King of Babylon for his horn. They were trying to force their entire congregation to vote for the future Red Dragon. Many people worst than fools called Antichrists put stupidity in front of their churches. Foolish George Bush won by the Supreme Court decision of the headline in the paper of Bush 5 to 4. That was five Republican Judges and they were against four Democratic Judges. The Holy Bible stated Satan would be in the Holy City and the Catholics even called President George W. Bush, Satan and had a picture of him with two horns on his head. Horns are what he would say not look like. I sent my only copy to Rome and I cannot find it again on the web, but the Catholics should put a copy of it in the Standing Historical or 666 beast books.

The Catholics were sending their Priests out to many church locations under former President William J. Clinton's administration to work against the Democrats. They achieved harming a hair on a child's head when President William J. Clinton and his wife ended up separated. If you heard their foolishness, you should have taught them a Vow of Silence, so his daughter could still have a father and mother married. The prophecy was God Save the Queen of the South and the Catholics through Pope John Paul II worked against prophecy and for his own foolish ideas. Where is the house divided amongst itself always fails? With all the foolishness of the

Catholic Church, they and others were able to get one third of Americans to vote for Republicans. They have not even taken a poll of the Catholic women to decide whether they need Pro-life or the victory of a desired child in the Catholic Church from a woman that is financially, spiritually, and physically able to bear that child. Then the Catholic Priest could work for that victory, not continue a House divided amongst itself always fails. The golden rule must be, "If God is for you who could stand against you." The only ones that can vote are the people that had an abortion and the will of the people prevails. So most of the religious leaders may realize the poverty of unneeded children is bad! I have tried to change the Catholics but they will not listen and violate Hosea 4:6. In the book of Hosea 4:6 "My people are destroyed for lack of knowledge: I will also reject thee, that you shall be no priest to me: seeing that you have forgotten the law of thy God I will also forget thy children." The Holy Bible states that lack of knowledge will destroy the church. The clergymen must be gatherers of all knowledge in order to satisfy the Tree of Knowledge in the Garden of Eden. All leaders I have contacted are rejecters of knowledge. I offered them to end all poverty through God's laws from the Holy Bible and they refuse to learn. As a woman, ask them what knowledge they have like Israel to turn all children into citizens at twenty-one years old. Is it foolishness or Catechism? The Holy Bible is written, so no man can boast.

What else do you know about Ireland and the foolishness of the Catholics and Presbyterian? Pope John Paul II when he stated he hated the Presbyterian, he did not have in mind the definition of "love less". His view would be dislike strongly or worse. In Ireland, the Catholic Priests must be sending the ones that kill the other congregation to Heaven for good deeds. They could be the second name on the door and allies against the Beasts. You may of heard the Catholic Church talk about the Italian Mafia back in the year of Our Lord 2000 AD. They stated that sometimes they become priests. You are not to send mass murders of children to the true Heaven because they give money to the church. Should all the Catholic Priests go to all clergymen types and convince them the women of your congregation (reform the church) should joy in their children dieing of drugs. Did the Catholics take a public opinion poll of all Catholic mothers whose child died from illegal drugs to determine if the Italian Mafia deserves to go to the true Heaven?

You have a passage that states, "I do not want you to do a job, you do not want to do." Is that part of Catechism? Since God's Plan requires zero Catholic children to take in Catholic schools studies that does not result in a Catholic doing a job they did not want to do, all other church locations would be interested in learning. They do not accept Catechism, so it must not be good. From what I have heard it should be one hundred percent rewritten not given to other church location to study and copy. With seven names on the door, much work is done as a workforce as the only goal is a life one thousand times better than the end. Since you are less than a decade away from the end, you should know the Catholics have to change all their literature. All their literature is deception. The Catholic Priests are not saved. The congregation should understand that if they go to any church location and double tithes, they still are not saved. King Jesus Christ will not save the Preacher Whores or today the Catholic Priests. If you ask the priest, he will tell you how good he is. They do not even know they are still in penance from back when the church disobeyed in Israel.

Did you hear the Vatican state they have one person that can really dig out your sins. One man for what they claim is two hundred million Souls. If they had one they should turn him into Paul and have him review the six other denominations. The purpose is to help their fellow man avoid sins and allow themselves to be keeping abreast of developments in other denominations. That covenant is critical to avoid their blasphemy mouths to return. They will be judged by Our Gods. They must use the Ten Commandments and church law to achieve the status of saints. Are they blaming the congregation today for being sinners? Since they called the congregation sinners, they require the blood of a just man to end the Black Plague or the word blame. That is well documented in the Old Testament the use of the word blame. The congregation is in jeopardy as pain in the families' lives. The Universal Church has the Cardinal Sins. King Jesus Christ will take care of the sinners and the clergymen's sins go up to the Heavens. Do not listen to someone that said I will forgive all your sins as a congregation member and he has a blasphemy mouth.

I have heard the Catholics state they have people assigned to Standing Historical, but I could not acquire any literature. In the United States, there are seven books one of which is titled, "Life of US (U. S.) Catholic" written like the Old and New Testaments. The clergymen are to be against the Beasts like the Republican Party in the United States. Have you heard of the Catholic Church in other countries where the economy is bad in the last two thousand years? In Italy since the Second World War, I heard they could not form a government. Has the Catholic Church read about the government of the Old Testament and King Jesus Christ stating there is no reason to change the Old Testament? Our King Jesus Christ did not do a good job of hiding the one world government, but the clergymen are reluctant to work together and are easily deceived in one hundred percent of everything Adam has achieved in King Jesus Christ's name. Only a true God could write a book called the Holy Bible that Adam has a copy of and because of his foolishness, he has done one hundred percent of everything wrong. Adam always had the answer of form the kingdom and he should learn how to talk. The Holy Bible does not change but you receive a little book from a man of European descent that has a little horn.

The Holy Bible is very clear to me that you are to split up the "Cows" wisely. In addition, the Antichrist came in an era of peace and prosperity or one hour past midnight on January 1, the year of Our Lord 2000 AD. Jacob was to be proven justified when he did not sell all his gold after seven years of creating Fat Cows in Egypt. President William J. Clinton created seven years of Fat Cows in the United States despite people like a billion Asians and the government of Mexico and South America having major problems with their economies. Good laws produce good economies. What should the clergymen teach? In the United States they are totally withdrawing from any form of General Welfare or telling the United States government through education to divide up the Cows wisely. The government had a two hundred and thirty two billion dollar surplus and the members of the congregation paying their taxes can satisfy the demands for money for the American people. The clergymen sat back and listened carefully to the promise keepers or campaign promises. The poor box in America should always be full through government policies since very little would come from church treasuries. The amount would be so minor that it is considered petty cash and the begging of the Antichrists finally ended.

The Holy Bible states all church locations are asleep at the Altar and they are not even ready for milk. The clergymen asked the congregation where they had money problems. The same group asked the politicians and courts to inform them of any law changes to resolve money problem among the congregation or beyond. Many sermons were created satisfying the demands of the congregation for information and value in what was being produced. No the beggars continued with their bad ideas and are worse than fools. They cannot achieve anything but failure. What did the Antichrist / clergymen achieve. They destroyed peace and worked against prosperity. Not bad for men the Holy Bible defines has gone backwards from New York in the year of Our Lord 1900 AD where the Federal Government was out of debt and it was a nation of love and marriage. What has the Catholics achieved in one hundred years or helping create the greatest debtor nation. The United States is the country where we have a currency that is green and is the wax location of the world and the wax is cold. The Catholics have to be justified by law not Grace because they cannot run their churches. Adam without God is just a fool and he has proven the Noah's Ark story is kind. It is better for Adam to be dead physically than go through the Battle of Armageddon over the penance of seven times longer. I do have to admit my past literature as to when King Jesus Christ will return is wrong. I did not know about the Second Advent story and even I have to plan as I learn the Words of the Holy Bible. My planning is such it would take a long time for Adam to do what is already on the table.

Have you heard the clergymen do not have to put any story to rest? They can write sermons where they are not ready for milk, let alone meat. They can sleep at the Altar.

Have they convinced you, they will forgive you for everything?

The Italian Mafia is attacking your grammar school children to have their workforce sell your children, drugs. Your children have more than a hair on their head affected. Did the Catholic priests do a public opinion poll to see if the women whose children died of drugs should forgive them? The Italian Mafia does not have to change. What should the Catholic priests do, if the public opinion poll does not agree with them? The will of the people prevails and may not believe the Italian Mafia should go to the true Heaven for good deeds. They have the wrong heart; however, they were baptized at eight days. They can go to church every day for the rest of their life, but they cannot reverse the jeopardy of the Catholic priests' unpardonable sins. The Catholic priests believe they can tell their boss anything and He must do it. They are teaching false witness and reach for pride in themselves in what they say is the word of God. The clergymen are the sinners to repent and the Son of Perdition.

The Republican Party through Vice President Richard B. Cheney desired to give people that did not have jobs assault rifles in the year of Our Lord 2004 AD campaign. A problem in the United States is guns killing American teenagers. What if a public opinion poll to provide assault rifles to certain people goes against the Republicans? How can we forgive the clergymen that allowed the guns in our children's hands? Why are they so ineffective on important issues? Many clergymen were boasting about the Republicans winning the elections and fighting against common sense in the year of Our Lord 2004 AD. The Republicans like the campaign money from the National Rifle Association. The Democrats were against guns in the hands of people without jobs and assault weapons.

The judges in American courts had a public opinion poll and they desired to be hanging judges. Do the clergymen desire the Death Penalty? Finding a person guilty in the church world is against God. Where is the mercy in the courts? The requirement is "In heaven on earth, do not send your policeman out to kill them because they do not want to go to school." Only the president of our country can end crimes. Where are the clergymen teaching the laws of liberty as the United States started out? We have lost the way. Do the clergymen desire the president to fail because of their words against God?

A committee was formed in the late 1990s. They reviewed why crime had gone down from President George H. W. Bush to President William J. Clinton. First the church should understand that committees are ineffective and not the way in scripture. The committee determined there was no reason why the results should be different. President Ronald Reagan and George H W. Bush took the money out of the poor neighborhoods and gave it to the wealthy. President William J. Clinton gave the states one hundred thousand new police officers and created wealth in the poor neighborhoods. The committee could not notice a difference. If all children were born of fathers that were not in want of money, our lives could be blessed. The prisons should disappear. Should we forgive all the people who vote for fools like the clergymen? Money in the poor neighborhoods is a deterrent to crime.

What should the clergymen do to a man who needs the feathers to eat up the flesh (Hawks and Doves)? Should the clergymen teach the politicians that a warlord is not a Hawk, but a dragon that needs to steal that woman's child? I heard a woman state that President George W. Bush killed her child. We would love to hear that through reincarnation, that the child was granted new arms and legs; however not hearing of the death would be better. King Jesus Christ states we cannot put that child back in her womb. Do the women state they do not mind a Red Dragon stealing that child from her? Is that the opinion and the will of the people? The Holy Bible asks the clergymen why Satan (Red Dragon) attacked. The answer was because he needed to win the presidential election. Is the clergymen forgiving the dragons and allowing them to kill that woman's children? Should the clergymen be forgiven that desire to be conquers as defined in the book of Romans? Does he have the right heart? The book of Romans is when the United States recreates the Roman Empire or what America is doing wrong. The church still teaches us King Jesus Christ is still only a prince and does he believe that as a clergymen, he can have the wrong heart. There is no hell like a woman scorned. She cannot get health care, daily bread, a good education, and/or a bright future for her children or the children of the land the government desires to conquer. The Preacher Whores running the church desire to help the government to kill her child and they forgive the Red Dragon.

President George W. Bush is doing what he did in Texas. In Texas, he took the money set aside for health care for children of Texas and gave the money to the rich. He violated the book of Mark. Should we forgive him for being a beast or a mass murderer of children from Texas? He is the beast of Revelation many clergymen Preacher Whores talk about and the woman is former President William J. Clinton's girl friend. Now, he is against children getting health care in the year of Our Lord 2008 AD. How many children will die because of him and yet many will say he is saved? Does he have the heart as Our God of Heart and we should forgive him? The Antichrist running the church would forgive. The congregation should question what heart the clergymen have. I say, the clergymen cannot be forgiven by the congregation or King Jesus Christ for their ideas of foolish religion. The church is disobeying one hundred percent of all instructions. They must obey the Holy Bible as salves or as a prince. Their cross to bear is the Holy Bible and they must teach us how to live by every word.

If you understand the above maybe, there is more to forgiveness than we have been taught.

I desire to document what I have learned on December 15, the year of Our Lord 2007 AD. I realize I am the best biblical scholar in the entire world. It took me thirty seconds to understand what I heard on the radio back in about the year of Our Lord 1998 AD. Do not let that dragon steal that woman's child. A dragon is a warlord and the soul does not die, but through reincarnation is reborn again, goes to the true Heaven, or somewhere else. The solution to understanding the words is the word "steal" and understanding John 3:16. You can ask the clergymen which of the Four Horsemen are to cut off his ugly head. I have been studying the Holy Bible with great intensity, because I desire to stop the Battle of Armageddon from starting in the United States. My family and the future of my grandchildren are at stake. The only people that can reverse the course of human events to the end shall come, are the clergymen. Many agree the end is near. As the Holy Bible states, I am to handicapped to do it myself. In the past, I have written to try to understand when the clergymen of the United States failed three times like Israel. Today I know, on January 1 in the year of Our Lord 2000 AD, the Antichrist came in an era of peace and prosperity. President William J. Clinton had the peace dividend in place and the federal government was approximately two hundred and sixty-seven billion dollars ahead in the future Heartland of the world. The final number turned out to be two hundred and thirty-two billion ahead that he granted a beast from Texas to accept the title of President of the United States. The Holy Bible states that unless you shorten the days (formed the kingdom) no flesh is saved (no John 3:16). In the Garden of Eden, it is written that once you are responsible for good and evil, you will surely die. The new beginning was the employees of King Jesus Christ to form the kingdom with seven names on the door, as this generation becomes the Age of Accountability.

What did I learn, today? I knew the Antichrist is the clergymen or employees of King Jesus Christ. They do not even understand what the definition of the word evil is. The church has created the definition as morally bad: profoundly immoral or wrong. The root of all evil is money; therefore, that has been translated into the "bad guys". On television, you may hear references to we also have crimes of passion. If they had to apply knowledge, they should learn the definition is wrong. I know evil means lack of knowledge and it takes money through time to discover. A passage states if you are not in a quest for knowledge, you are not priests of mine. Some say look we can go to outer space to prove that is what we are doing. King Jesus Christ states you talk like little children. We must learn the tree stories.

I use a story for me to understand about antilock brakes. When we focused on brakes over the last century for our cars, we developed great knowledge, but what does that have to do with driving on our highways safely as the government has lost control. The people say, we can all drive too fast because everyone does it. In addition, we have an accident every six seconds and our children learn from the adults, but do not have the experience. When you go to a hospital or see some television shows of reality in turns of technology, you see wonders. Yet, children die in America because their families cannot afford health insurance. King Jesus Christ did say in prophecies, we cannot go to Israel to learn how to raise a child, yet some churches state we require a law to teach the Holy Bible to the children. The reason is the children do not like organized religion or the clergymen have driven the children away. A country that does not properly raise its children has no right to exist. The children of 777 design (God's Children) should be great women at twenty-one or good men. I have heard the women state there is not enough good men to go around. They are either gay or married. Where is the quest for knowledge in the church like Israel? You must keep in mind that the Rabbis are to be the hunters and the church personnel are gatherers.

The above shows the church employees of King Jesus Christ were not saved on January 1, the year of Our Lord 2000 AD at one hour passed midnight. King Jesus Christ has named the Age of Accountability. The Gates to Perdition were opened at that time and they are the Son of Perdition. The religious leaders take pride in themselves, not humility for King Jesus Christ. All locations I have gone to use words like Jesus saves and they do not use His title. Read Luke 17:21 neither shall they say, Lo here! or, Lo there! for, behold, the kingdom of God is within you. Have you heard, I am the only one that understands this, but they have not formed the kingdom so they can learn how to talk?

When the Red Dragon went around to many kings in other nations, he convinced many others to join by using intimidation to start the war in Iraq, but first he said, "Let me seek the vengeance." not let God seek the vengeance. Once the Antichrist allowed the war to start in the Age of Accountability, their entire congregation lost John 3:16. As the Holy Bible states the Second

World War is a war to end all wars and we start another war. The Holy Bible states King Jesus Christ's employees shall be hated above all others. The answer is obvious. What heart does the Red Dragon or Satan have? He does not have the Heart of Our King. Satan or the Red Dragon and his wife cannot be saved and will die without having the possibility of salvation in this lifetime. King Jesus Christ will save the meek, not the preacher whore. You may have heard of a church without shackles or similar foolish ideas from the Son of Perdition, the clergymen. Have you heard about the saying; there is no fear in me? The words of the Holy Bible would mean there is no knowledge in you. Fear is the beginning of all wisdom (knowledge). A very foolish idea is King Jesus Christ is responsible for all divorces and a church law like the saints who run the church say, "If I have a problem in my marriage, I must seek the marriage counselors of the church." They can create a song like the Songs of Moses and sing in church and create sermons. The congregation would demand they handle their marriage problems too and the divorce rate would fall. King Jesus Christ does not create the divorces of church families, but the wrong heart of the clergymen and their unpardonable Cardinal Sins do. Many state come to my church, I can save anyone; however, the only one he can save is himself. Paul from the Holy Bible is out to help the clergymen maintain their story of salvation, not the congregation. King Jesus Christ saves, not the clergymen; however, through the actions of reform the church you can save others of His employees. The meek can end all killing wars, stop the drug lords, and many other miracles, if they form the kingdom and learn how to talk. Once they start to form the kingdom, the congregation gets John 3:16 back and the Battle of Armageddon will not start. If we live by the sword, we will die by the sword (guns) of our own citizens of the United States.

So what have I learned? The worst career to get John 3:16 through work is being the Pope in the year of our Lord now or the future. Unless he forms the kingdom as soon as a person joins the church, they will die. The congregation should realize King Jesus Christ saves souls, not the clergymen. King Jesus Christ judged you long ago because He loved you. The clergymen are to be the saints and they refuse to judge. Do they desire the congregation to forgive them for stealing John 3:16 from the entire world and letting the end come because they take pride in themselves and not humility for King Jesus Christ? They will never get John 3:16 back. The next step is the penance continues for seven times longer and King Jesus Christ returns with the Seven Horns of the Eternal Temple or Israel. One day the new clergymen again will be granted a chance to form the kingdom and learn how to talk, but in the mean time, they killed one trillion children because they refuse to obey King Jesus Christ by becoming royalty and wearing the color purple. Learn King Jesus Christ has told you all things and the church has a book that always ends up with a life one thousand times better than the end, called the Holy Bible.

Can you forgive them for their total failure as human beings? The Holy Bible states the congregation shall shoot them in the head (spiritually). They must experience death as King Jesus Christ did. They will not die physically but spiritually. They shall know what they did before they die. They died as stated in the Garden of Eden and must go through the story of resurrection of eleven hundred and fifty (42 months) or twenty three hundred (seven years) days.

Next, have you heard the clergymen stating, "I will forgive all your sins"? Do you believe in the foolish ideas about the Italian Mafia and forgiving? If the God Father from the Italian Mafia has a heart attack on the highway and he is taken to the hospital where the Catholic priest is there, he goes to the true Heaven for good deeds and forgiveness. Next time as he survived the first heart attack, he is driven to the hospital and is dead on arrival, before he sees the Catholic priest. Now, he goes by the way of Satan. What does the Holy Bible state to do with criminals like the Italian Mafia? They are to go to the true Heaven with one eye. What does "we the people" desire in return for that forgiveness? They must only have legal businesses and work hard to destroy the crime syndicates of your country. What does that mean work hard? Did the FBI receive all possible knowledge to stop illegal drugs (for example) from coming into our country and destroy all their ties with other drug lords? On the great and dreadful Day of the Lord, Good Friday, what do you cover for adults only? Their good deeds and desires give them a chance for them to go to heaven. Judgment Day is the day we die and death is beyond the scope of the saints. The clergymen have to teach the terrible reality that we have to forgive them for killing our children (what came before), because of their good deeds. All illegal drugs in the United States are planned to be over. Will the women understand or go after the clergymen for them to seek vengeance? You do not desire to explain to the congregation, yet forgiveness is a powerful tool to resolve problems. The Holy Bible states only a penance man can get off this world alive. You have to think about a rich crime boss and realize he will go through penance, but the pain in the future family lives ends with that generation.

I have written the judges in the courts are to correct the foolishness of items like property tax sales, living wills, being defined as hanging judges in courts. What will happen without the congregation learning to forgive? Have you seen people showing up at pardon review sessions to guarantee the courts maintain vengeance? How can a young man who killed your husband with a gun or on the highway be forgiven? The clergymen will have to learn how to convince people to let God seek the vengeance as I defined in the chapter on Dr Martin Luther King. The questions to explore are why the courts gave him a gun and why they lost control of our highways. Once the judge corrects the problem, we will forgive or blame will rise to overcome the ability of man to correct problems. Check my writings about Mayor Daily of Chicago and what blame can do. We must learn the correct use of the power of forgiveness or correcting and defining problems becomes impossible. The Holy Bible defines America requires ten thousand ideas to straighten out their country. The voice of the powerful drowning out the voice of reason can destroy even America, which started out designed by the Holy Bible. A land of freedom is a land of failure or "LAND OF FREEDOM LAND OF FAILURE" and a land of liberty to return as the laws of liberty. A land of liberty is a land you give up the right to fail yourself and all other rights are enhanced. The sermon to compare should develop LAND OF FREEDOM LAND OF FAILURE to LAND OF LIBERTY LAND OF SUCCESS.

I did not comment on their words or "I will forgive all their sins." Israel was a nation of priests. Priests have to obey the Ten Commandments and become the man of sin to repent. The clergyman that states you should obey the Ten Commandments and is critical of you, is wrong. Have you heard in the year of Our Lord 2000 AD where the Catholics stated I have a man that can really dig out your sins? He was blaming you and should not be forgiven. Only through the end of those foolish words can he repent. The Holy Bible states the clergymen must identify the man of sin. When King Jesus Christ stopped the Jewish man from killing that woman developed by Roman standards He said, "Let the man without sin cast the first stone." They knew if they cast the first stone, they would not be without sin. They were a nation of priests. How can you be blamed as a sinner and the Catholics are casting the stones? The Catholic priests are failing themselves as the congregation is in jeopardy. King Jesus Christ was too intelligent to call the people in the church world, who were not priests, sinners. The clergymen cannot be forgiven if they call the congregation sinners. That has a tendency to drive the congregation away at this time.

What should be the case where the Antichrists are out to kill the messengers? As the volumes of religious materials are great many would state my literature is the true living word. I

378

say the Catholic library, TBN, Pastor Murray, Gerald Flurry, Tomorrow's World and others all boasting their material is the true word are wrong. They have not formed the kingdom and learned how to talk. You should realize the Holy Bible states everything is one hundred and eighty degrees off or just the opposite of what should be done. All laws and religious material are wrong. Why would all important works of man be wrong, when we can invent antilock brakes? The answer is Adam is always trying to prove he is right. The Holy Bible gives all clergymen the answer to one hundred percent of all problems in the world. When Adam is faced with someone smarter than himself, he will argue and try to kill the messenger. I have a number of experiences with the Antichrist and their pride in themselves. One told me after I asked if he needed to end divorces, he said no. I believe a woman that is beaten up by her husband should have a divorce. When his congregation members are beating up their wives, he cannot be like King Jesus Christ and walk a mile in His footsteps; therefore, he does not have a heart for change to love the congregation. With that type of attitude, he is failing himself. He should just resign after he said those words and just sell shoelaces (Passover story). Adam only needs to do what Adam needs to do to take pride in himself, so he always believes if he is challenged, he must defend. He will always try to kill the messenger. When a teenager hears her parents arguing, he does not desire to hear from the child (the messenger) and for him to correct the marriage issues; therefore, Adam let the voice of the powerful drown out the voice of reason (common sense). The only answer is for the church to invent sixth sense or six words of common sense to let the Holy Spirit speak through them; however, they are all trying to prove their church location is the best without achievements or goals to work for. They must develop the stories to the small doors and that can only be achieved with the innocence and imagination of a small child. The tree stories are the quest for knowledge that strangers must learn in the perfect church environment. We cannot as the congregations forgive them. Only through them changing can we forgive them for all good intentions without good deeds that came before.

We had a public opinion poll that states the clergymen were the most believable and the attorneys were tenth. I can trust in the Italian Mafia's attorneys better than the clergymen. The Italian Mafia's attorneys, we should know stand for their own failures in turns of which heart they have. The clergymen are rejecters of all knowledge, do not know how to talk, but when a woman is being beaten up by her husband of their congregation, they have no solutions other than a divorce through Adam. When you petition a church, you would see a look of failure as the man does not even listen in the year of Our Lord 2000 AD to do a public opinion poll from our children to see if they desire good schools from President elect Al Gore. They allow a debate and let a beast violate the book of Mark. The Holy Bible states not one woman could vote for a mass murder of children from Texas who desires to steal the money required for schools and give it to the rich. His mother should not vote for him as he was about to gain the whole world and lose his soul. The clergymen do not learn because they tell you are to have eyes to see and ears to hear and they cannot learn. They do not desire to learn and are not priests of King Jesus Christ. It must be all heard in a church. How worse than foolish are they? I will go through a real conversation.

I go to many churches trying to get one to realize his responsibilities to King Jesus Christ. I am King Jesus Christ's representative and I am like Paul in the Holy Bible or a man that can improve the church. So I go to a Baptist Church, tell the clergymen who I am and what I need to do and naturally, with his pride in himself, he kills the messenger. He states, "You know, I have to wait for Jesus to return." Now, I intent to go back and teach; however, the church is locked (not open twenty-four hours a day) so I leave. He was to start on Wednesday night at 6:30 PM, but was not there in the afternoon that I could see. I had received the following letter from him to discuss. He apparently needs me to tell him how great he is. The Holy Bible compares him with the animal the ass or oxen, which know their own crib. I already knew by listening to him and understanding the Holy Bible, he is asleep on Sunday at the Altar. He could not tell me about the stories, he has put to rest, like he through the kingdom has eliminated ninety percent of the divorces in twenty years and is trying harder. The Holy Bible states he has gone backwards in the United States from the year of Our Lord 1900 AD to today and the wax is cold. Now, you have a background you can judge by as copied from the book he claims to represent. The book is called the Holy Bible. He cannot judge himself, but he can kill the messenger.

His letter to follow dated December 10, the year of Our Lord 2007 AD.

Mr. Richard Cartwright
430 Pembroke Road
Poplar Grove, IL 61065

Dear Richard

We were honored to have you with us at First Baptist Church last Sunday. I trust you felt welcome and enjoyed the service.

Because we seem to live in such a fast-paced society, we need a special time on Sunday to regroup. It is for this reason we strive to provide a service, which inspires and motivates us to establish and grow in a personal relationship with God.

We think people really feel comfortable in a church where-

The people are friendly and helpful,

The music is uplifting and encouraging,

There is a meaningful and inspiring message, and
A special time for the children is provided.

We are trying very hard at First Baptist to meet these objectives. You can help us by letting us know how we are doing. While your visit is still fresh in your mind, would you kindly write down your first impressions of us on the enclosed card and drop it in the mail? Your opinion is important to us.

If at any time I can personally be of help to you, please call upon me. I am delighted that you chose to worship with us Sunday, and I hope you will do so again soon. Our service times are:

Sunday School 8:45 - 9:30 Coffee Time 9:30 - 10:00
Worship 10:00 - 11:00

Your Friend;

original signed by Pastor Rex. A. Rogers
1255 W. Jackson
Belvidere, IL 61008

I finally was able to contact him on the telephone. I state I am answering his request to judge him. I ask if he needs to end all divorces and he states no. I hear he desires to blame King Jesus Christ for his own failure as he states King Jesus Christ is causing all the divorces. Next, I ask if he needs to end the unnecessary deaths of children all over the world. I state, "Do you need to make all the people in the United States rich?" All people of the world shall not want or be rich. He claims there is nothing he can do, because King Jesus Christ is causing all the unnecessary deaths and all that is bad, he implies. I tell him I am Elijah. He calls me a liar and refuses to meet with me to test if what I say I can do is true. He is required to be a gatherer and in a quest for knowledge and he refuses to learn. He just needed to kill the messenger. Is that what the congregation desires? A teenage child hears his mother and father yelling at each other. If he came to him, he would just kill the messenger. He like all others have accomplished less than nothing in the last one hundred years and the congregation can now learn why. If I am successful in creating heaven on earth, what he told me becomes part of Standing Historical as it is the way of all churches. They are required to be the Mother of Inspiration and all they desire to achieve is grandma (little old ladies writing sermons). They have not put a story to rest but have made life in our country worse. Have you heard those supporting wars, beasts, criminals, illegal aliens, bad schools, false witness and more unpardonable sins than man can count or a God would say? The Cardinal Sins go up to the heavens. They are the men of sin that must repent and obey the Ten Commandments. The most you will hear is they call you sinners and you must repent. They will imply they are perfect, but only one beast away from destroying the entire United States due to the pen.

Can you believe a clergyman would call a member of God's congregation a liar? That is blame and he requires the blood of a just man to end the "Black Plague" or the word blame. I believe if someone can reach for we shall not want (money or anything else) a clergymen should take time to listen. They are to take public opinion polls as well as except petitions. They are the only ones that can offer a divorce, not a judge in court one day. A judge should only divide the money.

He called me a liar and never called to apologize.

Let the man without sin cast the first stone. He throws a rock and now he should know he is not a man without sin. The Holy Bible states for a man to get the lost sheep, so I will try again with the letter I have sent. The letter to follow.

December 26, the year of Our Lord 2007 AD

First Baptist Church
Appleton Road & W. Jackson St
PO Box 276
Belvidere, IL 61008-5800

Rev. Rex A. Rogers

Regarding your letter dated December 10, the year of Our Lord 2007 AD, you asked me to judge you. You stated, "would you write down your first impression of us". King Jesus Christ has judged you in the Holy Bible long ago and I agree with the Holy Bible. He did it because He loved you. The book states for you to form the kingdom and learn how to talk. You like all your peers cannot tell anyone what stories you have put to rest.

Your defense is for example, King Jesus Christ is responsible for all divorces; however, the Holy Bible states for you to find Elijah to return fathers and sons back together. If you form the kingdom, the Holy Spirit words for you to use to learn how to talk is "FOR THE LOVE OF GOD'S CHILDREN". We are all children of God, but God's Children (Thy Children) are the angels and the ones you are to make special. When you create Church Laws (Moses Laws), one should be if the saints running the churches have a problem in their marriage, they must seek the marriage counselors of the church. The clergymen are the saints to judge the world. The older women that are to teach the younger women will force you to do the same for their daughters. I have invented a prophecy for the church and teachings in my literature for you to end ninety percent of the divorces in the United States in twenty years (777 design) and then try harder. I say you should be able to achieve the prophecy easily. King Jesus Christ has defined the answers. The Antichrist running the church would say, King Jesus Christ is responsible for all the divorces and there is nothing I can do in a kingdom. A prophecy is a future, the congregation will desire to inherit. Blind faith is the future you desire to create in His name, but you cannot see the results in our future like individuals have quoted in the Holy Bible like Daniel. You must create hope to make your commitment to the congregation come through.

King Jesus Christ has a requirement for you to stop sending Him little ones small and great. You say and all Antichrist states King Jesus Christ is responsible for all the unnecessary deaths and there is nothing I can do. If you trained the politicians and through a little bit of fear to recognize that daily bread are their responsibility, I say they would work hard to eliminate hunger. If you formed the kingdom in the year of Our Lord 1900 AD and made that a requirement for all politicians that represented King Jesus Christ, hunger as you know it would be gone or greatly reduced.

You can check the Holy Bible. If you abandon "THY" children of 777 design (born to twenty-one) I will abandon you and the penance will continue for seven times longer or He comes back with the Seven Horns of the Eternal Temple. You are in penance as the Holy Bible is clear and you do not even know it. The children do not like organized religion.

Since you believe you are a greater biblical scholar than I am, you can finish the Chapter on "The Word Forgiveness" that must be used by all church locations without exception. If you do not desire to learn from me, please leave the church and go sell shoelaces (Passover Story). All clergymen that refuse to form the kingdom or seven churches with the Universal Church format granted in the year of Our Lord 1200 AD, have the wrong heart. The Holy Bible states you worship Satan, which I can prove. You do not have the right heart for John 3:16.

The last statement for now is the Holy Bible always ends up with a life one thousand times better than the end. The eighth beast is next as you have failed and the end shall come. You will be responsible for a trillion unnecessary deaths in the future. Why, you refuse to create the greatest tribulation the world will ever experience by forming the kingdom and you become royalty.

NOW FINISH THE CHAPTER ON THE POWER OF FORGIVENESS WITHOUT ELIJAH. IF YOU CANNOT COMPLETE PLEASE APPLY THE MILLSTONE STORY TO YOU AND YOUR WIFE. THAT WOULD BE KIND FOR YOUR WIFE OR YOU COULD SEEK King Jesus Christ's TRUE MESSENGER ELIJAH.

Richard Cartwright
430 Pembroke Rd SW
Poplar Grove, Il 61065
Telephone 815-765-0161

Elijah is located at Candlewick Lake
Any major problem you can define, I can solve through planning or what the Holy Bible calls theology. The world must be developed through one hundred percent theology, which is planning from the Holy Bible.

I told him about the one world government of Israel of over 20,000 words. If he calls, I will give him this new part of the chapter on forgiveness and the documents so he can start to create heaven on earth or implement the Lord's Prayer. The start is he would be required to reproduce some papers, make a few telephone calls, read my book "The Antichrist- God's Version", and have his friends listen to a voice file on the presentation. The beginning of heaven on earth can be a reality.

Well, I did not wait. I wrote a new letter to him and copied the chapter I wrote on the Grace of God you are saved. He being the Antichrist, he must work with all clergymen to reverse the course of human events that leads to the Battle of Armageddon (biblical battle between good and evil: in the Holy Bible, the battle between the forces of good and evil that is predicted to mark the end of the world and precede the Day of Judgment. (Revelation 16:16) in the USA. Below is a copy of the letter. I will send similar letters to other Antichrists I have met.

January 6, the year of Our Lord 2008 AD

First Baptist Church
Appleton Road & W. Jackson St
PO Box 276
Belvidere, IL 61008-5800

Antichrist Rev. Rex A. Rogers

RE: Kill the Messenger

Now, you know whom the Antichrist is that is creating all that you see and hear as bad or as the Holy Bible states, Adam. What is good is nothing or the Noah's Ark story from God is kind. That I can prove. The new beginning can be only a few years away with your help. As Elias, I can form the kingdom and the book is complete or, "The Antichrist- God's Version". You should realize why the book has that title. As Elijah, I can end ninety percent of the divorces in a kingdom in twenty years and the prophecy will be found to be easy. You must get fathers back with sons or the fallen angels (boys) will be with the women. You cannot believe you will not reach for the greatest tribulation a clergymen can see or the return of King Jesus Christ, once you have no questions to ask. I have copied King Jesus Christ thousand-year plan for the government from the Holy Bible and you can prove it from scripture. Can you allow all the people you see to die in the Battle of Armageddon, which starts in the United States because you do not need to hold a meeting?

You are responsible to find Elijah if you believe you cannot form God's Kingdom by yourself. The Universal Church format, which was granted in the year of Our Lord 1200 AD, has seven names on the door and seven Holy Cities. If you understand reality because of your blasphemous mouth, you worship Satan. If you stay with the gospel about Christ as defined in the year 31 AD, as the book of Matthew states the end shall come. It is not the word of God. It is His plan. I have contacted you in the past and all you desired to do is kill the messenger.

The teenagers of America do not like organized religion so you believe that is not your problem. Let me kill the messenger. The teenagers do not like their parents getting divorces and you say I do not give a damn. I will kill the messenger. I am perfect. Why would I desire to change? All I have to do is con the congregation out of their money and I can tell them how great I am. The Holy Bible states, you are taking pride in yourself and not humility for King Jesus Christ. The Holy Bible states you are asleep at the altar. Why would you desire to change when you judge yourself as perfect? You must judge the world as saints. The Holy Bible states you have the wrong heart for John 3:16 as you worship Satan. I can prove that statement. Can you prove King Jesus Christ's messenger is wrong?

I am Elijah to teach you how to end divorces so you can get fathers back with sons or teenagers back to the church. I am a prophet that can end the millions of children dieing each year due to a famine (money). Do you desire to kill the messenger? A great amount of money is required and King Jesus Christ states I will double the best Adam can do. I have King Jesus

388

Christ's thousand-year plan for the one world government of Israel for the United States. Do you need to kill His messenger and tell the congregation, "You know I have to wait for King Jesus Christ to return?" The Holy Bible states He has told you all things, so you should know all the answers. Are you lying to the congregation and yourself? May you die without any possibility for John 3:16 as you desire to kill the teenagers that have a message or Elijah!

Are you killing the messengers of the Italian Mafia and lying to the men that are failing themselves? They are in shackles and as failures cannot be saved. Are you killing the messenger of the families whose children die of drugs? The Italian Mafia has the wrong heart and the church does not care or are the Son of Perdition. Do you judge the politicians violating the book of Mark and become the Mark of the Beast? No, you are the Son of Perdition.

King Jesus Christ has judged you long ago. The Holy Bible is clear. Do you have seven churches with the Universal Church format? Where is your Holy City? You are just the sinner that must repent and the Son of Perdition.

I have asked you and your peers to check the chapter you must teach on the great an dreadful Day of the Lord or Good Friday. If you desire to check, you can correct and send to me. If you agree you should ask Elijah, "What should I do next?" If you take no action, just resign from the church or do the Millstone Story. You will find it impossible to be saved. You have a heart that is different from your God of Heart as you have the heart of Satan or heart of failure of yourself.

What is required of you? I have created the presentation and a voice file. You must read, listen, learn, reproduce some papers and set up a meeting. The rest I have done for you. You will learn more about religion in less than one hour than you have learned in your entire lifetime. It is time for Adam to grow up and learn how to talk. King Jesus Christ will not return until you have no questions to ask. The seals are for communication within a kingdom. The 666 beasts are books of Standing Historical or the history of your denomination in each nation where you have a presence. The beasts are the politicians you start a war against to avoid their failures as human beings. The 666 beast books are to last longer than heaven and earth or from Here to Eternity a measure of time. May a thousand zeros of time be short in terms of the effective use of the Holy Bible to resolve any problem in this world through one hundred percent theology!

Elijah

Richard Cartwright
430 Pembroke Rd SW
Poplar Grove' IL 61065
Tel # 815-765-0161
Elijah lives at Candlewick Lake, has a daughter and grand children living in Elk Grove Village, and can prove all that he has written.
The four words of the millennium are fear, war, jeopardy, and joy. I have not heard your understanding of how they apply for the next thousand years.

The letters went to many other church locations.
January 8, the year of Our Lord 2008 AD

Immanuel Lutheran Church
1045 Belvidere Rd
Belvidere IL

Antichrist Rev Allen Buss Sr Pastor

January 6, the year of Our Lord 2008 AD

Cross and Crown Lutheran Church
7404 Elevator Rd
Roscoe, IL

Antichrist Pastor John L. Heins

January 7, the year of Our Lord 2008 AD

Poplar Grove United Methodist Church
105 E Grove
Poplar Grove, Il 61065

Antichrist Senior Pastor Lisa Kruse-Safford
(She told me you called me the Antichrist and you cannot learn from me and that is true. I have sent countless emails to her and the best she can answer is she is not capable or required to learn.)

I think about his sermon for the day I heard from the Baptist Rev Rex A. Rogers. He stated it was strange that the Rabbis of Israel did not go to Bethlehem (God's World) to witness the birth of King Jesus Christ. I was at the Bethel Church. Where was the commitment from the clergymen to find me? I wrote a book as the name Elias that is required per Mark 9:12. I am Elijah as defined to bring fathers back with sons and being the watchman for the United States. I being the watchman can only happen if the church is formed. The Holy Bible is clear. I must seek through Devine Intervention to become the president of the United States or the third power of eight.

I arrived at his church with great excitement in the belief he would be willing to learn. I just walk in and he runs to greet me. He states he does not desire to learn the teaching of Elijah despite the Holy Bible and knowing I can end divorces and what we call poverty today in the millions of children lives all over the world. All he needed from me is to state how great his sermons are. The Holy Bible has his judgment well defined, where King Jesus Christ compared him with the animal the ass or oxen and he lost.

What should the congregation expect God to do with men that can reach for such greatness by implementing the Lord's Prayer and all they desire to hear is how great they are? He is taking pride in himself, not humility for King Jesus Christ. Our God will meet us in the temple, not church. We cannot sit around and expect Him to return through our observation. The Antichrist reaction is what made the world of ours achieve one hundred percent of everything wrong. False witness of reality will cause the world to go into penance seven times longer and the Antichrists running the church will be responsible for the unnecessary deaths of a trillion children. What do you expect God to do to seek vengeance on Adam? All he has to do is continue the divorce from Israel and let Adam create a greater Hell or earth. He will return with the Seven Horns (what is said) of the Eternal Temple or Israel. One day a clergymen will be asked to create the beginning of heaven on earth again. The Lord's Prayer with seven names on the door and seven Holy Cities will be the answer. The answer is the same and shall always be the same. The greatest tribulation the world will ever see will be the church formed and the return of King Jesus Christ. What is required? The clergymen to obey King Jesus Christ, live by the Ten Commandments to become saints to judge the world, and commit to end the pain in the families lives like divorces. See the Chapter The Stairway to Heaven.

Going back to Antichrist Rev. Rex A. Rogers. The letter stated he desires to kill the messengers. He has another man that works with the young, but when the children do not like organized religion, he would say there is nothing I can do. When the children send a messenger they do not like divorces, he ignores. When the women see their children dieing all over the world, he cannot listen to the hunger of the messengers. How should God judge him? When he dies, he can judge himself as to what he believes and how he should be judged. If he lies to himself may the judgment be worst than Satan.

I have to go back to an old story. The clergymen where considered better than the attorneys in truth in an public opinion poll. I trust in the Italian Mafia attorneys more than the clergymen. We can easily believe they are not achieving anything other than their own failure. The clergymen were judged by God long ago, as Antichrists and they will lie to your face to prove they can be trusted with your inheritance or future. Many claim that King Jesus Christ caused all that is bad all over the world and there is nothing they can do in a kingdom as defined in scripture to resolve all problems. The Holy Bible states I have told you all things, so as a kingdom they can correct any social ills within any society. All they do is commit to false witness (sins) to prove they are justified to beg for your money to keep their church open.

We must include the Lord's Prayer in defining the word forgiveness. In the church side of the book of judges, the church shall include all the logic and wisdom defining the meaning of forgiveness as life evolves. What I am doing here is the foundation of truth, not the entire truth. I can use the judge in the court that stole your grandmother's house through a tax sale as an example. The answer was simple in the governor sending an attorney to grant a reverse mortgage to your mother. Countless number of people could have prospered from the new instruction; however, instead of blaming the court, the church must teach forgiveness. I can relate to my own family where under President Herbert C. Hoover. My father's family had two houses and money in the bank. The family was large and many men could work in the year of Our Lord 1928 AD. The local bank forecloses on the house and the family loses two houses yet they had the money in the bank. Many people have qualified for houses and under President Ronald Reagan and George H.

W. Bush lost their houses and farms. We should not forgive them. They did not attempt to avoid stealing our houses. Under Ronald Reagan, he had interest rates to twenty-one percent and the carpenters could not buy the house they are building for the government. If they built the exact house for sale, they could not afford a loan at twenty-one percent and many desirable houses for Americans where not built. There is zero reason for creating a depression or a recession type environment in our country. If you understand the Holy Bible, you should state neither condition could occur unless we had a large number of people retiring or other major reason for the number of workers decreasing (not unemployment). We cannot forgive losing our houses or the fools running government allowing a recession or worse. Now in the year of Our Lord 2007 AD, the parties and economists are debating and millions of lives are at stake. The answer is to raise the tax on greed and use the money to fix the roads and other sorrows. One social ill in our country is the roads are bad and we cannot forgive the politicians. With the tax rate so high today, the governments would receive more tax revenue than they spent on the roads. The value of the dollar would soar if the additional tax revenue were saved; thereby, the cost of gasoline could go down to half from the highs and inflation could go negative. Do not think of lower prices because of a bad economy is good. We should restrict the future spending of new tax revenue to fund Social Security as I have defined. Once the businessman understands the Holy Bible economic plan, they should say, "What are we going to fix next?" The problem arises only when you cannot define a social ill to fix. We shall not want. Once the congregation has their wants satisfied, they are rich. They must try to define more wants so the challenge can continue.

Only through the elimination of the social ills can the congregation forgive. Only through continual change will the clergymen reach the power of God.

The Tree of Knowledge and Tree of Life with the meaning of Good and Evil are covered in another chapter and you require a true understanding for the word forgive. The Holy Bible is the most complicated book in the world and only through a kingdom can be understood. The reason I can understand it is because I have created the requirements to form a kingdom years ago and my literature has evolved beyond just a new beginning. I know no one else in this world could do it without millions of men working together to learn how to talk. Since the church refuses to work together or hear from the messengers, King Jesus Christ had to send His representative back and he became the voice in the wilderness. He does not even have a secretary. He must rely on his memory and logic to write the companions and the sixty-seven book of the Holy Bible.

What shall be added to the books of Standing Historical for the United States with the thousands of memos I have originated to the Antichrist all over America. I have email through their web sites and email addresses countless number of solutions to mankind problems. The only hope I have left is the fact I did not learn of the name Elijah from Gerald Flurry of the book of Revelations liars of the Church of Philadelphia until about December of the year of Our Lord 2007 AD. That one item will keep me going. The Holy Bible states, I can be broken if I cannot use my hand. Hand in a colorful language of scripture means writing laws or being the president of the United States through divine intervention or the third power of eight. I must continue for the love of my grandchildren. On July 28, the year of Our Lord 2008 AD, you have two men that desire to be dragons as the eighth beast. Just like the year of Our Lord 2004 AD, if you voted for Satan or the False Messiah in the United States, you were wrong. Do not let the congregation make that mistake again. The end shall come.

I believe in the words of the Holy Bible. I would not try to save the Preacher Whores running the church. I would save the meek, which can end wars, stop crime syndicates and conquers the beasts that desire to rule and not satisfy the demands of people of their country in the want of health, wealth, and wisdom.

What are the church employees of King Jesus Christ to do with the Elders and the anointing oil? As written before, they are to do the Exorcist story. King Jesus Christ took the Demons out of the man's mind and cast them into the pigs. He who judges shall be judged and no one is judging the psychiatrist. How can we forgive them when they have turned American children from A and B students into D and E through drugs? In the year of Our Lord 1939 AD, the number one problem in school was gum. Today the children are not the same. What has America done but ruin countless numbers of children by bad deeds? King Jesus Christ shows the church employees to be board certified by the state and take over that role. The Demons that will come back in the minds of our soldiers of misfortune from Iraq. Our children through the church may through their medical science be better off and may we not have to forgive them for unkind medical views. King Jesus Christ on their side makes the church strong to do the exorcist story of the Demons in our minds. A person hurts a child by accident. May the Demons be removed and the power of forgiveness be effective! A child dies and mom has to work to continue life. Maybe an adopted child to replace like the Garden of Eden is the answer. Please clergymen have people certified by your area and end the pain of grieving as today and learn the power of mourning. Only through your change can the congregation forgive you. Easter Sunday is for teaching the meaning of the end of all death. Teach our children about the pain in grandma and she is waiting for the true Heaven to get new arms and legs. We can only forgive the clergymen when the congregation truly believes in John 3:16 and the cross was to show you the new beginning, the meaning of John 3:16, and a transfer of power. Please teach the people the meaning of caring for children and having the right heart. The clergymen cross to bear is the Holy

Bible. We must through the church teach to learn how to live by the words, not just read them with foolish concepts. We can start to forgive the clergymen only through their creating the one hundred percent theology.

Chapter 17. Bible Answer Man Test.

You find many people with titles of Pastor, PhD, Bishop, etc that claim they are qualified to teach the Holy Bible. Many have written books on various topics and have prospered from the sales of books. How many are really aimed at the clergymen for him to do? To my knowledge, my books are unique. The Holy Bible states that, "Some of the stories are so great, if you could get to the very elect, all you would do is deceive. I being the true representative of God, I have to prove that above is true. I have written countless memos and emails too many locations and have receive few replies. All the replies I have received defend their view that they do not have to change. The Holy Bible is clear as it states to form the kingdom first and learn how to talk. You should have been teachers, but the clergymen are what the Holy Bible defines as Preacher Whores. They read the word and guess at its meaning. They tell you to tell King Jesus Christ what to do and ignore providing any hope like becoming marriage counselors to end unnecessary divorces. I have and will include in this book some letters and memos, I have written trying to get their attention. The above states the word "some" or not many stories are great. The very elect is the clergymen doing God's Election and who has the right to vote and decide what is to be taught. You could understand why people do not write books for the clergymen to implement because they take pride in themselves, not humility for the King. They will not listen to anyone. They appear to be afraid to change, even though they have a passage that states, "It is not a sin to be afraid."

Below is a memo I have sent to many locations and not receive any answer. Many simply ignore anything that is hard because they are deceived. I can say that because I am like Paul trying to help the clergymen receive salvation, I understand.

Seeking a Church (Prayer Request)

Are you sure, you are justified by law and not by grace? You require a law to overcome a nation of abortion. I believe you still must find Mark 9:12. Are you better than King Jesus Christ? You should learn that the Pope John Paul II was condemned to this world. Are you better than Pope John Paul II or Archangel Michael? What have you done to create God's Kingdom? Any clergymen that does not implement the Lord's Prayer goes the way of Satan to Perdition. There are only seven church names. What is your Standing Historical or your books of 666 beasts that the Baptists and Lutherans agree to?

Please send me a copy of your Standing Historical or history that all churches in the United States agree to.

Original Message

Answer

From: <u>John Salsa</u>
To: <u>Richard Cartwright</u>
Sent: Wednesday, November 30, 2005 3:22 PM
Subject: Re: seeking a church

Dear Richard:

Jesus Christ only founded one Church: the Holy, Catholic and Apostolic Church. When you study the early Christians, they all claimed membership in the Catholic Church. It is only in the Catholic Church where you receive Jesus Christ, body, blood, soul and divinity in the Eucharist, through his ordained priests. It is the Catholic Church who gave us the Bible, and all the major doctrines of the Christian faith. I trust that when you do the research, you will discover the same thing and come home.

God bless you.
John Salza

To learn about the Scriptural basis for the Catholic faith, please visit <u>www.scripturecatholic.com</u>.

Original Message.
From: <u>Richard Cartwright</u>
To: <u>johnsalza@scripturecatholic.com</u>
Sent: Tuesday, November 29, 2005 7:13 PM
Subject: seeking a church

Seeking a Church (Prayer Request)
Any clergymen that does not implement the Lord's Prayer goes to Perdition. If you implement the Lord's Prayer, the

world achieves the greatest tribulation (JOY) the world will experience.

I am looking for a church and the experts state from the book of Revelation that the first through fifth church is bad. The sixth church in Revelation 3:9 is run by liars and worship Satan. Is your church better? Are the congregations of the six churches saved if God does not agree with their teaching methods? Are the church employees saved?

God calls our present churches whoredom. Matthew 24:14, "And this gospel of all the kingdom shall be preached in all the world for a witness unto all nations and the end shall come." God is stating the whoredom technique in our present church is bad and will end civilization as we know it. Does your church preach the gospel about Christ or the gospel of Christ? Does your gospel end the thirty thousand unnecessary deaths each day? Is the end 150,000 unnecessary deaths each day through the Battle of Armageddon? God states the famine is not for daily bread, but the word of God. The word of God is about money. Check the Old Testament about usury laws and the New Testament about the laws of liberty. The lawless ones are the clergymen, yet only the president (father of many great nations) can end crimes. Where are the judges trained on religion.

I have gone to many churches trying to find one that teaches a sermon with meat (substance). All I hear is they sing some songs, read a passage, collect money for Ames for the poor, or for daily bread (or equivalent), and then the congregation leaves. What is your format?

The end shall come that means now. What are your plans to overcome the end? What is the passage Mark 9:12 all about? What are you doing to help the churches that our Gods states are bad?

Thank you for answering my prayer request to find a church to welcome a new member of your congregation. Please do not disappoint me.

Please email me at carrichard@verizon.net with your commitment to God and me.

Another memo

What do you believe King Jesus Christ should do to a man that refuses to?

1. End all poverty? You cannot end all that is poor, but ending all poverty through creating a biblical economy is easy.
2. Commit to ending divorces through grace?
3. Commit to ending unnecessary abortions through grace not law?
4. Has determined a man in shackles is something he can tell God, He is wrong.
5. Refuses to end ten thousand unnecessary deaths a day by working with his peers and doing a public opinion poll?
6. The Italian Mafia should go to Heaven for good deeds.
7. Marriage is not important but encouraging twelve-year-old children to have children is the most important issue in the world.
8. Become a man that has eyes to see and ears to hear. He cannot learn from Standing Historical.

REFUSES TO IMPLEMENT THE LORD'S PRAYER

The Holy Bible teaches us how to achieve the above and I can easily read and understand God's requirements.

Refuses to implement the Lord's Prayer and become royalty? He must wear the color purple.

All they need to tell you is I forgive all your sins and the last thirty years in America the pain in the families life has become worse. They will tell you King Jesus Christ is in control and He cannot fail, yet sorrows in America have increased in pain for the families. The truth the congregation has to learn is Our Gods put us in penance back in Israel. If you were a true God and could put the world in a hellish mode, you would find one hundred percent of every thing wrong. If Adam is not one hundred percent wrong then Our Gods do not exist. Since I know, one hundred percent of all items that are major are wrong, that would prove Our Gods are true.

Here is an interesting Holy Bible answer man test for any biblical scholar. I know many are trying to guess, but none start out with form the kingdom and learn how to talk. That was the theme of my first book back in the year of Our Lord 2002 AD.

7/30/the year of Our Lord 2006 AD.

A challenge for the Holy Bible Answer Man.

KING JESUS CHRIST WILL RETURN WHEN YOU HAVE NO QUESTIONS TO ASK. I BELIEVE THE FIRST THING A clergymen WOULD DO IS ASK QUESTIONS.

WHAT IS YOUR FIRST QUESTION OR DO YOU HAVE
ALL THE ANSWERS. TRY THE TEST.

It all happens in one generation or 2999 minus 1007 or the
year of Our Lord 1992 AD to the year of Our Lord 2016 AD.
Man has five generations in one hundred and twenty years or
twenty-four years. The clergymen are to teach the world to live
by every word.

The Holy Bible contains many names the clergymen are
to recognize in their Standing Historical. If you do not have
a written Standing Historical, you are disobeying King Jesus
Christ and therefore taking King Jesus Christ's name in vain.
Since most locations do not believe the clergyman can go
to Perdition for disobeying, you must be able to answer the
following questions and know the real human being names.
Passing is all answers are correct. You must be sure of the will
of the people and what you are teaching. If you do not know the
answers, you should try to learn.

Question 1. Why is the Second World War a War to end all
wars? See the book "The Antichrist God's Version" Chapter
9.

Question 2. Millstone two names and one name left. In the
year of Our Lord 1981 AD Ronald Reagan. Now George H. W.
Bush in the year of Our Lord 1989 AD as president of the United
States. George W. Bush cannot be saved but the clergymen in
a house divided amongst itself will always fail. We should
be thankful to the clergymen that formed the kingdom in the
year of Our Lord 2000 AD, unfortunately clergymen did not.
Not one woman could vote for a mass murderer of children
from Texas as prophecy described. If the world only had God's
Kingdom and the clergymen knew how to talk, we could listen
to campaigns and hear reality. No the only interest was blame
in the election year or Pro-life from the church, not a new
beginning or implementing the Lord's Prayer.

Question 3. King of the north and south in the year of Our Lord 1992 AD held a debate and add their titles from prophecy. The answer is George H. W. Bush president of USA as he lived in Washington DC or north. Future President William J. Clinton was from a southern Baptist church. The debate was all about money and my literature will teach you about Starr and what the Republicans did to neutralize President William J. Clinton in the year of Our Lord 2000 AD presidential election. Many have taught about the beast of Revelation, but that is President William J. Clinton's girlfriend helping a beast or mass murderer of children from Texas, Governor George W. Bush.

Question 4. God save the Queen of the South. In the year of Our Lord 1993 AD, the Queen of the South's name is? First Lady Hillary Clinton. The Catholics covered much ground in Pro-life churches that I saw to condemn Pope John Paul II to eternal penance in his war against children. The part of the prophecy is what he did to hurt the daughter of former President William J. Clinton rather than use a Vow of Silence to let the Baptist leaders get involved as marriage counselors for President William J. Clinton. The Catholics may explain why all people of Catholic faith that have a problem in marriage should be front-page news. They should not of course, but the Catholic priests must train the people, the priests are to be the marriage counselors, not the divorce courts.

Question 5. What does it mean it all happens in one generation or 2999 (end of millennium) minus a strange number 1007 or 1992? King Jesus Christ has defined what He needs in the seven books of Standing Historical for the United States from the year of Our Lord 1992 to 2016 AD. It all happens in one generation. The new beginning is the Lord's Prayer or the end of modern civilization in the United States of America. My literature contains much to be covered, but the men of the cross in the United States must write the final books for publication.

Question 6. The one million plus Antichrists appear at one hour past midnight on January 1, the year of Our Lord 2000 AD. They came in an era of peace and prosperity in the USA. Since then, they have destroyed peace and prosperity. What is their generic title? This book answers the question many times but they are the employees of King Jesus Christ who as defined in Malachi 3:8 is stealing from Our Gods or taking His name in Vain through a blasphemous mouth and refusing to implement the Lord's Prayer.

Question 7. King Jesus Christ named the age. What is it from the year of Our Lord 2000 AD to the year of Our Lord 2399 AD? The Age of Accountability, where all are responsible for their actions and the Gateway to Perdition is opened. No church employee can close the gates by fantasyland. Do not listen to a man that believes he can forgive your sins and actions for example like divorces. Divorces are a form of child abuse and will require more penance for all involved. God hates divorces.

Question 8. Why did King Jesus Christ have to tell us the fallen angels have reappeared? Who are they and why did it happen? The women of the United States do not believe in marriage as the first thought and our Catholics are trying to encourage babies to have babies. Where are the fathers? A fallen angel is partly raised by a policemen and may end up being in prison for the rest of their lives. Single women raising sons is not a good idea as the fallen angels are with the women. Both the female and male children lose.

Question 9. The false prophet Archangel Michael goes to Israel in the year of Our Lord 2000 AD. What is his true name and title? Many saw Pope John Paul II making himself worse than a fool in Israel in the year of Our Lord 2000 AD and heard his fantasyland prophecy about striking Israel from outer space. He was going to burn down a city, not implement the Lord's Prayer.

Question 10. The Scarlet of Babylon is riding the beast in the year of Our Lord 2000 AD. What are the events that led up to that happening? What is her true name and does she have a title? Her true name I remember is President William J. Clinton's girlfriend and since he wrote a book about it, the church can record Standing Historical as public record. The king of the north, George H. W. Bush of the year of Our Lord 1989-1993 AD, stated history will judge me where I say the only mistake I made was raising the taxes during his administration. Since he is a beast and dragon, the churches must judge him and add to standing historical as he asked. The easiest answer can come from future President William J. Clinton's analysis during the election of the economy in the year of Our Lord 1992 AD, but include the impact of Ross Perot and his determination to reform the Republican Party. The abandoned building are from Supply Economics as created by a fool called Friedman and implemented by President Ronald Reagan. Allan Greenspan abandoned Supply Economics in the year of Our Lord 1994 AD, but the Republicans have brought it back under President George W. Bush. We the people of the world must be trained to listen to promise keepers of scripture or what we call Campaign Promises and learn to judge them, led by the church. The Republicans got Supply Economics back under foolish George Bush again and created the new abandoned building of the Year of Our Lord 2008 AD. The laws of Former President William J. Clinton rainbow economy was discarded.

Question 11. The beast maintains his title as a beast and adds the King of Babylon as he runs for public office in the year of Our Lord 2000 AD. What is his name and what public office did he run for? Governor George W. Bush as he blew his first horn in the tax cut will enable the people to donate more to the church. He like his father is incapable of managing the economy and should just resign as a mass murderer of children from Texas in the year of Our Lord 2000 AD. His own mother should not vote for him as the best he can do is go to Perdition in his administration.

Question 12. The King's Representative Elias writes the first book found in the book of Daniel and is ignored by the Antichrists. What was the title of the book that restored all things and the author's name? The Antichrist -God's Version by Elias of Mark 9:12.

Question 13. In the book of Daniel, the furnace was heated up but there was no smoke. Since the heat was created in a trial by fire as in the words of the first book. Whoever is not written in the book of life is cast into the lake of fire. The lake of fire is where the churches create value in His Name or trial by fire. What are the three modern names to replace the names in the Holy Bible? The year was the year of Our Lord 2003 AD. The three modern names are Pope John Paul II, former President William J. Clinton, and former Vice President Al Gore.

Question 14. Satan was created by what he said in public office. The two horns are not on his head as the Catholics put on their web site. The Holy Bible is clear as the horns are like a lamb or what the politicians say. What did Satan say to cause him to become Satan in the year of Our Lord 2003 AD? President George W. Bush stated to let him seek the vengeance not say let God seek the vengeance. The world achieved no flesh is saved as the mouths of people to become saints became the ultimate unpardonable sinners without forming the Lord's Prayer and must arise through the story of resurrection. See the chapter of the Stairway to Heaven in this book. The clergymen, Antichrist did not have John 3:16 at one hour past midnight in the year of Our Lord 2000 AD.

Question 15. Satan goes to a Holy City. What is the name of the Holy City? We only have one Holy City not seven and the press covered President George W. Bush as he visited the Vatican.

Question 16. In the Garden of Eden it is written, when you are responsible for good and evil you will surely die. When did all flesh die in the USA? When did all flesh die for the entire world (ten kings)? The answer is in Question 14.

Question 17. The false messiah runs for public office. What is his name and does he have a present title? Senator John F. Kerry runs in the year of Our Lord 2004 AD for president of the United States. What heart does he have when the theme of his campaign is, I can kill better than the Republicans as America recreated the Roman Empire as described in the book of Romans or the fourth beast from the book of Daniel. We have the metal teeth. Now the election of the year of Our Lord 2008 AD, the war will continue as both candidates represent the Roman Empire, not our best example of a president or President Franklin D. Roosevelt on peace. Senator John McCain campaign was insane and he lost by a small margin. Senator Barack Obama brought out a Dragon President John F. Kennedy, not President Franklin D. Roosevelt.

Question 18. Satan's darts are thrown at the false messiah. What could have happened? Who are his angels? President George H. Bush used blame against Senator John F. Kerry in the 2004 AD campaign. Senator John F. Kerry spent much time and money answering the blame. The church is to seek the blood of just men to stop the Black Plague or the word blame. If there was a kingdom, the election should have been stopped for the use of blame. Satan's Angels are the Young Republicans that will die as soon as they take office. King Jesus Christ judged you long ago and must be part of Standing Historical. He will return when you have no questions.

Question 19. Archangel Michael dies and was condemned to earth (reincarnation). Why did God use the word condemned/reincarnation? Only a penance man can get off this world alive. No penance is great enough for him to get off this world alive and he will never live in the true Heaven. He achieves unpardonable sins for his organization and employees of King Jesus Christ. They must be saints to judge the world and instead, he started a war against children. He desired the children to suffer for their faith, not the priests. Also Pro-life is against God. The church is to get children back with fathers and fathers back with children, not be justified by law.

Question 20. The second published book from the book of Daniel is this book. What is its name? Why does it mean restoreth all things from Mark 9:12 for the first book? What happened in Israel that forced King Jesus Christ into a divorce of His church? He had to send equivalent to John the Baptist called His Elias to restoreth all things. King Jesus Christ's true representative has a small horn. I published a book Life of US (U.S.) that I included in my second book The Antichrist God's Version. I realize what I thought was the second book in the book of Daniel The Antichrist God's Version is actually the first. The author's name is Elias from Mark 9:12. The second book from the book of Malachi and Revelation is the second book written by Elijah, the prophet. The Holy Bible states the prophets are death as the church writes no true prophecy. Many attempt by the best they have achieved is false prophet status. The first book forms the kingdom and the second book is prophecy that is included as a book in the Holy Bible or the sixty-seventh book. A book about the seven thunders or fear. Fear is the beginning of all wisdom (knowledge) and must be taught on the great and dreadful Day of the Lord, Good Friday. What happened in Israel was the church disobeyed King Jesus Christ three times and today the Antichrists running the church refuses to obey King Jesus Christ. They have to teach how to live by every word. What they refuse to do is to form the kingdom or Lord's Prayer. They cannot even listen to elections and determine if a fool they are about to vote for is the wrong person for the job. They as an organization can only represent one party. The clergymen are worse than fools or Antichrists and in denial as the only thing they achieve is they have moved the Roman Empire from Rome, Italy to Washington DC. The road to hell is paved with their good intentions but without good deeds.

Question 21. The mysterious messiah appears as the prophets are dead. What prophecy does he develop for the year of Our Lord 3000 AD as copied out of the Holy Bible? Read the chapter The Seventh Trumpet Story.

Question 22. Satan disappears in the year of Our Lord 2009 AD or earlier. Why did he have a big horn and lose all that power? Satan is foolish George Bush the president of the United States. He was a mass murderer of children from Texas and he promised to hurt the school system like foolish Ronald Reagan and his foolish father in the campaign. Eight years of Bush was and will always be recorded in Standing Historical as twelve years too many. The first four years should have taught America reality. In my first book Life of US (U.S.), I reviewed the election of the year of the Lord 2000 AD, three different ways and it always agrees with the Holy Bible. Our source document states there is not one woman that could vote for foolish George Bush. His presidential term is over in the year of Our Lord 2009 AD and if the kingdom is formed, his life would be better. He will return after the year of Our Lord 3000 AD and there is little the church can do. At that time, they will have to overcome again or the end may return. As the Mother of Inspiration, they must maintain hope in their hearts to overcome the infinite tyranny of man. Without God, Adam is just a fool.

Question 23. The Seventh Trumpet story is developed. What does the church expect of King Jesus Christ's, Christ? Why was the beginning stated in goals and prophecies? Why not just prophecy? That the story is included in this book, you can just read. King Jesus Christ's true Christ will work out of the seven Holy Cities.

Question 24. Why does the Seventh Trumpet story involve great knowledge about money? What generic titles would you list for the people involved? The answer is well covered in the Holy Bible and is a repeat of a story from the Old Testament. Which story did King Jesus Christ give us the story from? A clue King David is involved. King Jesus Christ stated, He can double the best economy Adam can create and that is money. The story is about King David's son and Our Father will give us a reprieve from killing wars. King Jesus Christ becomes the wall through the chapter, "The White Stone Story".

Question 25. Why does the Holy Bible state to form the kingdom first and learn how to talk? If you ever went to any church as Paul from the Holy Bible, did you know the answer? You can use chapter 17 from the book The Antichrist God's Version to audit any church. Paul saves the clergymen souls because he is an internal auditor sent by the six Holy Cities to audit the seventh or becomes one of God's Covenants. God's Covenants are the minimum requirement to run a church.

Question 26. If the clergymen refuse to form the kingdom, how long is the new penance? Since the clergymen have abandoned thy children (My children, 777 design) the penance continues for seven times longer or Our Gods come back with the seven Horns of the Eternal Temple or Israel. We have to wait for the church to start again.

Question 27. What does it mean only a penance man can get off this world alive? For example, if the church formed and ends ninety percent of the divorces in twenty years as a prophecy, your penance would be to go through reincarnation. You live a successful life as part of a loving and caring parent with good money. So, your penance is wonderful life for those that accept the way. The other ten percent will continue a bad life.

Question 28. The Holy Bible states to stay with reality. Why do clergymen love fantasyland when they talk about their witness of scripture? It allows the church locations to work against each other and never try to achieve anything. You can see the television station TBN with all the money they have stolen from God through tithes and offerings. They refuse to form the kingdom through the Lord's Prayer and have abandon Thy Children of 777 design. The only purpose for them to be on television is to tell you how good they are and tell God what to do. Where are their works to get the teenagers back and to work at the Altar, or become the marriage counselors. I have proven they are doing one hundred percent of everything wrong, yet they will say they do not have to change. They must go through the seven-year resurrection story for their salvation or John 3:16.

Question 29. We should pity the clergymen that stay with the gospel about Christ only as started in 31 AD. What should I say to start the GOSPEL OF CHRIST? I understand the real story of the White Horse for Christ the son of man? What is your answer on how to create the real stories? As the Holy Bible states, the clergymen that do not join the kingdom and learn how to talk, die at the second resurrection story and cannot be saved. The seals are for communication within a kingdom so King Jesus Christ will return with his Christ, who is the son of man. Christ works out of the seven Holy Cities.

Question 30. The Universal Church was granted to the world as the format for all locations. The Holy Bible shows the locations require twenty-five people to run it (clergymen and twelve and twelve). Much combining and staff positions for training must be started which all will take time. The people have to have eyes to see and ears to hear as it is all heard in a church location. Does your location conform to the biblical standards? Do you know of any church location that does? A small church may one day be fifteen thousand people with a large over fifty thousand. The church will have to reorganize over time to waste not want not as started in the chapter of the Seventh Trumpet Story for government.

Question 31. King Jesus Christ states you shall know what you did before you die. The Antichrist of over a million strong is refusing to obey God and become royalty. What is the modern name of the Antichrist and why are YOU refusing to become a prince and therefore royalty? You wear the color purple. The answer will be well covered in the seven books of Standing Historical. Each denomination should compare with the other six to complete the question. The answer must be believable by the congregation and may require King Jesus Christ to reread when He returns. Put your heart and soul into developing a believable story. Do not write a story of fantasyland and say you are saved. Each denomination shall challenge the other six.

Question 32 What does the title Holy Bible mean to you as a commitment from the true God our King in the future story of King of kings and Lord of lords? The word Holy is perfect and Bible as religion is away of life. So if the Mother of Inspiration is training the world to live by one hundred percent planning or theology, all citizens of the nation will one day have a life one thousand times better than the end.

Question 33 Who are the lords and what book do they use to judge for example the governments? The Lord will lord over the churches and the lords will lord over the courts by the book of Galatians where an attorney or judge seeking John 3:16 cannot be justified by law, he must have the right heart to be justified by grace.

Question 34 It would be good if the church trained the governments on how King Jesus Christ will judge them. The saints from the seven Holy cities shall judge the world but not attack the people in gospel armor. Do you know how to do that so we can talk? I do of course. All judgment is defined in the Holy Bible and the passages. My literature has given prime example, but I could not spend all the rest of my life on what is left, as real experiences are the best answer. You first must learn reality.

If you have interesting answers, please forward to me.
If you have interesting questions to add, please write.
I can grant you the true answers for all the questions, I have written.
email comfortinGod@hotmail.com

414

King Jesus Christ will appear after you form the kingdom and the one world government from the Old Testament and New.

Part of chapter Bible Answer man test. Information like below must be taught in the summaries and ongoing in church employees lives.

What do you believe King Jesus Christ should do to a man that refuses to:

1. End all poverty? You cannot end all that is poor, but ending all poverty through creating a biblical economy is easy.
2. Commit to ending divorces through grace.
3. Commit to ending unnecessary abortions through grace not law.
4. Has determined a man in shackles is something he can tell God He is wrong.
5. Refuses to end ten thousand unnecessary deaths a day by working with his peers and doing a public opinion poll.
6. The Italian Mafia should go to Heaven for good deeds.
7. Marriage is not important but encouraging twelve-year-old children to have children is the most important issue in the world.
8. Become a man that has eyes to see and ears to hear. He cannot learn from standing Historical.

REFUSES TO IMPLEMENT THE LORD'S PRAYER.

The Holy Bible teaches us how to achieve the above and I can easily read and understand God's requirements.

415

Chapter 18. The Word Blame

Much work in the Holy Bible focuses on how not to attack a person in gospel armor. Since the church is to teach the world how to plan or theology, we the congregation are in gospel armor. The saints are the priest in a quest for knowledge and require the blood of a just man to end the Black Plague, the word blame.

We have the concepts of the four winds in scripture or the force of the unseen. When the news uses blame to reach for marketing results of ratings for news shows, we cannot measure the negative impact on those that watch. I heard the physiatrists state not to watch the five o'clock news, because the impact hurts lives of people. Therefore, blame has a negative influence on people. The four directions of the winds can be abbreviated as n, e, s, and w but I would use it to the true works or the word n, e, w, and s or NEWS. King Jesus Christ was to smart to call the congregation sinners or blame. He will take care of the man of sin or as Israel was a nation of priests, His priests.

Have you heard Preacher Whores that cannot tell King Jesus Christ what to do like, "I forgive all your sins."? That is blame and they require the blood of a just man to end the Black Plague or the word blame in the church. How about the losers you see on television that state I am the only one that understands this and all other clergymen are deceived? They are to reform the church, but if they tried, all they would do is deceive. That is blame without reforming the church as King Jesus Christ has told you all things. King Jesus Christ judged you because He loved you, but this blame of people worse than fools or Antichrists is intended to convince people to follow their incorrect preaching. They must form the kingdom to learn how to talk as they talk like little children.

In politics, blame is used to convince something is wrong, normally because they cannot convince you, they are right. Many succeed like Satan's Darts of the year of Our Lord 2004 AD campaign. Foolish George Bush used extensive blame against Senator John F. Kerry as future Standing Historical must record.

Blame is stating something that is wrong and yet you do not have the solutions to correct. Sixty Minutes has been on television for decades and they define problems. To my knowledge, they have never carried a story through to correct what they defined is wrong. The same is for the newspapers. In addition, evil spirits are introduced as a solution but his answer will not work. He joys in hearing himself talk. The dictionary states criticize somebody, or I state you murdered that person. That did not correct the problem of why someone murdered a person. The Holy Bible calls that the Black Plague and states that was against what was allowed in Israel, but America, blame is part of normal conversation. The weatherman did not get it right today, when he said rain. The church was to correct this problem not create it in many situations. Adam does not know, what he does.

The requirement in the clergymen is, "Let the man without sin cast the first stone." If he casts a stone like, I forgive all your sins, that is blame and he is not without sin. How about the blame of Pro-Life? If I have the number right from memory, the employees of King Jesus Christ have seventy weeks to end their sins. I can understand seventy weeks of seven denominations working as independent organizations and them combining the knowledge before being put into practice, is a tremendous amount of work. One example, if they encountered greed within their land they must inform the Holy City as to their belief. The Holy Cities develops the corrective actions to take place. The seven Holy Cities must coordinate their efforts. Today the Catholics have to obey the Pope and he blames the other church names. That is wrong and they will never get John 3:16 as saints with that attitude. It is time for Adam to grow up and work against the tyranny of man even if that tyranny is themselves. The true story is against the beasts or politicians in 666 beast.

How would you end greed if you cannot blame? The Lord's Prayer states to forgive the debtors, which are the children. The American children are the greatest debtors in the world. I proposed a sixty to seventy five percent tax over three million dollars or income on greed. The congregation can compare an economy without property taxes for schools versus a passage that states never give people money that cannot use it wisely. The rich have trillions they cannot use wisely and the solution is a tax, not just state I believe the baseball players make too much money. Defining a problem without defining the solution is blame. The congregation will love Social Security funded and Elijah will get the rich to ask if we can do it faster, even though they pay. We will use the money to fund Social Security, forgive the debts of government on the children, and on Easter Sunday the clergymen will define what the rich man is achieving in His name to prepare for their return as the poorest child in their country. Where is the blame? Today many complain about Exxon-Mobile salaries and their is no solution that pleases.

Watch out for prophecies. If you write, "The congregation has to many divorces" that is attacking people in gospel armor. The way to write it is "The church will eliminate ninety percent of the divorces in twenty years (777 design for their theology on divorces) and then try harder." is good. You are taking responsibility, but do not fail yourself or use, "The church will eliminate one hundred percent of the divorces in twenty years." You are total and absolute failures if you cannot do it. Some I have heard state the problems are the congregation does not obey the Ten Commandments. Are all members of the congregation priests like in Israel? How could the church eliminate one hundred percent of the sins in seventy weeks? Many people do not even go to church and even after the kingdom is formed, may not. In Israel, the prophecies defined require more than seventy weeks to eliminate the sins of the Israeli man. The temple is far better run than any church I have gone to as God compared his clergymen with the animals the ass and oxen. At least the ass and oxen know their own crib.

The only answer is to develop a training course in the seminaries. First, a training course is required on how to avoid blaming people in gospel armor. The next step is to rewrite news articles that fail and are of importance. See the story on Mayor Daley of Chicago in the book Life of US (U.S.) contained in the book The Antichrist God's Version. You should encourage reporters and newspapers to conform to the standard of glad tidings. You publish a list of newspapers that have evolved.

You should expand the training courses to include the Vow of Silence. If you remember stories from old, you would have examples. When the basketball player, Michael Jordon's father was killed, what did the news do? They chased him around in his darkest hour at that time to ask, "What did you feel about your father dying?" Why, you may ask? I already knew the answer and I did not believe his family should be exposed. In terrorist, they desire to see their name in print, they work harder, and life is worse. How about a story out of Chicago where an eight year old boy threw a stone at a thirteen year old girl and she did not have a helmet. Her parents needed to revenge her death by the accident of a young child. Did the news make that life of that young child worse? Did you see Feed the Children trying to make us feel guilty instead of the good deeds of the politicians to correct the problem? You should

419

encourage through proclaiming good deeds not being asleep at the Altar. King Jesus Christ judged you because he loved you. What happens in a kingdom is you share your love with your fellow man and love conquers all!

What is the story you desire to see on television and in newspapers? How Adam desires to complete the Six-Day Creation Story and proclaim his glad tidings (good deeds).

Chapter 19. 666 Beast Books

The 666 beasts books are Standing Historical. Life of US (U.S.) Catholic is one of the seven names of the books in the United States. Life of Mexico or Russia would be a separate kingdom, as it has to be kingdom against kingdom and nation against nation. The reason is a challenge as to what country through a nation can satisfy the desires of the people best. A want is a demand the government must satisfy like ending poverty, problems in schools, health care, or the roads. A need is a desire at a new beginning of life to end that life with a desire for a new beginning of life. Government takes care of your wants, but only God can take care of your needs.

The format is the same as the Holy Bible where the history of the Church of the United States to the time of the Lord's Prayer is the Old Testament. The Holy Bible tells us some of what to write like King Jesus Christ will meet us in Spain (Christopher Columbus). How we started in Winston Salem and ended with a witch-hunt. The children of corn are the story we joy in the American Indians teaching our pilgrims how to plant corn and America ending with Thanksgiving. How America used the Universal Church format to create our form of government. We did not know how to write laws per the New Testament (the Generation of the FIG or the word love) but we started the laws of liberty, only to lose all of the works. A war brother against brother and sister against sister is the Civil War. Abraham Lincoln stated the wealth creation in the United States was incredible. The reason for the incredible wealth creation was we took our inventions (the trains in the year of Our Lord 1820 AD) and turned it into gold through interest free loans. Have you heard about airplanes or cars. After the war, it took until the year of Our Lord 1900 AD to get out of debt. The beast stories of our presidents and the works of, it all happens in one generation or the year of Our Lord 1992 AD until the year of Our Lord 2016 AD in the future Heartland of the world. Great writings will be required on how the seven churches formed, as we are the wax location of the world and the wax is cold. Much of my writings will be included in the Standing Historical books.

The new beginning or your story of the future you desire to inherit. How you desire to finish the 6-Day Creation story should be important to people beyond the church, like a temple. In The Seventh Trumpet Story, you are granted in this book is only for America, but you should know the story where the Eagles are. You must use the movie to help the other governments of the world to create a commitment to the taxpayers of their name. Again, you should add to films. I desire to see the faith of the unseen, even though I know the true vision will be incomplete. When you take over the schools in America in the year of Our Lord 2800 AD, you will not take over the schools in other countries. You are deciding when you will allow the government to include you running the schools for the nation of church beyond the year of Our Lord 3000 AD. Start another story of many mysteries and intrigue. You should add a word to Joy, Jeopardy, war and fear and you remember Satan comes back with greed. Are you going to be asleep again?

The future and past are well defined in your literature that you sell to maintain reality. How about the church creating some movies, written by you, directed by you, acted by you, and your film library grows. Just wait until your first space ship named the Star of Bethlehem and run as the Temple of Israel comes back with wondrous 666 beast books and music of the design of man. They will enhance man's way to a better way of life and praise to God for the glory of His vast Kingdom. Another prophecy of one thousand years waiting to learn more of God's vast Kingdom from outer space.

Man should always be intrigued with the wisdom of the churches inspiration. The church must sell their great works and use the text to help train future politicians, clergymen, and all the rest of mankind. How could a church consider running without Standing Historical and state they represent God? How could man finish the Six-Day Creation story, if every time he desired to achieve through the root of all evil (lack of knowledge) money became a hindrance to the success of man? May the clergymen train the wicked in shackles not to resort to becoming a beast and gain the whole world as the presidency or other titles, only to lose his soul. May that man rest without peace or in Eternal Death and go the way of Satan, Archangel Michael, or worse. May the church train and learn not to let beasts over come, what is good again. Certainly, God does not desire the Son of Perdition, the Antichrist in the year of Our Lord 2000 AD to maximize the lost of souls.

Chapter 20. Additional Letters.

The clergymen are to have eyes to see and ears to hear. On the surface, they would tell you they are perfect. In a church, it is to be all heard and if you talk to a clergymen about scripture, you learn what little they have learned. After two thousand years of Adam saying he represents the Holy Bible, what he has achieved is he has moved the Roman Empire from Rome, Italy to Washington DC. As Hosea 4:6 states, "If you are not in a quest for knowledge you are not priests of mind." The only church a person can go to is a perfect church where a stranger enters and he does not know the door stories, the congregation will not drive him away. The trees are the Tree of Life and the Tree of Knowledge from the Garden of Eden. I have been waiting for one man that desires to be like Peter. He leads the way to achieve 1000 and five for Peter to return to Rome, Italy as a concept. He becomes as if a conquering hero to lead the world to a level of life man does not believe he can achieve.

BELOW ARE NUMEROUS MEMOS WHERE YOU DO NOT DESIRE TO BE ME AS I AM TRYING TO HELP MY GRANDCHILDREN AND HAVE KNOWN FOR MORE THAN A DECADE THE TRUE END WILL COME. ALL I DESIRED WAS TO FIND PETER OR A MAN THAT

DESIRED TO REPRESENT KING JESUS CHRIST IN THE CHURCH AND IMPLEMENT THE LORD'S PRAYER.

I have never met the likes of the clergymen that we believe in, yet they have created a total fantasyland for religion. They are about to create the end and they are in denial that they require any change. They state they understand the Holy Bible and cannot judge themselves as scripture defines as men that have gone backwards and are doing one hundred percent of everything wrong. They do not even understand they are in penance and Our Gods refused to help them. All they are doing is disobeying the Holy Bible and violating the following by stating, "You know, I have to wait for Jesus to return." They cannot even call Him King. He is still the Prince of Peace as they promote killing wars and do nothing to stop them. They were never saved at the beginning of the Age of Accountability or one hour past midnight in the year of Our Lord 2000 AD. What they work for is observation or a time where Our Gods will do everything for them, which violates the Holy Bible. They are quick to declare King Jesus Christ is causing all the problems in the world through their blame. They achieve nothing for the tithes and offering we provide, as the Holy Bible is stating they are stealing from God.

The proof is the Holy Bible or

Luke 17:22 And he said unto the disciples, The days will come, when ye shall desire to see one of the days of the Son of man, and ye shall not see it.

Luke 17:20 And when He was demanded of the Pharisees, when the kingdom of God should come, He answered them and said, The kingdom of God cometh not with observation:

Malachi 3:8 Will a man rob God? Yet ye have robbed me. But ye say, Wherein have we robbed thee? In tithes and offerings.

The above must be clearly written and part of Standing Historical for all Seven Churches. We, the congregation must understand, but not until they go through the story of resurrection as defined in the Holy Bible and my literature.

I sent to more church locations all over the United States. The only answers I received were the type implying Elijah is wrong and the Antichrists running the church are right. The are to be gatherers of all possible knowledge and not reject any input at all. It shall be all heard in the church and a big size church should be fifty thousand people not run by one-person worst than a fool or what God calls the Antichrist.

Sent May 5, the year of Our Lord 2008 AD
Question.

WE ARE TO LIVE BY EVERY WORD. Do you know any church location or organization that desires to implement the Lord's Prayer so the Second Advent can occur?

The Lord's Prayer is a prophecy of King Jesus Christ and must be implemented by the church for salvation.

In a kingdom, no one worries about money if the kingdom understands what a famine is.

Sent January 23, the year of Our Lord 2008 AD.

Chapter By the Grace of God You Are Saved from the book Voice of Vengeance -Fear by Elijah (Now the sixty-seventh book of the Holy Bible).

With the Antichrists running the churches, what shall we learn on the terrible and dreadful Day of the Lord or Good Friday where only adults can attend? The reality is all adults must attend if they joy in the meaning of the end of all death or John 3:16; however, God did not promise everlasting life but eternal life. There is a big difference. Do not be deceived! The four words of the millennium story must be understood which are war, jeopardy, joy and fear. For one thousand years, you will be learning the true meaning of the four words and how the words apply.

We must have the clergymen go back to the Garden of Eden and think of why the Flaming Swords were guarding the Tree of Life and the Tree of Knowledge. Adam told God, "God, I need to do it myself." Adam started much penance of pain such as the pain of childbirth, viruses, and the pain of many tongues. We know the Antichrist speaks many tongues, as the language of the church is to be English. How else, can the most powerful organization the world will ever experience, the church, communicate through language and computers? The only reason the Son of Perdition desires to keep the church ineffective is so as a nobody, he can do it himself. The Antichrist takes pride in himself, not humility for King Jesus Christ. Pride is a deadly sin. Working together for common goals to overcome the social ills of his world is the problem and the solution. Now, you should understand the importance of the Tree of Knowledge and the Tree of Life. The Holy Bible and God's Plan evolves around Adam learning how to work together to achieve common goals like no child is hungry, or without health care, or has a bright future. In God's Kingdom, they are not dying due to bad laws. If you heard Senator Hillary Clinton speak, she said. "The Republicans and Democrats have opposing views." What that will achieve is the voice of the powerful drowning out the voice of reason. That is how Adam desires to be in the church as well. A house divided amongst itself will always fail. What does the Holy Bible say about life in the year of Our Lord 2007 AD? Adam was put in penance back in Israel for disobeying and Our Gods refused to help us. In the year of Our Lord 2007 AD, you find great social ills all over America and we cannot work together to resolve. Adam after 2000 years without God's help is doing one hundred percent of everything wrong. Adam without God is just a fool. The Holy Bible is clear. You write down in column A what the church, government, and businesses are doing today. In column B, you write down the opposite. You work to resolve the social ills of any nation by working on column B. You can write what is good and what is bad in two separate columns. When the column of good only contains the Holy Bible and the love of parents for a two-year-old child, you can stop. When you get tired of writing down what is bad, take something that is bad and put that story to rest once what was bad can be put under the column of good. You must work to change and put stories to rest. You do that with all other social ills or what is poor. You have a church with seven names on the door with the Universal Church format granted in the year of Our Lord 1200 AD. "Why is all bad?" you say. It is because Adam never learned the meaning of the two trees. Yet the Holy Bible defines them clearly.

I have originated memos like the ones the church should communicate by and sent to the people that Americans and beyond are very dependent on. What have they written me when I explain and copy the Holy Bible for them to understand? They write I believe in John 3:16 and therefore I am saved. In the book of Luke is where they quote from and believe they have a heart from Heaven. The Holy Bible states because of their blasphemous mouth they worship Satan. They should explain what terrible knowledge they have relied on and teach on the great and dreadful Day of the Lord or Good Friday. The Road to hell is paved with good intensions. There is no hell like a woman scorned. She cannot get daily bread, health care, good education, or believe in a great future for her children. The women are King Jesus Christ's educators or the ones the clergymen must hear. You should cover what procedures they are going to use in the future to become saints to judge the world. You will guard against repeating evil spirits, they have created in man's mind to deceive the congregation and themselves. The church employees do not even know what the word evil means. As a church of enlightened power, you never admit defeat, but rely on pending victories. Can you teach the congregation to do the same?

Now, you should teach what the Grace of God is. Fear is the beginning of all wisdom (knowledge). The church will go through extreme fear when they realized what they did before they died. The Holy Bible proclaimed the church personnel should experience death, which is fear. For those that should get involved on the first great and dreadful Day of the Lord, you explain what locations are staffed with people that cannot be saved. Now, you are developing and have in the last forty-two months the techniques of Paul from the New Testament and review what the Holy Bible states. Paul is like a Quality Assurance person that comes from the seven Holy Cities. You can explain that your fear is your quest for knowledge to avoid Hell on earth and your calling beyond your calling or your true death (unpardonable sins). Do not go too far and try to cover too much. Next year you know you will be better and have new areas you are going to explore like, "Some governments are taking you on the Road to Hell" or you will try to send the Italian Mafia to Heaven with only one eye. You may have to keep the congregation for more than one hour and ask them to use a Vow of Silence for the Love of God's Special Children or 777 design His angels.

What is happening right now? Antichrist Ken Copeland on TBN states there is no fear in me. I will state the truth about his show in that no knowledge is coming from his mouth. All he states is a deception on his viewers to get them to love him for all the skills he possesses, yet he never accomplished anything for the children of 777 design (born to twenty-one). What can he tell you about what he thought about the government taking you on the Road to hell, which has happen all over the world? Famines (money) are killing millions of children each year due to the pen. The Holy Bible states I do not care what they eat but stop sending me little ones small and great. Fear in politicians could end hunger in America over night. Now, you suffer for what you have faith in the unseen and the actions of Hope. The children will get food from the politicians all over the world. All you had to do was teach that is fear. The "White Stone Story" I have copied out of the Holy Bible will end hunger where there is a kingdom of the church. Antichrist Ken Copeland has no fear and therefore no knowledge. The Antichrist can stop wars in eighty-two percent of the countries led by a man of European decent. The angels (children 777 design) are King Jesus Christ's peacekeepers. They are not the angels of death or adults that can shove the bodies under the Altar. The requirement is, "I do not want a hair on a child's head harm." Yes, that means a child in Iraq too. Killing a child's father in Iraq is worst than harming a hair on a child's head. The Antichrists running the church could have ended wars centuries ago. You must learn that the Second World War was a war to end all wars. I covered the subject clearly in the book "The Antichrist God's Version" and was born in the year forty-two or during the war. The clergymen must become the meek that inherit the earth. The meek are very powerful in correcting social ills like unnecessary deaths of children with hair on their heads.

Have you gone to a church that teaches, by the Grace of God you are saved? There is nothing you have to do. How about the churches that only teaches the New Testament? In those types of churches, they require you do nothing. Yet when a man told King Jesus Christ, "I can barely take care of my wife and child." What did King Jesus Christ say, "You are doing all that I asked." What if a dad abandons his family? Is that individual doing what King Jesus Christ stated? All should say, "You must take care of your wife and child." Is that doing something more than nothing?

In the book of Luke, it is written you must have the right heart for John 3:16. You can ask the Catholic priest if the Italian Mafia has the heart of the God of Heart or King Jesus Christ. If they answer, you must be baptized at eight days, is that more than nothing? In addition, the Holy Bible states the crime syndicates can go to heaven with one eye. In the church world, it is an eye for an eye and shove the bodies under the Altar, or fear. The religious leaders are to teach that is legal businesses only. So generation after generation of Italian Mafia children die at eight days because their fathers teach them to live in the wrong world of success for themselves.

Now, you should learn from a clergymen what the Grace of God is and what that passage means. First, you can start with the saints that run a church. King Jesus Christ judged the world long ago, because He loved you. The saints are to judge the world or do they have the right heart? Before the clergymen are ordained and lose their citizenship in the country they live in, they should start learning what it means to live by the written instructions the seminaries have for King Jesus Christ's employees on the Ten Commandments and how they apply. Once they officially are part of the church, they receive real life experience training from their peers and bosses. Once they reach the age of the King where He started the concept of His kingdom, they are reborn again and should reach the total sainthood commitment and be prepare to judge parts of life because of their love of the congregation. Now, they are the right age to judge on their own merits. Many in the church should love the celebration of their ministries being reborn again, but their own family members being reborn again will make other celebrations seem small. What becomes the hardest to judge? It will be themselves and what function they should perform for the enlighten power of all humanity or inheritance. The man that holds the book and is the very elect in God's election on how the church is to be run is his challenge. The best man to run the church must always be the best man to run the church. What happens if a man has a stroke and does not recover one hundred percent of all he had? How can those below him judge? What if he was in perfect health and someone is better? Should the new man say, "God, how come you have forsaken me?" He has the responsibility for all souls before him and the challenge becomes great. The church employees must develop the ways. How can you teach the politicians something you have not learned yourself? Are people like George H. W. Bush (king of the north) capable of judging himself in comparison to William J. Clinton (king of the south) to manage the wealth creation in the United States in the year of Our Lord 1992 AD? President George H. W. Bush stated, "We have to watch out for Governor William J. Clinton, because he is good." Prophecy defined the pot of gold at the end of an Irishman's administration or tremendous wealth creation (rainbow). The Holy Bible requires the church to divide up the fat cows of President William J. Clinton and not allow the skinny cows of President George W. Bush to do what his father did to the economy. In addition, you were to learn Jacob was to be justified in the year of Our Lord 2000 AD. You can read about him walking through Egypt without selling all his gold and giving it to the poor. Did you hear Allen Greenspan (Federal Reserve Governor and accountant), when he stated it normally takes three month to count the money and in the year of Our Lord 1999 AD, it will take six months longer? They must learn and lead the way. Who are they going to send to the Holy Cities to judge the world and select the right people to lead the way? You have a young child or teenagers. Are they willing to move or are you going to put God's work above your children? You must find the creative minds to become Christ the son of man in the Holy Cities. He must have the innocence and imagination of a two-year-old child. So much for the saints to learn and teach us how we can judge ourselves and the future we desire to inherit. Does the unskilled mind of George W. Bush Senior and Junior desire to take a critical role in judgment only to achieve, "If a man gains the whole world and loses his soul, he gains nothing at all."? Millstone two names George Bush and Ronald Reagan and one name left George Bush. God warned you ago and Satan cannot be saved in this lifetime.

I thought we started out with, there was nothing to do. All the answers to the above are available in the Holy Bible. You have to reach for a perfect way of life as saints and become the role models for those without your extreme training. Over many millenniums let all that follow King Jesus Christ ways in the kingdom gain until all reach a perfect way of life. That challenge may take a hundred thousand years or longer, but will it be lost again to divorce. Life is like a circle, what comes around goes around. The true saints will find one person requesting a divorce will have to start a new beginning or the end may return. Now, you should realize King Jesus Christ has told you all things. So your judgment on your organizations becomes essential. They even provided Paul to keep you informed and provide mercy when you go astray.

What is the next part of one hundred percent theology? We should take a passage like, "I do not want you to do a job, you do not want to do." Since a want is a demand the government must satisfy, how would the Grace of God qualify. You must understand King Jesus Christ is the trunk of the Tree of Knowledge. Presently, King Jesus Christ admits the trunk and even the roots are dead. One branch off that tree is the above passage or a path to a small door. You cannot create lives one thousand times better than the end unless all people in His kingdom are doing jobs, they desire to do. In America, I heard half the people do not like their jobs. A large percent do not even have a job to dislike. How are the parents of the children dying due to a famine (lack of money) love their jobs all across the world? They are back to the old saying, "Hey buddy, do you have a dime, I cannot buy a job." The one hundred percent theology requires the men to be able to care for their families with a job they desire to do. You may ask the Catholic priest in Mexico, "Why do the Mexicans come to America, when the Catholic Church is to teach all the people to love their jobs? The church, government, and businesses are the branch and the seeds of knowledge are the leaves. Each passage that applies has a branch and the fruit of our labor is the success of the congregation. Anything short of perfect is short of the glory of God and must be considered poor until corrected. By the Grace of God, you are saved. How can a politician fail himself when he is working to produce happiness? All the people of his nation will get the right education in schools and churches and the businessperson will help provide the information and feed back as to the success of the theology. The businessperson has a great part in the jobs and wisdom on the branch or the path to the small door. All the children are working their way to a small door where their paycheck is more important than the sheep (product), yet their loyalty to the business is well accepted as the way, truth, and light. Nearly a billion jobs to go and all jobs the people must shine in. Where is the Grace of God in the year of Our Lord 2007 AD? It is in the Holy Bible as each church location works against their success.

Where is the information to be stored on the Tree of Knowledge? In the Garden of Eden, it is stated that once you are responsible for good and evil you will surely die. The existing poor format of people stating they represent King Jesus Christ has created no flesh is saved from a spiritual view. One hour past midnight in the year of Our Lord 2000 AD, became the

Age of "Accountability" or you are responsible for your actions. Once you know how to manage good and evil, you will be like Gods of saints as the Holy Bible defines. The Catholic Church is good at storing data as they where hired by the United States government to straighten out records; however, the Holy Bible defines the true way, which has been hidden since the beginning of time. The answer is in programming a computer. The Holy Bible grants the way to the church as held in trust for the love of our children so the church can afford to grow to satisfy the demands of the congregation. The procedure was covered in my first book, "Life of US (U.S.)". A reprint is included in, "The Antichrist God's Version" as part of chapter 24 or subchapter 13 of chapter 24. The program has been committed by me to be developed by the Federal Government of the United States and put on their computers with the fees granted to the church. All businesses, universities, associations and all the rest will demand training through the church seminaries and fees applied. The church will become well off as they train the world on theology or planning from the Holy Bible.

In the Garden of Eden, we were denied the Tree of Knowledge and King Jesus Christ has the wisdom already in the Holy Bible. I have heard Antichrists trying to teach me the table in front of them is not there. I suggest they sit on it so it will not disappear. The desktop is just what you normally put as the first screen on a computer. We have one tree left or the Tree of Life.

The purpose of life is life not unnecessary deaths because of bad laws that kill millions of children each year. The prophecy is, "The problem near the end times is the problem with the rich." Which party represents the rich in the USA? Normally it is due to the rich being elected and serving the rich at the expense of the poor (social ills of the country). The Tree of Life is the temptations we encounter like a clergymen hires a beautiful secretary and she is richly endowed. He looks at her and sees more than he should. A blessing is coming forward and the temptation was too great. The types of temptation like discussed is to be developed and through fear to be overcome. Fear is the beginning of all wisdom (knowledge). You never fear an American soldier but a God that can cut off the dragon's (warlord) ugly head is powerful. Through the church, the Tree of Life must be taught and the reality of our decisions noted in the book of life (666 beast books). Today, we require many millenniums of work to overcome the lack of wisdom in our example. Temptation must be delivered from evil and the consequences of our decision through fear be understood. For example, the clergymen are to teach what their mothers need for their grandchildren. Does she desire her son as a clergymen not to understand the emotions of man? Penance is desired, when her grandchildren are affected. The clergymen can teach what his wife desires from the Tree of Life for her grandchildren. Does the average mother desire less for her children? The will of the people will prevail. When God's will and the people's will agree, no penance is required and the clergymen have effectively taught the Tree of Life. The divorces in a church environment are the same as the Old Testament, but you must update for John 3:16. I have covered the answers in other works, so the church can get fathers back with sons and not create fallen angels or boys in prison. The fallen angels are in general with the single mothers. The clergymen can easily develop the teaching for the Tree of Life as they are responsible for the deadly sins and must live by the Ten Commandments as saints and role models.

I just learned how easy it is to understand. I wrote a definition of a need or want in my book "Life of US (U.S.). A need is a new beginning of life that ends with a desire for a new beginning of life. Only Our Gods can take care of our needs or spiritual view. A want is a demand the government must satisfy. We in the congregation shall not want or the congregation will demand the government make them rich. I have covered how to achieve in past writings. We learn the Tree of Life is a need.

The Tree of Knowledge is a want. There is overlapping in the two. I covered how the church is to determine whether a desire is a want or need in chapter 2 of the book of life titled "Life of US (U.S.).

The end of this chapter should include we have to live by every word and the Holy Bible is a planning book where through theology you plan the future you desire to inherit. Fear is the children teaching the religious leaders what information they must learn to achieve their success or spare the rod, spoil the child will be the failure of the clergymen. The senators are to hear what is required from the children (angels) to meet that demand of the child to reach happiness in his career and God helps those who helps themselves. All church children (777 design) are to be doubled blessed or special. Do not let the wicked senator ignore the wishes of our most important citizens or the children! A country that does not properly raise its children has no right to exist. The United States has gone the way of the Roman Empire.

January 23, the year of Our Lord 2008 AD

Shepherd's Chapel
PO Box 416
Gravette, Arkansas 72736

Pastor Arnold Murray

Re: Elijah

Do you imply you have found Elijah and you are getting sons back with their fathers? You must obey the Ten Commandments and watch out for your false witness. Most locations say if I do not do anything, all will turn out good. King Jesus Christ is doing nothing.

Since I am the true Elijah, I do not believe what should be the most powerful organization the world will ever see can be based on doing nothing. What stories has the church in the United States put to rest. Was it poverty, divorces, or maybe abortions? If we continue with the Gospel about Christ (31 AD) as defined in the book of Matthew, the end will come.

Are you interested in starting the greatest tribulation the world will ever see or God's Kingdom? I grant you the knowledge of the Trees from the Garden of Eden. If you have been listening to the politicians on what they would do to reverse the word recession, you should realize they talk like little children. I can also teach you King Jesus Christ storage retrieval system that has been hidden since the beginning of time.

The seals are for communication within a kingdom. The 666 beast books are Standing Historical or the history of the denominations within a country to form the church. Life of US (U.S.) Catholic would be one name of seven. Where is your Holy City as required by the Universal Church format granted in the year of Our Lord 1200 AD?

If you write me, I will grant you the chapter "The Word Lust" which will get fathers and sons back to the church and end the divorces. You will be able to end the abortions not through law but through a true religion. The result will be the beginning of the end of the Fallen Angels (sons) growing up with the women and being helped by the police officers, but without fathers and husbands. Where are you?

I will grant you a copy of King Jesus Christ's economic plan for the one world government of Israel for the United States. All politicians will be trained by the church on the one world government. The results will be kingdom against kingdom and nation against nation. What nation will be the best to develop life for its citizens and end the social ills of the nation and thereby country? The kingdom of the United

States is separate from the kingdom of Mexico and so on. Each country will have to develop a thousand year plan and use it in their country. It is possible the church of India with one percent of the people will win all the national elections, because King Jesus Christ's economic plan as defined will double the best economy Adam can do. The world can finish the Six-Day Creation story, which will require tremendous wealth creation. When you read the plan, you will realize money is the problem today, but the reason is the laws are bad and the wicked (rich). The title of the chapter from the book "The Sixty-seventh Book of the Holy Bible" is "The Seventh Trumpet Story". The story comes from the Old Testament where Our Father granted Israel a reprieve from killing wars and Israel started a tremendous wealth creation story.

The greatest tribulation the world will ever see is the creation of heaven on earth by the church forming with seven names and seven Holy Cities. That kingdom will last longer than Heaven or planet earth. The millennium story was a new beginning or implementing the Lord's Prayer or the end where the church stays with the gospel about Christ (31 AD) and the end comes. The Holy Bible is not God's words but His plan.

The Holy Bible is clear or the famine at the end times is not for daily bread, but the word of God. If you study the Sign of the Times of today, you would say the big problem in government is money. The Famine (money) is for the word of God. We are at the seventh beast and the eighth beast is already a beast, but he has the wrong title to qualify as the eighth beast.

I have attached the answer to overcome the word recession of today. The "Seventh Trumpet Story" has the permanent end to the word depression in economics. Why would a country want money to be a problem in God's Kingdom? We shall not want. The Battle of Armageddon starts when it is buyers and sellers remorse.

Elijah
Richard Cartwright
430 Pembroke Rd SW
Poplar Grove, IL 61065
Email carrichard@verizon.net
Telephone 815-765-0161

God does not need your burnt offerings.

Sent January 23 the year of Our Lord 2008 AD

Since I have written the Seventh Trumpet Story based on the Holy Bible, what I said in my first book "Life of US (U.S.) of the year of Our Lord 2002 AD is coming true. I stated if you desired to understand President George W. Bush's economy, all you have to do is study his father's economy. Many social ills of the country have had the funding removed; thereby, violating the book of Mark. The church can find great sorrows all over the country and it will become worse. A trumpet is what a president would use to explain important economic or other type issues.

First, the economists on market analysis television were criticizing the Federal Reserve for not lowering the interest rates as quickly as possible. The Bush administration is going to use the old theme of tax cuts to avoid the recession. I hear a number like one hundred and fifty billion dollars. In an environment where citizens are greatly in debt and their jobs are possibly affected, we will have a tendency to save. Even some professionals on television are telling people to do that. A greater decline will occur if you issue tax cuts, which further cause the dollar to decline. Inflation at the present high rate can expand and cause what is called stagflation or high inflation without good growth. The last time the Bush administration lower the taxes, the layoffs continued at three hundred and fifty thousand a month for the next year. The money above one hundred thousand dollars a year in income was government waste. The change did not work. If you lower the interest rates the professionals are stating, "What are you going to do to get the banks to borrow money and put the money to work?"

What would King Jesus Christ representative teach you to do or explain? First, you have to start out with what is known or the Sign of the Times. You must define a future you desire to inherit or lower inflation, strengthen the American dollar, and take care of an important social ill of the country. A possible recession is over and consumer confidence soars. What is known? Give me a sign.

1. Much greed is found in the United States.
2. A greater budget deficits will devalue the dollar further and increase inflation.
3. We should not take a chance and do nothing.
4. Many construction workers are without jobs caused by housing.
5. America is 1.6 trillion dollars behind on their roads.

A new tax must be imposed on people earning over ten million dollars a year. Some people state our sports players earn a lot of money. Have you hear about the Exxon Mobil executives earning four hundred million per year? We collect one hundred billion in new tax revenue from greed. The congress uses the tax money to fix the roads. We are 1.6 trillion dollars behind. In California, I heard sixty per cent of the roads are bad in a county. You must build confidence, define a long-term project, but it must be an important social ill of the country. If you do the tax cuts, which will weaken the dollar inflation will consume most of the money. Have you heard of one hundred and fifty dollar oil if you further weaken the dollar and the associated inflation?

The construction commitment creates many millions of new jobs and a commitment to add more tax revenue by reversing Bush tax cuts for people earning over one hundred thousand dollars a year. Again, the money is added to road construction absorbing the construction workers. They spend and buy items like trucks, housing and food. The governments all over the United States are collecting additional tax revenue. The Federal Government at our present tax rates will collect almost twice the monies spent on roads and must save the money for Social Security benefits. The value of the dollar soars and causes a corresponding decline in the cost of oil. A higher value of the dollar will cost Americans less for imported oil. As oil prices decline all products delivered and many produced will decline lowering inflation. Electricity and natural gas costs decline along with oil causing inflation to drop. The house owner may end up with over five hundred dollar less cost between gasoline and utilities. The saving may be much higher.

You review what you desired to inherit in the future. Inflation is way down, the American dollar increases in value. You are starting to fund Social Security with new tax from the present tax rates. People who receive pay raises will actually receive real consumption dollars not inflation dollars. You must get many non-inflation taxed dollars in the hands of the consumers. We shall not want. You created millions of jobs and the word recession is behind you. The last time a president raised taxes on the wealthy or on the group over one hundred thousand dollars a year, you were starting to hear the stocks going up as under the Democrats and the wealth creation in the country was being restored. In a few years, we may hear the rich complaining again, "I made so much money, do I have to pay taxes?" The answer is to get the governments out of debt as the word of God is, "Do not give people money that cannot use it wisely".

Road construction is so far behind, you should try to get the labor unions to get people from hot areas in the summer to go north and in cold climates months to go south. America can put the story of recession and bad roads behind us and fund Social Security at the same time.

Without the church, correcting the bad roads cannot be done. What a surprise for the people that run or goes to church. Have you heard of the passage, "Some governments are taking you on the road to hell?" King Jesus Christ judged the world long ago because He loved you. What are you doing to judge the world so your love can shine on the congregation? You must be the saints that judge the world. I can teach you how to do that.

Please send to other church locations so we can avoid a government taking us on the road to hell. Make your sermons count!

Sent January 7, the year of Our Lord 2008 AD.
January 7, the year of Our Lord 2008 AD

Poplar Grove United Methodist Church
105 E Grove
Poplar Grove, Il 61065

Antichrist Senior Pastor Lisa Kruse-Safford

RE: Kill the Messenger

Now, you know whom the Antichrist is that is creating all that you see and hear as bad or as the Holy Bible states, Adam. What is good is nothing or Noah's Ark story from God is kind. That I can prove. The new beginning can be only a few years away with your help. As Elias, I can form the kingdom and the book is complete or, "The Antichrist God's Version".

You should realize why the book has that title. As Elijah, I can end ninety percent of the divorces in a kingdom in twenty years and the prophecy will be found to be easy. You must get fathers back with sons or the fallen angels (boys) will be with the women. You cannot believe you will not reach for the greatest tribulation a clergymen can see or the return of King Jesus Christ, once you have no questions to ask. I have copied King Jesus Christ thousand-year plan for the government from the Holy Bible and you can prove it from scripture. Can you allow all the people you see to die in the Battle of Armageddon, which starts in the United States because you do not need to hold a meeting?

You are responsible to find Elijah if you believe you cannot form God's Kingdom by yourself. The Universal Church format, which was granted in the year of Our Lord 1200 AD, has seven names on the door and seven Holy Cities. If you understand reality because of your blasphemous mouth, you worship Satan. If you stay with the gospel about Christ as defined in the year 31 AD, as the book of Matthew states the end shall come. It is not the word of God. It is His plan. I have contacted you in the past and all you desired to do is kill the messenger.

The teenagers of America do not like organized religion so you believe that is not your problem. Let me kill the messenger. The teenagers do not like their parents getting divorces and you say I do not give a damn. I will kill the messenger. I am perfect. Why would I desire to change? All I have to do is con the congregation out of their money and I can tell them how great I am. The Holy Bible states, you are taking pride in yourself and not humility for the King. The Holy Bible states you are asleep at the altar. Why would you desire to change when you judge yourself as perfect? You must judge the world as saints. The Holy Bible states you have the wrong heart for John 3:16 as you worship Satan. I can prove that statement. Can you prove King Jesus Christ's messenger is wrong?

444

I am Elijah to teach you how to end divorces so you can get fathers back with sons or teenagers back to the church. I am a prophet that can end the millions of children dying each year due to a famine (money). Do you desire to kill the messenger? A great amount of money is required and King Jesus Christ states I will double the best Adam can do. I have King Jesus Christ's thousand-year plan for the one world government of Israel for the United States. Do you need to kill His messenger and tell the congregation, "You know, I have to wait for King Jesus Christ to return?" The Holy Bible states He has told you all things, so you should know all the answers. Are you lying to the congregation and yourself? May you die without any possibility for John 3:16 as you desire to kill the teenagers that have a message or Elijah?

Are you killing the messengers of the Italian Mafia and lying to the men that are failing themselves? They are in shackles and as failures cannot be saved. Are you killing the messenger of the families whose children die of drugs? The Italian Mafia has the wrong heart and the church does not care or are the Son of Perdition. Do you judge the politicians violating the book of Mark and become the Mark of the Beast? No, you are the Son of Perdition.

King Jesus Christ has judged you long ago. The Holy Bible is clear. Do you have seven churches with the Universal Church format? Where is your Holy City? You are just the sinner that must repent and the Son of Perdition.

I have asked you and your peers to check the chapter you must teach on the great and dreadful Day of the Lord or Good Friday. If you desire to check, you can correct and send to me. If you agree you should ask Elijah, "What should I do next?" If you take no action, just resign from the church or do the Millstone Story. You will find it impossible to be saved. You have a heart that is different from your God of Heart as you have the heart of Satan or heart of failure of yourself.

What is required of you? I have created the presentation and a voice file. You must read, listen, learn, reproduce some papers and set up a meeting. The rest I have done for you. You will learn more about religion in less than one hour than you have learned in your entire lifetime. It is time for Adam to grow up and learn how to talk. King Jesus Christ will not return until you have no questions to ask. The seals are for communication within a kingdom. The 666 beasts are books of Standing Historical or the history of your denomination in each nation where you have a presence. The beasts are the politicians you start a war to avoid their failures as human beings. The 666 beast books are to last longer than heaven and earth or from Here to Eternity a measure of time. May a thousand zeros of time be short in terms of the effective use of the Holy Bible to resolve any problem in this world through one hundred percent theology?

Elijah

Richard Cartwright
430 Pembroke Rd SW
Poplar Grove' IL 61065
Tel # 815-765-0161
Elijah lives at Candlewick Lake, has a daughter and grand children living in Elk Grove Village, and can prove all that he has written.
The four words of the millennium are fear, war, jeopardy, and joy. I have not heard your understanding of how they apply for the next thousand years.

Sent August 7, the year of Our Lord 2007 AD.

Question

What does the Holy Bible mean in Mark 9:12? Jesus said, "Elias will cometh first and restoreth all things."

August 8, the year of Our Lord 2007 AD
United Methodist Church
Reverend Richard Carl Wisdom
Telephone 1-815-399-5910

I was at your church and you stated in song the kingdom was formed.

The Holy Bible states there should be seven churches with seven names on the door. In the United States there are thirty-six names on the door and half the church locations have no alignment.

The Universal Church format granted you in the year of Our Lord 1200 AD requires each name to have a Holy City. Where is your Holy City?

You are required to reform the church if that format is not in your eyes to see and you do not have ears to hear their great accomplishments.

Read Mark 9:12 where King Jesus Christ stated Elias will cometh first and restoreth all things. Has your church found Elias?

The teenagers do not like organized religion. The Holy Bible states if you abandon Thy Children (777 design), I will abandon you and the penance will continue for seven times longer or fourteen thousand years. In the year of Our Lord 16,000 AD He will return with the Seven Horns of the Eternal Temple or Israel. Your thirty-six denominations with half nonaligned has disappeared or your church is gone. The whole world is down to the Lord's Prayer and Elias can restoreth all things. Did you know you are in penance for two thousand years and the beginning of the end of penance is the Lord's Prayer?

The end is the eight beast and we are on the seventh. Please tell me the names of the first six if you can. I can verify your answer.

The seals are for communication within a kingdom. Have you ever used the Angel of Death to cut off his ugly head of a dragon that desires to steal that woman's child? Please explain what a dragon is and I can verify your answer.

King Jesus Christ will return when you have no questions to ask. The Holy Bible is a way of life. Religion is a way of life and always ends with a life one thousand times better than the end. The end is near and the church requires a new beginning. What is the plan of the seven churches of the United States to end the divorces or pain in the children's lives (777 design). What do the other six names desire to achieve?

I would love to talk to you about the above and your call to action prayer to reform the church.

Richard Cartwright
430 Pembroke Rd SW
Poplar Grove, IL 61065
815-765-0161
email comfortingod@verizon.net
MEMO TO OTHER METHODIST CHURCH LOCATIONS TO SEEK THE PRAYER

Sent December 30, the year of Our Lord 2007 AD
The Seventh Trump.

I had an email from your peers that asked who I am. I am Elias of the year of Our Lord 2005 AD. My role is to restoreth all things. You determine something that is bad and I can correct. I desire to end the war in Iraq before it started (the year of Our Lord 2002 AD) because I represent the Prince of Peace or King Jesus Christ. I know why King Jesus Christ called the Second World War a War to End All Wars. In the Year of Our Lord 2005 AD or whatever you desire to, end the war in Iraq so the congregation has a gift from the religious leaders to overcome

82% of the standing armies by who the clergymen. What does that make you? You should decide before you die and the King has no choice but to send you to Hell.

You desire to learn about the sixth trump and the meaning of the seventh. If you represent King Jesus Christ the answer is yes. The six are men against the King or War Lords as the Holy Bible describes the crown leader of a country where the currency is green, the greatest debtor nation, and the wax location where the wax is cold (USA).

The six trumps or warlords are dragons or men against the Prince of Peace. You have achieved in the one-generation all that will happen or the end of the millennium 2999 minus 1007 or the year 1992 (near the end times).

The six trumps are dragons or warlords against the Prince of Peace:

1. President Dwight D. Eisenhower 1952.
2. President John F. Kennedy 1960.
3. President Ronald Reagan 1980.
4. President George H. W. Bush 1988.
5. President Bush 2000 who became Satan and cannot be saved.
6. President Elect John F. Kerry or the heart from Hell and achieving through a victory in election The False Messiah.

So you must represent the Prince of Peace and create a peace president in the year of Our Lord 2008 AD and wait for January 20, the year of Our Lord 2009 AD. If you do not the Divorce or the King's penance stays in place for 14,000 years and He comes back with the Seven Horns of the Eternal Temple or Israel. The church is gone for their pestilence. I am Elias represent the King Of kings and Lord of lords in a period before the war started. If the war started you recreated the Roman Empire in the book of Romans and worship Satan. All this is covered in the book "The Antichrist God's Version".

Original Message
From: "Chris Skowronek" <cchapel@snet.net>
To: "'Richard Cartwright'" <carrichard@verizon.net>
Sent: Wednesday, December 28, 2005 1:12 PM
Subject: Read: A PRAYER REQUEST

Sent December 1, the year of Our Lord 2007 AD

Seeking a Church.
Understand the word "this" in Matthew 24:14.

You did not answer, so it is a good chance you now realize, you are a church that King Jesus Christ does not want in His Kingdom. The book of Revelation is clear. Being afraid is not a sin but if you continue your call to inaction. Judgment day is the day you die. You should know the answer before you die. It is apparent.

If you write me I will give you or I have given you the story of the White Stone as the form of gospel God desires. The White Stone ends the war in Iraq. God has used the bombs from Heaven or Smart Bombs from airplanes. Once the war started you lost John 3:16 for my three grandchildren. They are more important to me than you, but I cannot run all churches and teach the White Stone story, which ends the war. You as a clergymen cannot be stopped. Future war where there is religion cannot turn into nation against nation.

The Holy Bible states you worship Satan because of your blasphemous mouth.

Satan has a short time left or 1/20/ the year of Our Lord 2009 AD and will make a real millstone story.

Archangel Michael has been condemned to planet earth for his war of 777 design against the children (Pro-Life). Pope John Paul II was the false prophet that was drunk with power. God used the word condemned because without you the Battle of Armageddon starts in the United States in less than ten years. God does not respect a person.

450

The famine in the end times is not for daily bread but for real money. Read buyers and sellers remorse.

There are to be only seven churches and the angels are our children. Any clergymen who fails to implement the Lord's Prayer goes to Hell. The congregation should move to the seven churches that agree to form God's Kingdom through the technique of 1150 and 2300 days in the book of Daniel in a silent war or a Vow of Silence. Today none of the seven church types meet the standard of King Jesus Christ.

The clergymen is the Antichrist that King Jesus Christ directs the congregation to shoot in the head (Spiritually) and this is your answer. You are not an acceptable religious location. Please change so my grandchildren do not live on planet Hell or planet earth.

Please let me know when you will implement the Lord's Prayer as King Jesus Christ had to meet His Father's requirement from the Old Testament or the book of Daniel you do once in all church locations. Once you start the Lord's Prayer you will receive John 3:16 back as of today all flesh is dead.

Judgment day is the day you die physically. You should know the answer before you die. It is apparent.

CAN YOU BELIEVE THE PEOPLE LIKE YOURSELF EMAIL ME THAT WHERE OUR GODS USE CHRIST AS THE SON OF MAN THAT THEY BELIEVE THE PASSAGES ARE REFERRING TO THE SON OF GOD? WHEN YOU CREATE THE WORDS OF THE HOLY SPIRIT FOR ALL CHURCHES TO TALK THROUGH YOU ARE CALLED CHRIST IN THE STORY OF THE SEALS OF THE WHITE HORSE. YOU EMAIL THE INFORMATION FROM THE SEVEN HOLY CITIES TO ALL CHURCH LOCATIONS WITH SECURITY CODES.

Please email to your peers that will help you implement the Lord's Prayer or go to Hell for your failure as a man representing King Jesus Christ. Without Elias you are on your own. You should know what you did before you die spiritually. You should not try to kill the messenger.

Original Message

From: Richard Cartwright

To: admissions@csj.edu

Sent: Thursday, November 17, 2005 11:52 AM

Subject: A CHURCH

Seeking a Church (Prayer Request)

I am looking for a church and the experts state from the book of Revelation that the first through fifth church is bad. The sixth church in Revelation 3:9 is run by liars and worship Satan. Is your church better?

God calls our present churches whoredom. Matthew 24:14, "And this gospel of all the kingdom shall be preached in all the world for a witness unto all nations and the end shall come." God, I believe, is stating the whoredom technique in our present church is bad and will end civilization as we know it. Is your church that teaches King Jesus Christ' Gospel and uses it to create a true gospel? Does your gospel end the thirty thousand unnecessary deaths each day? Is the end 150,000 unnecessary deaths each day? God states the famine is not for daily bread; therefore the only answer is money.

I have gone to many churches trying to find one that teaches a sermon with meat (substance). All I hear is they sing some songs, read a passage, collect money for Ames for the poor for daily bread (or equivalent), and then the congregation leaves. What is your format?

The end shall come that means now. What are your plans to overcome the end? What is the passage Mark 9:12 all about? What are you doing to help the churches that our Gods states are bad?

Thank you for answering my prayer request to find a church to welcome a new member of your congregation. Please do not disappoint me.

Please email me at carrichard@verizon.net with your commitment to God and me.

Sent on July 28, the year of Our Lord 2007 AD
Friday, July 20, the year of Our Lord 2007 AD
For your attention

You should study unless you shorten the days no flesh is saved alive. Shorten the days is implementing the Lord's Prayer. No flesh is saved alive means no John 3:16 is in the world. The Antichrists (clergymen) have killed all flesh. Check the Garden of Eden about once you are responsible for good and evil you will surely die. Once you know how to manage good and evil you will be like Gods. King Jesus Christ will make you royalty as you become the meek that inherit the earth as a prince like in the Prince of Peace. Today the Holy Bible defines you as a preacher whore or one that reads the Holy Bible without trying to get your congregation to live by every word. The Holy Bible states by now you should be teachers. I guarantee the Holy Bible is correct, not you. The clergymen are to become the saints that judge the world. You become a saint in the church world when you obey and live by the Ten Commandments. The congregations are in jeopardy and not sinners. Where is your color purple and knowledge to raise the children of 777 design? In the church world like the Catholics, they call their congregation sinners, which means they are blaming. King Jesus Christ is to smart to fail at calling the congregation sinners, but He will take care of the sinners or clergymen. Their sins go up to the heavens.

As a test from the Holy Bible of your success judge yourself. The church has gone backwards from the year of Our Lord 1900 AD to today in New York City and the wax is cold. New York City of the year of Our Lord 1900 AD was a land of love and marriage where the federal government was zero dollars in debt. Today New York is a land of divorce and abortion and as the Holy Bible defines America with our green currency is the greatest debtor nation of our world. In the last thirty years/ what story have you put to rest like you have ended ninety percent of the crimes, poverty, divorces, your success of marriages or what pain has been eliminated through you? If you say John 3:16, but the Holy Bible states you are not saved.

If you abandon Thy Children (777 design) I will abandon you and the penance will continue for seven times longer. The clergymen do not even know they are in penance. Please do not ask King Jesus Christ to heal the sick of your church because He will not listen. He will not turn stones into food yet He states for you to stop sending me little ones small and great which are His children that where born alive and are dead. I believe the Holy Bible is a good book for the Lutheran's Mission to study and change their evil ways. You are allowing crimes by the governments against King Jesus Christ through the foolishness of the Lutheran's Mission and not developing the true words of God. The Mark of the Beast comes from the book of Mark. Faith healing is ending the unnecessary pain in people's lives. If you say John 3:16 you better pray you have enough time to learn what the Holy Bible means. You define yourself as a saint judging the world? I and the Holy Bible defines you as a preacher whore and not saved. Please explain to me in person why King Jesus Christ should save any Lutheran clergymen or any other with your disobedience of all that is written in the Holy Bible.

The Lutheran's, Catholic's, Baptist's and all the rest are total and absolute failures. Why, because you have been in penance and do not even know it. You worship Satan and I can prove it.

The clergymen must change from their evil ways as they do not even know the definition of the word evil. You can add many more words like hate, nation, hope, etc.

If you could read the Holy Bible with understanding, you know the Antichrist is the clergymen taking pride in themselves and ignoring form the kingdom first and learn how to talk or humility for King Jesus Christ. They came in an era of peace and prosperity or one hour past midnight in the year of Our Lord 2000 AD. What did their failures achieve but a killing war and increased poverty for the lower one third of income? This is the Age of Accountability or you are responsible for your actions. Actions speak louder than words.

The Holy Bible states if you abandon Thy (is mine) Children I will abandon you and the penance will continue for seven times longer or fourteen thousand years. We are all children of God but the ones twenty-one and less are more important or 777 design. You are to let the angels (Thy Children of 777 design) talk at the Altar and be heard by the senators; instead you have driven them away from the church. You are to put the children on a pedestal of man's design. Children of 777 design can learn, but a seventy five year old should be saved and you have stolen John 3:16 from your congregations.

You will know what you did before you die. That will be the Battle of Armageddon or being forced or planning to implement the Lord's Prayer. The clergymen can turn planet earth into planet Heaven on earth or Hell on earth. Through reincarnation in planet Hell, no flesh can get off this world without penance. John 3:16 is not like you waving a magic wand and all is good. The gift is true but the actions of hope through the actions of work and education is required to achieve.

King Jesus Christ will return with the Seven Horns of the Eternal Temple or Israel if you fail to implement the Lord's Prayer and become royalty in the year of Our Lord 16,000.

Study Mark 9:12 or King Jesus Christ stated "Elias will come first and restoreth all things." I am Elias.
Richard Cartwright or Elias to restoreth all things.
430 Pembroke Rd SW
Poplar Grove, IL 61065
815-765-0161
email comfortingod@verizon.net
or comfortinGod@hotmail.com

The Battle of Armageddon results in the clergymen being responsible for killing about a trillion children. You have proven the Noah's Ark story is kind. That is not fantasy that is reality. The answer is for the clergymen to regain John 3:16 by implementing the Lord's Prayer and becoming royalty. The King will return when you have no questions to ask as the Holy Bible states, "I have told you all things." and Elias agrees. Today you would stay with the Lutheran's Mission and the kingdom would never form and He would have to leave.

Please send a copy to your peers for their comments. I would joy in their success.

All the information required to implement the Lord's Prayer is at
Mount Olive Lutheran Church
2001 N. Alpine Rd
Rockford, IL 61107
815-399-3171
Where Pastor Kenneth E. Krause has the knowledge from Elias of Mark 9:12 by him doing the Supper Story. What is lacking is the knowledge of the great and dreadful Day of the Lord or Good Friday.

Sent February 8, the year of Our Lord 2007 AD
2/8/ in the year of Our Lord 2007 AD
Preliminary copy thousands of words to go.
Who is the Antichrist?

The History Channel had a two hour show named "The Antichrist: Zero Hour" written and produced by Sean Dash in the year of Our Lord 2005 AD. The biblical scholars interviewed in the film include such names as Track Griswold Presiding Bishop, US Episcopal Church and Pastor Benny Hinn of Benny Hinn Ministries as shown on TBN and various others as listed below that claim the Antichrist is one man. If they stopped to think, how could one man, worse than a fool, achieve that status? He would have to build an organization of extreme size and we could simply ignore that one person. They would be able to identify the time by their fantasyland version of the Rapture. How could you run the church, business or government where a billion people would disappear and the world continues to function? That in the Holy Bible is impossible as King Jesus Christ states I will not turn stones into food. So He will not use the power of creation for their views. The Antichrist would have to have a negative impact in all countries, where there is a church. The only power he would have is the power of work, not creation.

Satan was a real human being that came on the political challenge with a woman riding on him as a Scarlet Beast. He becomes the King of Babylon and yet the religious scholars never recognize who he is. He was in the only Holy City. The Red dragon is someone of military failure to overcome the King who was the Prince of Peace and is King Jesus Christ of the Church. The Holy Bible states Satan cannot be saved. The clergymen never learned who he is and allowed themselves to worship him, rather than our true Gods. He will be around for a short time, but many have been blaming Satan for the world problems for a long time. Many claim they have overcome Satan; however that is not true because of their blasphemies of the Antichrists. Satan is the seventh beast and the eighth is the end or next. The clergymen do not even know the names of the first six beasts and dragons. So they ignore rather than try to learn. The United States lives by the sword, they will die by the sword. Maybe we should revisit the Holy Bible for the true understanding of the Antichrist. The biblical scholars are so easily deceived.

As the Holy Bible states King Jesus Christ has told us all things. We should be able to use the Holy Bible to overcome any problem on the planet that mankind has determined is bad and turn it into good. The Holy Bible states it is 100% theology or planning from the Holy Bible for government, business, or church. We have to live by every word not read every word. The Antichrist came in a way we should be able to determine who he or they are. King Jesus Christ named the era of one-hour pass midnight in the year of Our Lord 2000 AD as the "Age of Accountability". The Antichrist came in an era of peace and prosperity at that time. This is the era for Adam to grow up and become responsible for his actions. Our God, King Jesus Christ has divorced the church and put them in penance through divorce for their failure to obey Him in the Church of Israel. The way back to be in favor with Our Gods, His Father and King Jesus Christ is to implement the Lord's Prayer or cover the book of Daniel we do once. Our failure to learn will make the penance seven times longer. Most clergymen seem the say, "If I do nothing, everything will turn out great." That is not true.

The Antichrist came in an era of peace and prosperity or one hour past midnight on January 1 in the year of Our Lord 2000 AD in the Heartland of the world or the USA. President William J. Clinton had the best economy in modern times and he was committed to maintaining the peace dividend. By the year of Our Lord 2007 AD, the Antichrist had destroyed the peace dividend and the economy is not close to the Year of Our Lord 2000 AD in material wealth. The first four years of President George W. Bush created less than zero jobs. Job creation is a big part of wealth creation. Only President Herbert C. Hoover the Years of Our Lord 1929 to 1932 AD did worse. Under his presidency the economy will never achieve the 232 billion dollar surplus or the 3.5 % unemployment number. In addition millions of Americans fell below what we call the poverty level. Some foolish economists state the economy is good, but a quick review is that it is based on borrowed money which one day will end. Have you notice the number of credit cards you are being offered. Have the Antichrists read the Old Testament lately? They will want you to pay the money back. The Holy Bible called America the greatest debtor nation whose currency is green. King Jesus Christ has told you of a serious problem. The clergymen ignore the Holy Bible or have simple non-workable solutions. You think of why they allowed it to happen when King Jesus Christ told them all things. The wealth creation over the last seven years in the United States is negative. Go back to President Abraham Lincoln and learn what a true wealth creation should be until Adam picked up the "Sword".

The power the clergymen derive is, "If God is for you, who can be against you." So in government the clergymen cannot allow presidential debates, all laws are to be written per the New Testament, be veto proof in the new beginning, or the Generation of the Fig for the church world.

I have written to the Catholic clergymen and they state there is only one name on the door and that is Catholic. The other six names from the book of Daniels and Revelations do not exist. Their six new Holy Cities are not to be created in the King's Name as part of the greatest tribulation the world will ever experience. The Catholic Church appears to have a problem recruiting and their average age is high. The fantasyland view of the world may turn the Catholic Church into many locations run by men who do not qualify to be ordained until they will down size. Under President Ronald Reagan poverty rose so high the Catholic Church abandoned the poorer neighborhoods in the United States. They still maintain a church law that if you do not go to church you commit a mortal sin, yet they abandoned many people for money issues.

What is amazing is the Antichrist reads that passage where, "unless you shorten the days no flesh is saved". They claim the tribulation is bad. The definition of Joy is the trials and tribulation of man. The Antichrists change their ways and forms the Lord's Prayer and they believe that tribulation is bad. I can understand no flesh is saved as the Antichrist worships Satan; therefore, what should they believe they have in terms of John 3:16? They are still heard to say that after the Second World War where the Russians and Chinese won, they are waiting for one third of the world to die (no John 3:16).

The Catholic Church appears to disobey their Gods by trying to attack teenagers in gospel armor and trying to overcome the will of the people. The Holy Bible states to stop sending Our Gods little ones small and great. The Catholic Church is against, "If God is for you, who can be against you." For forty years they argue that God needs the children having children and grow up without the gifts the teenage girls deserves like the chance for a good job, college education, and an easier time to find a husband. The Holy Bible would define these children as fallen angels, since poverty creates a climate where prisons appear to be the answers, and the police help to raise the children without the gifts children richly deserve like a dad. The will of the teenagers are against the Catholics trying to impose their will on the teenagers. The only ones that can vote are the teenage girls that had an abortion. If they believed at the time of their action, they were correct; the Catholic Church is wrong and should change. Do not try to make the teenage girl feel guilty. Forty years of penance by the Catholic Church is enough. The Catholic Church is desperate to be justified by law not grace. Not a court in any land can be justified by law and the Catholic Priests need that right. When Pope John Paul II was still alive, he populated the Vatican with pro-life; therefore the Catholic Church does not have agreement. One of the greatest problems on the planet is there are too many children dying due to lack of money or a famine in their land. The correct answer for the clergymen is they desire children to be born from women that are financially, spiritually, and physically able to bear that child. The church should teach financial planning to the nation to overcome the unnecessary deaths because of lack of money and jobs created by the politicians claiming they represent the church. The Holy Bible that Our Gods granted us will always end up with the rich demanding the poorest child in a country has the money problems for his family over as satisfied by the government. Just because a family has the poorest children to raise does not mean that the family has to be below what the economists define as below the poverty level. The Catholic Church is increasing famine (lack of money) by not obeying King Jesus Christ. The Holy Bible will always end up with a life of 1000 times better than the end, which is only the next beast away (by or before the year of Our Lord 2016 AD). Understand the King refuses to help the Catholics or any church location until the Lord's Prayer is complete and the one world government is accepted by the clergymen from the mysterious messiah.

The Catholic Church appears to misunderstand the judgment by Our King. The Holy Bible contains all judgment yet the religious ordained love to take the passage out of contents of, "He who judges shall be judged." The saints sent by the church to the seven Holy Cities are to judge the world. The clergymen state, "I need the death penalty.", but they do not need the hanging judges of American courts to judge which they do without mercy. The politicians have to judge on what laws to write but the clergymen need them to write laws and not worry about how to write their judgment of laws by the New Testament requirements. Only some Adams, worse than fools, would invent that fantasyland view of do not judge because you will be judged. All humans will be judged by the saints and Judgment Day is the day you die. When the saints die, they are to bring with a book of good deeds of their congregations. Our Gods will always joy in the good works of all mankind. The book is buried in their Souls that go to the true Heaven for new arms and legs.

The actual requirement of the church world comes from the Old Testament where Our Father did not want any pits or American prisons. The Antichrists claim they need the death penalty of Israel. The requirement is, "In Heaven on earth, do not send your policemen out to kill them because they do not want to go to school." The Antichrist should explain how effective the death penalty is when the first thing the police have to do for major crimes is to stop the volunteers from being executed. All the confessions and none may have done it. That is the church view of fear. The true version is they should shove all beasts under the Altar. Many argue that is not the meaning of God's words in that they can save anyone. Satan is real, goes to a church and cannot be saved. The true words of God have to be created by the seven Holy Cities. In the United States under the laws of liberty, the clergymen have a moral responsibility to eliminate all crimes, therefore all prisons. The Holy Bible already defines how to do it. Only the Antichrist would state he needs prisons and death penalties.

You can hear the clergymen asking the politicians for immigration. During the first four years of President George W. Bush the number of immigrates were approximately a million a year and less than zero jobs created. How about our graduates from high school and universities? The rich were thankful on one stock market station, because they could exploit the workers. The new jobs are like President Ronald Reagan days where the hamburger expansion was creating poor paying jobs. Again the jobs are poor paying and our college graduates end up with high student loans and little good job environment. The clergymen are still demanding immigration to a future poor country. What will they desire to do next? Should all our sixteen year olds leave their families and go to a foreign country to find work. Did we find many illegal aliens in our country and the Catholic Priest asked, "Do you desire to make me a criminal?" Are they teaching the congregations to violate the laws? I hear on television the latest is for richer countries like America to pay for the health care costs of third world nations. Should the Antichrists realize America is not close to providing health care for its own citizens? The Catholics had to experience the wealth creation under President William J. Clinton and realize the problem as the Holy Bible defines is with the laws. Good laws produce a good economy. If the church forms the seven Holy Cities, King Jesus Christ can produce an economy in all nations greater than President William J. Clinton. All people that are dying due to a famine (lack of money), the church has the ability through the Holy Bible to make rich. Adam can start to complete the Six-Day creation story from the Garden of Eden. May 1000 zeros of time be short living in God's Kingdom.

Have you heard of shackle less churches? One hour past midnight on January 1, the year of Our Lord 2000 AD King Jesus Christ put the rich in shackles. The losers say the King is wrong and I can send the rich to Heaven. Executives like Exxon Mobil appear to have greed in their salaries, yet the Antichrist would say that is King Jesus Christ's problem. Let all of them go to my church and I will save them or in reality go the way of Satan. King Jesus Christ saves not the clergymen. He must teach how King Jesus Christ will judge.

The clergymen have defined a dragon as Our Gods fantasyland or a fictitious character of no meaning. Actually, the dragon is what is called a hawk in the USA. The fantasyland view of religion has clergymen as warlords or conquers as defined in the book of Romans. The book of Romans defines the fourth empire. The first is Rome. The second is the British or look at the shield of Richard the Lion Heart. The third is the Russian Bear or the Soviet Union and the fourth does not have an animal but has a bird of prey.

The Holy Bible defines there is no fear. What I have witnessed is you do not need to mention the word fear or grandmas will have a heart attack and the Italian Mafia will laugh. The Holy Bible states it is faith, and wait, with a little fear. The clergymen define the death penalty of Israel, which does not apply where there is a possibility of John 3:16. Of course, Adam has done 100% of everything wrong in terms of judgment, which creates problems Adam by disobeying the Holy Bible, cannot overcome. There is no difference in fear between the Old and New Testament except on how you apply it. The Old Testament, you would kill the Italian Mafia as you extract an eye for an eye, a tooth for a tooth, and extract a pound of flesh. In Israel the Jewish man learned not to be the crime syndicate. In America, you extract and eye and send the Italian Mafia to Heaven with only one eye or just legal businesses. If they refuse to change the Catholic Priests and others shove the bodies under the Altar. They go by the way of Satan. Others like a single woman that destroys a marriage with her new husband will be condemned to planet earth (reincarnation) until all divorces are over where a single woman goes out with a married man. The requirement is, "I do not want a hair on a child's head harmed." She is not in shackles, but only a penance man can get off this world alive. Fear with end countless divorces but the Antichrist has to stop violating the ninth Commandment for the love of God's Children of 777 designs. Teenagers may trust the churches, if they believed the religious leaders took marriage seriously instead of stating come to my church and I will send you to Heaven and bore them with bible studies. God has forgiven all your sins as only losers would say. King Jesus Christ included the sins of Israel where He had to use the word jealousy to make the prophecy come true. The clergymen cannot save their congregation's Souls as the only Soul they can save is their own. King Jesus Christ saves Souls. No flesh is saved when they worship Satan. The Antichrist created their own form of religion through use of their blasphemies. The clergymen's sins go up to the Heavens. The latest some clergymen have said I am required to be justified by law to bore the teenagers with their form of bible study. Which religious bible types do they need in public schools by law? Is it Indian, China, Korean, or Old Testament only? Why would you believe people who teach the Darwin theories are qualified to teach 100% theology or planning from the Holy Bible to business and government officials?

If you were a true God and you needed to put the people in penance, you could do the story of the forty years in Israel. You are talking about the church world, which reaches the four corners of the world. What would you do? Could you as a human being write a book that would cause Adam to be

465

deceived and refuse to help him? The clergymen are about to create the end which turns this planet into planet Hell. There is no Hell like a woman scorned as she sees her children dying right in front of her eyes. The Antichrist will kill one trillion children before they can answer the question, "Do you need to form the kingdom and learn how to talk?" The clergymen are to know what they did before they die. It could be the end of their natural life as they will live through the beginning of the Battle of Armageddon in the United States caused by the pen. The second way is they realize what they did and die when they understand they must implement the Lord's Prayer.

The Battle of Armageddon will prove the Noah's Ark story in the Holy Bible is kind but not available due to the Ark in Greece. The Antichrist will kill one trillion children through reincarnation with the new penance seven times longer or 14,000 years. King Jesus Christ comes back with the seven horns of the Eternal Temple or Israel. Buy a copy of the Holy Bible and read it yourself. Do not listen to people that have created their own religion. Once you implement the Lord's Prayer you will through me understand the Holy Bible and the book will never change. So one of the greatest miracles a true God can do is put you in penance for two thousand years and yet you use the same book to create Heaven on earth.

The Antichrists should review the passage that states, "Some governments are taking us on the Road to Hell." If you were to do an analysis of the words from the Holy Bible what would the clergymen teach? I am like Paul in the Holy Bible that I am not paid by the church, but I go to many different types and learn. I studied the Holy Bible for seven years and know the difference between fantasyland and reality. The Holy Bible instructs the clergymen not to go into fantasyland and not to lose the Holy Bible. We have to live by every word, not just read it. Have you heard of New Testament only churches? Have you heard of clergymen saying in principal, "It is my responsibility to read the Holy Bible and it is the King's role to do everything else?" If you live in His kingdom and any place King Jesus Christ states He will do something that is the responsibility of the clergymen up to Judgment Day. The Holy Bible already defines the answers. A planner like myself finds, if there was a kingdom something like ending poverty in the United States is easy. I already know how the do it and is contained in my writings.

I am in a Baptist Church in the Late 1990s in Mount Prospect, Illinois. The preacher whore reads a passage, "Some governments are taking us on the Road to Hell." He states to join him in a prayer to Our Gods that the United States does not take us on the Road to Hell. What other words should he and all other Baptist Churches have to discuss. Their is no Hell like a woman scorned as her children are forgotten in money, health care, daily bread, job creation, bad schools, good fathers, great mothers, prisons, and the list can continue. The requirement of him is to understand elections so not one hair on a child's head is harmed. That also includes smart bombs in Iraq to kill a child's father or Vietnam to kill children through the Hell of American foolishness. I asked the Pastor if he needed to learn what the passage meant. I just heard it for the first time. He asked me to leave because I had a pack of cigarettes in my shirt pocket and I did mention the word fear, which caused grandma to have a negative reaction. In all churches it is to be all heard. A clergymen cannot learn if he refuses to see and refuses to hear. The religious leaders are not to drive the congregation away even if they declare gay or are of the wrong color as the Ku Klux Klan of white trash would do. The Holy Bible is clear, do not kill the messenger. Before that he did what I have grown to believe all churches would pray to King Jesus Christ that He would avoid that from happening. The Baptist went to pro-life campaigning at their churches in the year of Our Lord 2000 AD election. My analysis of the year of Our Lord 2000 AD election is that George W. Bush was against funding for good schools, wanted to increase military expenses, which would help his campaign funding from the defense industry and have produced laws in Texas that should be bad from the church view as it violated the book of Mark. He has continued to write laws that violate the book of Mark and others.

The Holy Bible does not allow the kingdom in the United States to represent two parties. A house divided amongst itself always fails. So he never learned anything from the Holy Bible that he could use. He did start out the meeting in the back room with, "Aren't you glad you came to my church as I can read the Holy Bible better than the church down the street." Just saying that violates the Holy Bible because if it were true he is required to evangelize the other locations. By the church in the United States allowing the congregation to have two parties is against itself. If the only reason many churches said to vote for the failure of the Republicans is pro-life that is continuing to build the clergymen sins higher in the Heavens. They refuse to repent.

The Catholic Church apparently would vote for President Herbert C. Hoover in the year of Our Lord 1932 AD if they thought he would grant them pro-life. They may pray to Our Gods that the United States government does not take us on the Road to Hell in the Years of Our Lord 1929 to 1932 AD. After two thousand years, the clergymen do not know that if the Hell is caused by a beast like Herbert C. Hoover, he took us on the Road to Hell, he should go like Satan. If 1.4 million Americans went below the poverty level in the year of Our Lord 2004 AD, the women are scorned and the Road to Hell becomes the way of our government. Where is the seven Holy Cities working together in the year of Our Lord 1932 AD or before with the Terrible Swift Swords coming on the scene and relying on the passage, "I will take you by the hand if one person dies." in the year of Our Lord 1932 or 2004 AD. "By the hand", meaning writing new laws to overcome the poverty in 1.4 million American lives or President Franklin D. Roosevelt putting five billion dollars in our banks. Think if you had a kingdom, the rich would demand the government correct the problem. The rich become the poor through reincarnation as defined in scripture. You would need to believe that would happen before you created Fear. The people in greed in America become, "A friend in need is a friend in deed." Only God can take care of your needs, which are spiritual. It is extremely difficult to believe if we continued the wealth creation before the Civil War and the rich demanded the poor families were granted money through jobs, pay raises, and any gifts children richly deserve, the gifts would not be lacking in America or any country where God's Kingdom has a presence. Only the Antichrists focusing on daily bread as their only commitment to end the famine (lack of money) by disobeying the Holy Bible could result in such foolishness on the part of government and wealthy. King Jesus Christ will take care of the greed through the kingdom as His Father. The Holy Bible is clear. The famine at the end is for the Word of God not daily bread. The Antichrist should review the Old Testament. The clergymen that con the congregation out of money for daily bread does not understand the words want and need. A children's dictionary would help the people with a PhD in religion to understand the two very difficult words for them to comprehend.

The number one problem on planet earth is the clergymen refuse to obey King Jesus Christ by giving Him the Lord's Prayer, God's Kingdom and the clergymen becoming a prince and therefore royalty.

The following biblical scholars were interviewed in the two-hour History Channel presentation.
Pastor Benny Hinn Benny Hinn Ministries
Track Griswold Presiding Bishop, US Episcopal Church
Joel Rosenberg Author, The Last Jihad
Ted Haggard Founder & Sr Pastor New Life Church
Timothy Weber, PhD Author on the Road to Armageddon
Alan F. Segal PhD Professor of Religion Barnard College

Paul Apodaca PhD Professor Social Science Chapman University
Chris Chapel PhD Professor Theology Loyola Marymount University
Rachel Fell McDermott PhD Professor Eastern Cultures, Barnard College
Robert Fuller PhD Professor of Religion Bradley University
Hal Lindsey Author The Late Great Planet Earth
Ronald Farmer PhD Dean Wallace All Faith Chapel
David Sanchez PhD Biblical Studies Loyola Marymount University
John Wilson Director Inst for Study of Archaeol & Rel
Bernard McGinn PhD Professor History Theology, University of Chicago
Marvin Sweeney PhD Professor of Hebrew Bible Claremont College
Paul Boyer PhD Professor of History University of Wisconsin
Randall Balmer PhD Professor of Religion Bernard College
Ronald Farmer PhD Dean Wallace All Faiths Chapel
The above will be a chapter in my new book "Voice of Vengeance –Fear"
Elias (like from Mark 9:12) is CHRIST son of man since King Jesus Christ divorced you.
You will know the true Word of God by the representative of the King not the preacher whore who reads without understanding, cannot site the many miracles of stories he has put to rest, and must be justified by law not Grace.
Author of "Life of US (U.S.)": a book that forms God's Kingdom (Lord's Prayer).
Author of "The Antichrist God's Version": a book of God's miracles that people would say cannot be done like ending all poverty. Author's name Elias.
Present writing Voice of Vengeance – Fear: author's name is Christ (Son of Man) a book that takes books like the book of Revelation and turns it into a present day reality. No man

of today could avoid the wrath of God without penance. I have gone to many different types of churches like Paul from scripture and I guarantee the Holy Bible is correct. The church of today went backwards from New York, NY in the year of Our Lord 1900 AD to today and the wax is cold. The church must be justified by law because grace is gone. Have you heard of a nation of divorce or abortion and the church desires to be justified by law not grace?

email comfortinGod@hotmail.com

First two books published listed on www.iuniverse.com and other locations.

I have King Jesus Christ patented planning technique of knowledge on how to get to a small door.

Sent on June 9, the year of Our Lord 2007 AD.
I am interested in the Lutheran Mission on God's Plan. The Holy Bible states King Jesus Christ will return when you have no questions to ask.
I will be at your service on Saturday night. If you are not ready give me a date.

Sent on November 17, the year of Our Lord 2006 AD

You must implement the Lord's Prayer or you are taking God's name in vain.

King Jesus Christ will not return until you have implemented the Lord's Prayer.

Please explain to the congregation the downside of you becoming royalty and them living in a kingdom of God.

The Holy Bible states you shall know what you did before you die. You die when you realize you must implement the Lord's Prayer. All problems in the world can be solved when you have completed forming the kingdom. The problems only exist because you are failing God. King Jesus Christ put you

471

in penance back when you failed yourself in Israel about two thousand years ago. They wrote prophecy and the other words of grace for a kingdom, not an individual.

The advantage of implementing the Lord's Prayer is the beginning of the end to:

1. Divorces.
2. Abortions.
3. Killing wars.
4. Poverty by making all people rich.
5. Or end all pain in family's lives.
6. You can easily end the unnecessary deaths of six million children by forming the kingdom.
7. You define a problem and the kingdom can resolve.

I have created a presentation that would allow any church location that has a presence in Asia as part of its denomination to implement the Lord's Prayer. In addition I have created a voice file that can be heard through any free program that can play music. One file is in music form but does not contain music and can be run on a free system like Windows Media Player. The voice file is the words of the presentation and in a way all your work is done except a few telephone calls. The others can be opened by the program like Words. Also you will receive a thousand year plan for the one world government of the USA. All the rest of the governments are the same format.

Any church location from the smallest to the largest can start. If you can talk to your peers, you can start the beginning of implementing the Lord's Prayer. If you state I have to wait for King Jesus Christ to return, because I need to ask Him questions, you are wrong. The Holy Bible states I will return when you do not have any questions to ask. The end is the eighth beast and his failure is close to creating the real end for the penance continues for seven times longer.

I will send you the presentation, literature, and a voice file. If you require or desire me to be involved, just ask. If you have a fast internet connection the information will come like any download. If you have a very slow connection, I will send a disc.

To start send me your email address to start the download. If you have a dial up connection send me your address. Do not fail yourself.

Richard Cartwright
430 Pembroke Rd SW
Poplar Grove, IL 61065
Telephone 815-765-0161
email comfortinGod@hotmail.com

Sent December 18 the year of Our Lord 2006 AD.
12/18/ the year of Our Lord 2006 AD
Help

If you had a presentation and voice file so you do not even have to talk, would you be willing to start to implement the Lord's Prayer. All you have to do is make some telephone calls, reproduce some papers and play a voice file. You can start to end the pain in all families' lives. Is that to much to achieve such greatness?

You have to make a few telephone calls and host a meeting.

Write to comfortinGod@hotmail.com for the information.

If I was the true Gods and you failed to try, I would suggest you seek a new career like selling shoelaces. You should realize who you worship (Satan) and John 3:16 is gone for all that refuse to implement the Lord's Prayer. I would consider that fear for the clergymen.

Sent on December 7, the year of Our Lord 2006 AD.
You have not told me and your congregation why you refuse to obey Our Gods and implement the LORD'S PRAYER> TELL ME WHY> TELL ME WHY AT comfortinGod@hotmail. com

Maybe I can help you get John 3:16 back

----- Original Message -----
From: "Cahalan, Anne" <Cahalan.Anne@aod.org>
To: "Richard Cartwright" <carrichard@verizon.net>
Sent: Thursday, December 07, 2006 10:35 AM
Subject: Not read: Re: Question?
Your message
To: Cahalan, Anne
Subject: Re: Re: Question?
Sent: Mon, 4 Dec 2006 20:29:46 -0500 was deleted without being read on Thu, 7 Dec 2006 11:35:41 -0500

Sent October 2, the year of Our Lord 2006 AD
Re: Heaven on earth.

In the book of Hosea 4:6 "My people are destroyed for lack of knowledge: I will also reject thee, that you shall be no priest to me: seeing that you have forgotten the law of thy God I will also forget thy children." The Holy Bible states that lack of knowledge will destroy the church. The clergymen must be gathers of all knowledge in order to satisfy the Tree of Knowledge in the Garden of Eden. All leaders I have contacted are rejecters of knowledge. I offered them to end all poverty through God's laws from the Holy Bible and they refuse to learn. The Holy Bible is written so no man can boast. So you have an economy in Israel that even a fifty percent increase in tithes or taxes could not destroy. When I asked the clergymen how they would eliminate poverty not all concepts of poor, they said and I have in writing (emails) that I do not believe it is possible and yet in the United States it is so easy for those that need to try, you will wonder why anyone spent any time on it. Other countries like Mexico will require you to have Faith and Wait (suffer) for the poverty of those that need to try for it to happen.

In reviewing Standing Historical it all happens in one generation. The generation starts near the end times with wars and roomers of wars. The generation started in 2999 minus 1007 as defined in the Holy Bible or the year of Our Lord 1992 AD. You have the King of the North and of the South debating all about money. The King of the South wins and when the Age of Accountability starts at one hour past midnight on January 1, in the year of Our Lord 2000 AD, what occurs is Hell is opened up and all are responsible for their actions. At that moment the rich are put in shackles and the million plus Antichrists are defined as coming in an era of peace and prosperity. President William J. Clinton had a commitment to the peace dividend and the economy in the Heartland of the world was reaching a level of unemployment that should make the clergymen love. The King has written He could double that economy. The Garden of Eden defines that once you are responsible for good and evil you will surely die. I have not met a clergymen that understands what evil means. Also, it states that once you can manage good and evil you will be like Gods. King Jesus Christ needs you to become a prince and wear the color of royalty or purple.

In the Year of Our Lord 2000 AD you heard the King of Babylon on television as well as the false prophet was in Jerusalem. Satan appears in the year of Our Lord 2003 AD and will be around for a short time and cannot be saved. He started out as a Red Dragon and beast and appeared in the Holy City on television. He created the church failure as judged by King Jesus Christ in the book of Romans. We are past the false Messiah and Satan's Darts and stand at the point of looking for the Mysterious Messiah.

The church has been in penance since the church disobeyed King Jesus Christ in Israel and He divorced the church. Prophecy is written the penance will begin to end once the kingdom is formed as in the book of Daniel and the Lord's Prayer. There are seven names on the door not thirty-six with half-nonaligned with gays and demons running to marry. The 1150 days are for the church types that have a presence in Asia. The 2300 days are for the rest. The church should understand the prophecy, "Some of your stories (OF ALL ADAMS, CHURCH, GOVERNMENT, AND BUSINESS), if you could get to the very elect (GOD'S ELECTION OR THE clergymen ELECTION to determine if the stories are good) all you will do is deceive. So when King Jesus Christ put Adam in penance when he disobeyed in Israel the penance was complete. Yet, King Jesus Christ has told you all things, so you have the answer to overcome everything that is bad, by the use of the Holy Bible and teaching of one hundred percent theology (planning from the Holy Bible). We have to live by every word and Adam has done every thing wrong. The Noah's Ark story would be kind if the kingdom does not form. The church is about to create the end.

What are the future prophecies? I will start with the bad news or the end of civilization in the United States by hiring a politician (eighth beast and Satan is the seventh) that will create the ultimate famine or lack of money similar to the old Testament, but the United States cannot recover as the electricity, water, gas, and essential services close in America. Then the poor inherit the earth through the use of internal conflict with guns. You have created buyers and sellers remorse. The penance never ended since the kingdom did not form or the church implemented the Lord's Prayer. What destroys America is the pen to create bad laws. The penance continues for seven times longer or fourteen thousand years.

The passage that creates the end is he is a beast, he is not a beast, yet he is a beast. Some believe in their fantasyland that Satan which is the seventh beast and the eighth beast are

476

the same person, but the answer is no as the church will allow both to go to Hell and they took the entire United States, then the world with them. The penance continues for seven times longer or fourteen thousand years and leads to the prophecy of His return with the Seven Horns of the Eternal Temple or Israel. The clergymen are responsible for approximately one trillion unnecessary deaths of children. If you had Standing Historical, you would know the names of the first six beasts and the reason they did not go to Hell. A beast cannot be saved. A beast started as a real person, but failed himself and the church refused to help him. You read prophecies to me and most have already happened.

The passage that creates the new beginning is the Seventh Trumpet where the King will give us a reprieve from wars as His Father did in the Old Testament through King David's Son. That will create the greatest tribulation the world will see as the Seventh Trumpet is part of forming the kingdom and is the one world government commitment through the church. King Jesus Christ makes all people rich as He doubles the best Adam can do through a biblical economy. The part about all flesh is dead if you did not shorten the days is where the church failed to form the kingdom until after the False Messiah appeared and disappeared. In the Year of Our Lord 2006 AD all flesh is dead and the answer is to give King Jesus Christ His Virgin Bride back or the Church. You receive John 3:16 when you develop a plan to implement the Lord's Prayer. All Antichrists that refuse to implement the Lord's Prayer dies a second time and cannot be saved. You remember the church has been in penance since the clergymen disobeyed approximately two thousand years ago. The following passage applies that some of your stories (not many) are so great if you can get to the very elect (God's election through the clergymen) all you will do is deceive. Since you where in penance and the end will come, you have to realize all of Adams work is wrong (100%).

King Jesus Christ states you cannot go to Israel to learn how to raise a child since the knowledge was destroyed. So the greatest knowledge a clergymen can grant the world is how to raise a child of 777 design and continue his education through the book of needs until he is reborn at the right age. One million plus leaders all develop the greatest of technology and share the techniques with all that go to any church location.

You say health care is great technology but where is the end of malpractice and the beginning of universal health care in the United States, so all children can afford a doctor and dentist as they grow up. Many live on the streets and eat from the garbage cans.

You say cars are great technology but how are you going to end the unnecessary deaths on the highways. The police hide in the bushes to see if you desire to save your life by wearing seat belts.

The courts are the land of chaos and confusion from the man that holds the gavel.

The seventh and eight beasts are in government.

The Second World War is a war to end all wars. How well did the church do to end all wars?

You can go on with reality as the Holy Bible states the Antichrist went backwards from New York City in the year of Our Lord 1900 AD as a land of love and marriage to today or a land of abortion and divorce. The clergymen are to end all pain in the families not bore them with their sermons or writing sermons for "grandmas". In the year of Our Lord 1900 AD the United States government was free of debt and You fulfilled a prophecy of becoming the greatest debtor nation in the world. Your currency is green. The approximate cost of interest for government debt is about two thousand dollars per person per year or eight thousand dollars of taxes just for interest for a family of four. You are allowing the government to gamble with the economy, so a fool can win elections.

I have audited churches like Paul in the Holy Bible and find many do not know how to start a prayer as well as end. You start all prayers to Our Father which art in Heaven, Hallowed be Thy name. Next is your call to action as to what you will commit to like reviewing all elections so the passage, "Some governments are taking us on the Road to Hell." like the seventh and eighth beast and you will stop him. The end in His name King Jesus Christ as He stated you made Him King back in Israel. To date you had seven chances to stop the beast and six chances to stop the dragon.

I can give you is the only presentation required for you to start the beginning of Heaven on earth. After you talk to twelve of your peers and they present to twelve of their peers, you cannot go any further and must carry the message forward to the leaders of your denomination. You will know God's Plan, how to get the teenagers back to your church, and have Church Law equivalent to Moses Laws. You should be invited to carry the message forward to other denominations especially the Catholics. If you need I will give you the knowledge on how to determine God's Covenants.

One thing you should not do is kill the messenger that copied the answers out of the Holy Bible. I need to give my grandson a chance to grow up without the Hell of the Battle of Armageddon in the United States. You live by the sword; you will die by the sword.

Richard Cartwright
430 Pembroke Rd
Poplar Grove, IL 61065
Tel # 1-815-765-0161

King Jesus Christ is not going to return until you have no questions to ask. If you are telling the congregation (false witness) He will return now, you are wrong. The Holy Bible states, "I have told you all things." The problem is you have not worked together to achieve what King Jesus Christ has stated He...will shorten the days to forth-two month for the church to restart after implementing the Lord's Prayer. The entire world is down to one prayer.

Add to your copy of the Seventh Trumpet Story or King Jesus Christ Thousand Year Plan for the One World Government of the United States from Prophecy.

You remember you have to form the church with seven names on the door to make the Seventh Trumpet story real. You are living in fantasyland by believing the tribulation of the beginning of Heaven on earth is bad. All flesh is saved is true (no John 3:16).

In the book of Galatians you in His kingdom become the lord in the Lord of lords. You are to teach the judges of our country in a training course to live by Grace and not by law. As you teach from the Holy Bible you ask the judges of the court to send you a copy of how grace applied in reviewing the laws of America and use the material to train the future Scripture Attorneys the reality of theology or planning from the Holy Bible. As an example as the judges correct the problems they caused by their rulings on Living Wills, you desire how and what was accomplished. Always rely on the courts to develop the future training package. As the government creates the laws of Liberty and uses the format of the New Testament, you will teach. The watchman will use the concept that all Supreme Court Judges will have a term limitation of six years and will be granted a chance to go to a lower court, where they can review the knowledge that they developed. As the courts develop reality, you forgive them for the mistakes that came before. If you do not, the news will blame (black plague them to refuse to try). Their corrections are the only way you can forgive them, but they do not have to go to church. That right is still up to them, but the vast majority will try.

In the book of Timothy you are to train future politicians in a training course on how to coordinate the work of a governor or king as a bishop would. Age will be covered as age or experience is required, not a man without experience covering the role of a president like Jimmy Carter without having the chance to grow into the position. The government will develop the King's computerized planning technique, develop the training courses and turn future training in the one world government over to the Seven Holy Cities. I would enjoy teaching the King's business design to the organizations of Social Security, US Post Office, and the IRS. The Federal government and others will pay the church to use the bottom up planning technique program in the Holy Bible or the path to the small door. The government will realize the program will be used by all people in business as it is the business design of God and the work of Adam. For example the computerized Holy Bible technique is invaluable to a doctor to help overcome malpractice and he will Joy going to a training session and taught by his denomination.

In the example of my training course to the clergymen on the passage, "I do not want you to do a job you do not want to do." make sure you cover the technology from the Altar, so the politicians have a clue of what you are doing to complement their efforts.

As describe in the Holy Bible, if the one world government writes bad laws, the sins of the clergymen will be all over the country. The problem will result in the rod of iron to be used. The officials of the government will be required to blow the trumpet. If they fail to do so and one person dies, the King will take them by their hand (fail to write laws to correct). The congregations are very interested when the government takes the country on the Road to Hell.

The clergymen are to end the pain in the lives of people. Under President George H. W. Bush of the year of Our Lord 1992 AD, there were forty million children in jeopardy. That is forty million Cardinal Sins of American clergymen. Under President William J. Clinton before the end of his term, I heard the number of Cardinal Sins went down to twenty seven million. As the politicians eliminate the jeopardy of famine (money), you desire to encourage them to continue by having them send you each of their efforts. In God's Kingdom of New Testament Law, all laws must follow the rules of argument as trained and be veto proof. The New Testament Laws are dynamic action plans and begins the Generation of the Fig. Their achievement will be summarized by the church staff, reviewed from the Altar, added to the local book of good deeds, and sent to the right Holy City to be granted their leader to die and carry the message forward to Our King in His name King Jesus Christ.

Lawrence E. Couch of the Archdiocese of Washington, DC sent me emails where the Republicans are violating the Holy Bible in the book of Mark by eliminating the money to solve the Social Ills of the country. That type of law violates the laws King Jesus told the leaders will make Cardinal Sins increase and if you understand the King's economic model

Chapter 21. The Election the Year of Our Lord 1992 AD.

The prophecy is the problem near the end times is the problem with the rich. As you learned earlier, the election was between the King of the North and the King of the South. What did the King of the North or President George H. W. Bush state? "We have to watch out for Governor William J. Clinton because he is good." What he should have stated, "The Republicans have no man that could match the skills of future President William J. Clinton and we should make him president of our great country and not debate." The Holy Bible and my literature describe what foolish George Bush did as scripture proclaims. Between the Years of Our Lord 1928 AD until 1993 AD, we never had a successful Republican president.

The election must be part of Standing Historical as the Holy Bible tells you to explain all the abandoned buildings and poor economy under President George H. W. Bush and Ronald Reagan or Supply Economics. Do not forget to put the information in your museums. I will not go into writing the Standing Historical for the churches, but they can learn a great deal by studying history and my literature. This is the starting time generation or it all happens in one generation from the year of Our Lord 1992 AD until 2016 AD. What makes the United

States more important than any other country? The United States must become the Heartland of the world where the God of Heart will make a stand. What does He stand for? By the grace of God, we are saved. We must live by every word of the Holy Bible, not just read it. The grace of God is His work or the entire Holy Bible. What is missing is the grace of the clergymen as all they have is good intentions, but no good deeds. John 3:16 is at stake for the preacher whore who reads and never tries to help the congregation live by every word.

I should end this chapter with the wisdom, President William J. Clinton talked about money. The Republicans always work against the wealth creation of our country to deceive the people for their vote. President George H. W. Bush campaign was based on read my lips no new taxes. The words are only fools gold, but the only commitment the rich use to con the clergymen out of their vote along with the foolishness of Pro-life or the blame of our children since the church cannot overcome what is called fallen angels. The Holy Bible requires great wealth creation beyond what Adam can do to finish the Six-Day Creation Story started by Our Father. The Six-Day Creation Story is now called Heaven on earth with the power of work, not creation. The Republicans greatly increase the sorrows the churches are to eliminate in our lives. A summary of future President William J. Clinton words are if we kept President George H. W. Bush in power, we could end up with a depression and at best a recession by the year of Our Lord 2000 AD. Bad laws in a land of freedom produce a bad economy and a story of negative wealth creation. If the church only had the Standing Historical words of Abraham Lincoln of the year of Our Lord 1860s AD on the wealth creation in the United States to fall back on. Where was the church in learning and teaching the world to avoid, "Some governments are taking us on the road to hell"? The wisdom was all Republican presidents from the year of Our Lord 1928 AD and later created hell on earth by increasing the sorrows and being failures as human being or what the Holy Bible calls a beast or dragon. They no longer had the right to be called men.

Chapter 22. The Election the year of Our Lord 2000 AD.

Satan was a man where by appointing a Soul, Satan was granted much wealth and name recognition. He should be easy to identify by the clergymen as the Holy Bible defines the four horns of Satan and he must be a politician to derive such power. He will start with all the advantages most people in politics would desire in name and wealth. Satan as prophecy defined was in the only Holy City of our world. Many saw him in the Holy City of Rome on television. You have some passages that state, "Do not let that dragon steal that woman's child. If a man gains the whole world and loses his Soul, he gains nothing at all. In heaven on earth, do not send your policemen out to kill them because they will not go to school. If you fail to blow the trumpet and one person dies, I will take you by the hand. Some governments are taking you on the road to hell. Let God seek the vengeance said the Lord." The passages go on and on for what the saints in the Holy Cities of seven are to use to judge the politicians. Have you heard of the Mark of the Beast from the book of Mark? A politician must understand the book of Mark, so he has the mark of the beast in his forehead. What that means is if you see him, you know he understands he cannot violate the book of Mark. Now, you know the sorrows will not increase because of bad laws. The judgment of the saints covers all governments in the world, where there is a church. The nations where they have a physical presence and politicians that claim to represent the church, the judgment of the clergymen (saints) shall be unbelievable in comparison with what anyone does today. In the United States, we do not even know some of the names on the ballots. When the seven Holy Cities review our past presidents, they will notice the Republican Party never had a successful president from the year of Our Lord 1928 AD until present. Yet, the clergymen worked against the best economy in modern times under President William J. Clinton and he had the "peace dividend" in place. As the Holy Bible states, "The Antichrist came in an era of peace and prosperity" or one hour past midnight on January 1, the year of Our Lord 2000 AD. The clergymen allowed peace and prosperity to be lost. The politicians should move up the ladder of success like the Catholic Church finding the best man to run the church or the Holy City. As the clergymen learn they must train the politicians.

What occurred on January 1, the year of Our Lord 2000 AD? King Jesus Christ named the age as the Age of Accountability. All congregation and employees of King Jesus Christ are responsible for their actions. The Holy Bible discusses the future invasion of Iraq or by the army of two hundred million led by the one-third dead. We will have two hundred million in gospel armor or the Salvation Army to bring salvation back to the world led by the USA. The one-third dead were the people that represent hell on earth or the people that voted Republican in the United States. They love hawks, which are the dragons that desire to steal that woman's child. The Red Dragon will attack Iraq. The Republicans came out in force to vote for a man that is the beast in Revelation with the King of the South's girlfriend on his back. If you study the election, the numbers would state approximately one third of the people are Republicans, one third Democrats, and one third do not vote at all in America. Foolish George Bush will take us from an era of peace and prosperity and recreate the Roman Empire of the book of Romans. The world will lose John 3:16 and move closer to the end shall come as defined for the church in Matthew 24:14.

The warnings of God in scripture are great as He gave us many signs. 1007 is seven years to create the kingdom or I saw seven churches from the book of Revelation and His thousand year plan. We are to divide up the cows wisely as President William J. Clinton gave us seven years of fat cows and the rainbow economy or a pot of gold at the end of the rainbow or 232 billion dollar surplus and he talked about funding Social Security with the surplus. King Jesus Christ would return to Israel and all knees bow down to Him. The clergymen were warned it would be God or Satan they would worship as the opened up the Holy Bible before the year of Our Lord 2000 AD and learned to obey God like a slave including teaching the wicked they are in shackles. They knew about the beast of Revelation, King of Babylon, and Satan, but what did they somewhat worked together to achieve? They desired more fallen angel through Pro-life and ignored all God told them to do. Some talked about the end but we only had six beasts and President William J. Clinton did not qualify to be a beast. So many choices and all the clergymen decided to do was to work against each other even men of the same denominations like the Lutherans or the Catholics against everyone including the immigration laws and child abuse.

What was important to many churches? The Antichrists were to be discovered. They are the sinners who must obey the Commandments of God like Thy Kingdom Come, become the Prince in the Prince of Peace, and as saints judge the world politicians and congregations for the passages quoted above and others in the Holy Bible. All judgment is in the Holy Bible. Instead, what did they work for? A war against our children or Pro-life. This memo below was written in the year of Our Lord

2008 AD for the Antichrists blaming our children for not having enough babies having babies, but is required here to learn what the church thought was important in the year of Our Lord 2000 AD. You should be able to understand why Our Gods started a new name for the clergymen or the Antichrist. You remember our present clergymen were compared to the animals the ass and oxen and the review must be part of Standing Historical. That is critical to the survival of our world. May they never fall asleep at King Jesus Christ's Altars again.

Right to Life or Pro-life by Elijah, the prophet.

First, you should study the Holy Bible to end the controversy of babies having babies. You should not take pride in yourself but humility for King Jesus Christ. The Antichrist is within you if you do.

Some fools believe that one political party is more morally correct because they talk about Pro-life. If you studied history, you would learn the Republican Party of the United States of America for the first time in history increased the number of their party in Congress in the year of Our Lord 2002 AD with a member of the same party as in the White House. If the Republican desired more children the people did not need, they could have voted in Pro-life in the year of Our Lord 2003 AD. They controlled both houses of Congress, the Supreme Court, and the White House. All they desired is your vote. The year of Our Lord 2008 AD, foolish George Bush said our children do not deserve health care because there are too many. He is against new schools in his works and only the Democratic Party put in the school luncheon programs. Daily bread hunger in the United States has increased and all the Republicans desire is more "Hell Machines" as warlords or Hawks. Today the Holy Bible states the feathers are eating up the flesh or John 3:16. A Hawk is a bird that celebrates eliminating government waste like hell on earth through wars, not people that represents the false messiah. The Bird of Peace is the only view of the church.

All of the above is to be written in Standing Historical all church locations should have. All location must agree on reality not live in fantasyland.

Now scripture has the Archangel Michael condemned to this world for his war against children. Only a penance man can get off this world alive. Since you do not know about anyone living on the world for thousands of years, you have a story of reincarnation from the Holy Bible. Archangel Michael was Pope John Paul ll and he died, but will never see the true heaven. He cannot receive enough penance to qualify for the true heaven for his war against children or Pro-life. Only a penance man can get off this world alive. One thousand zeros of time is not enough penance for what Pope John Paul II did to the children. From here to Eternity is his penance.

You can read, you cannot attack people in gospel armor and especially children. Let the man without sin cast the first stone and since you are casting stones (blame), you become a sinner. You have to identify the man of sin. Since God did not forgive Archangel Michael, you had better work for the right heart. Do not invent your own religion. Now, you desire to be justified by law, not grace. The grace of God is His work or the entire Holy Bible as you are sending killers of children to heaven in your fantasyland religion. God will judge by the Holy Bible, not by shackles less church foolishness.

If you worshipped King Jesus Christ, what would Elijah, the prophet teach you? King Jesus Christ has told you all things. First, the church has driven away the teenagers because they do not like organized religion. Boring, boring, boring the teenagers will tell you. The Holy Bible states you have gone backwards from the year of Our Lord 1900 AD in a new city called New York and the wax is cold. There is no inspiration from the church to get the teenagers back. They refuse to work on 777 design as one voice or all church locations the same. 777 is zero to twenty-one years old to teach, not preach to the new generation of children. King Jesus Christ stated, "You cannot go to Israel to learn how to learn how to raise a child." Elijah would copy from scripture where God loved you so He judged you. The clergymen are to judge the congregation for the same reason, so they are prepared for Judgment Day or the day you die.

Second, Elijah, the prophet would teach you to get all children born from a woman that is spiritually, physically and financially able to bear that child. King Jesus Christ has told you to get children back with fathers. The reality of scripture is the opposite of a man would teach that has pride in himself and not humility for King Jesus Christ. Please study the Holy Bible because false witness and failure to let the Holy Spirit speak through you correctly will cause you and your wife to go to Perdition or Eternal Death. The hardest role for a man to get John 3:16 is to be an employee of King Jesus Christ and continue with false witness. The clergymen did not have John 3:16 at one hour past midnight on January 1, the year of Our Lord 2000 AD.

Third, what would King Jesus Christ tell you to do? He stated to stop sending Me little ones small and great. Your foolish hawk morality is causing the government to spend resources on hell on earth rather than daily bread. King Jesus Christ desires to be the wall and you refuse to form the kingdom with the Universal Church format or seven names on the door. Elijah, the prophet can teach you how to receive the blessing of peace on earth, good will towards men. Millions of children die each year and you work against parties that desire to provide school luncheons. King Jesus Christ stated, "He did not care what they ate, but you are working against the politicians providing daily bread." If you form the kingdom and trained the politicians, they must provide daily bread to serve King Jesus Christ and have the right heart for John 3:16, you could achieve greatness in His Name. Next, you train the congregation to listen to the

491

politicians desiring to provide daily bread. Now, you have the congregation report to you where the leaders are doing good or bad. Now only the people that want to provide daily bread win. Now, you have the right heart for John 3:16. King Jesus Christ did not put the people in prisons in shackles, He put the rich and politicians (wicked) in shackles.

What does the Holy Bible teach about the babies having babies? King Jesus Christ pities the women of suck. The fallen angels are the children of Pro-life. If you talk to the police department, ask them what a profile of a man in prison is all about. King Jesus Christ has told you to get rid of prisons and you are filling them up. The fallen angels are with the women. In addition, babies having babies have fallen too. The power you get in the kingdom is "If God is for you, who can stand against you." The only ones that can vote to determine if your story of Pro-life is any good, are the teenagers that had an abortion. Eighty percent of the babies having babies end up on general welfare. All you are doing is making all worse. You should try teaching in a church to have a child born from a woman that is spiritually, physically, and financially able to bear that child. If God is for you, who could stand against you. Thirty-five years plus of failure and your foolishness is not ending. Now, you are trying to be justified by grace, not by law, when you get children back with fathers. The clergymen do not care about the one-half million poor children in the orphanages. That is just in the United States. They cannot even get a toy at Christmas. You desire to make the total fifty million children without hope. How many more prisons do you desire? The church should try teaching the way of Our Gods or a baby born from a woman that is spiritually, physically, and financially able to bear that child.

Your greatest challenge is to find Elijah, the prophet and learn through him. King Jesus Christ put you in penance back in Israel and He desires His virgin bride back, the church. Elijah can copy the answers out of the Holy Bible in a plan form, we can achieve. My work in planning is about over until you can find the voice in the wilderness or Elias and then Elijah, the true prophet. For your love of John 3:16, you should seek Elijah. King Jesus Christ will meet us in Israel or the temple, not church.

Your greatest tribulation (reward) would be in forming the kingdom and realize the sorrows of the world can be corrected through your inspiration. The Holy Bible if applied properly will always end up with a life one thousand times better than the end. The end is less than nine years away in the year of Our Lord 2008 AD. The world must learn that fear is the beginning of all wisdom (knowledge). What you teach people to fear, they will avoid like a plague. It worked in Israel or with the Roman Empire running the nation, they had a life nine hundred times better than the end. Once the children of Israel gave up on God, they lost everything.

If you desire to obey King Jesus Christ, you must find Elijah, the prophet. I will make it easy on you, I am Elijah, the prophet as God did not abandon you but He will if you abandon His Children of 777 design. Elijah will teach how to create heaven on earth from the Lord's Prayer and eliminate any sorrows you can define anywhere.

WHY CAN PAUL SAVE SOULS WHEN KING JESUS CHRIST IS THE SALVATION? Paul can save souls because he is reforming the church. The clergymen cannot save the congregation' souls only the other clergymen through reform the church. You must have the right heart to gain John 3:16, not have the heart of the False Messiah and represent hawks or warlords. President George W. Bush is a hawk or the Red Dragon you are looking for. John McCain is a hawk and a dragon and has promised to disobey the book of Mark and become the Mark of the beast as he was to be trained by Satan. He cannot be saved. President Elect Barack Obama used hell on earth in his speeches and became a dragon and cannot be saved. The Son of Perdition is shoving many bodies under the Altar. They will all go by the way of Satan and the clergymen that refuse to go through the story of resurrection.

The United States is critical in prophecy, as the Heartland of the world or the location where Our Gods are going to make a stand. What do they stand for, but every word of scripture. The Holy Bible states King Jesus Christ will meet us in Spain. He has granted us a beautiful land. We are the children of corn and the wisdom continues. King Jesus Christ through the Holy Bible has given us a wealth of "Give me a sign." That inspiration makes our presidents more important than other countries as the future Heartland of the world.

What did President William J. Clinton create despite what the King of the North did to him? He created the best economy in modern times. He is an Irish man, who granted a pot of gold at the end of the rainbow. The clergymen should check the word rainbow in scripture. He beat President Franklin D. Roosevelt on the economy, since in the year of Our Lord 1937 AD, we had a recession and the Second World War pulled us out, but left many debts behind. We have an election between another foolish George Bush and former Vice President Al Gore. Again, I have covered this in previous writings. That must be part of Standing Historical like the Old Testament of King Solomon and David. You have President William J. Clinton's girl friend that allowed a beast from Texas to run into the White House. Al Gore tried to explained the government waste the Republicans left behind.

What America did to Congress during the term of President William J. Clinton is crucial to understand the Holy Bible and how the end will come. To prove we know how to vote, we will work against the party in the White House. That must change. In the future under President Elect Barack Obama the same thing will happen.

Chapter 23. The Election the year of Our Lord 2004 AD.

What an interesting election. I heard after many clergymen state how great it was that foolish George Bush won by three and one half million votes. Senator John F. Kerry became a dragon to prove to America he was a bigger fool then foolish George Bush. As I discussed earlier, he became the False Messiah. We had an election between Satan and his Satan Darts (blame) and the False Messiah. The world had lost John 3:16 as the war started and Satan became our god of this world when he said, "Let me seek the vengeance." The church must learn to let God seek the vengeance. Now, the Antichrists or the clergymen because of their blasphemous mouths worship Satan. They shall be hated above all others for My name's sake because they invented their own religion of failure. The religious leaders are doing one hundred percent of everything wrong and are totally deceived. They are in penance from back in Israel and never worked together to get out. Only a true God could grant you a book that always ends up with a life one thousand times better than the end and the clergymen in penance are working for the end shall come. The end is the end of civilization in America, as we know it. The give me a sign in the museums of the seven

Holy Cities should be great on this era. Even Elijah the prophet would joy in visiting your Holy Cities of seven.

Great works of Standing Historical should be written on the prophecy of Satan' Darts.

Chapter 24. The Election the year of Our Lord 2008 AD.

Again, this election is in the one generation. As the Holy Bible states it all happens in one generation. You had Satan training the beast John McCain. How did he train, but to use the concept of Satan's Darts as developed by foolish George Bush's marketing team that won him previous elections! Usually the man with the greatest amount of money wins elections except where there are unusual circumstances. This is only the third time a Democratic candidate has won without the involvement of people like Ross Perot to reform the Republican Party in the year of Our Lord 1992 AD. In the year of Our Lord 1932, we had Hoover Ville versus future President Franklin D. Roosevelt. In the year of Our Lord 1964 AD, President Linden Johnson won after the death of President John F. Kennedy. Now the economy that foolish George Bush created was just the same type as his father. The professionals in Standing Historical should have determined this easily; however, they do not exist.

What the financial markets stated before President Elect Barack Obama first speech on November 7, the year of Our Lord 2008 AD, was he won the election, but we never heard his economic plan. He does not apparently understand how economies work and had no view except what was already defined but not completed. He is the eighth beast and cannot be saved. I heard him mention Universal Health Care, but when he was asked to solve the sorrows of a lack of doctors, he had no ideas. Universal Health Care and an aging population may require doubling the number of doctors.

Former President William J. Clinton established goals for the country and increased the taxes on the wealthy. The Holy Bible described the rainbow of an Irish president. We ended up with a pot of gold in the year of Our Lord 2000 AD and the peace dividend was in place. President Elect Barack Obama should have developed his economic plan before the election and not copy the technique of the Republicans through the word, blame. He will never recreate the best economy in modern times. In Israel, Our Father did not allow the word blame or the "Black Plague" to be used. The financial station states we may be another trillion dollars behind next year and his only plan was tax cuts. When a society is in jeopardy of income, when they get more money, they love to save. The last plan to give the money out as I forecasted ended up mostly saved and could not work. What will happen is the beasts will come back as in President William J. Clinton's administration. The future of indebtedness cannot and will not be embraced by the world and our government will recreate Hoover Ville. President Elect Barack Obama or Senator John McCain are the wrong men and could not be successful. He will do better than Senator John McCain will but will cause the Battle of Armageddon to start in the United States of America as the Holy Bible foretells. The curse of God will occur all over the world. Adam without God is just a fool.

Earlier in the campaign, it was stated he never originated any new legislation. He may not be an idea man that is require to correct America with the ten thousand new ideas required as scripture explains. Since all laws of importance are bad in America, we require a prophet that can plan anything like:

1. Fund Social Security so the businessperson will ask, "Can we fund it faster?"
2. Get America out of debt completely.
3. Grant America a new education system with new techniques for buildings.
4. Grant us the beginning of energy independence and reverse global warming.
5. Grant the US Universal Health Care at a cost the businesspersons would agree to.
6. Develop the plan Our Gods demand to eliminate prisons and add the people to the taxpayer role.
7. Start the beginning of the end of the penance of viruses as the Holy Bible states.
8. Grant a plan where one hundred per cent of the people will be above the poverty level, if they try.
9. Start the beginning of the end to the serious problem of medical malpractice in our country and beyond.
10. End the illegal alien and children on milk cartons. We will have to pay to get rid of the wall of fool, but visiting the site as a tourist must be considered.
11. Start a war against drug lords that America must win.
12. Train and staff all hospitals to overcome the doubling of people going into Social Security. Also, solve the problem where the doctors will not accept Medicare payments.
13. The more I try to list, the more I realize I would have to list. I have always been an idea man.

As I wrote earlier I even gave President Elect Barack Obama the technique to end killing wars and the church representing the poor in the year of Our Lord 2004 AD, could have set up the way. All Senator Barack Obama wrote back to me is he cannot represent religion. Elijah, the prophet can plan anything and is the right choice as King Jesus Christ has written for the first watchmen elect and can write laws per the New Testament.

I will leave the election of the year of Our Lord 2012 AD up to the clergymen. May the movie be well accepted.

Chapter 25. Life is Like a Circle.

What do the last four chapters mean? First Americans are so use to blame, we cannot learn what the politicians stand for. As I have written, we must vote after their term in office to release the shackles. In eight years, a Republican failure, Senator John McCain lost by a few percentage points. It was only a vast amount of money and adopting blame that a Democrat won. The marketing plan was Senator John McCain and foolish George Bush, what a team. There was not one reason to vote Republican as they are beasts and cannot be saved. We the people of the United States and the world are fortunate that Our Gods wrote the prophecies for us. The end is buyers and sellers remorse or Hoover Ville being recreated: however, we cannot recover.

President Elect Barack Obama has made statements in the past that makes him a dragon and he brought up the failure of President John F. Kennedy to aid in his victory. Where was a clear campaign without blame to compare a party where there are zero reasons to vote for and President Elect Barack Obama? The Democrats should win by a ninety-seven percent majority. The United States must form the church of seven names and get rid of the Republican Party to get John 3:16 back. As the Holy Bible states, we must identify the man of sin and the Son of Perdition. The church has become killers as many politicians are like the lawless ones and cannot be saved.

Why is the name of this chapter "Life is Like a Circle"? The Holy Bible continues with what comes around goes around. Americans do not know what they are doing, when they vote. To prove to themselves, they have created a very clear policy. Whatever party is in the White House, many will vote against our leadership. Now, they know how to vote. President William J. Clinton created the best economy in modern times and he discussed the voter put in the rich men that were against the view of his party. Vice President Al Gore tried to explain in his election campaign about the government waste, but people do not care and cannot understand. The Holy Bible will tell you Americans put beasts in place to work against America to win the election in the year of Our Lord 2000 AD. Foolish George W. Bush as the beast of Revelation was the King of Babylon. Then he went on to become the Red Dragon and Satan. Not one woman could vote for him. I covered earlier, why his mother should not vote for him.

What will happen now without Divine Intervention or the third power of eight in life is like a circle? The Americans will send beasts to represent them. The Republicans will regain Congress like under former President William J. Clinton. President Elect Barack Obama cannot handle as he does not understand how economies work. The economy will grow at first then continue to fail until the end will come. If you notice, his main idea is tax cuts. As I explained earlier that would not work as people in financial jeopardy will have a tendency to save. The economy will not grow as quickly as it did under President William J. Clinton. First, you have to straighten out the budget or tax the rich that cannot use the money wisely or greed. The Holy Bible does explain. His reversal of foolish George Bush tax cuts is not enough. Then invest in the sorrows or social ills of the country to create a business and job creation environment. The Holy Bible contains the ideal economy or

Consumption Economics. Anyone who believes money is not part of religion had better get a Holy Bible and study. If we fail now in fourteen thousand years, Our Gods will come back with the seven horns of the Eternal Temple or Israel. Again, since America again looks like the America Indians had it in the year of Our Lord 1492 AD, the story will be the same.

I WILL END WITH. KING JESUS CHRIST WILL MEET US IN ISRAEL, NOT CHURCH. WHAT THE TWENTY FIVE PERCENT PLUS OF THE HOLY BIBLE IN PROPHECY IS STANDING HISTORICAL OF COMMANDMENTS FOR THE CHURCH. THE CHURCH IS WHERE THE SINNERS HAVE TO REPENT. ONCE THAT IS COMPLETE, ISRAEL WILL BE NEXT.

Chapter 26. A Refiner's Fire, and Like Fullers' Soap

Hosea

In the book of Hosea 4:6 "My people are destroyed for lack of knowledge: I will also reject thee, that you shall be no priest to me: seeing that you have forgotten the law of thy God I will also forget thy children." The Holy Bible states that lack of knowledge will destroy the church. The church leaders must be gathers of all knowledge in order to satisfy the Tree of Life and the Tree of Knowledge in the Garden of Eden. All leaders I have contacted are rejecters of knowledge. I offered them miracle after miracle and they refuse to learn.

A miracle is a future to inherit that people would say is impossible. Examples provided by Elijah and Elias are amazing. The answer for the church to teach is all is possible in a kingdom. If the end result is good then the world can achieve. The best example is a life one thousand times better than the end in the church world. The title of the Holy Bible is holy is perfect and bible is a religious way of life. So, the Holy Bible will always produce a life one thousand times better than the end. Elijah has just copied the answers out of scripture as the Holy Bible is written so no man can boast. The plan is already there. Even fear could be developed by the kingdom, had it formed.

Since God has told us all things, then the Holy Bible teaches us how to form the kingdom to minimize the lost of souls. God admits we will lose some. Every story the church creates seen to maximize the lost of souls and lives unless you go into pure fantasyland. The observation techniques are like God will snap His fingers and all will be good. If you listen to a man worse than a fool called a Antichrist that claims this, I would be will to offer all the money in the world against his soul that will not happen. The penance of eternal death will be Adams work for the next fourteen thousand years or the penance will continue for seven times longer.

What Elijah has developed in the Chapter Stairway to Heaven is summarized now to clarify what the Holy Bible states is required. The wisdom is complete.

February 26, the year of Our Lord 2009 AD

Cross and Crown Lutheran Church
7404 Elevator Rd
Roscoe, IL 61073
Pastor John L. Heins

Immanuel Lutheran Church
1045 Belvidere Rd
Belvidere, IL 61008

Pastor Kurtis Bueltmann.

I was asked indirectly by a clergyman, what is the procedure necessary for King Jesus Christ to return. I have a chapter that covers the procedure as copied from the Holy Bible. The chapter title is called "Stairway to Heaven". I will summarize here how easy it is to start and actually to complete. God will never give us more to do than we can do.

King Jesus Christ will not return through our observation but good deeds.

From the book of Luke 17:20. And when He was demanded of the Pharisees, when the kingdom of God should come, He answered them and said, The kingdom of God cometh not with observation:

He will join us in the temple of Israel not church.
From the book of Malachi 3:1.
Behold, I will send my messenger, and he shall prepare the way before me: and the LORD, whom ye seek, shall suddenly come to his temple, even the messenger of the covenant, whom ye delight in: behold, he shall come, saith the LORD of hosts.

Procedure:

Step one is we must first identify the Antichrist. The work is complete.

Step two is we must have a common ground to get together with the chosen ones. I have written the first meeting and the future work to review. What are included are the presentation material and the words. No additional work is required unless you desire to read some background material. If you can make a sermon, you can present the material. I can explain the seventh day He rests like His Father, so you require the material from the mysterious messiah for a thousand year plan from the Holy Bible. The church must be run like the temple of Israel in mystery and intrigue. The work is very detailed and is covered as a wall of hope for each church location. Do not try to add detail now, just read. Only God can provide hope. Hope is the actions required to fulfill faith through people like you. Forgiveness is provided after the social ill is resolved, not before. You cannot forgive people that have the power to change and refuse. You must think about it like deadly sins. They must repent to be forgiven. The Holy Bible is clear.

Step three is to start church laws like Moses laws that the clergymen must obey. I have covered a number of them and you should encourage others to think about what maybe required. An example is, "If the clergymen have a problem in their marriage, they must seek the marriage counselors of the church." The result will be the congregation will force you to end divorces in their marriages. Finalizing anything now is not to be tried, but the principles to be learned.

Step four is to get the signatures of the clergymen and ask them to try the same with others and get their signatures. When you are satisfied, you go to your upper management, make the same presentation, and show the wall of hope unfinished and some preliminary church laws. Have your upper management contact another denomination and do the same. Do not contact the Catholics.

Step five is to get five denominations and one thousand signatures. Now you are ready to carry forward to the only Holy City we have, the Catholics. You do the same thing.

Step six is you gather in a storage web site all the churches you can find all over the world. The Holy Bible states to even check the caves or places you would not expect to find what someone called a church. You are trying to contact all to do the same as above. In addition, you will ask them to do a public opinion poll and the sermons that are created. You will have to find someone in the five denominations to write the two to five sermons for the power of one voice. Now you have ended future killing wars. The existing ones of the United States will stop and killing wars will never come back. This is a requirement in the Holy Bible and will be joy to achieve. In addition, you will help millions of children with daily bread. You will go to the temples to ask them to take the public opinion poll in addition to the church. Upper management should be able to arrange that easily with the powerful voice of your God leading the way.

Step seven is the church opens up the Holy Bible and learns what tasks must be completed. Since my literature covers most and many answers, I would start there. For example, you must complete God's Covenants or the minimum requirement to run a church. You require a physical structure called an Altar to be used at all locations. You would design what education requirements are necessary. When you divide the tasks, you should get as many people as possible to get involved. If there is a sermon to be written, you do not desire one million plus men to all write that one. So you pick some people and the task and meet with the other denominations to agree as one voice. So think small and get as many as possible you can to develop the great tribulation (reward) or work on the return of King Jesus Christ. He does not expect you to be perfect as written, the first time you try something new it is not very good, but your work over the millenniums makes all your works appear perfect. The task is complete when you, not He has no questions to ask. So all clergymen must consider questions and have the taskmasters complete the work. Again, I repeat you should make each tasks small so many can be involved.

Elijah
Telephone 815.765.0161
Email comfortingod@mchsi.com

Pastor John L. Heins, I have met with many times in the past. Even thou he is doing one hundred percent of everything wrong, he told me on the phone he is doing some of the items I have mentioned. He refuses to try for the story of his salvation and gaining the same heart of the God of Heart. The best his religion of Lutheran design can achieve is his eternal death. Eternal death means you wish you were dead the rest of your live, the only thing you cannot do is die. When I met with him he laughed at God or I do not want A HAIR ON THE CHILD'S HEAD HARMED. He has no chance for John 3:16.

Pastor Kurtis Bueltmann as of April 15, the year of Our Lord 2009 AD. I have a meeting with to teach him how to write laws per the New Testament as we did not know in the year of Our Lord 1776 AD. To me the concept is clear in the Holy Bible if the clergymen would try. They know God has a plan and the laws must be a plan. The church has faith and wait and all that is left is love. So all that is left in the forty two or seven year law plan is love. Over two hundred years and the clergymen could not learn because all they desire is for example Lutheran church location versus Lutheran Church location. The temple of Israel is in contact with the temples in Chicago, Illinois to work together. What a difference between the training of Our Father and the legacy left behind, then the church that disobeyed God in Israel and is doing one hundred percent of everything wrong and believe they are good. All clergymen are working hard for eternal death. They require Elijah the prophet to be like Paul and reform the church. Once they agree to work on implementing the Lord's Prayer in earnest, they get John 3:16 back for the entire world and the end will not occur.

More letters to gain their love. I have written the book and now I am like A Refiner's Fire, and Like Fullers' Soap, just as the Holy Bible foretold.

Christmas, the Day of Our Lord 2008 AD.

Immanuel Lutheran Church
1045 Belvidere Rd
Belvidere, IL
Antichrist Rev Allen Buss Pastor

Kenneth Copeland Ministries

Fort Worth, Texas 76192-0001

Antichrist Ken Copeland

Jim Swaggart Ministries
8919 World Ministry Ave
Baton Rouge, LA 70810

Antichrist Jimmy Swaggart

Breakthrough with
Rod Parsley
PO Box 100
Columbus OH 43216-0100

Antichrist Rod Parsley

Benny Hinn Ministries
PO Box 162000
Irving, Texas 75016

Antichrist Benny Hinn

Antichrist Gerald Flurry of the Church of Philadelphia
Post Office Box 3700
Edmond, OK 73083

Cross and Crown Lutheran Church
7404 Elevator Rd
Roscoe, IL 61073
Antichrist Pastor John L. Heins

The Sixty-seventh Book of the Holy Bible by Elijah the Prophet as God Promised from the Book of Malachi.

Mount Olive Lutheran Church
2001 N. Alpine Rd
Rockford, IL 61107

Antichrist Pastor Kenneth E. Krause

North Loves Baptist Church
5301 E. Riverside Blvd
Rockford, IL
Antichrist Senior Pastor Paul Kingsburg

Shepherd's Chapel
PO Box 416
Gravette, AR 72736
Antichrist Pastor Murray

First Baptist Church
Appleton Road & W. Jackson St
PO Box 276
Belvidere, IL 61008-5800
Antichrist Rev. Rex A. Rogers

Poplar Grove United Methodist Church
105 E Grove
Poplar Grove, Il 61065
Antichrist Senior Pastor Lisa Kruse-Safford

Tomorrows World
PO Box 3810
Charlotte, NC 28227-8010

Antichrists at Tomorrows World

What you are about to read is information sent to the people above.

Before the world can progress, the clergymen must find the Antichrist.

We must review what should be part of Standing Historical knowing the clergymen are the son of perdition or causing eternal death. Let me repeat, the clergymen are the son of perdition and the lawless ones. Who is stealing tithes and offerings, but the clergymen. Fear is the beginning of all wisdom (knowledge) and must be taught on the great and dreadful Day of the Lord or Good Friday. Let us review the politicians and understand which ones King Jesus Christ can save. King Jesus Christ put the wicked in shackles or the rich and most of the politicians, not the people in prisons. The problem near the end times is the problem with the rich. The Antichrist came in an era of peace and prosperity as the United States had the peace dividend and the unemployment rate was well below four percent. Job creation is wealth creation.

ELECTION YEAR	POLITICIANS
• 2000	Vice President Al Gore versus Governor George W. Bush
• 2004	President George W. Bush versus Senator John F. Kerry
• 2008	Senator Barack Obama versus Senator John McCain

In the year of Our Lord 2000 AD, King Jesus Christ named the age as the Age of Accountability. All humans became responsible for their actions. If the clergymen had Standing Historical, it would include the kings and governors. The text would be like the Holy Bible, which covers many politicians.

The answer to the test is only former Vice President Al Gore can King Jesus Christ save. He can only achieve former

Vice President Al Gore's story of salvation if the church forms the kingdom. All clergymen that refuse to form the kingdom go by the way of Satan for the one thousand years. What do you believe Our Gods should do with the old bones? It becomes a story of reincarnation, when Our Gods grant them, new arms and legs.

Contained within the names above you will find the following from scripture

1. The beast of Revelation.
2. The king of Babylon.
3. Satan, yes the god of the church is Satan.
4. The Red Dragon.
5. The false messiah.
6. The eighth beast.

If you had Standing Historical of the United States, when would you learn about the bad economy of President George W. Bush of the year of Our Lord 2001 to 2009 AD? I wrote in my first book in the year of Our Lord 2002 AD that eight years of Bush is twelve years to many. The first four years of Bush was a financial disaster. You would have recorded what occurred in the Presidential Debates by then Governor William J. Clinton and President George H. W. Bush, which would partially explain why the economy would be bad, today. Governor William J. Clinton explained the great indebtedness would cause a depression or a recession at best by the year of Our Lord 2000 AD. The clergymen cannot represent a fool that reaches for the passage, "Some governments are taking us on the road to hell." Since Governor William J. Clinton won, you ended with a good surplus for the Federal Treasuries and an unemployment rate well below four percent. Good laws will produce a good economy. You had the peace dividend in place.

You must also understand the book of Mark. The debate of the year of Our Lord 2000 AD would partially explain why

Satan would be created, take America on the road to hell, and recreate the Roman Empire. The congregation will agree with the Holy Bible and agree with the lost of foolish George Bush's soul, once they understand. The clergymen cannot say let it be I, as both will lose their souls. I heard Pastor Murray of television state he needed to be a conqueror. That is just the opposite of what it would take to have the right heart for John 3:16. All men are brothers.

Why is fear so important to the congregation? When you read the addition to the Holy Bible, you will realize King Jesus Christ will not create the fear, except for the clergymen. The will of the people prevails. The congregation in a kingdom forces the clergymen to create fear. The clergymen do not impose their will on the people like Pro-life. The people impose their will on the clergymen. The clergymen do not desire to be in church on Good Friday because they will have to describe their failure to use knowledge to help all the people. King Jesus Christ has imposed fear on His employees or the clergymen to create the kingdom. You heard of unpardonable sins. The clergymen must know what they did before they die. That will lead to, they will be hated above all others for My name's sake. You have lost John 3:16 for all humans and all that is left in a church is the greatest beggars in the world. If you love fellowship, you can join the VFW, it will cost you less. No clergymen should believe people that worship Satan have John 3:16. There is little time left before the end and you must do Divine Intervention or the third power of eight. Elijah has your instructions in literature as copied from the Holy Bible. You can have a copy free. You can reproduce some pages free.

You are killing members of the congregation and they cannot be saved. You will have to shove their bodies under the Altar and explain why on the great and dreadful Day of the Lord or Good Friday. Good clergymen would not desire to be in church that day, but must be there.

Fear is the beginning of all wisdom (knowledge) and you must work for there is nothing to fear but fear itself. You can achieve that in the thousand-year plan for the one world government of Israel for the United States of America. In my literature, it is chapter 3 and 4 of over twenty-five thousand words. The plan is very detailed. You cannot do it by your fantasyland view of religion, but Elijah has given you a story of reality as copied from the Holy Bible. The chapter title is "The Seventh Trumpet". God will not give you more to do than you can achieve. He has selected me and I can do it. He knew me before I was born. The miracles because of faith and wait with a little bit of fear is incredible. The clergymen of today will be jealous of the people who live in the year of the Lord 2050 AD, because life is great, as many important sorrows have disappeared. The children in America will get the gifts of daily bread, the best education system in the world, the best health care system in the world, and a bright future that is unbelievably good. Elijah has developed the plan from the Holy Bible. I cannot boast since the wisdom came from scripture, give me a sign, and took many years of my life. Anyone that believes money is not part of religion should study the passages on money. In addition, King Jesus Christ has joined us in the temple of Israel long ago by the year of Our Lord 2050 AD. The tests of scripture were completed by the clergymen and Our Father has allowed His Son to return.

How you create the greatest tribulation (reward) the world will ever be involved in is covered in the chapter titled "Stairway to Heaven". The tribulation is part of the definition of the word joy. You go through the trial of creating the kingdom and then you receive the great tribulation.

The Holy Bible is not complete. Revelation 10:1 to 10:10 is clear. The seven thunders are fear. The cross the clergymen have to bear is the Holy Bible. You must teach the congregation to live by every word. Elijah, the prophet can teach you how. You should request an advanced copy if you desire the story of salvation for yourself and the world. When the will of the people and God's will agree, you will achieve a life one thousand times better than the end, the Holy Bible always accomplishes.

How can you best describe the story of the world completing the Six-Day Creation story? All the world is a stage. We are all actresses and actors. The problem we have is when we are born; we do not know the script. The church teaches the world the reality of, "The IQ I possess, how can I serve myself best. Yes I said serve myself best." Therefore, all the congregation defines a future they desire to inherit and all the world becomes a stage where we the people serve the will of the people. Do not let the rights of a few people interfere with the masses as today. When God's will and the people's will agree, we are getting closer to a perfect way of life for all. Once the people reach that level, then all should take time for a great tribulation or party for the entire world. Do not become impatient as that may take one hundred thousand years. Life is like a circle, what comes around goes around as we humans reach for perfection, we can go asleep again. Where is the Mother of Inspiration, the church?

Elijah, the prophet
. The voice in the wilderness is Elias.
430 Pembroke Rd SW
Poplar Grove, Il 61065
Tel 815-765-0161

Email to comfortingod@mchsi.com for an advanced copy and provide an email address you desire the book to be sent.

From the book of Hosea

In the book of Hosea 4:6 "My people are destroyed for lack of knowledge: I will also reject thee, that you shall be no priest to me: seeing that you have forgotten the law of thy God I will also forget thy children." The Holy Bible states that lack of knowledge will destroy the church. The church leaders must be gathers of all knowledge in order to satisfy the Tree of Knowledge and Tree of Life from the Garden of Eden. All leaders I have contacted are rejecters of knowledge. I offered them miracle after miracle and they refuse to learn. The only acceptable church is a perfect church with one of the seven names on the door. Anything less will not reach the glory of God. The small churches of one thousand or less must combine when forming the kingdom. You must stay at the Altar, not take pride in your television failure to provide communion and teaching so the congregation can be reborn at the age of the King.

Hint on the purpose of some of the books of the Holy Bible.
Timothy to train the politicians.

Do not forget the book of Mark in their foreheads. What that means is when you see the politicians representing King Jesus Christ, you know they have been trained by the church not to violate the book of Mark and end with a bad economy and eternal death. The will of the people is fear if they create a bad economy through violating the book of Mark. The clergymen is forced to shove the bodies under the Altar. If you do not, then you shove your own body under the Altar.
Galatians Clergymen to lord over the courts.
Romans when a country recreates the Roman Empire.

Look for the country with metal teeth or great military and no merchant marines.

A miracle is a future to inherit that people would say is impossible. Examples provided by Elijah and Elias are amazing. The answer for the church to teach is all is possible in a kingdom. If the end result is good then the world can achieve. The clergymen must maintain the future in prophecies or major and minor challenges for all. Where is the challenge in, "You know, I have to wait for King Jesus Christ to return?" What would He say, but form the kingdom and you learn how to talk. He has told you all things, so you already have the answers to all sorrows if you work and not sleep at the Altar. The best example is a life one thousand times better than the end in the church world. The title of the Holy Bible is holy is perfect and a bible is a religious way of life. Therefore, the Holy Bible will always produce a life one thousand times better than the end. Elijah has just copied the answers out of scripture, as the Holy Bible is written so no man can boast. The plan is already there. Even fear could be developed by the kingdom, had it formed. All judgment is defined and must be used by the saints. King Jesus Christ will rule with a rod of iron. A rod is a measurement of success and iron is the Terrible Swift Sword. The clergymen must judge the politicians on, "Some governments are taking you on the road to hell." There are many passages the government must be judged on for the clergymen to receive the gift of eternal life. If the clergymen voted in the election, they are judging. A house divided amongst itself always fails, so you know the church can represent only one party. If you believe some voted Republican or Democrat, you must find the Antichrist who speaks many tongues. The language of the church is English. Any clergymen that voted for the main candidates in the year of the Lord 2004 AD or 2008 AD and believes the congregation has John 3:16, would be wrong.

THE ENTIRE WORLD IS DOWN TO THE LORD'S PRAYER AS THE ONLY HOPE. ANY CHURCH LOCATION THAT DOES NOT HAVE THE UNIVERSAL CHURCH FORMAT INCLUDING THE HOLY CITY IS TAKING GOD'S NAME IN VAIN. That location is stealing tithes and offering from God and is run by the Antichrist. The Antichrist came in an era of peace and prosperity. What did he do? He destroyed peace and destroyed prosperity. The United States is the Roman Empire and financially we are in a very serious financial situation and the country will be run by the eighth beast next year. The pen is mightier than the sword and will destroy America by the Battle of Armageddon.

King Jesus Christ was born to become the God of Heart Our Father stated He required. As written in the sixty-seventh chapter of the Holy Bible, you will read the following:

The prophecy of the crucifixion in one thousand years.

The purpose was to inspire Israel in longing for a savior, to show us the meaning of the gift of John 3:16, to write a new beginning for the world, a transition of power to the meaning of the heart in judgment, His only begotten Son to rule with a rod of iron, and to forgive the Israeli man for his sins as King Jesus Christ used the word jealousy against us to make the prophecy come true. This is the second power of eight.

What does a prophecy of today state? The church is losing to an egg. The Easter Bunny is bringing Easter eggs to the children of the church and that is more important than the sermons without milk being taught. When you read the sixty-seventh book, you will learn you are not to teach God's Children of 777 design of the crucifixion. Today, the church is still teaching grieving, not mourning. You can read the literature from Elijah, the prophet to get the love back for John 3:16 on Easter Sunday. The day must become a great day for God's Children to learn the reality of mourning and the meaning of new arms and legs. Do not teach about the cross and you must burn the idols of the Catholic Faith showing Our God on the cross. The clergymen's cross to bear is the Holy Bible, as they must teach us how to live by every word.

What is true about Christmas? I have gone to your sermons without meat and have seen a person bring in a crossword puzzle. The sermons are boring and not worthy of such an incredible day in the lives of our children when the congregation learns the importance of a birthday through the children. The children must run the church in a sense and desire to be there as their first choice. The Jewish Faith has twelve days in December. The church will bore you with one. Clergymen of the nation of church must develop the twelve days of Christmas. You notice the children have the days off plus more time. If any do not desire to go to your church where your Ball Room can hold a dance for ten thousand people and serve wine, the clergymen think small. The twelve days of celebration or He was born to rule as a gift from Our Father must encourage all that are able to celebrate with their families, that is the greatest time to be alive in the nation of church and love in the kingdom of that country.

The Antichrists are running the church and they lost in so many countries like Cuba, China, the Soviet Union, Mexico, and the United States or should I just list all countries. Now their sermons cannot compete for the hearts of our children and they are losing to an Easter egg. Without the church forming, they will lose the church and the penance will continue for seven times longer. The clergymen shall know what they did before they die. That is an extremely important prophecy.

ALL MUST LEARN THE ENTIRE WORLD IS DOWN TO ONE PRAYER OR THE LORD'S PRAYER.

The first item of great importance for the clergymen is to find the Antichrist. I have a number of pages that cover the topic, but first let us examine the Antichrist will neutralize eighty-two percent of the standing armies.

The Second World War was a war to end all wars. Many claim the United States won the war, but President Franklin D. Roosevelt stated we became tired of fighting. He desired to continue on why you put him in office or work on the wealth creation in our country. Therefore, he declared unconditional surrender to the Communists. They won the war and Communist China and the Soviet Union formed. I joined with God in the year of Our Lord 1989 AD. The only request I made was the Soviet Union would break up. Two weeks later, it was over.

Let us look at all the wars the foolish Americans have won. The First World War was used to start the second. We lost the war in South Korea and Vietnam. Many in the church only talk about the dust in the wind or MIA. Nobody I heard, gave a damn about all the lives we foolish Americans destroyed in Vietnam and surrounding countries. In Central America, they will tell the foolish Americans that they hate you. They imply send your money but you stay at home. Iraq is a war that foolish George Bush found his father to be an idiot, as he did not complete the task. Now the al Qaeda is stronger and American soldier's lives are worthless. So now, you again can call Americans fools and members of the Roman Empire. A land without hope for our children. There is no call to action for 777 design or the angels to talk at your Altar and for the senators to listen to God's Children. All the church is doing is abandoning God's Children.

Why would the Holy Bible call that a war to end all wars? President Franklin D. Roosevelt formed the United Nations so the governments could learn how to talk. A nation is a religious order and the title should be United Countries. I heard Pastor Murray on television and he stated the United Nations never learned how to talk as American politicians talk like little children. The Holy Bible states for the kingdom to form and the clergymen learn how to talk. Then the clergymen can teach the politicians on how to talk. Elias covered in the book, "The Antichrist God's Version" what the world lost by continuing killing wars and not learning how to talk. That book is the first book from the book of Daniel that did not sell. Now the clergymen have to find an organization large enough to neutralize eighty-two percent of the standing armies. We know King Jesus Christ will meet us in Israel once the clergymen have no questions to ask. King Jesus Christ will come back with the power of work, so we know the Antichrist only has the power of work, but Judgment Day is the day you die. John 3:16 must be important to politicians, the day they die. They must have the right heart.

If we explore the world without the advantage of religion, we find in Communist China, no one can talk from the Altar. With North Korea, Vietnam and others, where there is not an established religion is the eighteen percent left (100-82 equals 18). We look at the United States and we find a country with metal teeth and no merchant marines. The US is the wax location, the greatest debtor nation, and its currency is green.

In the Chapter "Stairway to Heaven" from the new book of the Holy Bible, Elijah is thankful to God for the story of the Antichrist to neutralize eighty-two percent of the standing armies, which will greatly aid in minimizing the lose of souls for the clergymen. The men of the cross to bear or the Holy Bible should realize that military does not produce peacekeepers. The Antichrist is to find the peacekeepers and they are God's angels. Elijah, the prophet is a man of European descent that God knew before I was born in a war to end all wars and my hair has turned white.

If you have a question, you have to do it yourself or think. King Jesus Christ will not turn stones into food or He will not return with the power of creation. He would never get out of the hospitals and thereby would violate the stories from the Garden of Eden. You as a clergymen think big as to what many talk about but do not believe in the world of peace. The clergymen can create the miracle of King Jesus Christ becoming the wall through fear. Yet you can teach the fools that run America, we have nothing to fear but fear itself if we believe in the King of Peace or King Jesus Christ. We must have the right heart for John 3:16.

Elijah, the prophet has copied the peace plan from the Holy Bible to minimize the lose of souls for the clergymen that go by the way of Satan. The angels are God's Children of 777 design and the peacekeepers. The passage is peace on earth, good will towards men. When a politicians talk about peace, we all listen. The church gathers all he said and writes sermons about meat from the Altars. We call a dragon a hawk in America. When a dragon shows his ugly head, the Pale Horseman is there to cut it off. The only king the clergymen can represent is a leader like President Franklin D. Roosevelt. The hawks like President John F. Kennedy will have the pale horse from the seven Holy Cities cut off his ugly head. The women will demand fear when a dragon desires to steal her child. My mother is still mad at President Franklin D. Roosevelt for allowing her brother to die in the WW II. Where was the fear in Germany? The women will and should demand fear. The Chapter "Stairway to Heaven" contains the plan copied from the Holy Bible to form the kingdom. The Holy Bible is written so no man can boast. The scripture is the grace of God and there is nothing you have to do in planning, since He gave you all the answers. The grace of King Jesus Christ is perfect. The grace of the clergymen is applying the knowledge of scripture, so we can live by every word. The plan is written by Gods and cannot fail to create a life one thousand times better than the end, but perfect takes time. The clergymen can start now or kill a trillion children before Our Gods come back with the seven horns of the eternal temple or Israel. King Jesus Christ will meet us in Israel, not church. The church is going to Egypt. As published in the book, "The Antichrist God's Version", "God stated he will turn men into women—not physically but spiritually as in Egypt. They started the Six Day War (the Russian Bear) and now Anwar al-Sadat and Prime Minister Menachem Begin agreed on peace between the two countries." Should the United States through our church leaders be more like Egypt? I have covered the story of Anwar al-Sadat of Egypt going to Israel and working on the Commandment of Love thy neighbor. What a peace plan the Antichrists can create in Our God's name. The Mother of Inspiration must work to protect the children even to the view of I am going to die to help. Elijah, the prophet has granted you the biblical answers. You must provide the knowledge and work to teach the beginning of heaven on earth. It shall be done on earth as it is in heaven, but you have what is possible, not probable or the power of creation. Adam told God in the Garden of Eden, "God, I need to do it myself." Today, Adam is telling God to do it all, so he can stay asleep at the Altar. God will never give you more to do than you can achieve in His name.

Let me cover their responsibility to reform the church. TBN, Tomorrow's World, and Shepherd's Chapel are on television. TBN can be defined as great beggars but refuse to develop sermons that can teach the children. If you watch they desire their customers to have money. They have nothing for the teenagers and have abandoned thy children or God's Children. All there work is directed to King Jesus Christ to return through observation not deeds that I have seen. Pastor Murray has covered in his view that if he does nothing all will turn out good. Tomorrow's World is teaching the sword is mightier than the pen and the end is very close. All have different views on the same subjects. Where are they reforming the church or creating one voice so they can save each others souls. If Tomorrow's World and Shepherd's Chapel do not work together, neither can be saved as at least one is false witness. All refuse to form the kingdom and learn how to talk; thereby none have the right heart for John 3:16. Pastor Murray and Tomorrow's World are blaming others or lo here and lo there. All differences must be resolved in the church. The only one that I have met or heard is Elijah and Elias. I am sorry, but that is true.

From the book of Luke 17.

Luke 20 And when He was demanded of the Pharisees, when the kingdom of God should come, He answered them and said, The kingdom of God cometh not with observation:

Luke 21 neither shall they say, Lo here! or, Lo there! for, behold, the kingdom of God is within you.

The Sixty-seventh book of the Holy Bible
By Elijah, the prophet from Malachi 4:5.

The book is from the book of Revelation that St John was told not to write but we had to wait for Elijah, King Jesus Christ Prophet of Malachi 4:5. Elijah is a man of European descent and his hair has turned white. When you read it, you will realize how important it is too write now not in the days of old.

I can be reached at
Email comfortingod@mchsi.com
Or telephone 815-765-0161

now see the chapters that will be turned into Elijah 1:1 until the clergymen reach to end.

I was going to list more letters I sent out but the knowledge will be left on my computer for the clergymen to sort and read. The Wall of Hope must be in every church location and I will help develop parts to be shown in the movies.

Chapter 27. The End

THE END

February 1, the year of Our Lord 2010 AD.

Matthew 24:14 And this gospel of the kingdom shall be preached in all the world for a witness unto all nations; and then shall the end come.

Please learn how the end occurs. Now you can achieve in His name.

Many clergymen have fantasyland views on how the end comes, yet God has given us a clear view. It appears many answers are designed for an individual to do nothing. If all the clergymen work together, you can avoid the end. The only people that can avoid the end are the clergymen. They have a chance to create heaven on earth (Lord's Prayer) or the end (eternal death for all mankind). God is waiting for your decision.

How does the end occur? The famine at the end times is for the word of God. The problem near the end is the problem with the rich, wealthy. Nostradamus told you as scripture defines it all will happen in one generation. The start is the year of Our Lord 1992 AD and the end of the generation is the year of Our Lord 2016 AD. December 21, the year of Our Lord 2012 AD is a political event or a house divided amongst itself always fails. The United States currency is worthless in the year of Our Lord 2014 AD and the gangs of America rule. The United States and the world cannot recover. God comes back with the seven horns of the eternal temple, Israel in fourteen thousand years and gives Adam another chance to obey God. You will find the penance worse than the Noah's Ark story.

You are looking to find a country from the book of Daniels with metal teeth and is the wax location of the world or America. How could the banks fail? You must learn. Today they are borrowing out money at what today is defined as low interest rates. As the budget deficit of America continues the rich will raise their demands for interest and devalue the American currency. The banks again cannot support its loans and fail. President Ronald Reagan had the interest on the US thirty year bonds at sixteen percent to attract money, but the banks cannot afford that with the numerous low rate loans in place. Inflation takes over and the government will raise the rates. The United States government became the greatest debtor nation in the entire world and the rich has by buying political seats with money lower the taxes on the wealthy extremely low, historically. The rich will pay approximately forty percent next year and have much surplus money. They can borrow the money to our government and receive interest. You are under taxing the wealthy, so they can buy your bonds and the average man has to pay more taxes. The Republicans are claiming the wealthy will get more tax breaks if they are elected and the rest of the world gives up lending money to America. The Holy Bible states buyers and sellers remorse from the book of Revelation. You must question why the church represents two parties. The problem at the end is with the rich and the party representing the wealthy across the world is bad. A house divided amongst itself (the church) will always fail. The church cannot represent the rich at the expense of the poor. The easiest thing to do is feed the children in blessed are the poor, not the failure of greed for the rich. Nostradamus states you cannot get your money out of the banks like the time of President Herbert Hoover. Finally the printing press print big money commitments and the only thing you can do with the money is burn it, as it is worthless. The Holy Bible of God's warning and second through Nostradamus is true. The Holy Bible proclaims not one woman could vote for a mass murderer of children from Texas, who was working against reducing the cost of schools in property taxes and made our public school system worse, like his father. The congregation and clergymen must learn how to judge the politicians all over the world as to which ones are representing the God of Heart and the King of Peace.

Now you desire to know how it will happen. I will go back in time to explain further or start with President Jimmy Carter. Much came before in Standing Historical before but I will start here. President Jimmy Carter campaigned he required more tax revenue to continue overcoming the sorrows of the country. I will use biblical terms when possible not the actual words. A grain of sand changed the results and a man that believed in strong fiscal responsibility called Governor Ronald Reagan took office. He was almost impeached in California by raising the taxes to straighten out budget concerns. Now he changed to a man representing the wealthy only. He changed the highest tax rate for the rich from seventy percent to under twenty eight. He goes on television and explains his foolish ideas. The economy fails and the year of Our Lord 1982 AD became a good time to buy stocks since the rich lost fortunes.

What happened by the year of our Lord 1984 AD. First President Ronald Reagan violated the book of Mark in a big way. He worked against the money to improve the sorrows of the country. The rich were complaining they could not make any money, so he had a foolish economist create what is called Supply Economics. The minimum unemployment number was to be six percent. The Holy Bible states the unemployment number must be zero as a mind is a terrible thing to waste. Through the economy of the Holy Bible as God has defined not only is zero unemployment the only answer, but the families whose children are dieing like in Haiti, must live on a piece of land, their families own. One third of Americans live in apartments, which is a sorrow. President Ronald Reagan raises the taxes on the wealthy in capital gains, not income. The next election occurs and the Democrat tells America the true we must raise the taxes on the wealthy and President George Bush wins. He does raise the taxes to twenty eight percent. That is over sixty percent less than the 1950s and forty-two percent less than President Ronald Reagan started with. America is going greatly in debt, the unemployment number is high and the saving rate is poor. In Arlington Heights, Illinois I met a man going to open his property tax bill and he knew it was going to be bad. So America changed the tax on the rich to higher property taxes and others types all over America. The wealthy did not use the money to create jobs but what the Holy Bible describes as gambling. The church may have talked about a man gambling and losing hundreds but the government and wealthy losing a trillion dollars was not their words.

Now we have a bad economy under a man called President George Bush, with Supply Economics in place and the King of the North, George Bush and the King of the South, William J. Clinton were debating money. We had abandoned buildings of office and housing type all over America. Future President William J. Clinton explained that if we continue great indebtedness under President George Bush (three hundred billion, but getting worse), we would have a depression by the year of Our Lord 2000 AD or at the best a recession. Again Supply Economics forces the government to violate the book of Mark which God gave as a gift since when you violate the book of Mark, you weaken the economy and collect less tax revenue. The country will lose both ways. What a gift our Gods have given the world but the clergymen never use. The Mark of the beast from the book of Mark. When you see a politician, you know by his face, he was trained by the church in the seminaries.

Now the King of the South wins and the churches were to work for God save the Queen of the South for the love of her child, but the Catholics worked hard to destroy the president's daughter instead of using a vow of silence. By the end of his administration, he spends fifty million dollars to defend himself. On the church radio station, I remember the rich even complaining about a new aircraft carrier. Also on a church radio station, they complained he destroyed the education system before he was elected. The schools were bad because of the Republicans. You can read what the King of the North did to the King of the South in the book of Daniels. President William J. Clinton raises the taxes on the wealthy to approximately forty percent. He proceeds to work on the social ills or sorrows of the country and that created a great environment or business. They establish a simple goal of a minimum growth on the economy of 2.3 percent and try to hold it under three, so it can continue. The Holy Bible describes the economy as a rainbow or an Irishmen in the White House will leave a pot of gold at the end. He creates twenty six million jobs so Congress should already know how to achieve or blessed are the poor they shall inherit the earth as you resolve what made them poor. Many mayors are giving tax money back on property taxes. The average American was not concerned about their property tax bills. All people must be in a group of they shall not want or money problems are eliminated in a kingdom.

Now in the year of Our Lord 2000 AD or the new beginning requirement to avoid the end occurs. The unemployment number is about 3.5 percent. Many companies have help wanted signs on the business locations. I remember going into a Jewel food store in Mount Prospect, Illinois and that location had fourteen job openings. If you worked part time (20 hours) at Jewel you receive a good health care plan. The Federal government had a pot of gold from an Irishman president of two hundred and thirty two billion dollars. As President William J. Clinton reported the people that created the economy were losing their jobs to the rich men or Republicans. One way an American proves he knows how to vote is work against the party in the White House and many bad laws were written to get good ideas through a growing rich man congress. The rich on average have proved in the past they have more money than brains, but Americans cannot refuse a foolish plan of bad tax cuts for people that cannot use the money wisely. What were the rich saying at this time, "I made so much money, do I have to pay taxes?" The answer is the American children are the greatest debtors in the world and the clergymen should check the Lord's Prayer. God told the clergymen the truth. Allen Greenspan, our accountant threw away Supply Economics in the year of Our Lord 1994 AD, as fools gold, but no new economic book was created. One book on economies from scripture is required as God told you there are a number of books to write.

The election is between a man from Texas whose father could not manage the economy and a Vice President Al Gore that was involved in creating seven years of fat cows. The Holy Bible instructed the clergymen to divide the cows up wisely. So Governor George Bush, a mass murderer of children from Texas that stole the money allocated for children's health care and wasted it on the rich, runs. The Holy Bible would call that the Mark of the beast. Now he also worked against the tax payer getting property tax relief by the government paying for new school buildings. Near the end he states the American children do not deserve health care because there are too many. Does this mean he does not have the same heart as the God of Heart from the book of Luke? He becomes the Red Dragon and Satan when he starts the foolish war. Now he opens up the treasuries to the rich, goes four trillion dollars in debt in the first four years, and creates less than zero jobs. The next four years are worse. Job creation is wealth creation for a country. The Holy Bible would describe that as seven years where the skinny cows ate up the fat cows. Satan stopped the rain in America by biblical definitions. He gave the money to the people that cannot use it wisely, started a foolish war, and violated the book of Mark in a big way. I heard a man on financial news stating he may be the worse president we ever had and his education in the Republican Party is still there. It all happens in one generation and we are at the eight beast. December 21, the year of Our Lord 2012 AD is a political event. You find out what God told you to do or the year of Our Lord 2014 AD is the end and two hundred million Americans (future salvation army) will die quickly and the number will increase as the poor without hope and guns take over. The gangs will rule and since we have nothing to offer the police or military man, some may join with the gangs to survive. ·

If the church only had Standing Historical they could create heaven on earth. Oh, I just gave you the start. If you only have a hundred thousand men in the United States to complete, all could be good. All the above is covered in scripture and you ask where are the training of politicians in the seminaries of the church on the book of Mark. Now when we see them as graduates, we know the picture on the web means they know about the great gift of God on economies. If you solve the sorrows of a country, and it is done correctly at our present tax rates, the government ends up with more tax revenue. If

President William Clinton was not forced to listen to foolish Republicans ideas, we could have more saved.

Can you believe if foolish Ronald Reagan did not change the tax code, we could have Social Security funded? Today the wealthy have ten trillion surplus dollars to buy stocks but very little new money invested to create jobs. Have you heard the consumer does not have enough money and America's infrastructure is falling apart? All that work on the books and the government through the eighth beast cannot create jobs. If you had half the money the rich have that they cannot use wisely, you could invest in rebuilding America, but the amount of money you have could not be spent because you would run out of workers. The rich require a big tax increases to cover the Lord's Prayer in America and the rest of the world and avoid the end. All you would hear from the rich is more greed through blame, and the end will come. The Democrats cannot do it. It must come from the clergymen to create heaven on earth and see the return of King Jesus Christ. Until you prove you desire to live in a kingdom where it is being planned that none worries about money, the God of Heart will not return. He has told you all things, so you know the clergymen already have the answers.

Had Senator McCain won the economy would not be able to make it through the year of Our Lord 2012 AD as his only idea was to open up the treasuries more and give it to people that cannot use it wisely. The rich are the wicked in shackles and the church must try to help them. If you hear of a shackle less church, all I can say is I feel sorry for the congregation, but very little for the foolish clergyman. Can you believe many are teaching not to judge and leaving people helpless on Judgment Day or the day you die? Today, the congregation is trying to judge the politicians when they vote but are doing a bad job. They were judged by God as no flesh is saved or no John 3:16.

An antichrist in Israel was a clergyman that disobey God in the smallest detail. Who do you believe an Antichrist would be today? The clergymen must spread out the Holy Bible and study what God told them to do. I believe if they can find the true Elijah, he could help them.

Elijah has more details in his literature. If you can host a meeting with your peers, you can create heaven on earth. Without the clergymen finding the true Elijah, the end will come. You can have eternal life instead of eternal death for checking to see what Elijah has to offer. You cannot lose if you try.

I have below what I will send to as many organizations as I can. Since the clergymen are reluctant to change, the Holy Bible tells me to work with the chosen and faithful.

August 1, the year of Our Lord 2010 AD

Glad Tidings

The sixty-seventh book of the Holy Bible has been sent to the publisher. The title is The Sixty-seventh Book of the Holy Bible written by the author Elijah, the prophet as covered in the book of Revelation.

The time is now for Adam to write the greatest love story the world will ever be involved in and the return of King Jesus Christ. The clergymen must prove they desire to live in His Kingdom.

God has completed all He has promised in the Holy Bible and the book is now complete. The time is now for Adam to work to create heaven on earth. What will the last book of the Holy Bible enable you to achieve in His name? You can end any sorrow any clergyman can define. The great tribulation (reward) for your works (grace) is the return of King Jesus Christ to the temple of Israel, after the year of Our Lord 2020 AD. The clergymen will start to create the greatest religious revival the world will ever see and return of Our God, the God of Heart, Lord Jesus Christ for church work. Please use His correct title. The clergymen are the lords and lord over the world as royalty or saints.

What the church must work for is to overcome the end, which the Holy Bible and Nostradamus 2012 agree, it all happens in one generation or the year of Our Lord 1992 to 2016 AD. Only the clergymen can overcome the end, which will occur in the year of Our Lord 2014 AD. No one knows the date as defined in scripture, so the clergymen realize December 21, the year of Our Lord 2012 AD cannot be the end. We are in the eighth beast so it is a political event. The god of the church is Satan, so we know there is no flesh saved or John 3:16 has even disappeared from the unborn children. The question must be, if I represent the God of Heart, should I let earth turn into a land of hell or heaven? The end is less than four years away and only the clergymen can stop it. The poor in the gangs with guns takes over America and civilization as we know it will disappear. The end as defined by God is real and will last seven times longer than the penance from Israel.

I am sorry but any clergyman that refuses to create heaven on earth will go by the way of Satan the present god of the church.

As an organization, the church can end all the sorrows as God has told you all things or the answers to all the sorrows. With the sixty-seventh book of the Holy Bible you will work on faith healing or ending the pain in lives of families. The sorrows include:
1. All divorces.

535

2. Babies having babies.
3. Poverty.
4. The unnecessary deaths of children all over the church world.
5. The pain of dying in wars.
6. The pain of prisons.
7. Any other pain you can define like the meaning of death.

Elijah will teach the world on how to write laws per the New Testament. Today it is the laws of failure or static laws of freedom. The Generation of the Fig is the new laws of liberty or forty two months or seven years of dynamic action plans that you measure the success and all that is left is love.

Now this great religious revival will result in King Jesus Christ returning to the temple of Israel to enable the Jewish Rabbi to work for a life one thousand times better than the end and to receive the gift of eternal life by John 3:16 for himself and his ancestors. Any clergyman that refuses to obey the God of Heart must go by the way of Satan.

If you are a major denomination call your peers and host a meeting. If you are on television, tell your viewers to buy the book and go to their local church locations and tell the clergymen to start the greatest love story Adam can create.

The web site to order will be www.iuniverse.com. Again the title is The Sixty-seventh Book of the Holy Bible as written by Elijah, the prophet as defined in the book of Daniel and Revelation.

Elijah
430 Pembroke Rd SW
Poplar Grove, Il 61065
Tel 815-765-0161
Email comfortingod@mchsi.com

The Sixty-seventh Book of the Holy Bible by Elijah the Prophet as God Promised from the Book of Malachi.

The cover of the book is as follows.

Cover

Title The Sixty-seventh Book of the Holy Bible by Elijah the Prophet.

Back cover

Revelation 10:9 And I went unto the angel, and said unto him, Give me the little book. And he said unto me, Take it, and eat it up; and it shall make thy belly bitter, but it shall be in thy mouth sweet as honey.

Revelation 10:10 And I took the little book out of the angel's hand, and ate it up; and it was in my mouth sweet as honey: and as soon as I had eaten it, my belly was bitter.

Here is the mystery of God, where He will train an angel to write about the seven thunders in modern times or fear. Fear is the beginning of all wisdom (knowledge), yet we have to reach for, there is nothing to fear but fear itself. How can a book result in my mouth sweet as honey when I speak and my belly was bitter as I tried to swallow my pride and the wisdom made me sicken? He told us to eat of the book as He has told us to eat of His body. A location that does not teach fear is not a valid church location, since fear is the beginning of all wisdom (knowledge).

537

About the Author

Malachi 3:1 Behold, I will send my messenger, and he shall prepare the way before me: and the LORD, whom ye seek, shall suddenly come to his temple, even the messenger of the covenant, whom ye delight in: behold, he shall come, saith the LORD of hosts.

Malachi 3:2 But who may abide the day of his coming? and who shall stand when he appeareth? for he is like a refiner's fire, and like fullers' soap.

Malachi 3:3 And he shall sit as a refiner and purifier of silver: and he shall purify the sons of Levi, and purge them as gold and silver, that they may offer unto the LORD an offering in righteousness.